Volume 3

by
Minetaro Mochizuki

HAMBURG // LONDON // LOS ANGELES // TOKYO

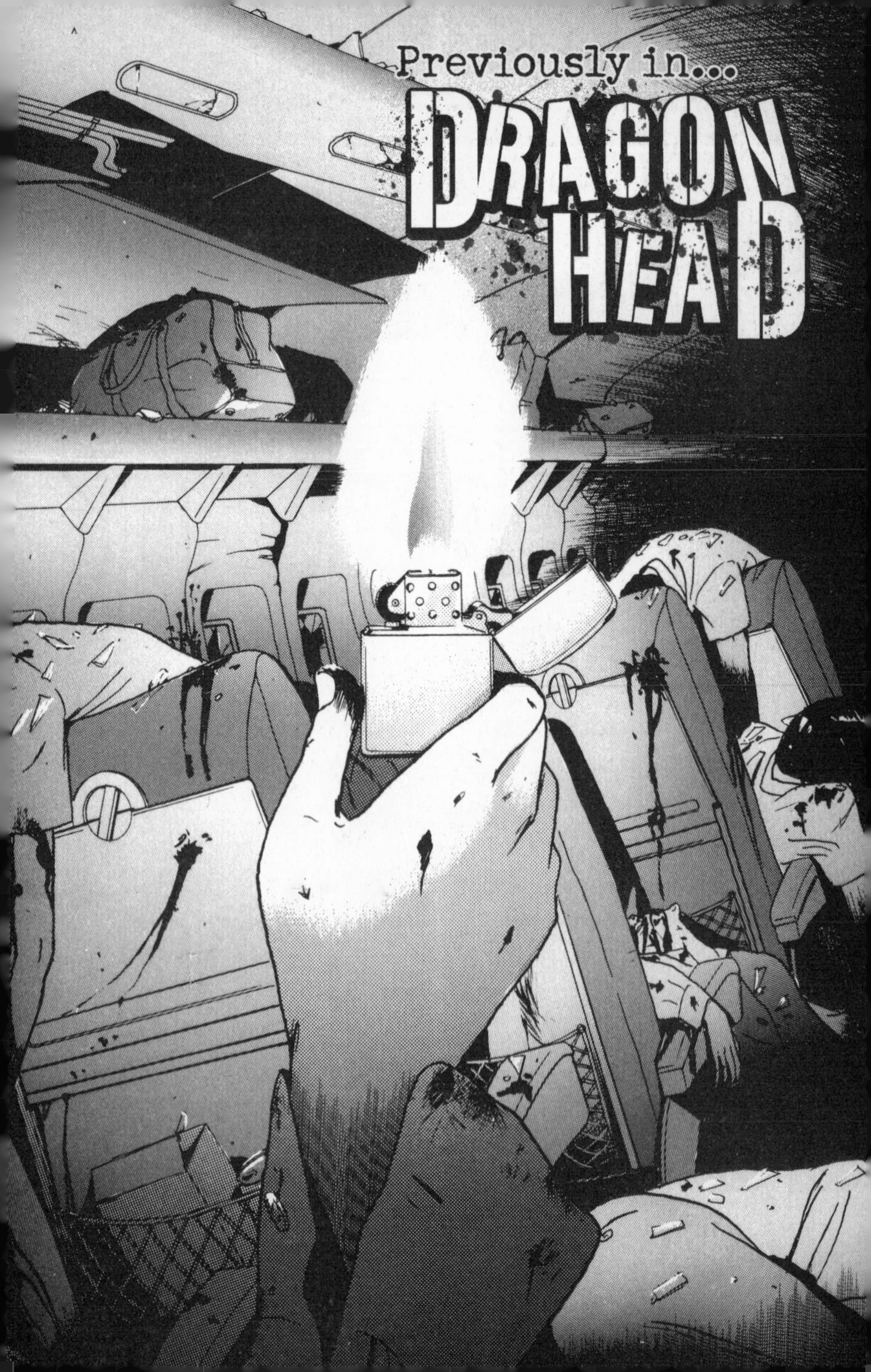
Previously in...
DRAGON HEAD

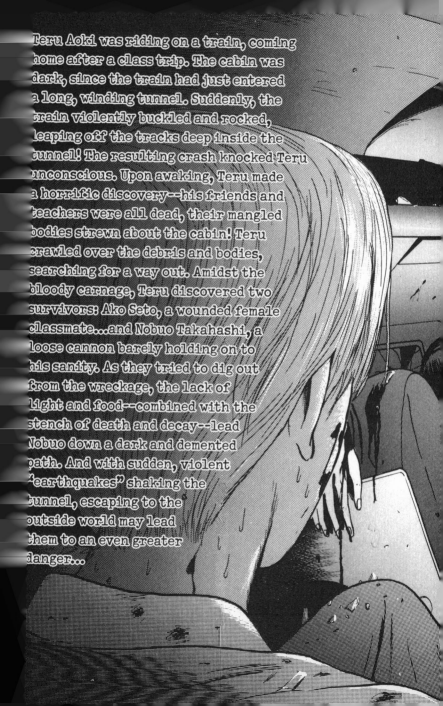

Teru Aoki was riding on a train, coming home after a class trip. The cabin was dark, since the train had just entered a long, winding tunnel. Suddenly, the train violently buckled and rocked, leaping off the tracks deep inside the tunnel! The resulting crash knocked Teru unconscious. Upon awaking, Teru made a horrific discovery--his friends and teachers were all dead, their mangled bodies strewn about the cabin! Teru crawled over the debris and bodies, searching for a way out. Amidst the bloody carnage, Teru discovered two survivors: Ako Seto, a wounded female classmate...and Nobuo Takahashi, a loose cannon barely holding on to his sanity. As they tried to dig out from the wreckage, the lack of light and food--combined with the stench of death and decay--lead Nobuo down a dark and demented path. And with sudden, violent "earthquakes" shaking the tunnel, escaping to the outside world may lead them to an even greater danger...

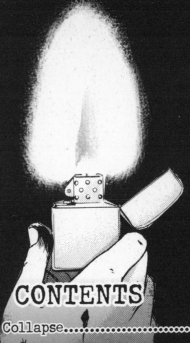

CONTENTS

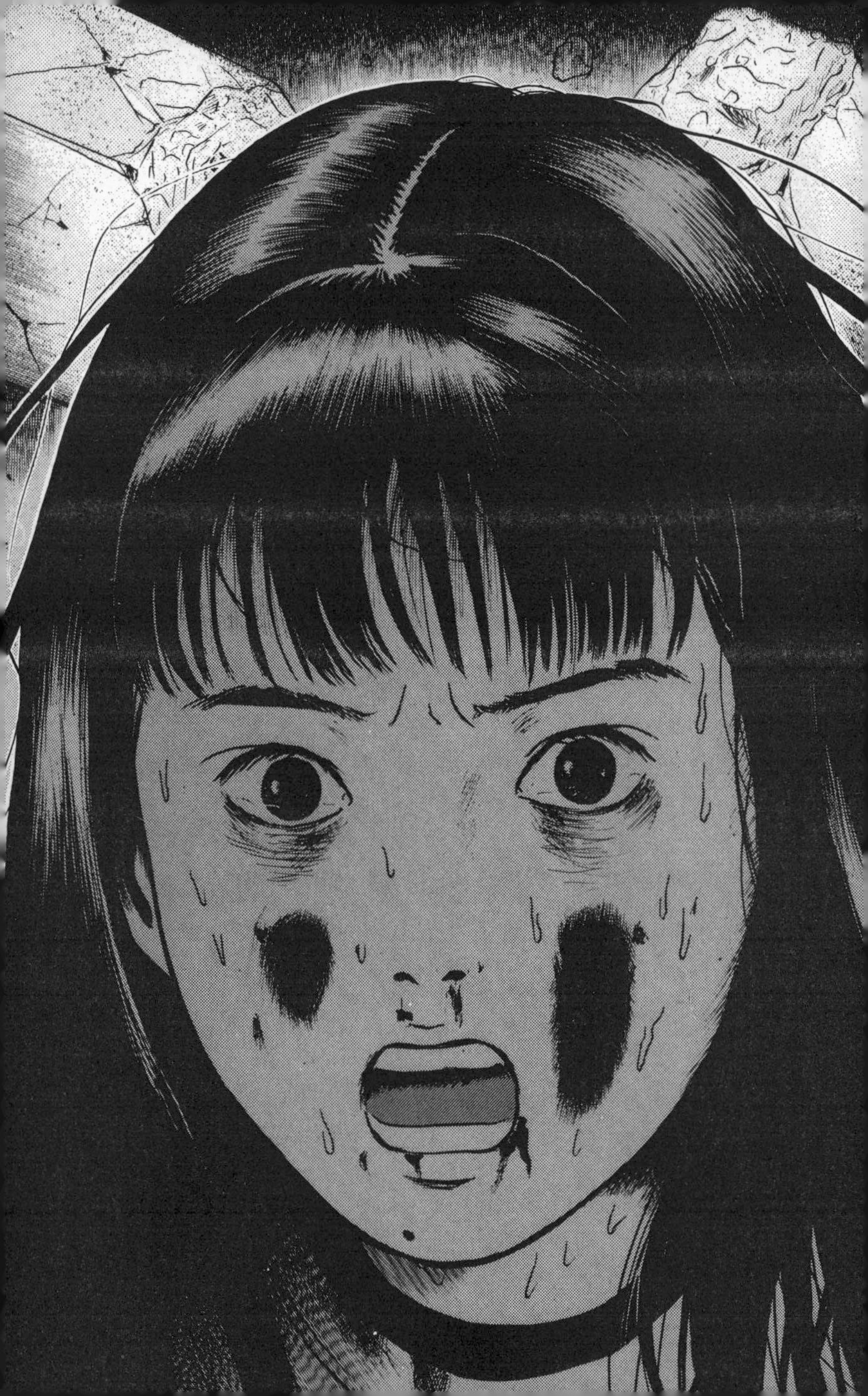

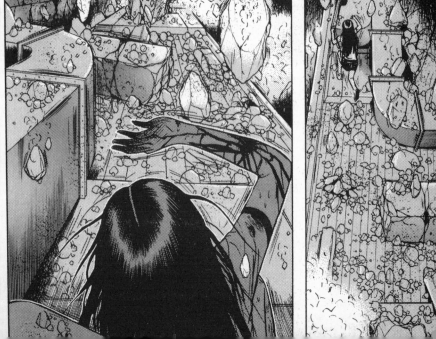

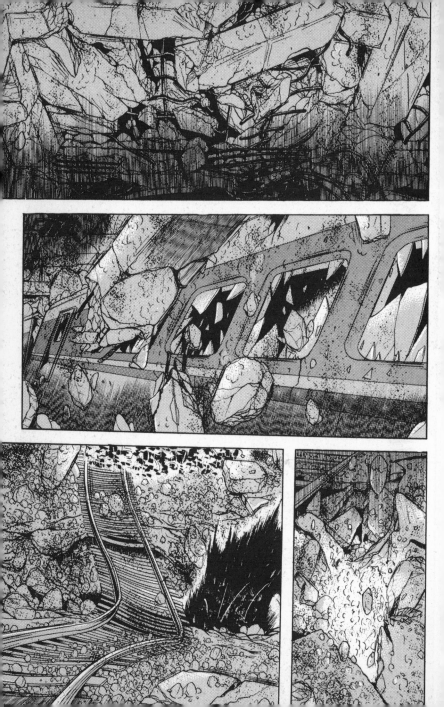

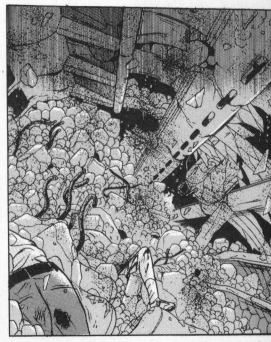

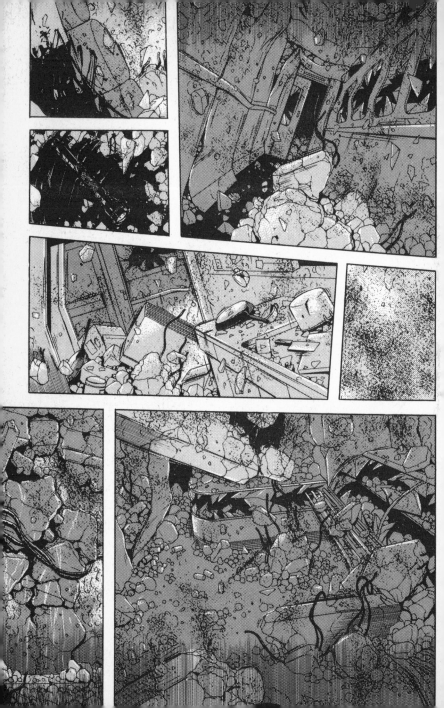

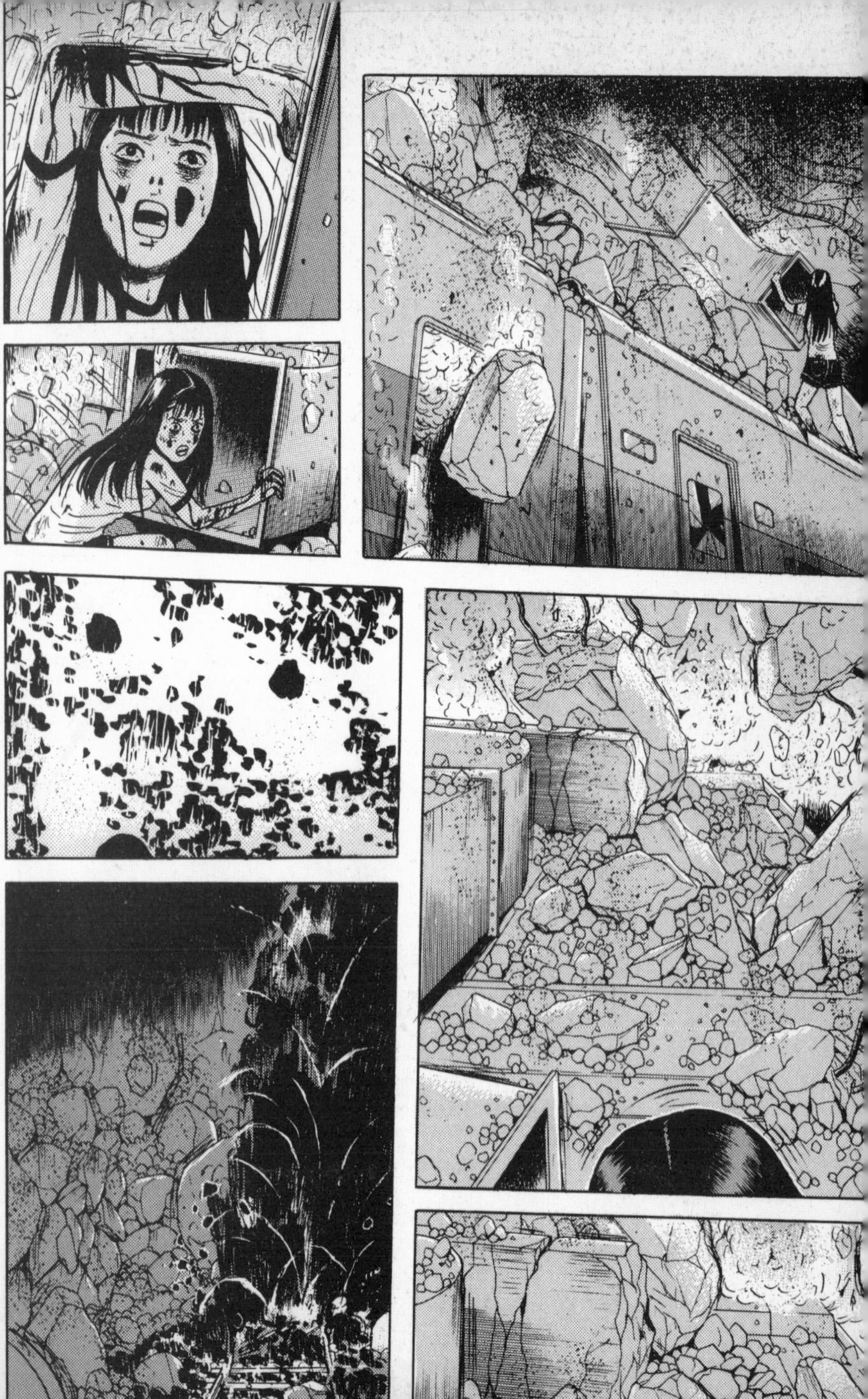

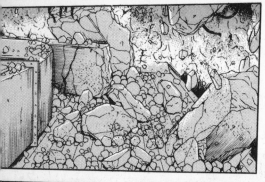

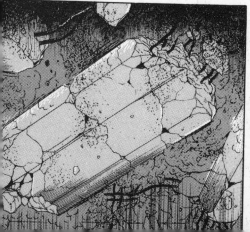

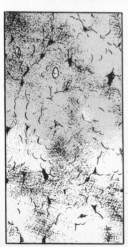

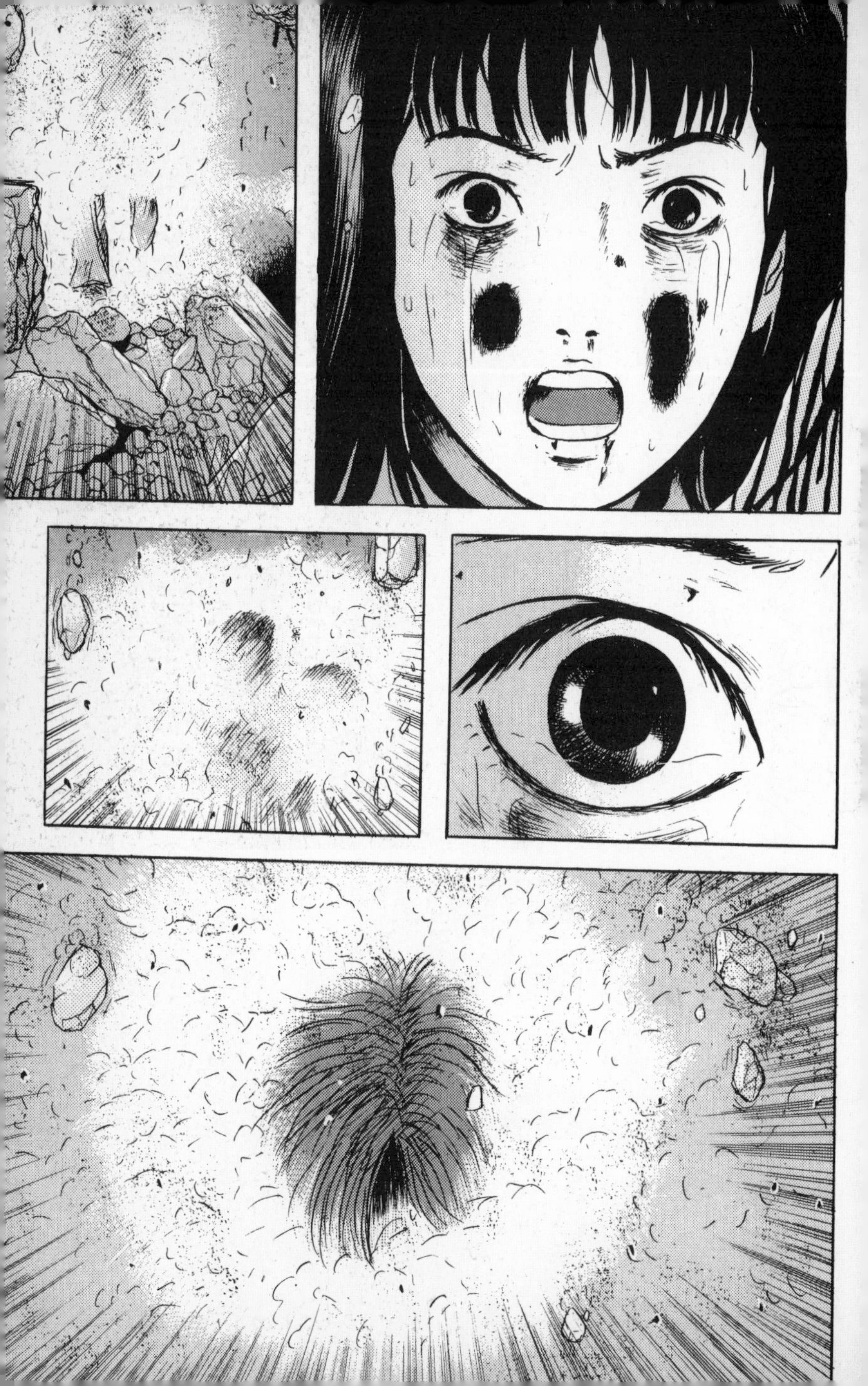

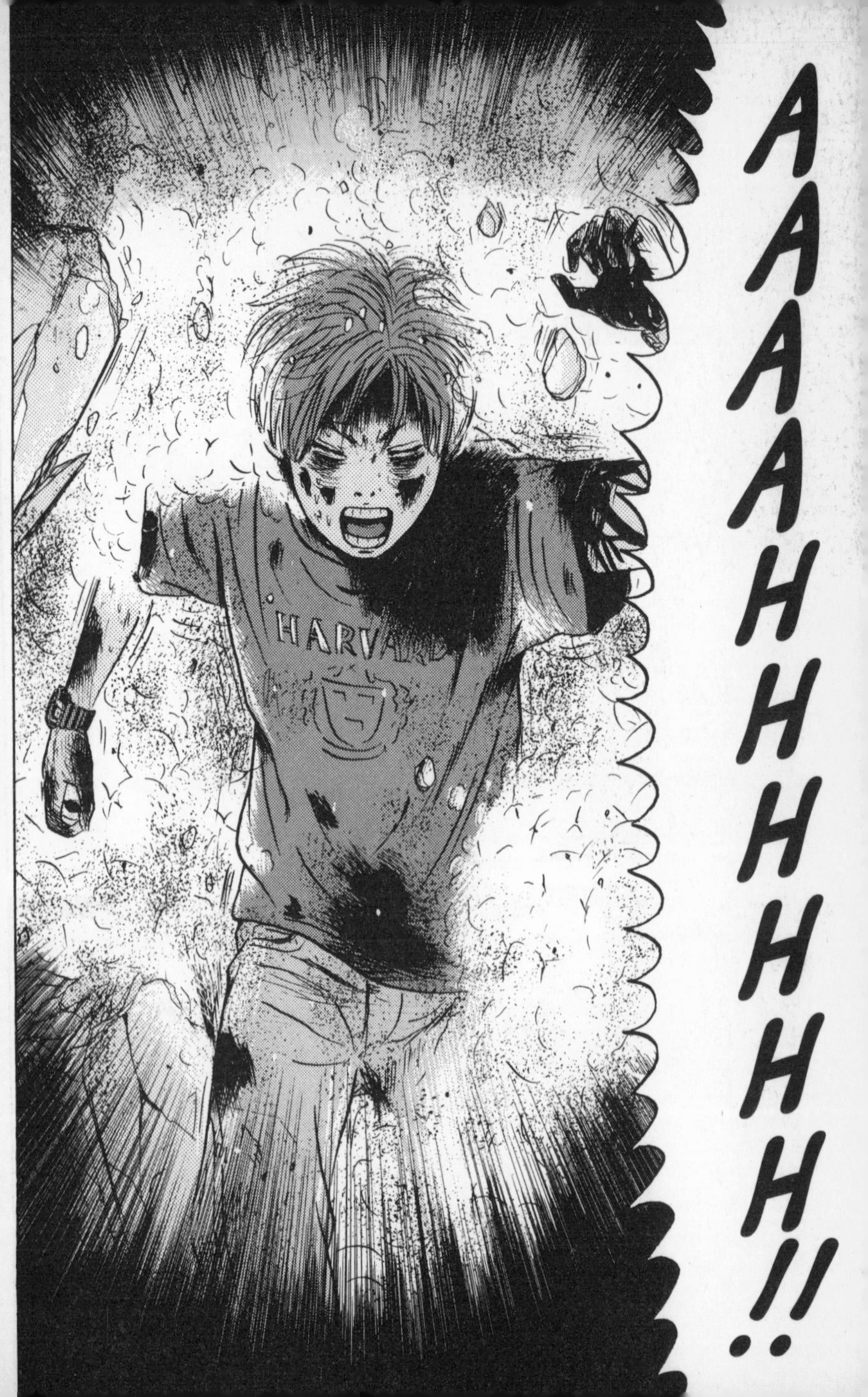
AAAAAHHHHHHH!!
HARVARD

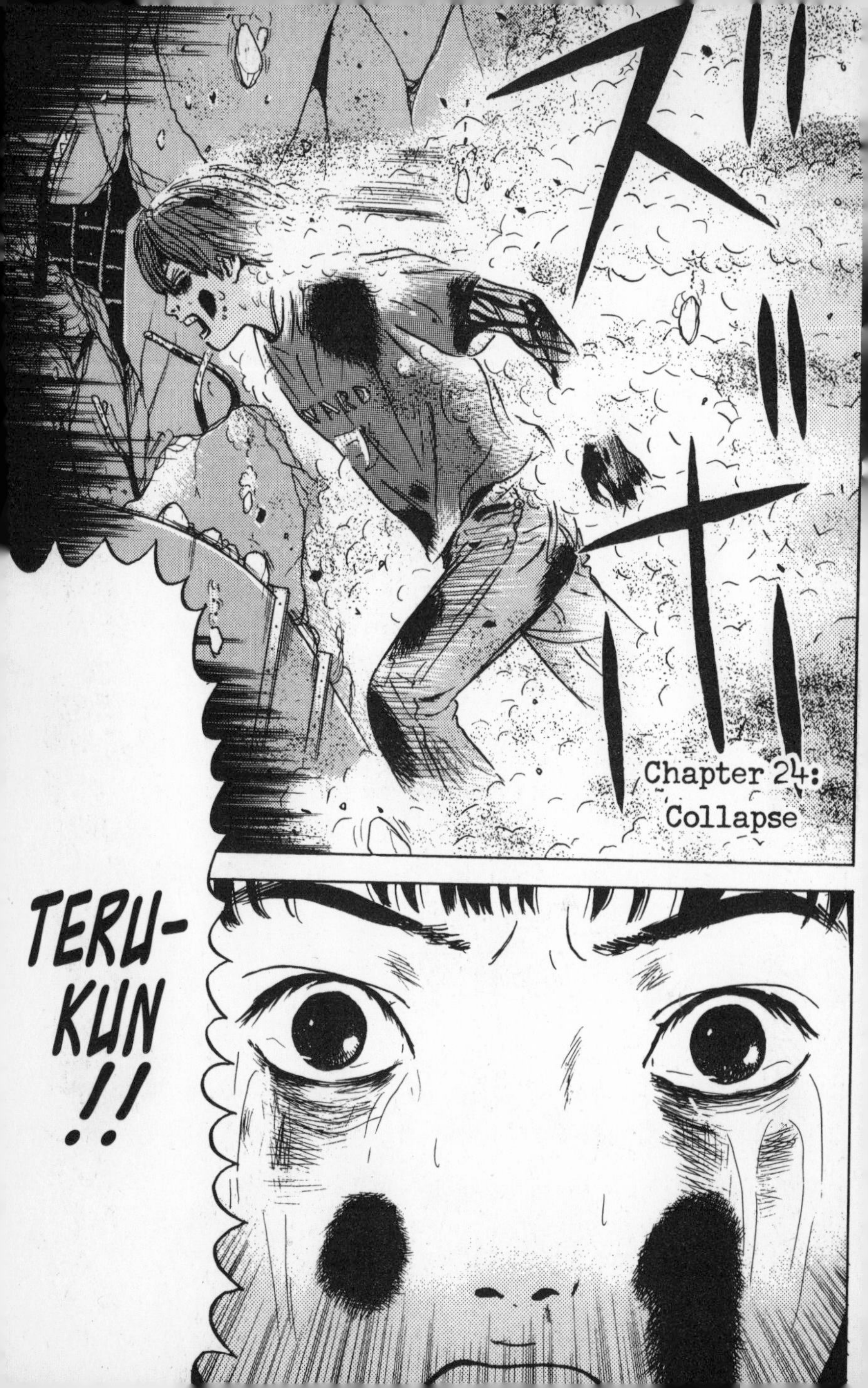
Chapter 24: Collapse
TERU-KUN!!

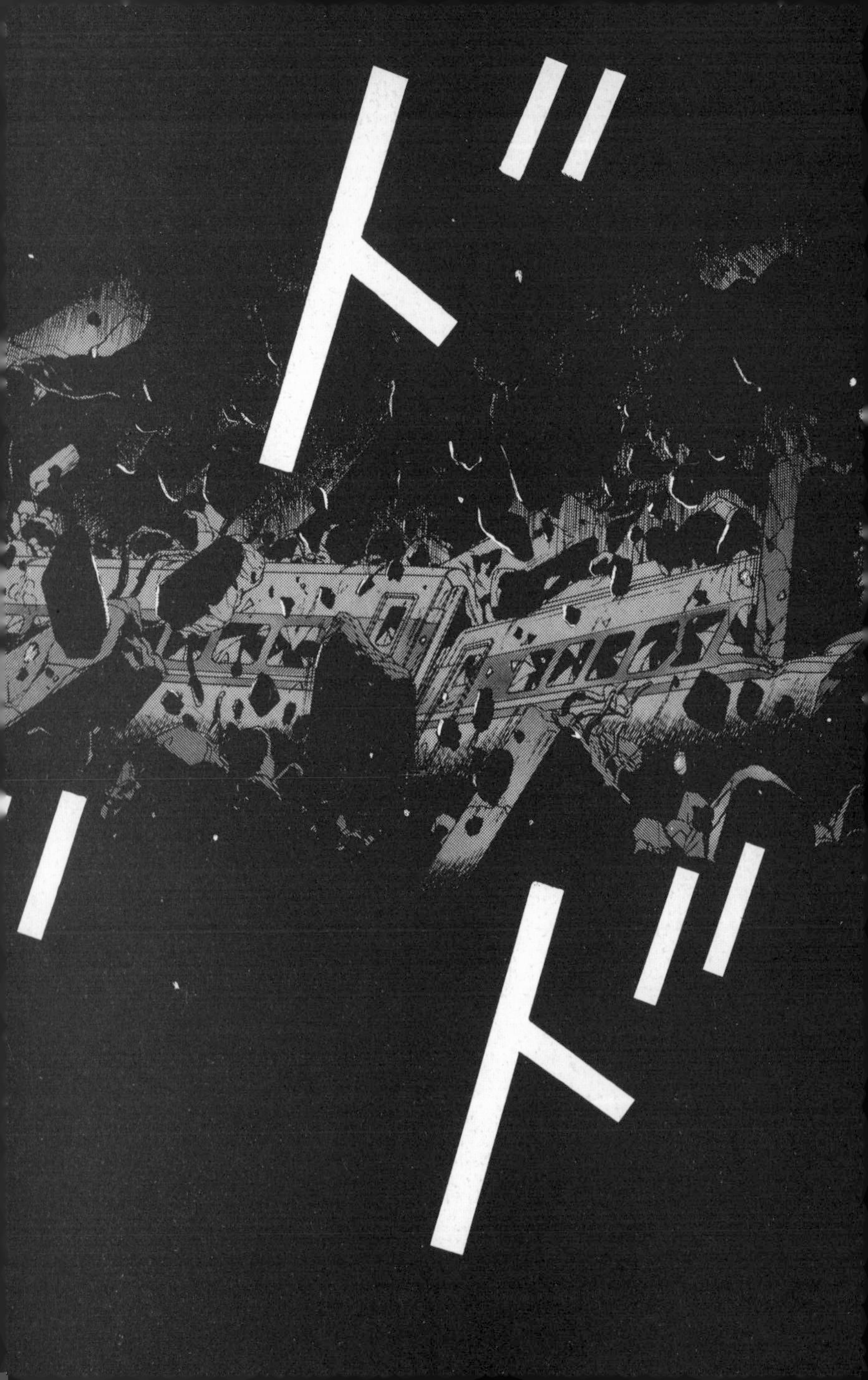
ドドー

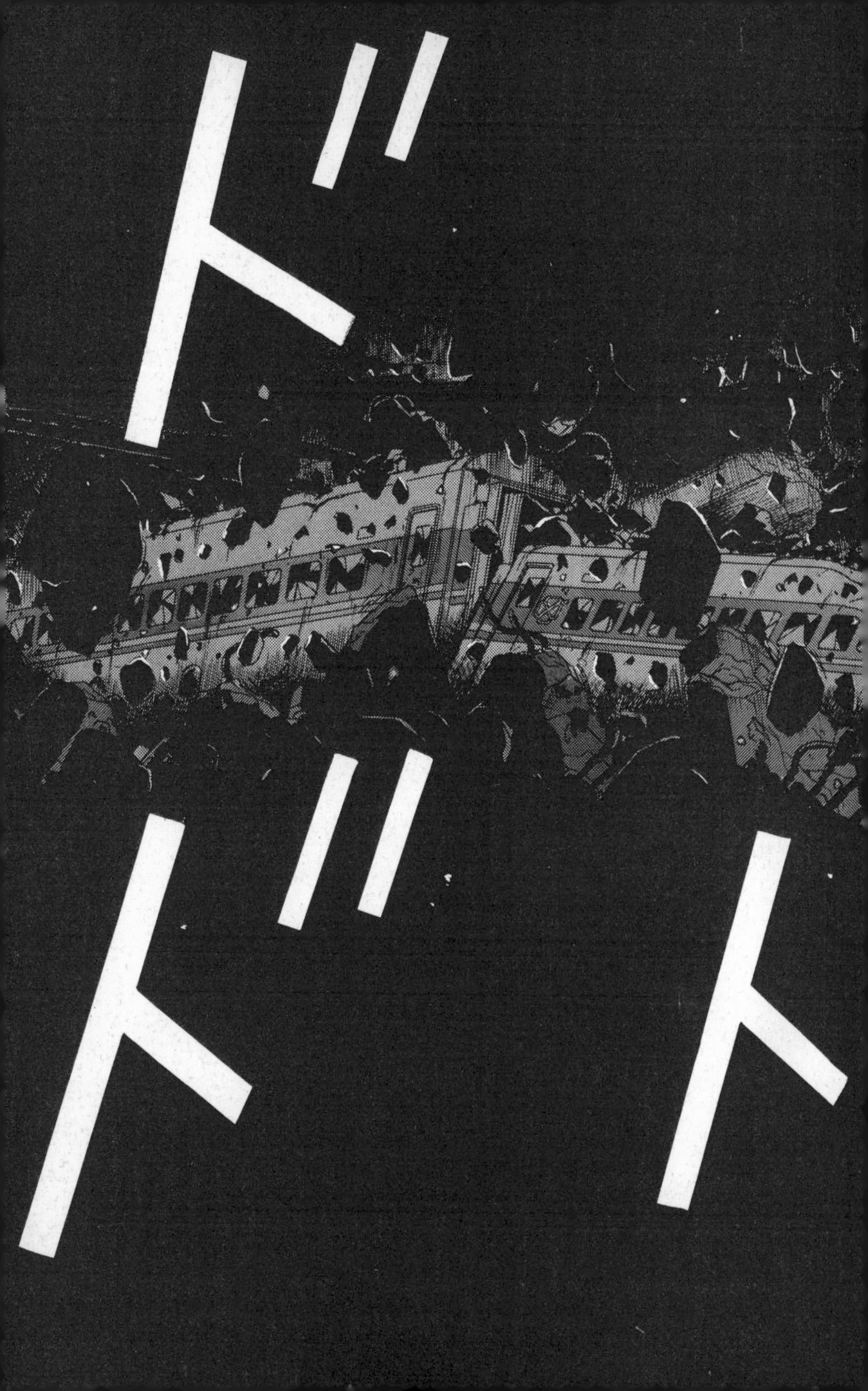
ド
ド
ト

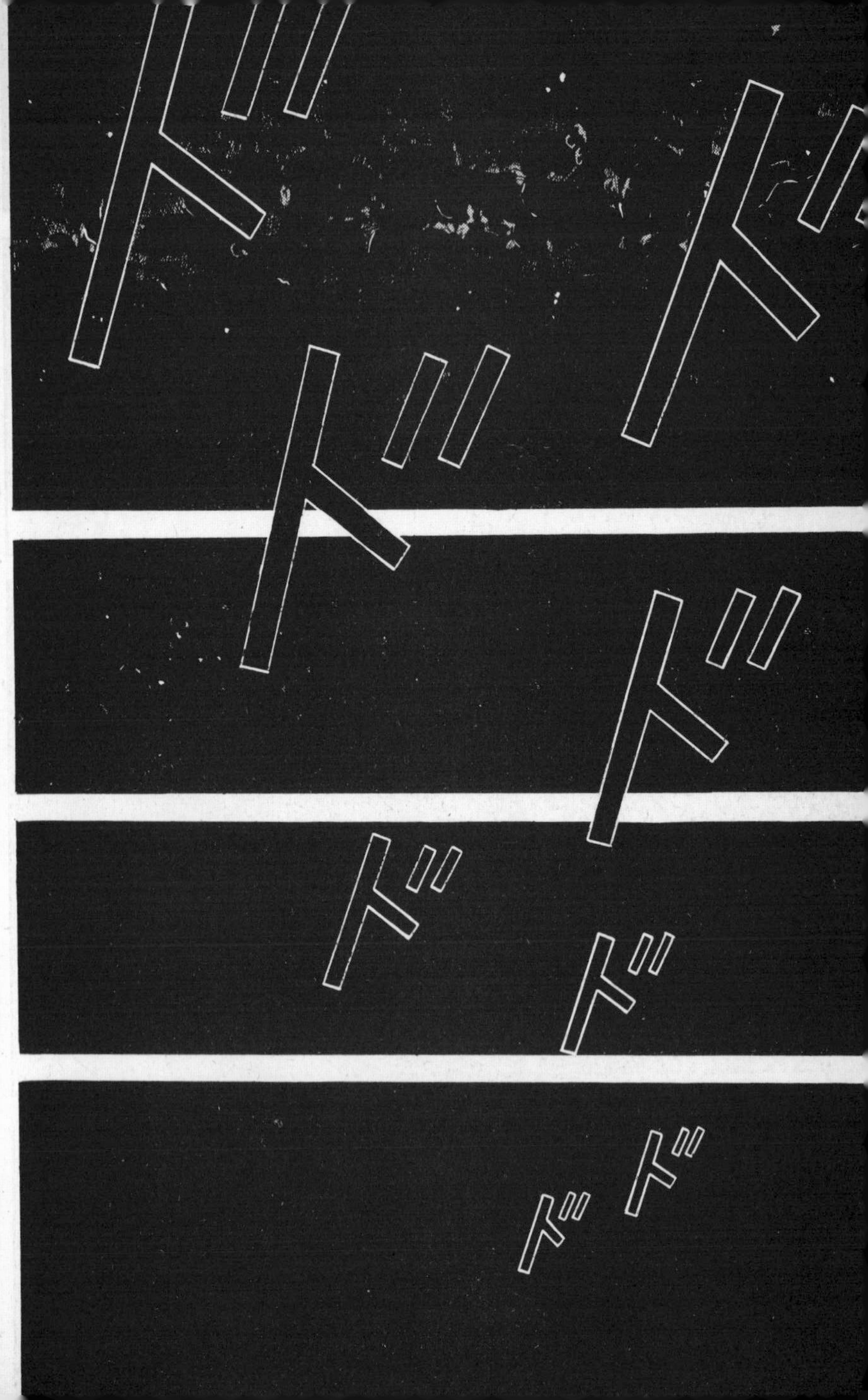
ド ド ド
ド
ド ド
ド ド

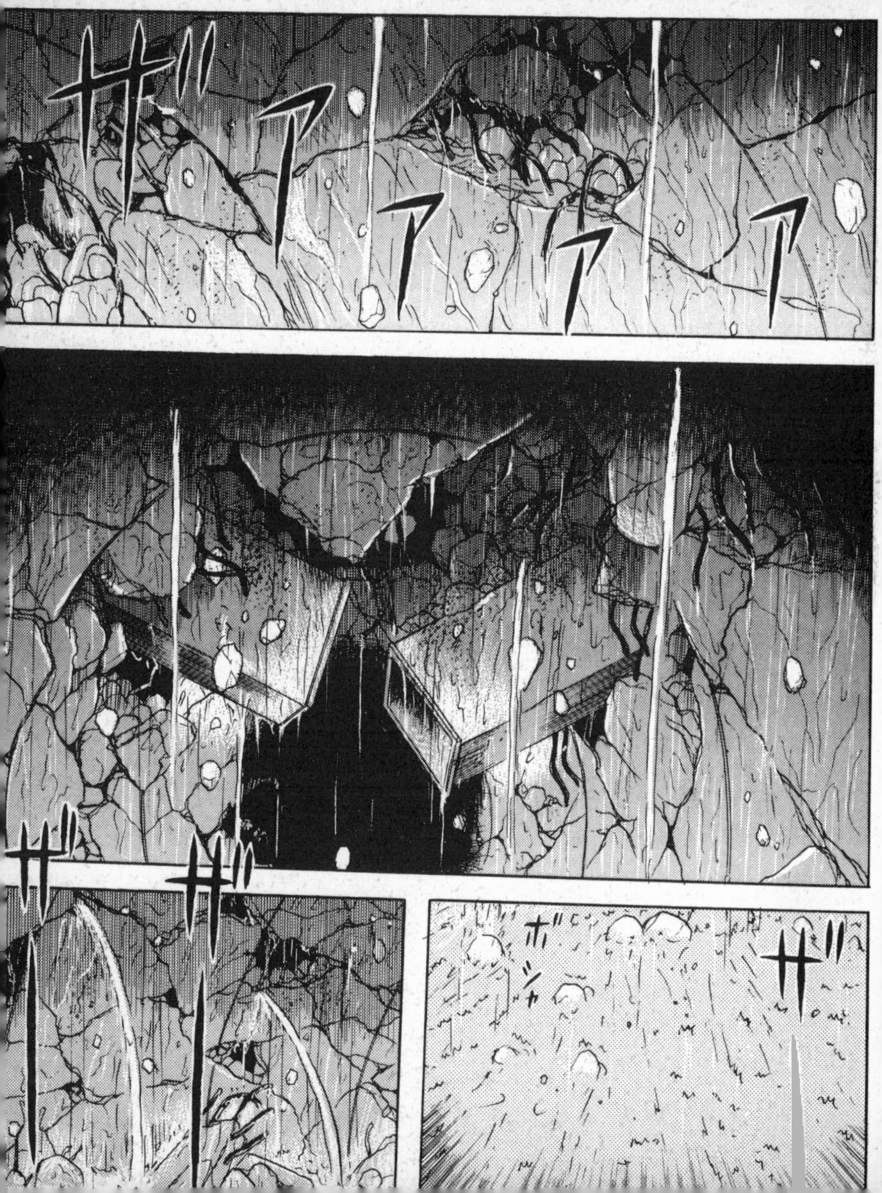

ザアアアア
ボシャ
ザ
ザ
ザ

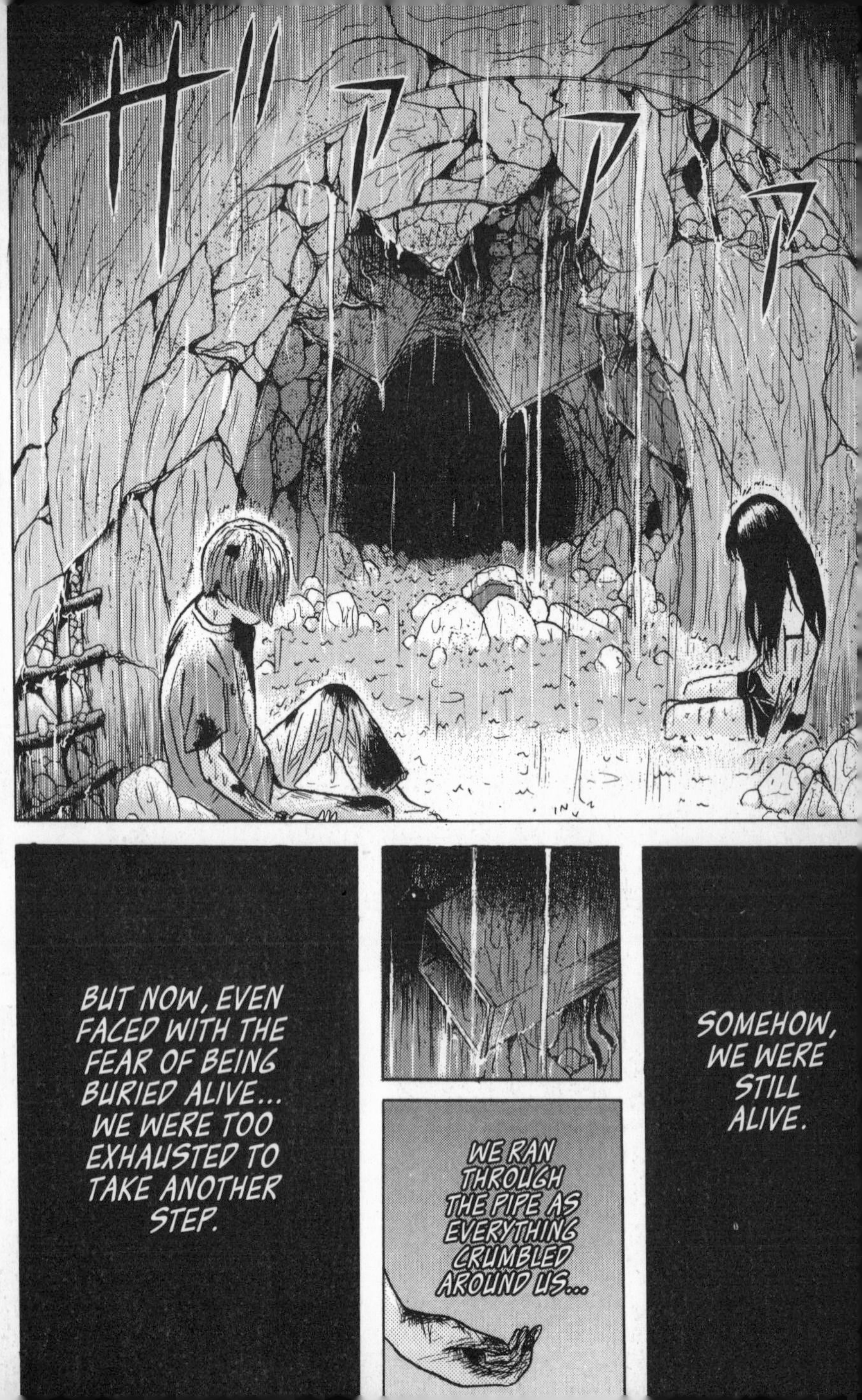
SOMEHOW, WE WERE STILL ALIVE.
WE RAN THROUGH THE PIPE AS EVERYTHING CRUMBLED AROUND US...
BUT NOW, EVEN FACED WITH THE FEAR OF BEING BURIED ALIVE... WE WERE TOO EXHAUSTED TO TAKE ANOTHER STEP.

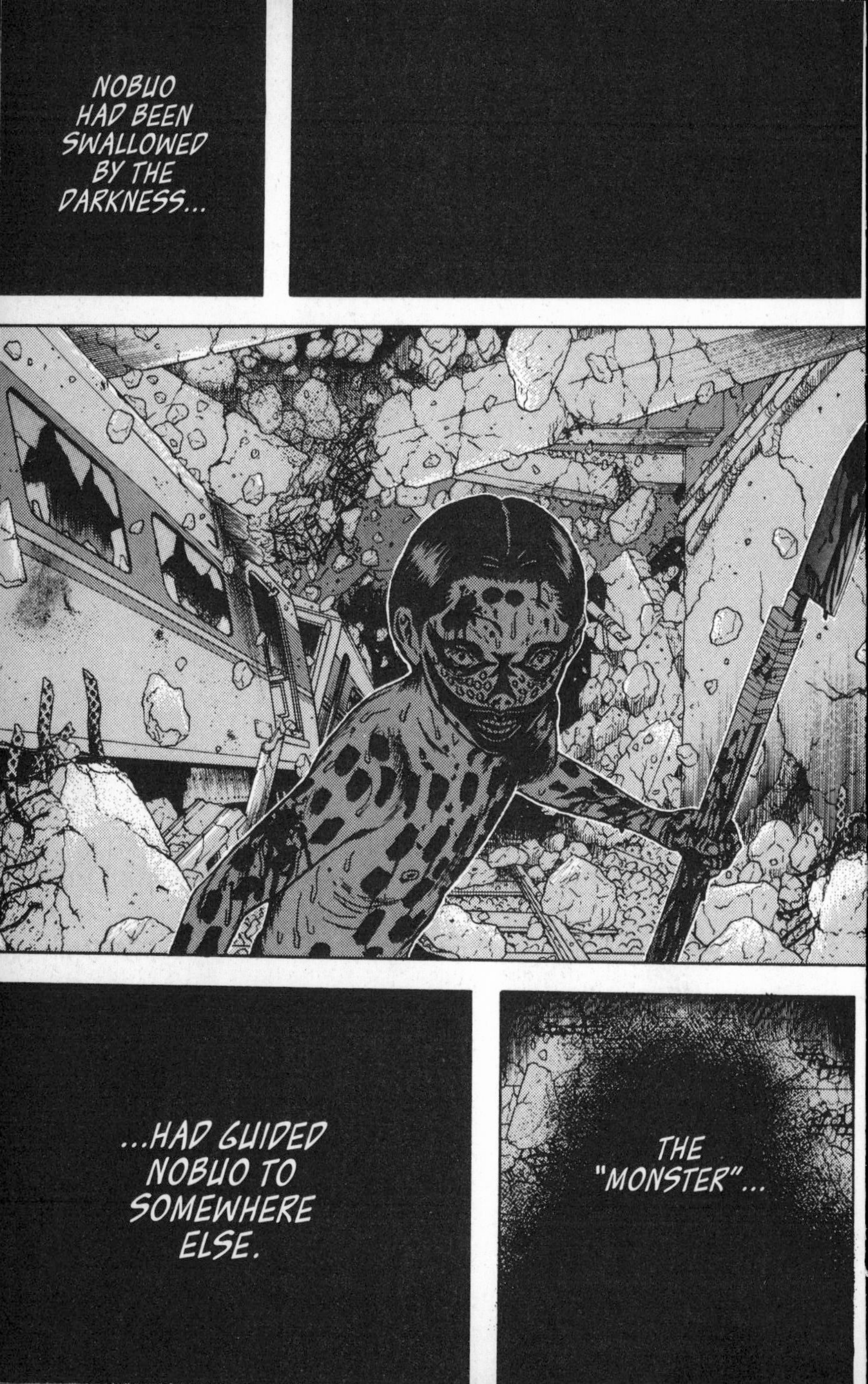
NOBUO HAD BEEN SWALLOWED BY THE DARKNESS...
THE "MONSTER"...
...HAD GUIDED NOBUO TO SOMEWHERE ELSE.

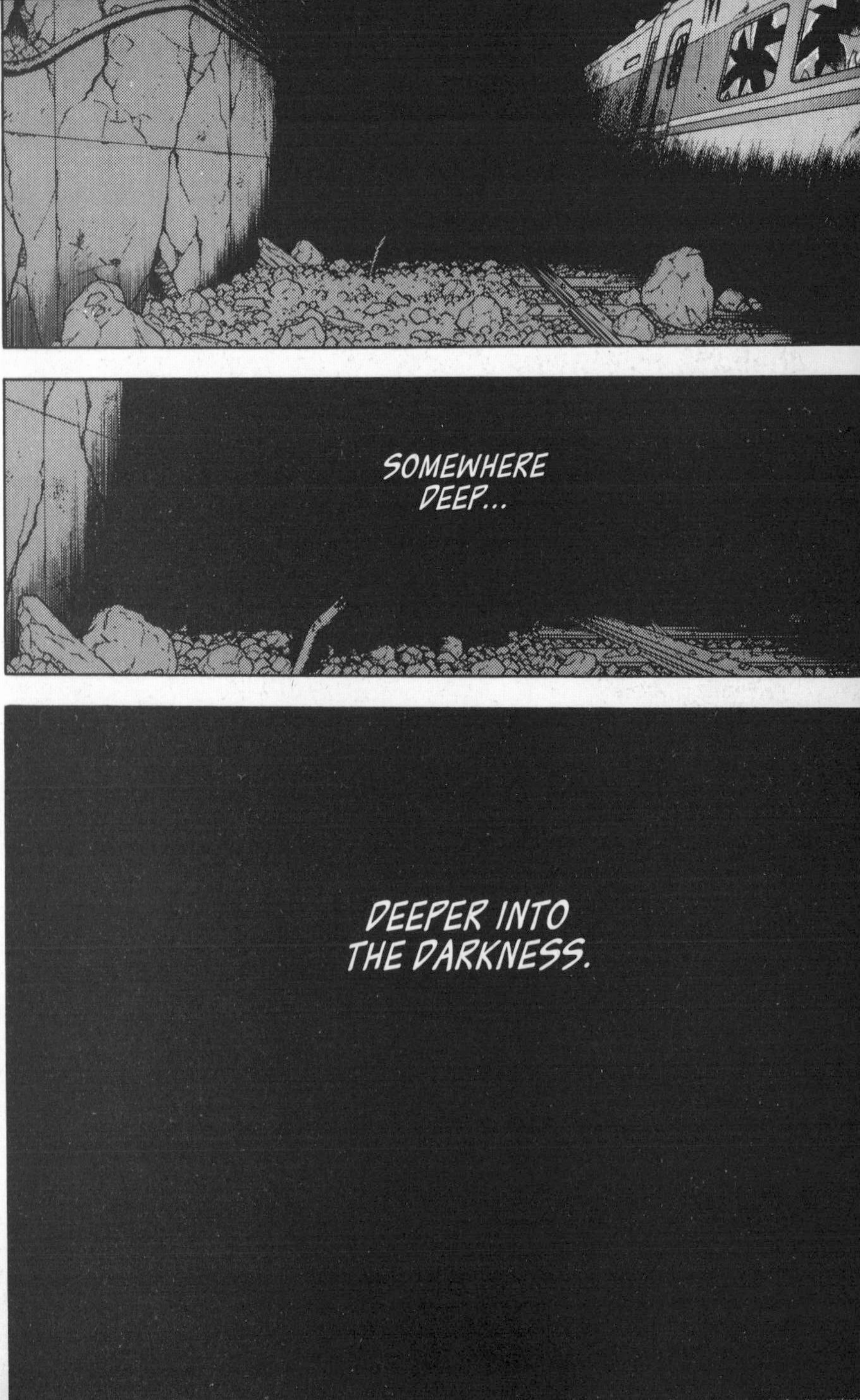
SOMEWHERE DEEP...
DEEPER INTO THE DARKNESS.

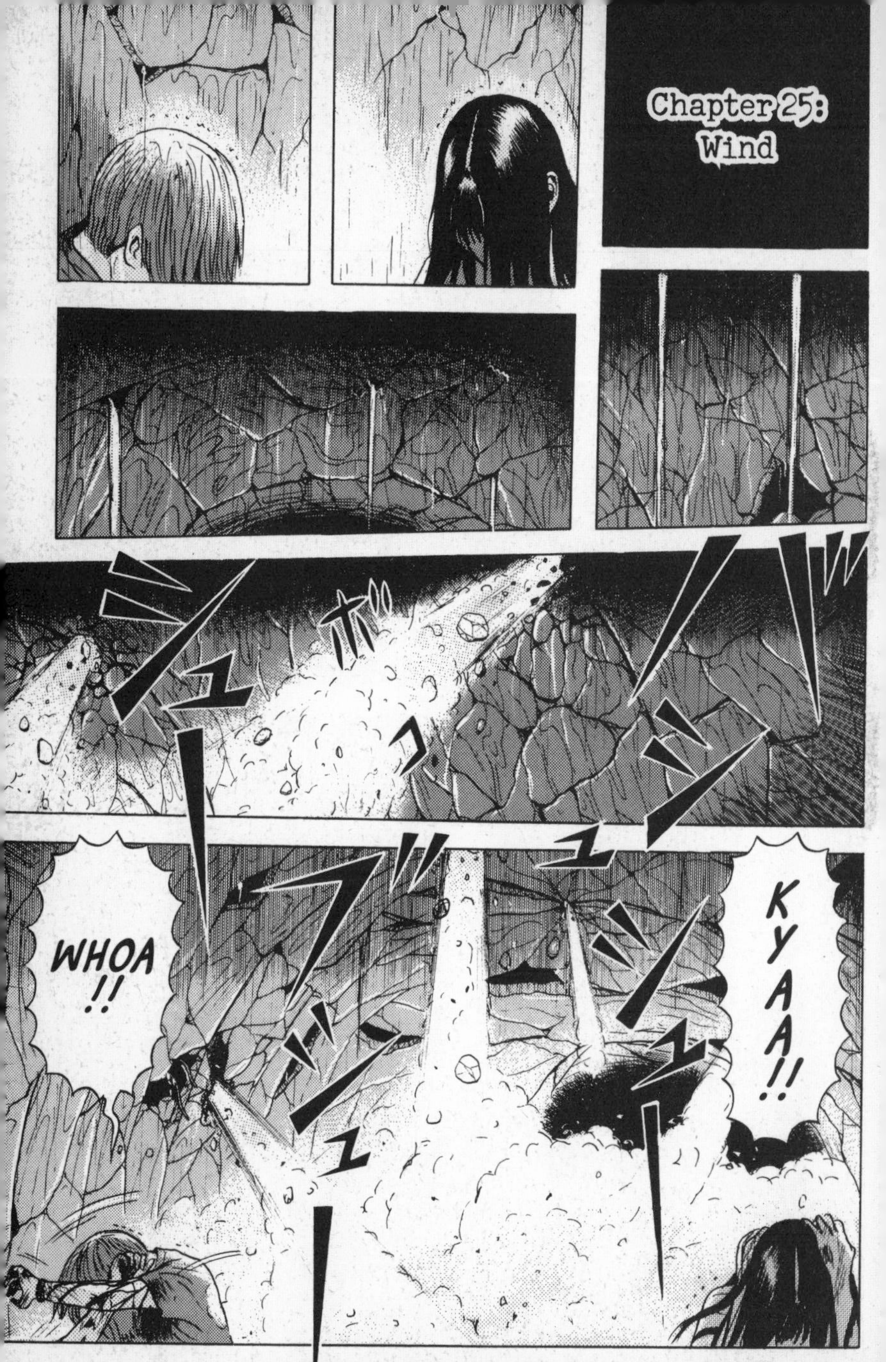
Chapter 25:
Wind
KYAA!!
WHOA!!

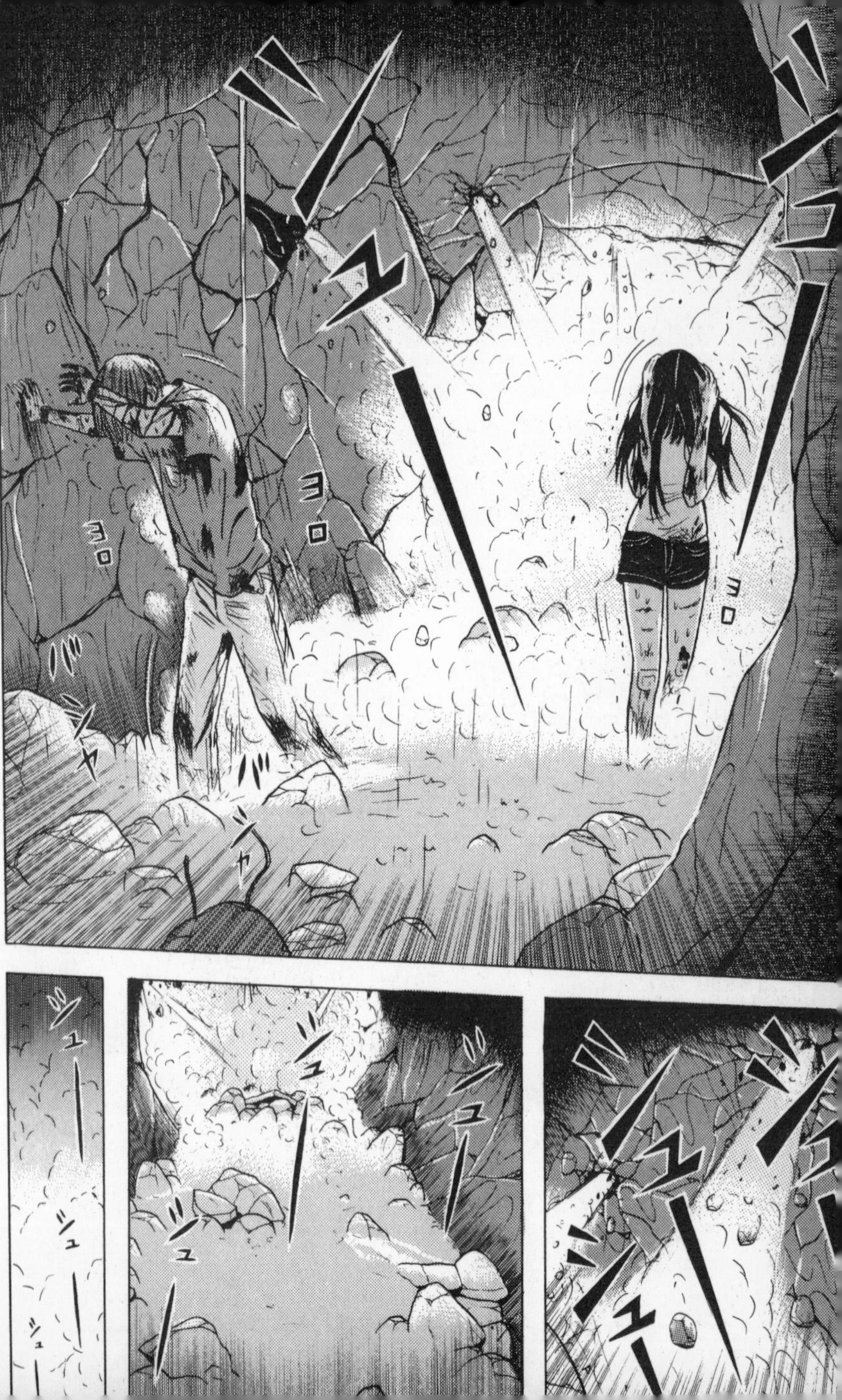
ズン
ズン
ヨロ
ヨロ
ヨロ
バシャ
バシャ
ズン
ズン
ズー
ズー
ズー
シュー
シュー
シュー

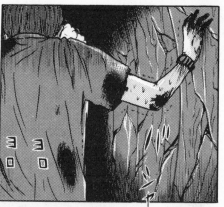

WE WERE IN PAIN, HUNGRY, THIRSTY...SO THIRSTY. OUR ENDURANCE HAD REACHED ITS LIMIT.

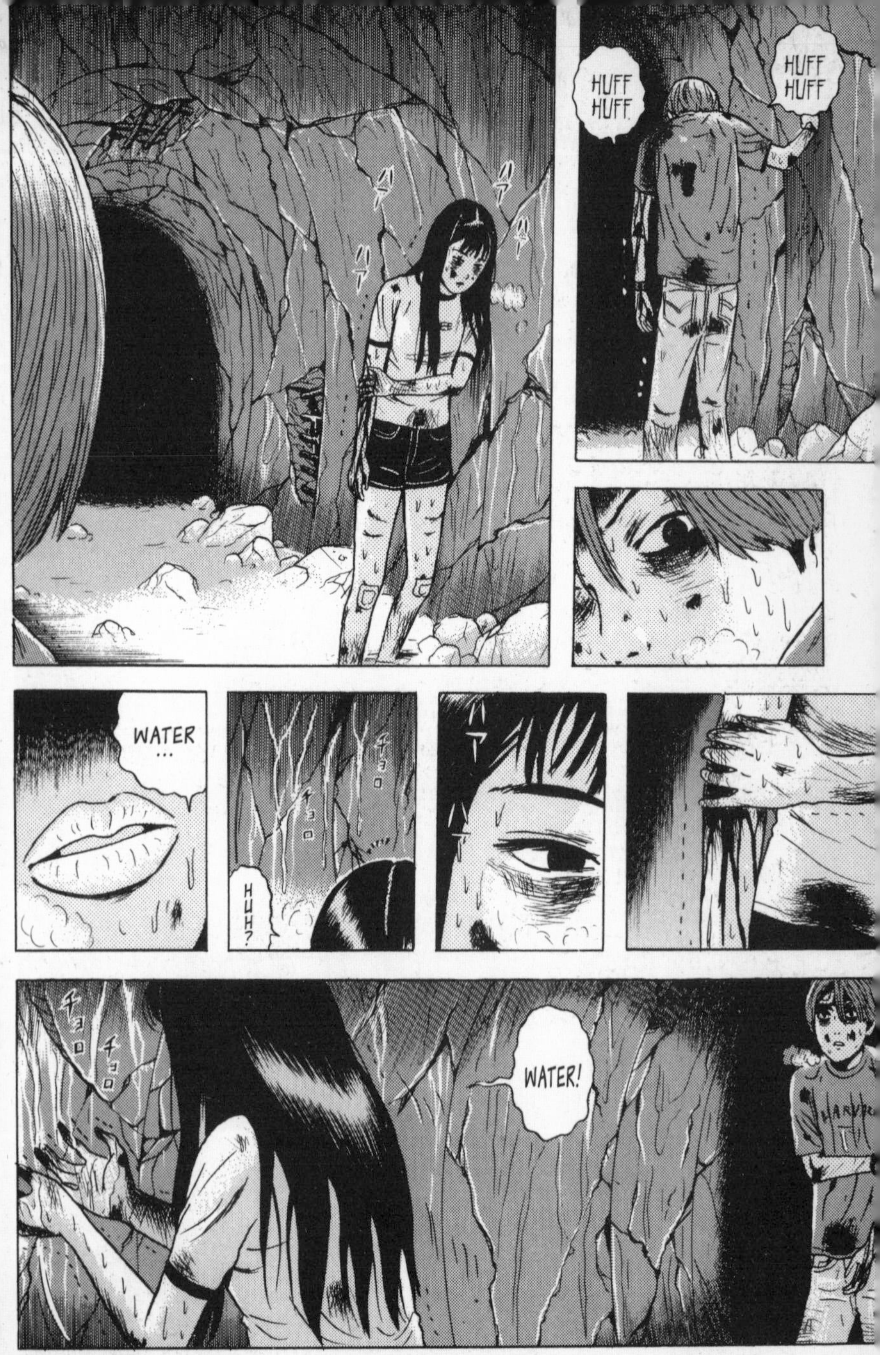
HUFF HUFF
HUFF HUFF.
HUH?
WATER ...
WATER!

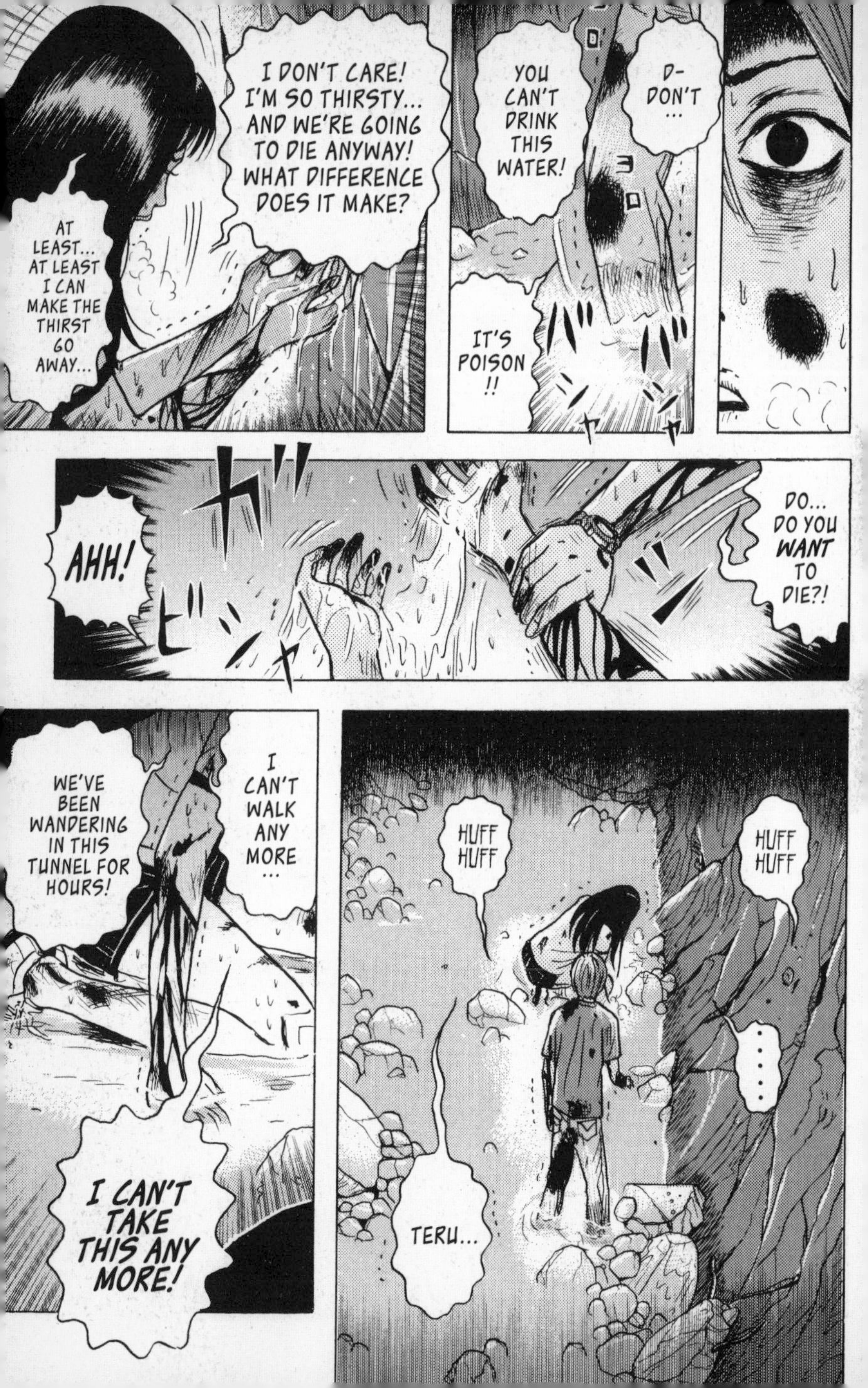
D-DON'T ...
YOU CAN'T DRINK THIS WATER!
IT'S POISON !!
I DON'T CARE! I'M SO THIRSTY... AND WE'RE GOING TO DIE ANYWAY! WHAT DIFFERENCE DOES IT MAKE?
AT LEAST... AT LEAST I CAN MAKE THE THIRST GO AWAY...
DO... DO YOU WANT TO DIE?!
AHH!
HUFF HUFF
HUFF HUFF
.....
TERU...
I CAN'T WALK ANY MORE ...
WE'VE BEEN WANDERING IN THIS TUNNEL FOR HOURS!
I CAN'T TAKE THIS ANY MORE!

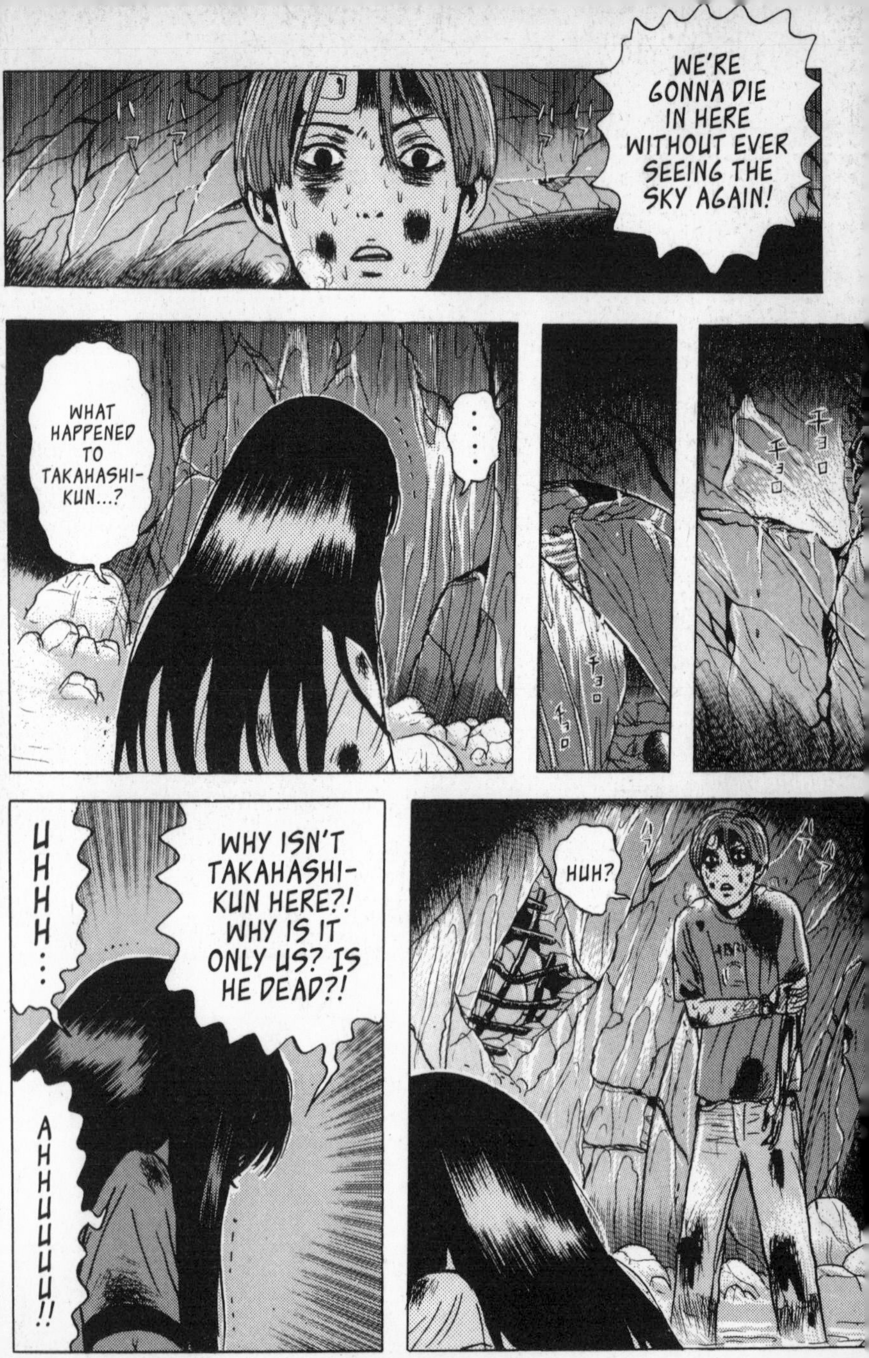
WE'RE GONNA DIE IN HERE WITHOUT EVER SEEING THE SKY AGAIN!
チョロ チョロ
チョロ チョロ
...
WHAT HAPPENED TO TAKAHASHI-KUN...?
HUH?
WHY ISN'T TAKAHASHI-KUN HERE?! WHY IS IT ONLY US? IS HE DEAD?!
UHHHH...
AHHUUUUU!!

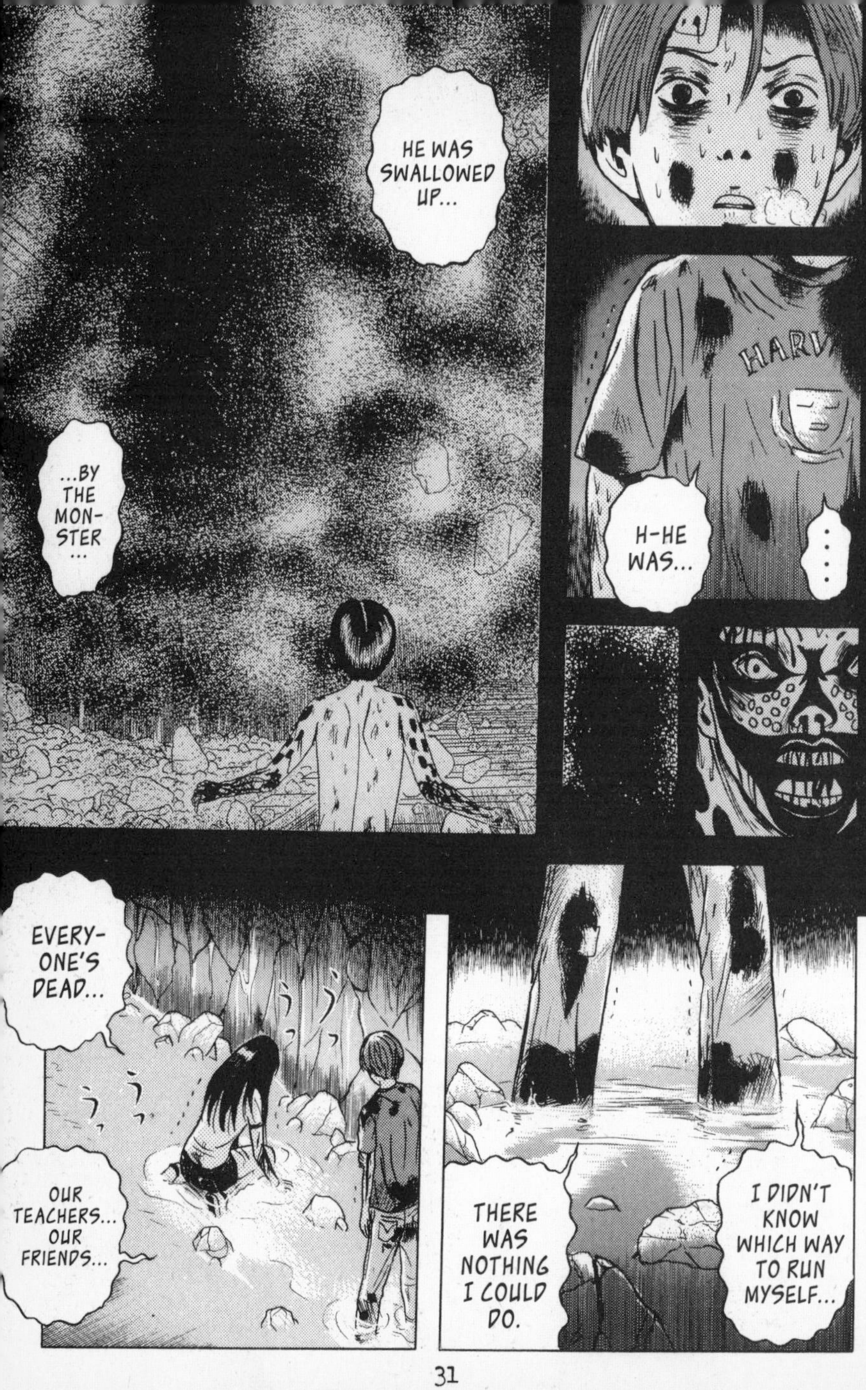
....
H-HE WAS...
HE WAS SWALLOWED UP...
...BY THE MON-STER...
I DIDN'T KNOW WHICH WAY TO RUN MYSELF...
THERE WAS NOTHING I COULD DO.
EVERY-ONE'S DEAD...
OUR TEACHERS... OUR FRIENDS...

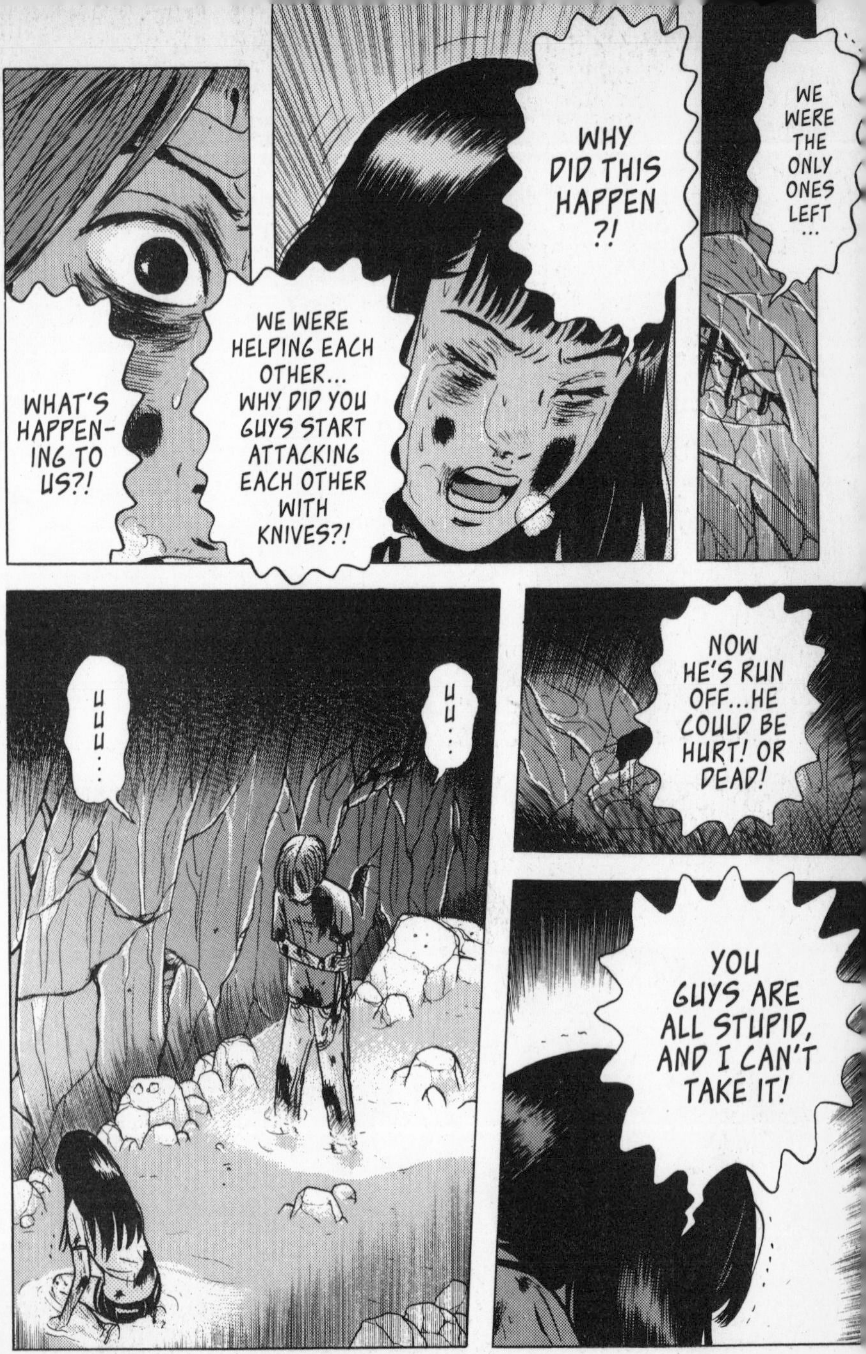
WE WERE THE ONLY ONES LEFT...
WHY DID THIS HAPPEN?!
WE WERE HELPING EACH OTHER... WHY DID YOU GUYS START ATTACKING EACH OTHER WITH KNIVES?!
WHAT'S HAPPEN-ING TO US?!
NOW HE'S RUN OFF...HE COULD BE HURT! OR DEAD!
YOU GUYS ARE ALL STUPID, AND I CAN'T TAKE IT!
UU...
UUU...

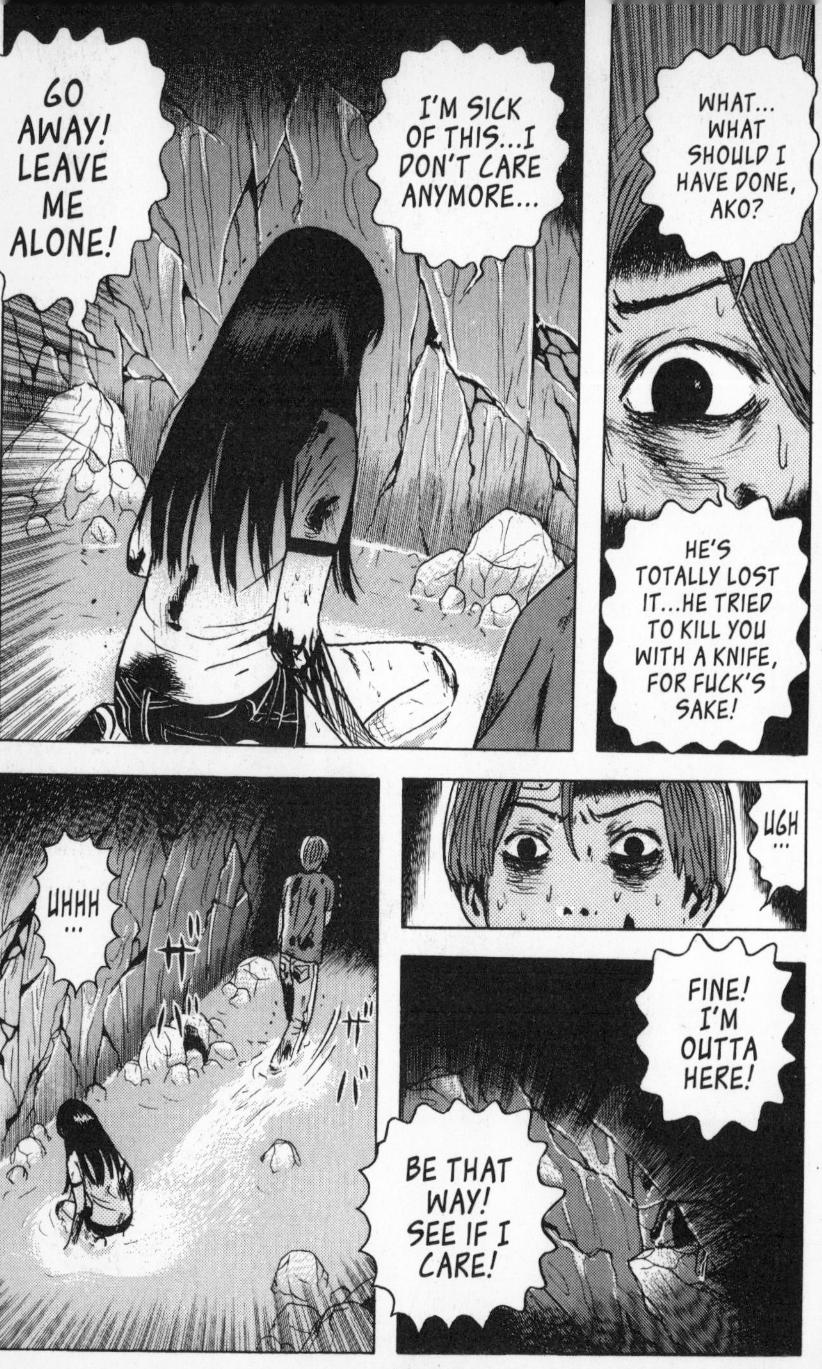
WHAT... WHAT SHOULD I HAVE DONE, AKO?
HE'S TOTALLY LOST IT...HE TRIED TO KILL YOU WITH A KNIFE, FOR FUCK'S SAKE!
I'M SICK OF THIS...I DON'T CARE ANYMORE...
GO AWAY! LEAVE ME ALONE!
UGH...
FINE! I'M OUTTA HERE!
BE THAT WAY! SEE IF I CARE!
UHHH...

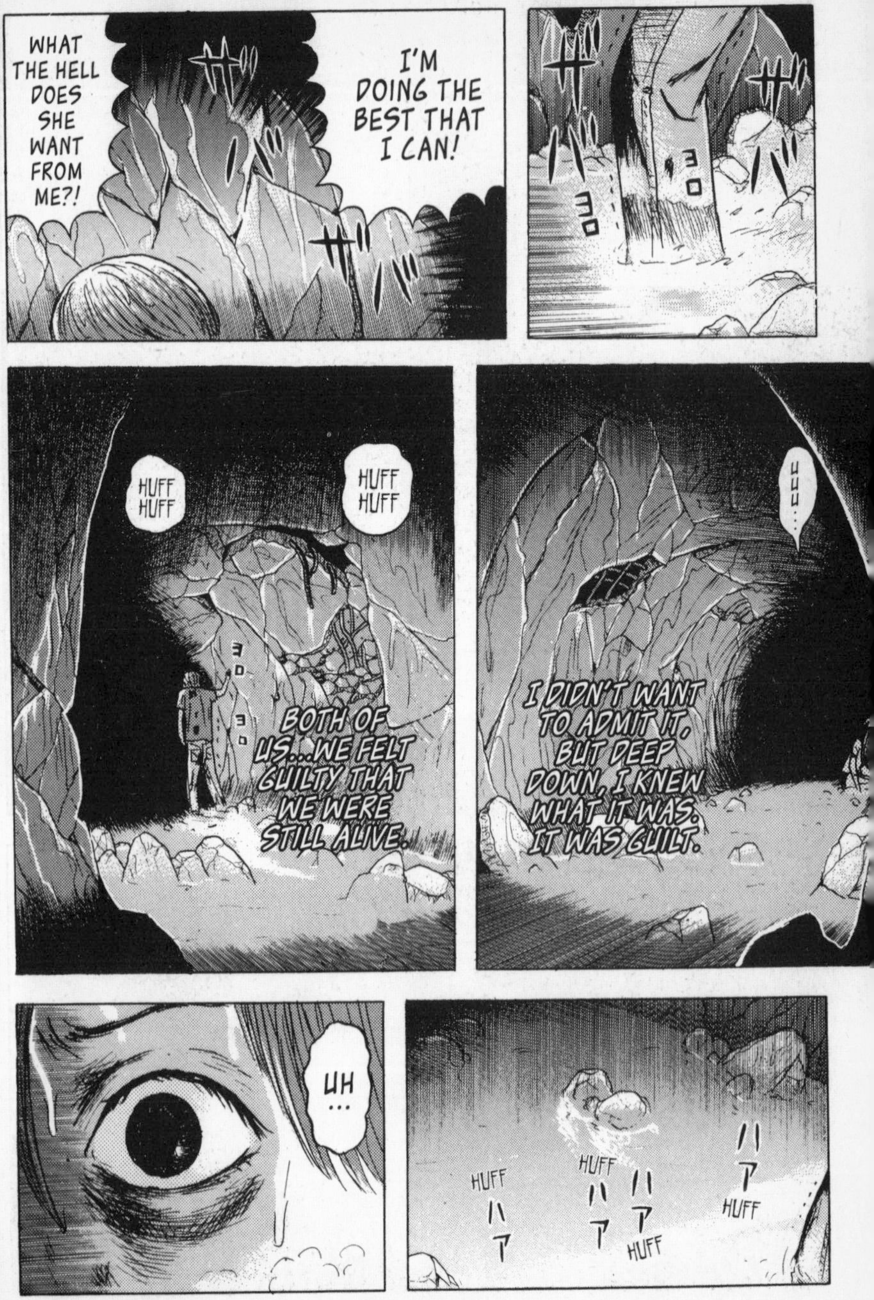
I'M DOING THE BEST THAT I CAN!
WHAT THE HELL DOES SHE WANT FROM ME?!
UUU...
I DIDN'T WANT TO ADMIT IT, BUT DEEP DOWN, I KNEW WHAT IT WAS. IT WAS GUILT.
HUFF HUFF
HUFF HUFF
BOTH OF US...WE FELT GUILTY THAT WE WERE STILL ALIVE.
ハア
HUFF
ハア
HUFF
HUFF
ハア
HUFF
ハア
UH...

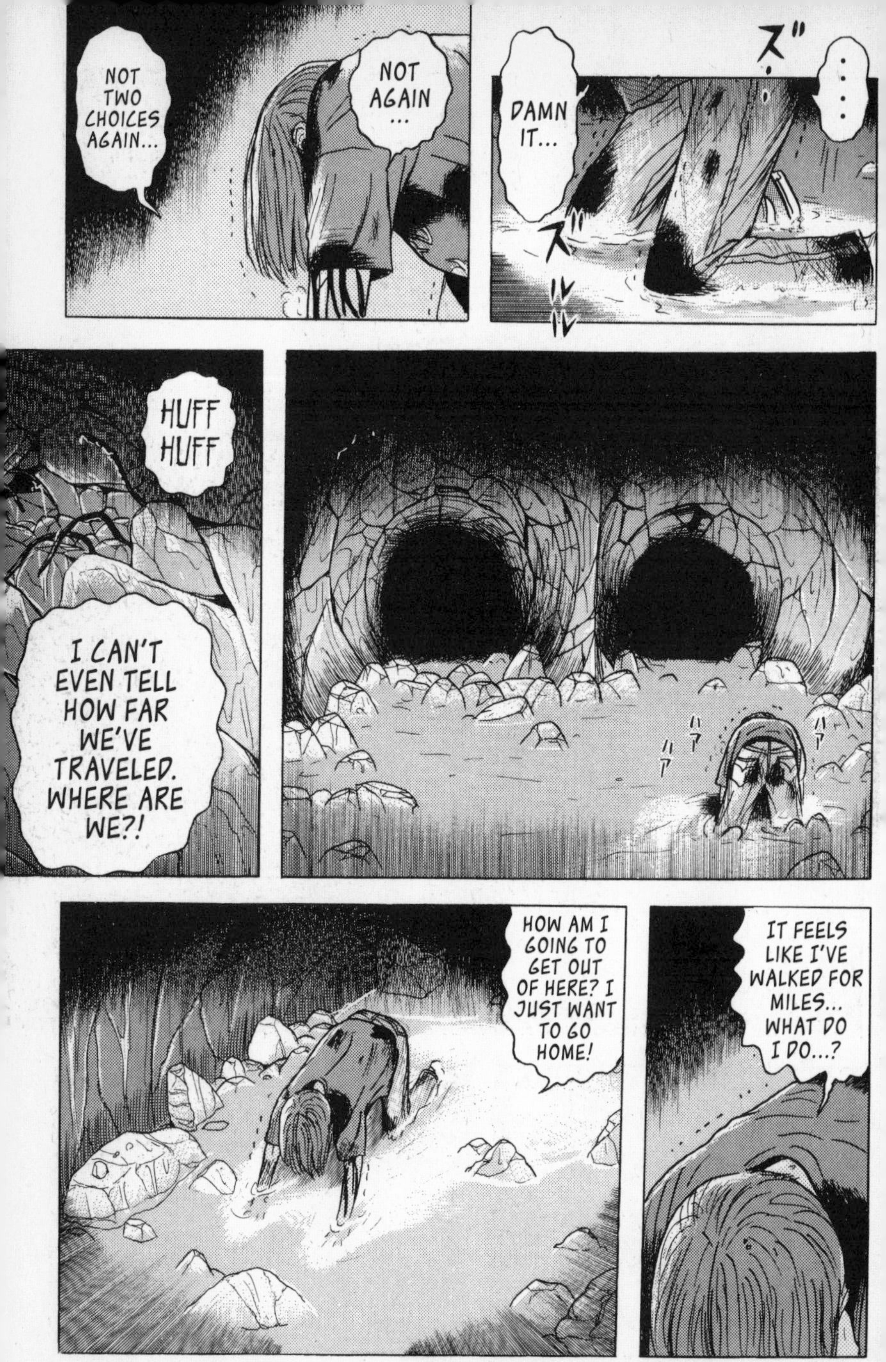
ズ
...
DAMN IT...
ズル ズル
NOT AGAIN ...
NOT TWO CHOICES AGAIN...
ハァ ハァ ハァ
HUFF HUFF
I CAN'T EVEN TELL HOW FAR WE'VE TRAVELED. WHERE ARE WE?!
IT FEELS LIKE I'VE WALKED FOR MILES... WHAT DO I DO...?
HOW AM I GOING TO GET OUT OF HERE? I JUST WANT TO GO HOME!

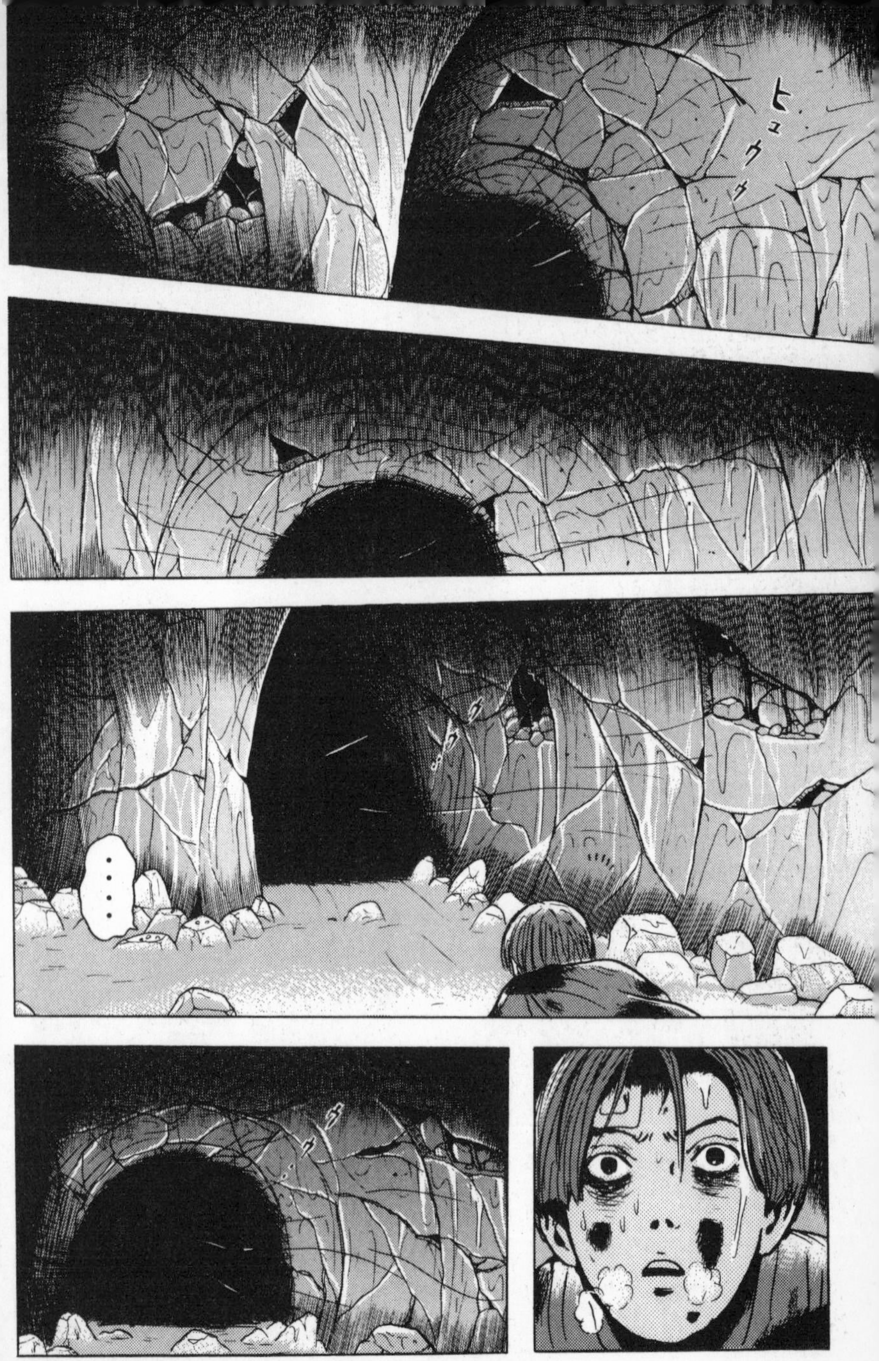
ヒュウゥ
…

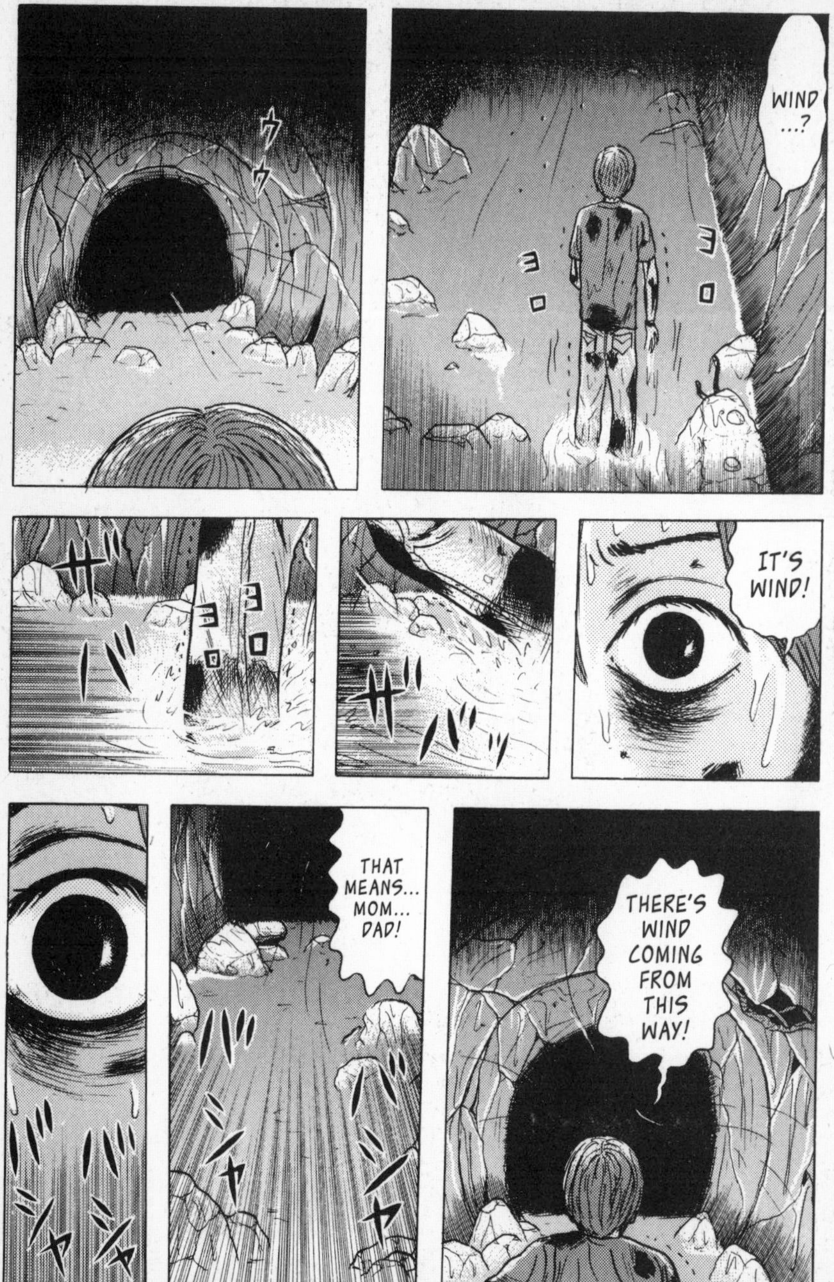

WIND ...?
IT'S WIND!
THERE'S WIND COMING FROM THIS WAY!
THAT MEANS... MOM... DAD!

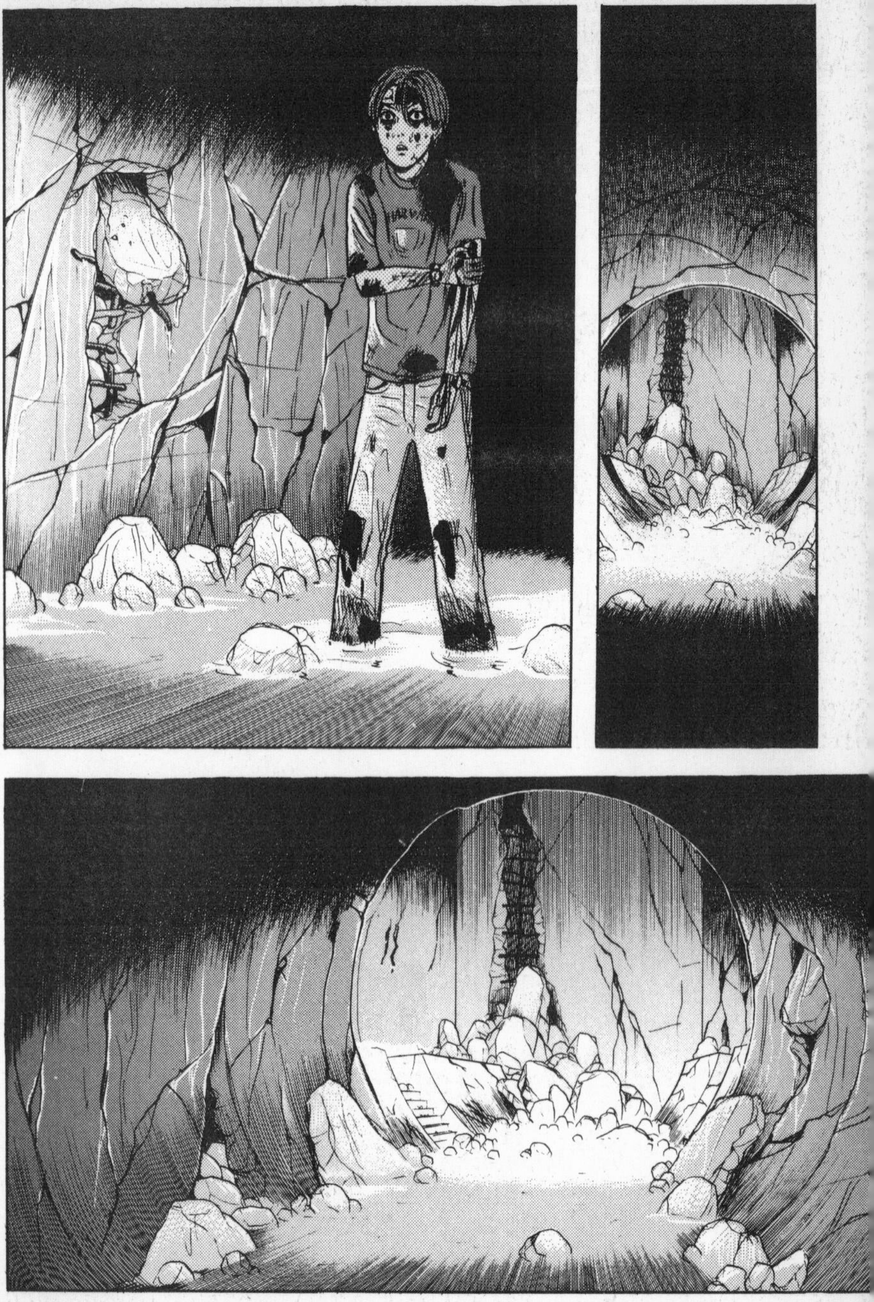

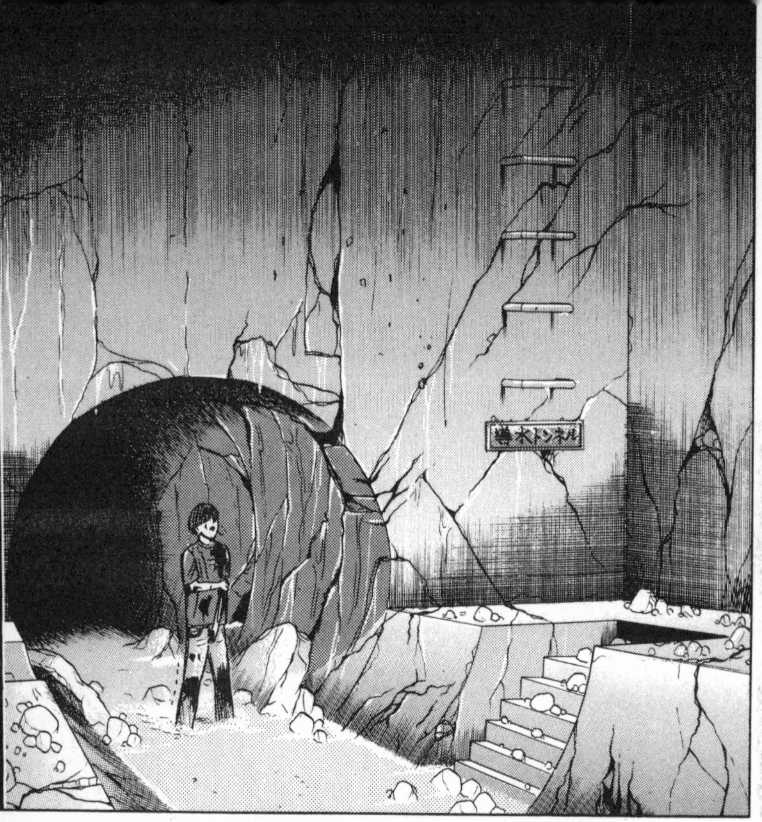

Sign: Sewer Tunnel

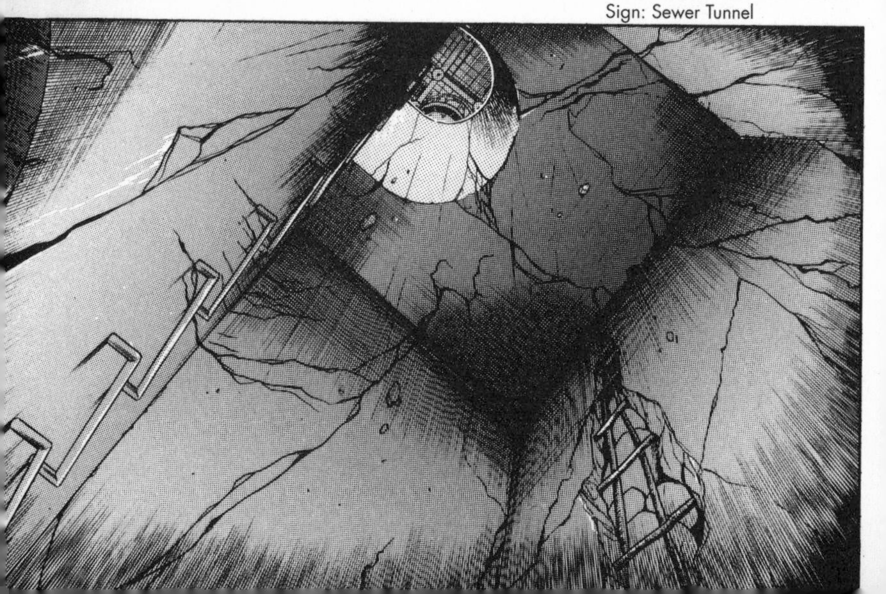

ヒュゥ
HEEEEEY
……
わ

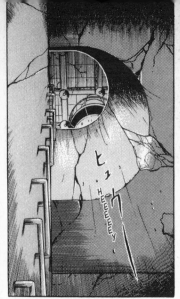

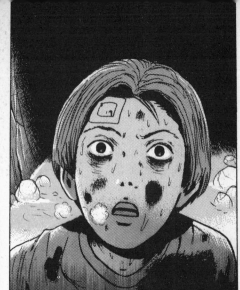

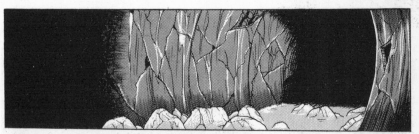

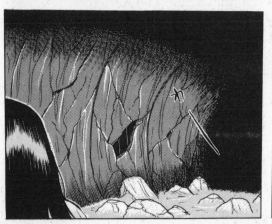

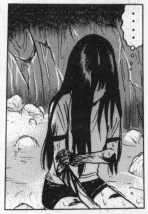

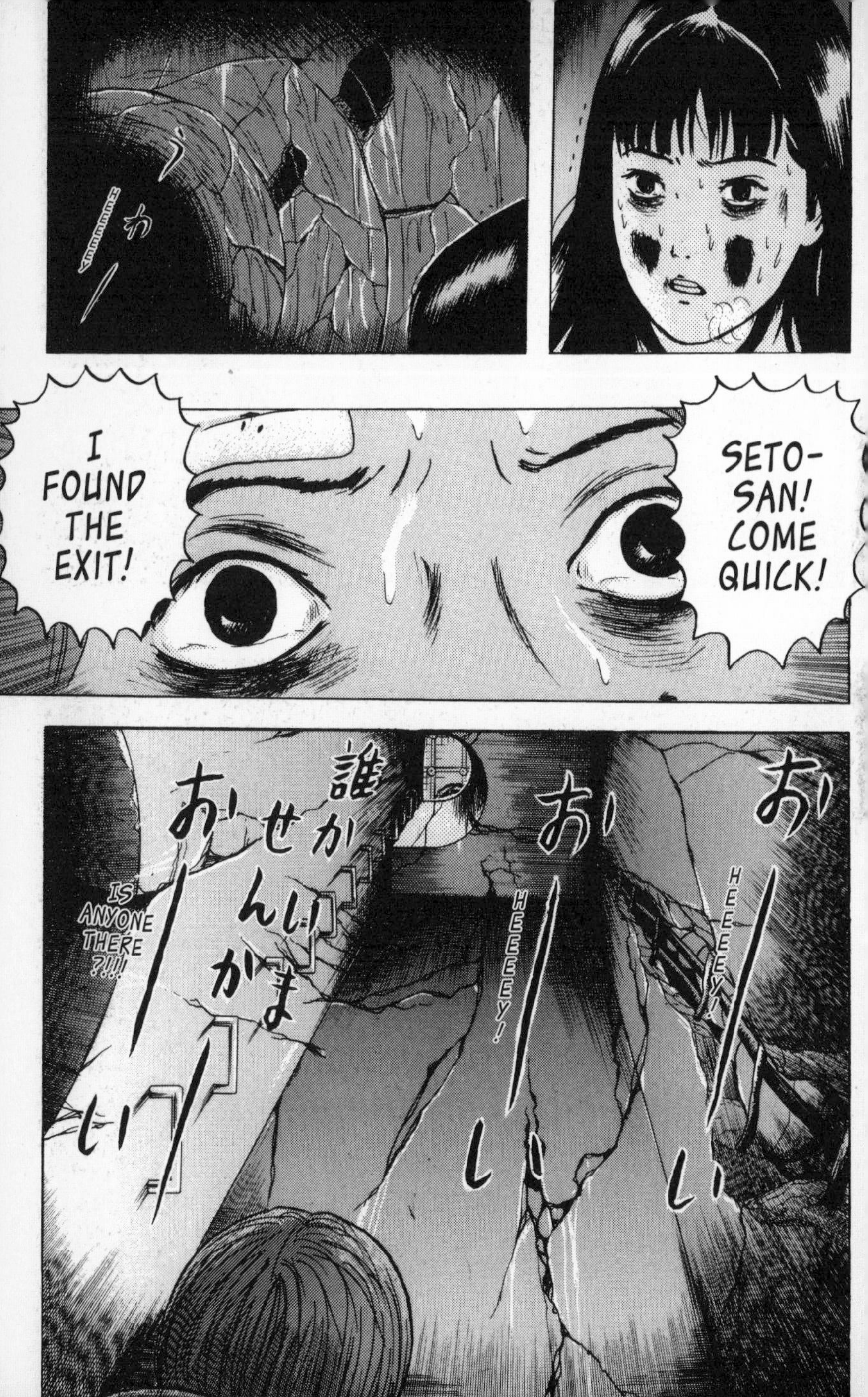
HEEEEEY!
SETO-SAN! COME QUICK!
I FOUND THE EXIT!
おーいー
HEEEEEY!
おーいー
HEEEEEY!
誰かいませんかーっ
IS ANYONE THERE?!!!
おーいっ

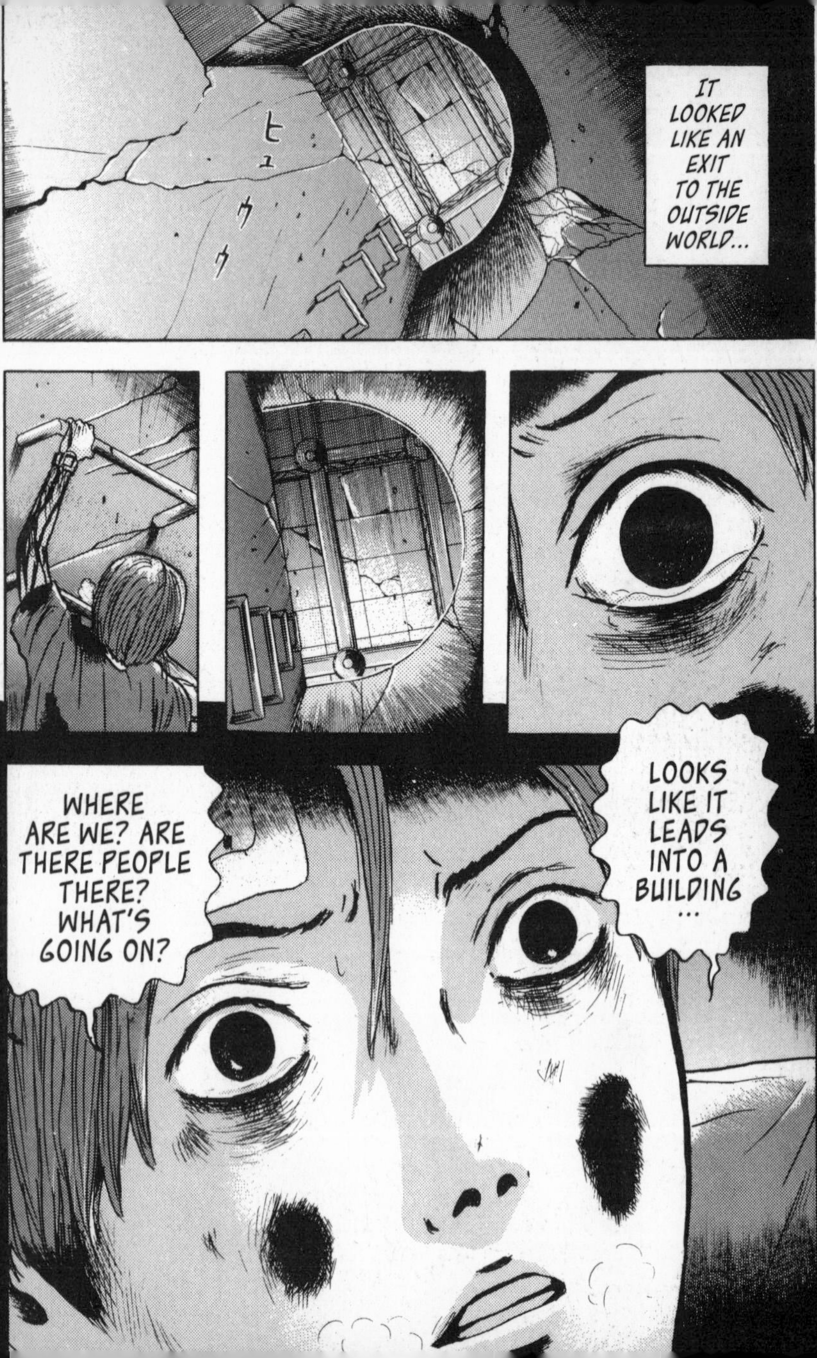
IT LOOKED LIKE AN EXIT TO THE OUTSIDE WORLD...
ヒュウウ
LOOKS LIKE IT LEADS INTO A BUILDING ...
WHERE ARE WE? ARE THERE PEOPLE THERE? WHAT'S GOING ON?

Chapter 26: Ruins

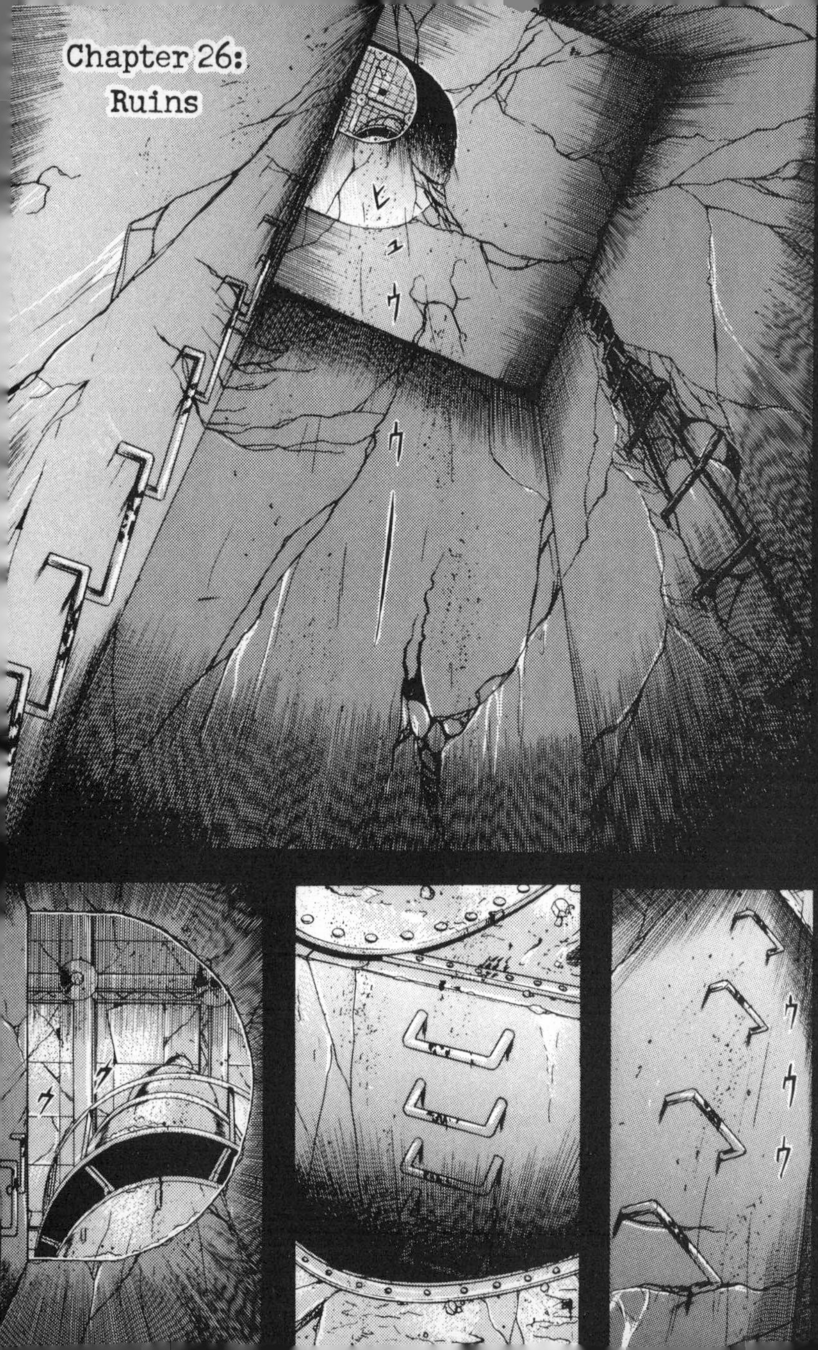
ヒュウウ
ウウウ

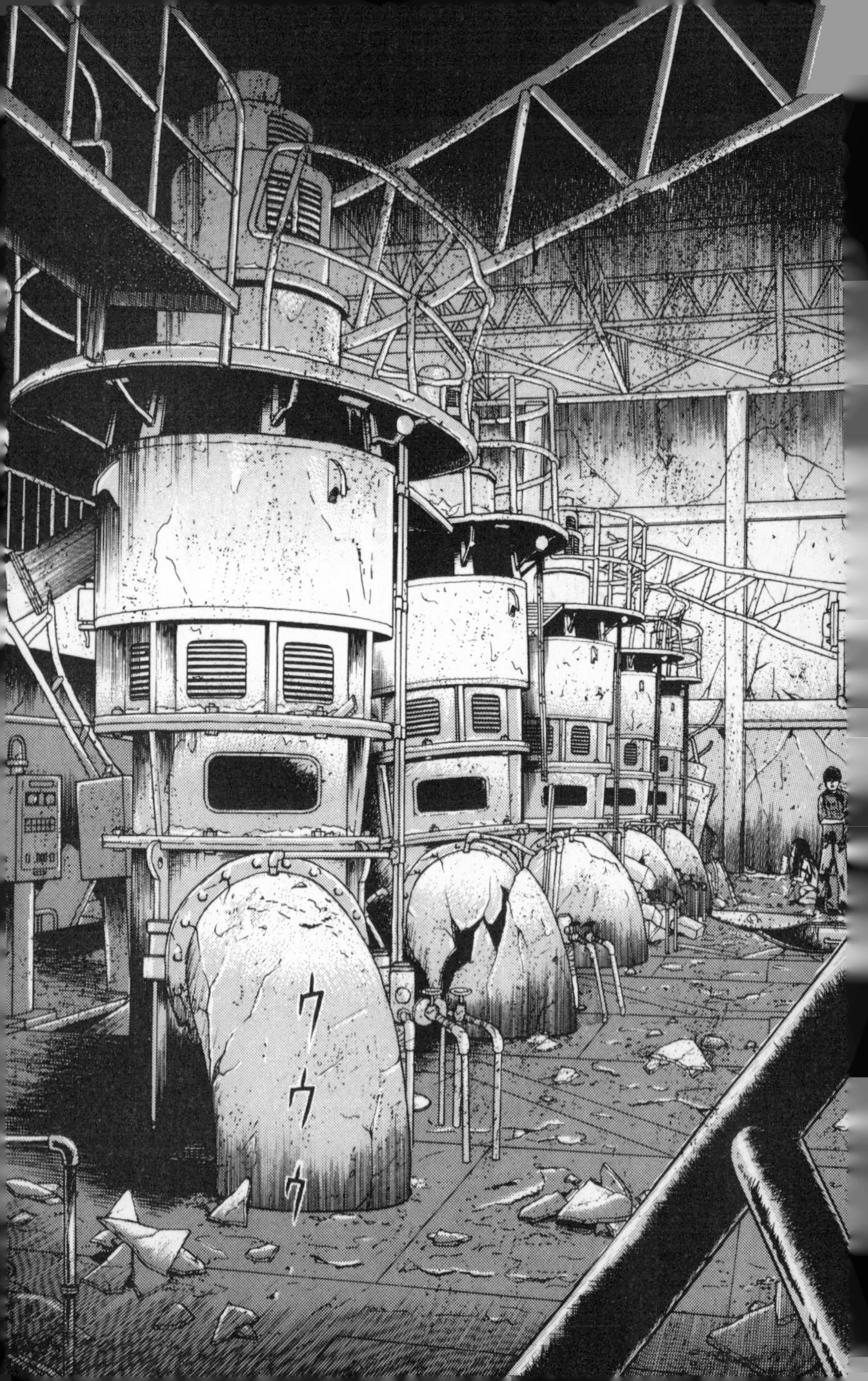
ウウウ

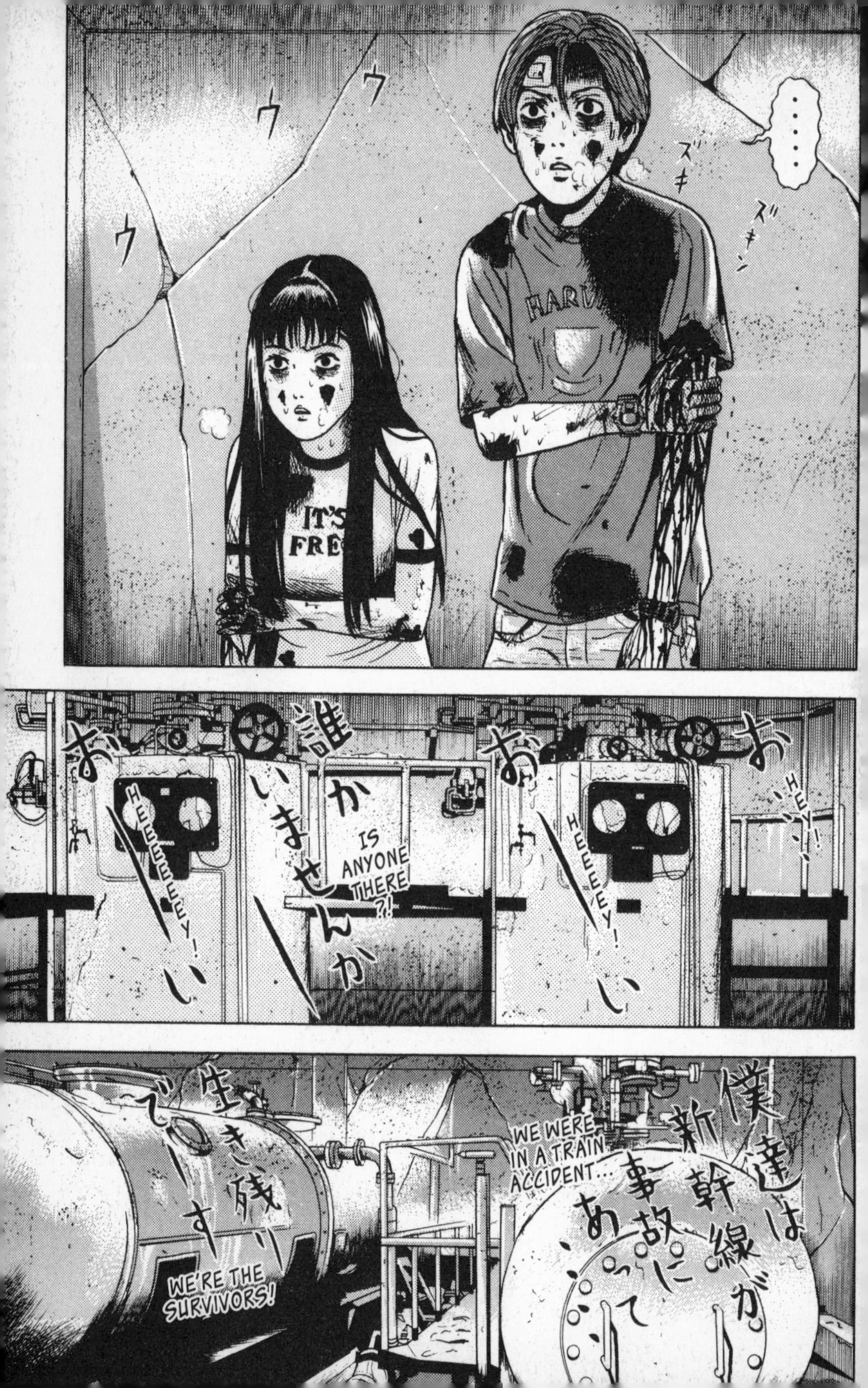

……
ズキ
ズキン
ウ
ウ
ウ
お、
HEY!
おーい
HEEEEY!
誰かいませんか
IS ANYONE THERE?!
おーい
HEEEEEEY!
僕達は新幹線が事故にあって
WE WERE IN A TRAIN ACCIDENT...
生き残りです
WE'RE THE SURVIVORS!

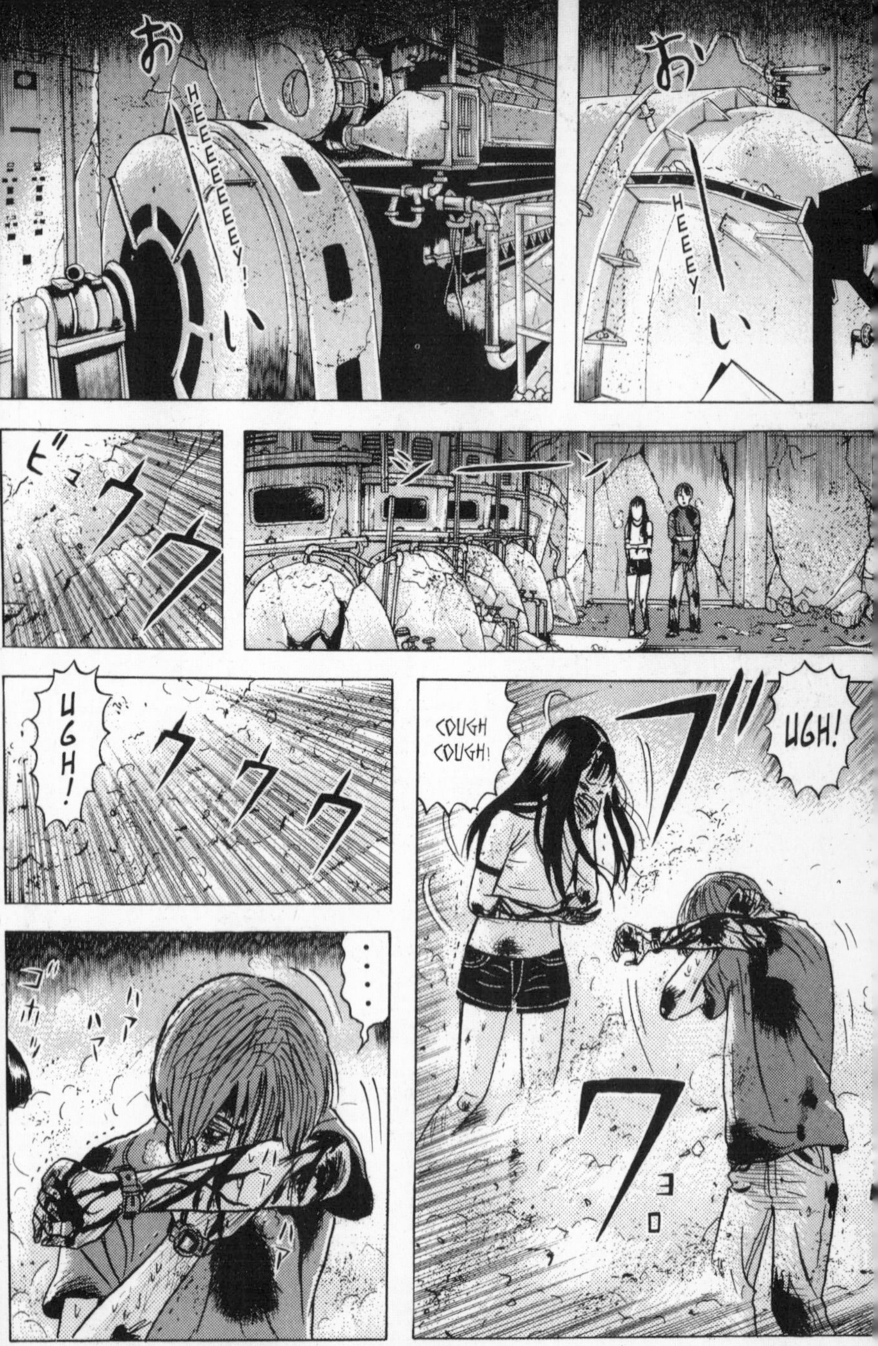
おい
HEEEY!
おい
HEEEEEEEY!
UGH!
COUGH COUGH!
UGH!
....

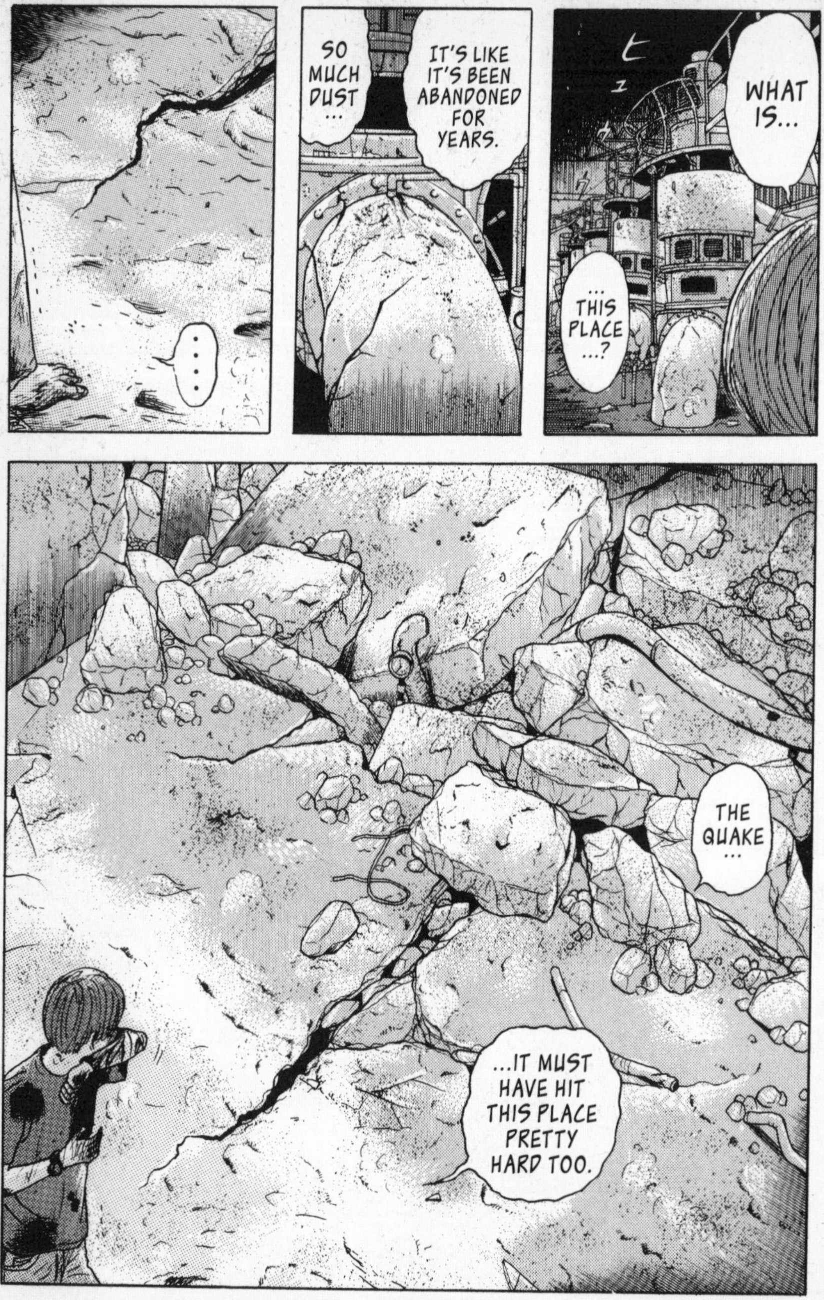
WHAT IS...
...THIS PLACE...?
IT'S LIKE IT'S BEEN ABANDONED FOR YEARS.
SO MUCH DUST...
....
THE QUAKE...
...IT MUST HAVE HIT THIS PLACE PRETTY HARD TOO.

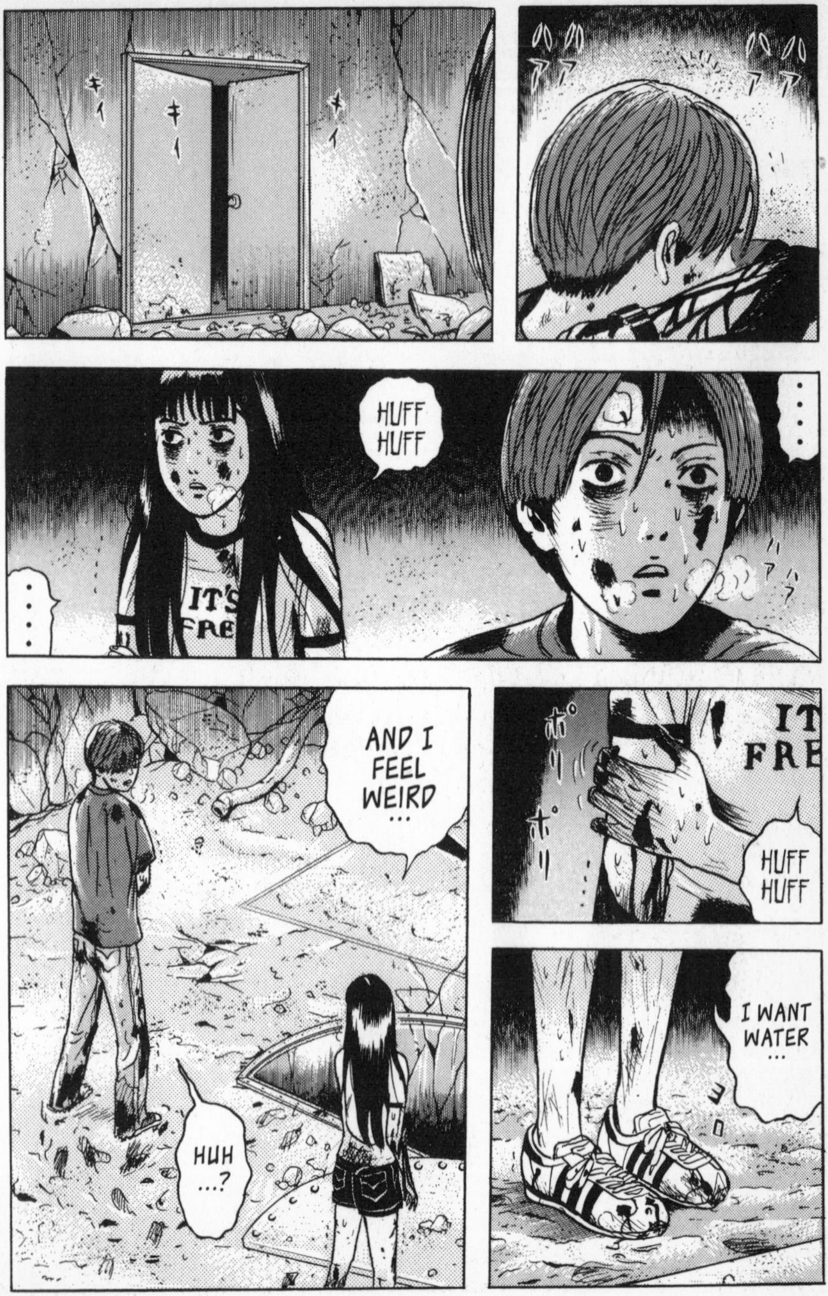
...
HUFF HUFF
...
AND I FEEL WEIRD ...
HUH ...?
HUFF HUFF
I WANT WATER ...

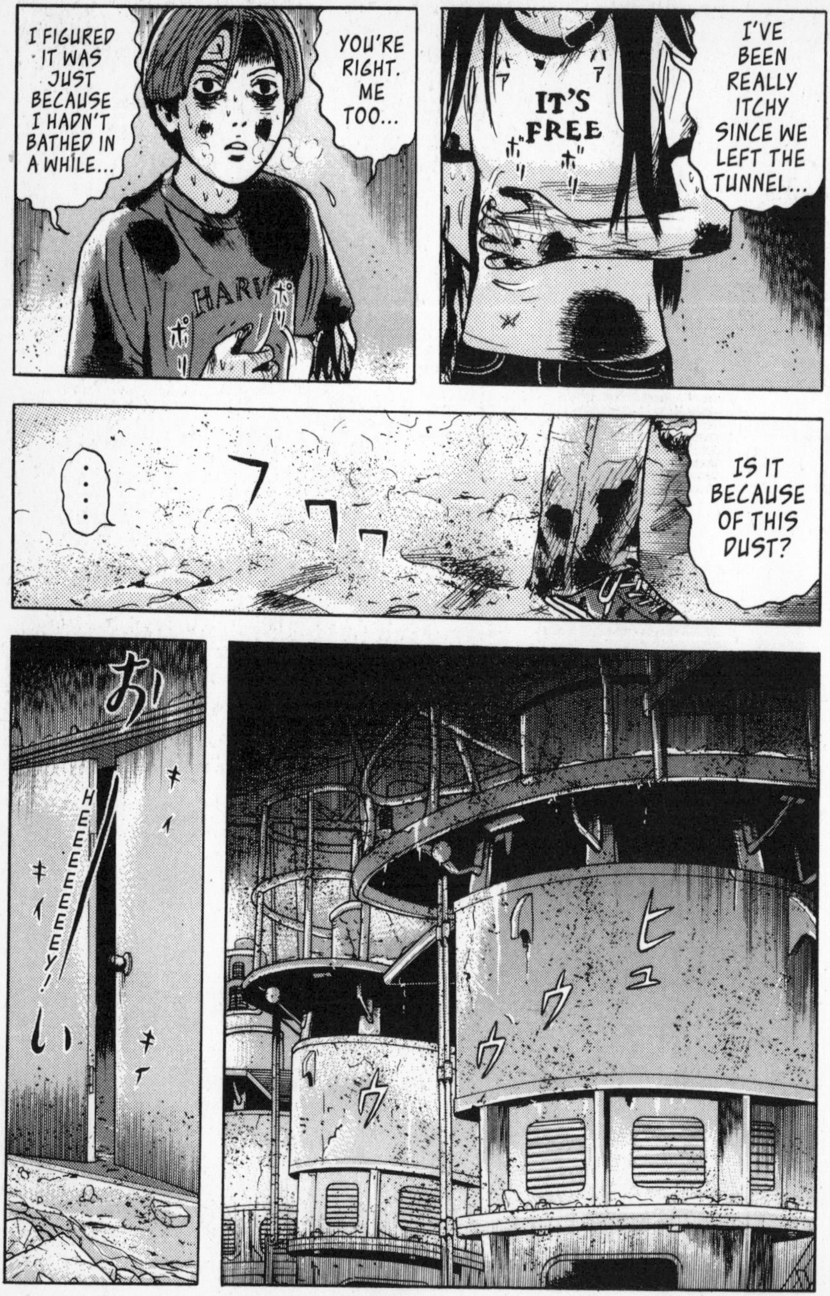
I'VE BEEN REALLY ITCHY SINCE WE LEFT THE TUNNEL...
IT'S FREE
YOU'RE RIGHT. ME TOO...
I FIGURED IT WAS JUST BECAUSE I HADN'T BATHED IN A WHILE...
HARV
IS IT BECAUSE OF THIS DUST?
....
HEEEEEEEEEY!

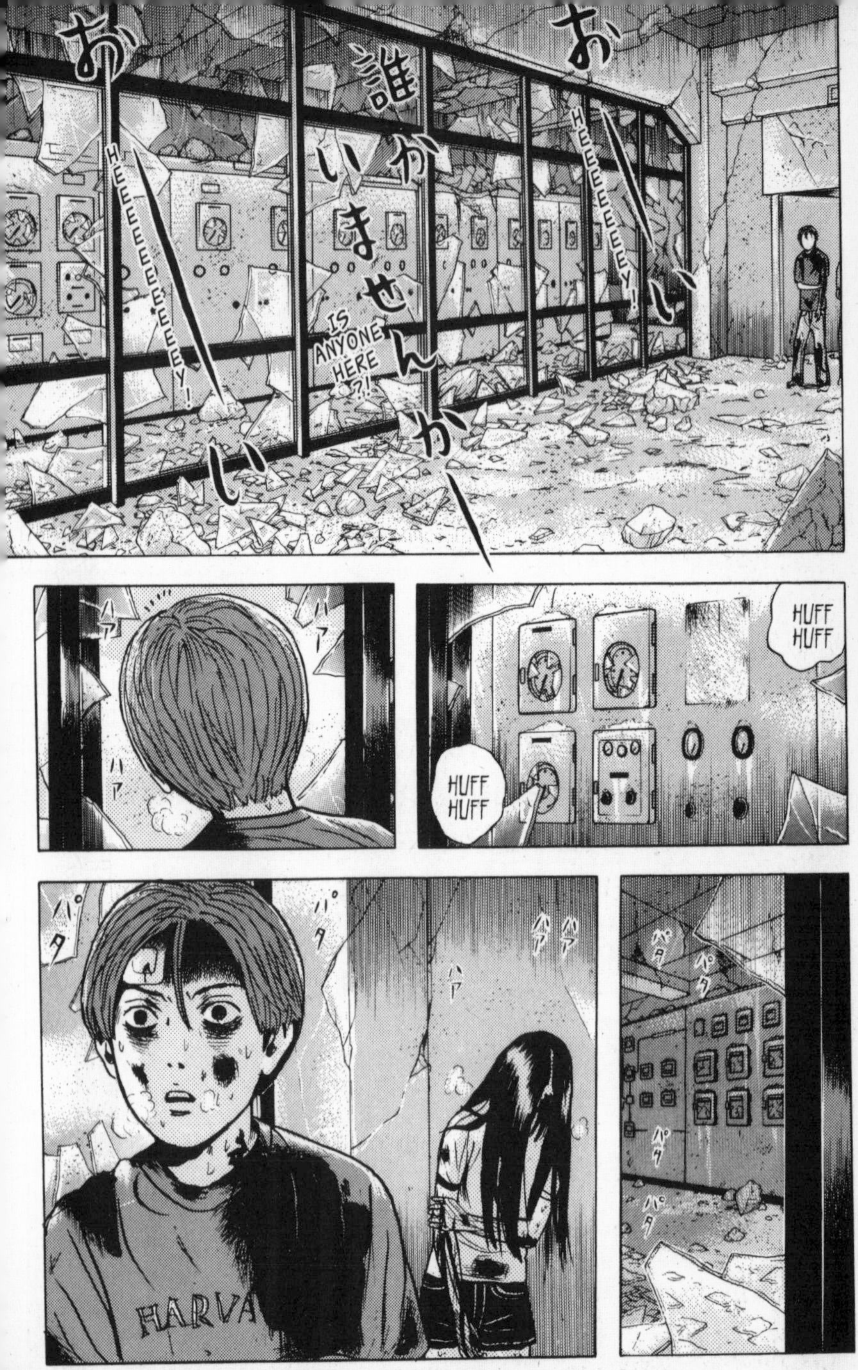

おーい
HEEEEEEEEY!
誰かいませんか
IS ANYONE HERE ?!
おーい
HEEEEEEEEEEEEY!
HUFF HUFF
HUFF HUFF
ハア ハア
パタ
パタ
パタ
パタ
パタ
パタ
ハア ハア
ハア
HARVA

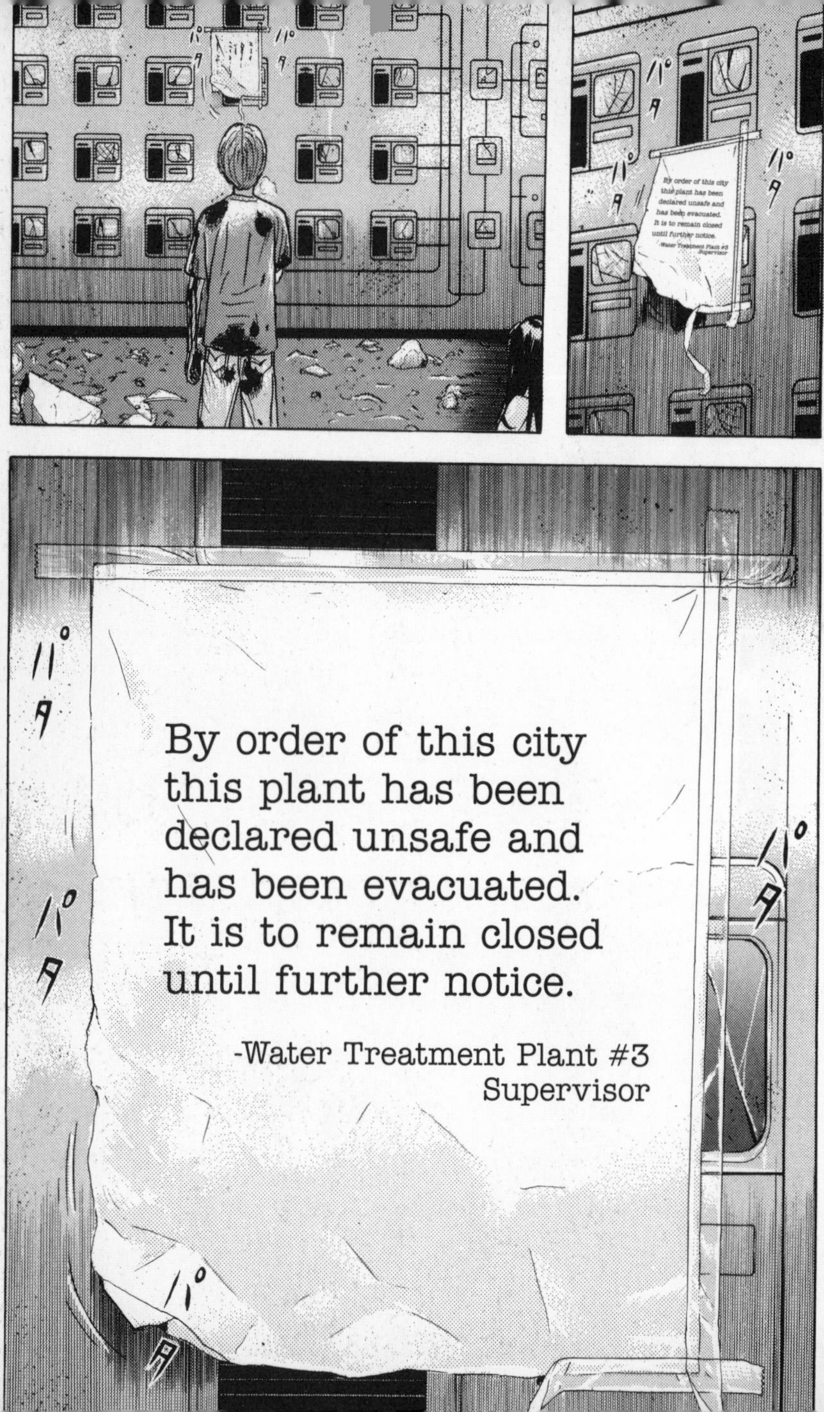

パタ
パタ
パタ
By order of this city this plant has been declared unsafe and has been evacuated. It is to remain closed until further notice.
-Water Treatment Plant #3 Supervisor
パタ
パタ
パタ
パタ
パタ
By order of this city
this plant has been
declared unsafe and
has been evacuated.
It is to remain closed
until further notice.
-Water Treatment Plant #3
Supervisor

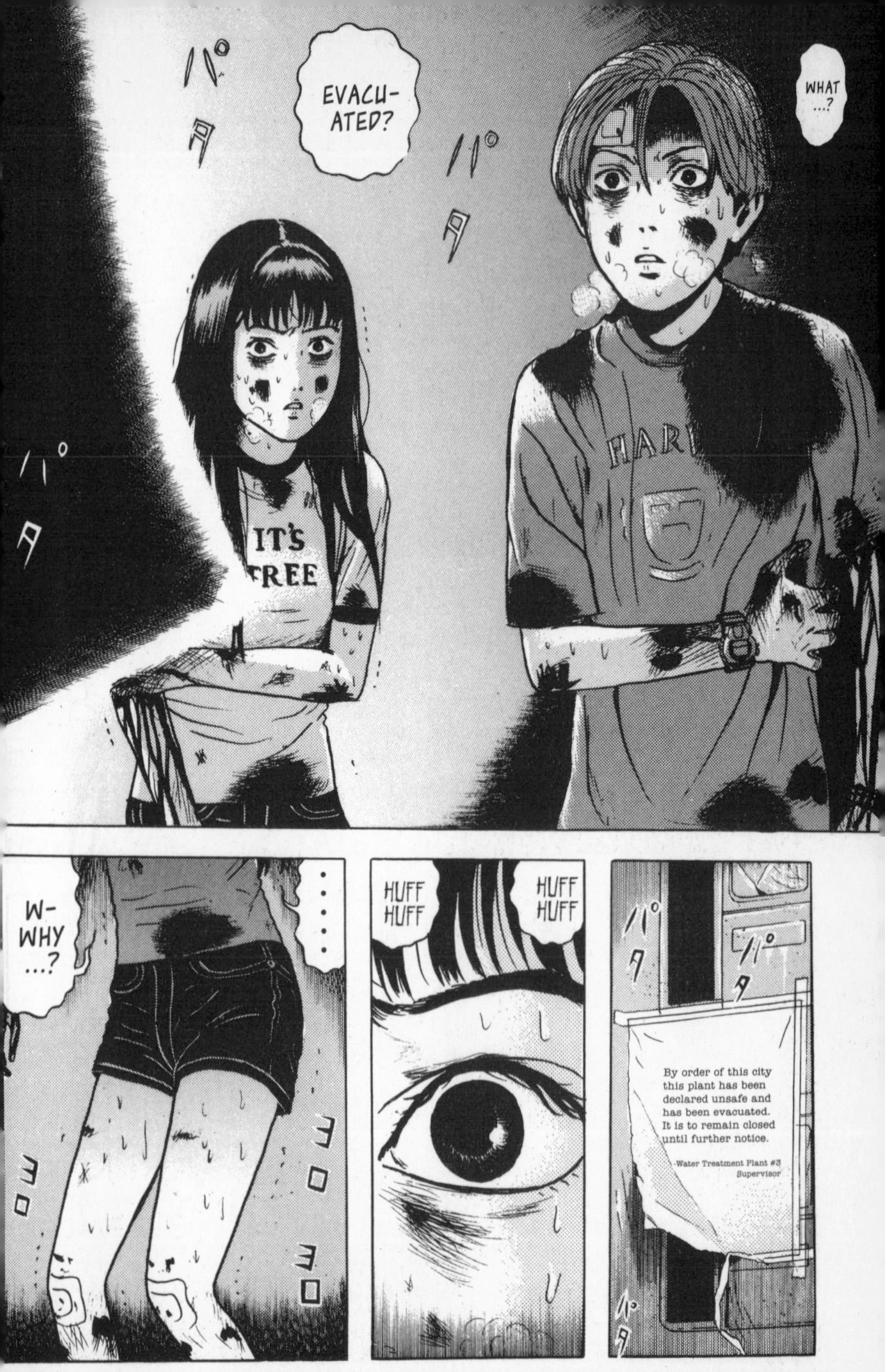
WHAT ...?
EVACU-ATED?
パタ
パタ
パタ
IT'S FREE
HAR
パタ
パタ
By order of this city this plant has been declared unsafe and has been evacuated. It is to remain closed until further notice.
-Water Treatment Plant #3 Supervisor
パタ
HUFF HUFF
HUFF HUFF
......
W-WHY ....?
ヨロ
ヨロ
ヨロ

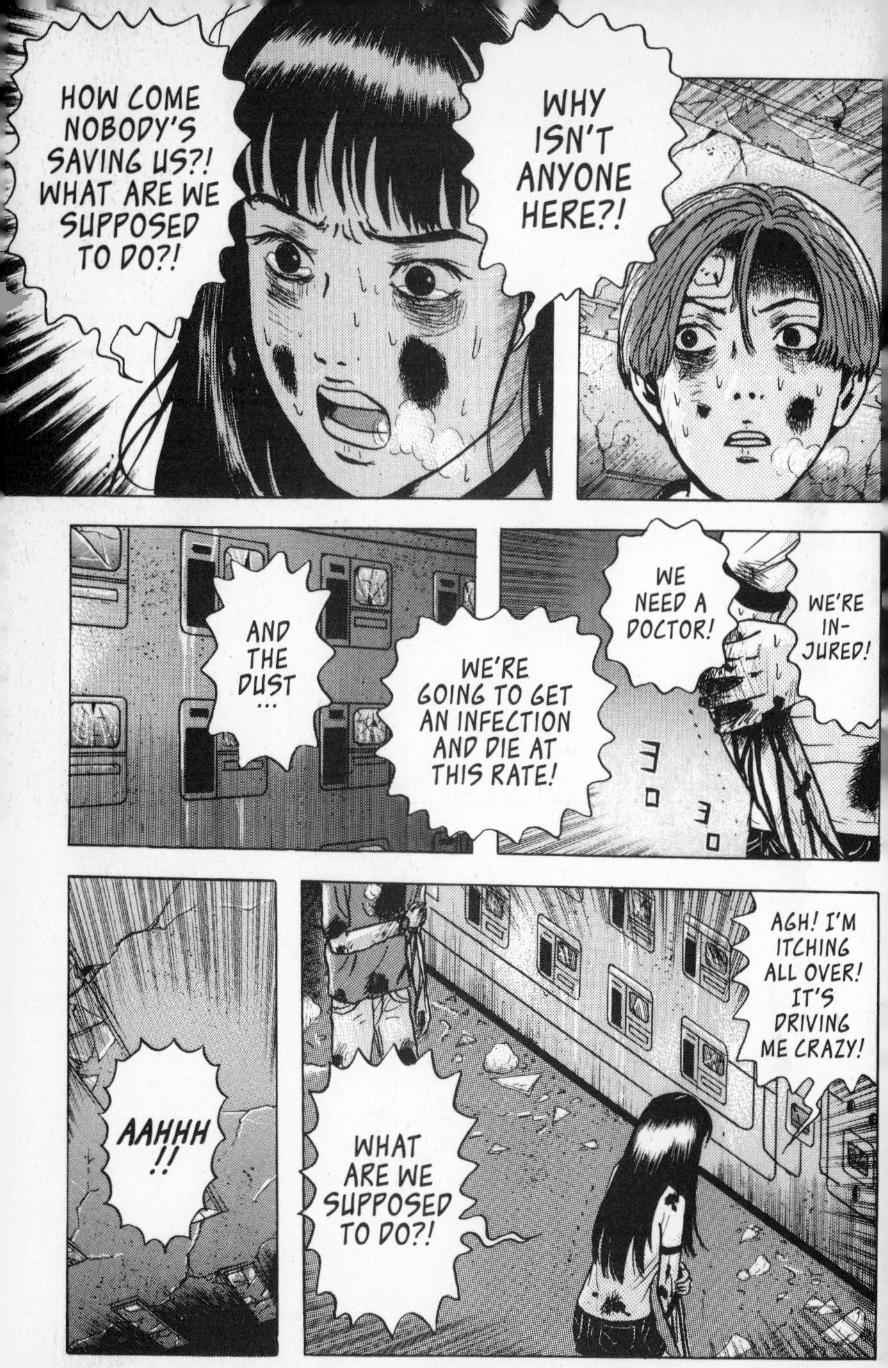
WHY ISN'T ANYONE HERE?!
HOW COME NOBODY'S SAVING US?! WHAT ARE WE SUPPOSED TO DO?!
WE'RE IN-JURED!
WE NEED A DOCTOR!
WE'RE GOING TO GET AN INFECTION AND DIE AT THIS RATE!
AND THE DUST ...
AGH! I'M ITCHING ALL OVER! IT'S DRIVING ME CRAZY!
WHAT ARE WE SUPPOSED TO DO?!
AAHHH!!

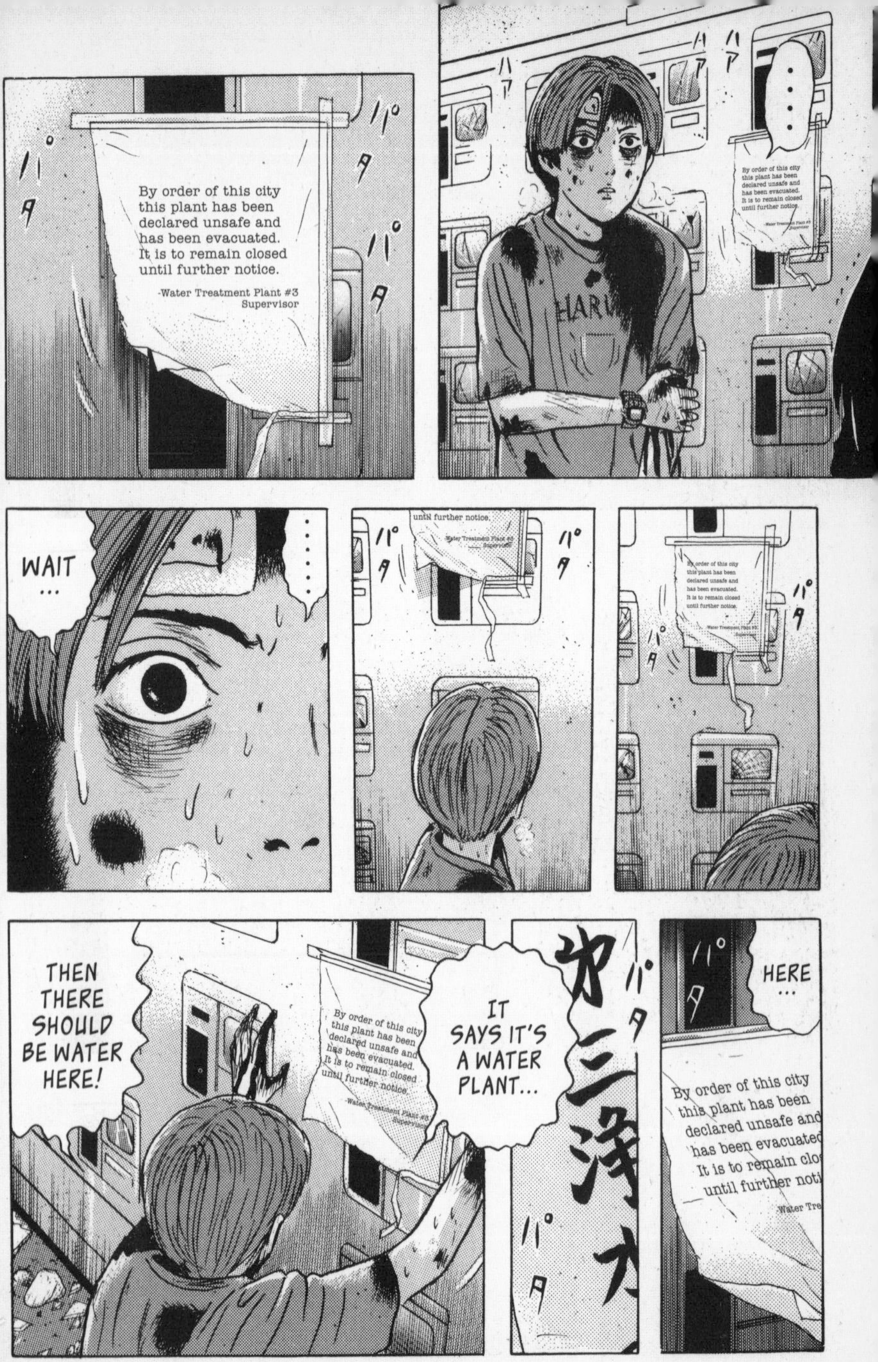
ハァ ハァ
.....
By order of this city this plant has been declared unsafe and has been evacuated. It is to remain closed until further notice.
-Water Treatment Plant #3 Supervisor
パタ パタ
By order of this city this plant has been declared unsafe and has been evacuated. It is to remain closed until further notice.
-Water Treatment Plant #3 Supervisor
パタ パタ
By order of this city this plant has been declared unsafe and has been evacuated. It is to remain closed until further notice.
パタ パタ
until further notice.
.....
WAIT ...
HERE ...
パタ
By order of this city this plant has been declared unsafe and has been evacuated. It is to remain clos until further noti
パタ パタ
IT SAYS IT'S A WATER PLANT...
By order of this city this plant has been declared unsafe and has been evacuated. It is to remain closed until further notice.
-Water Treatment Plant #3 Supervisor
THEN THERE SHOULD BE WATER HERE!

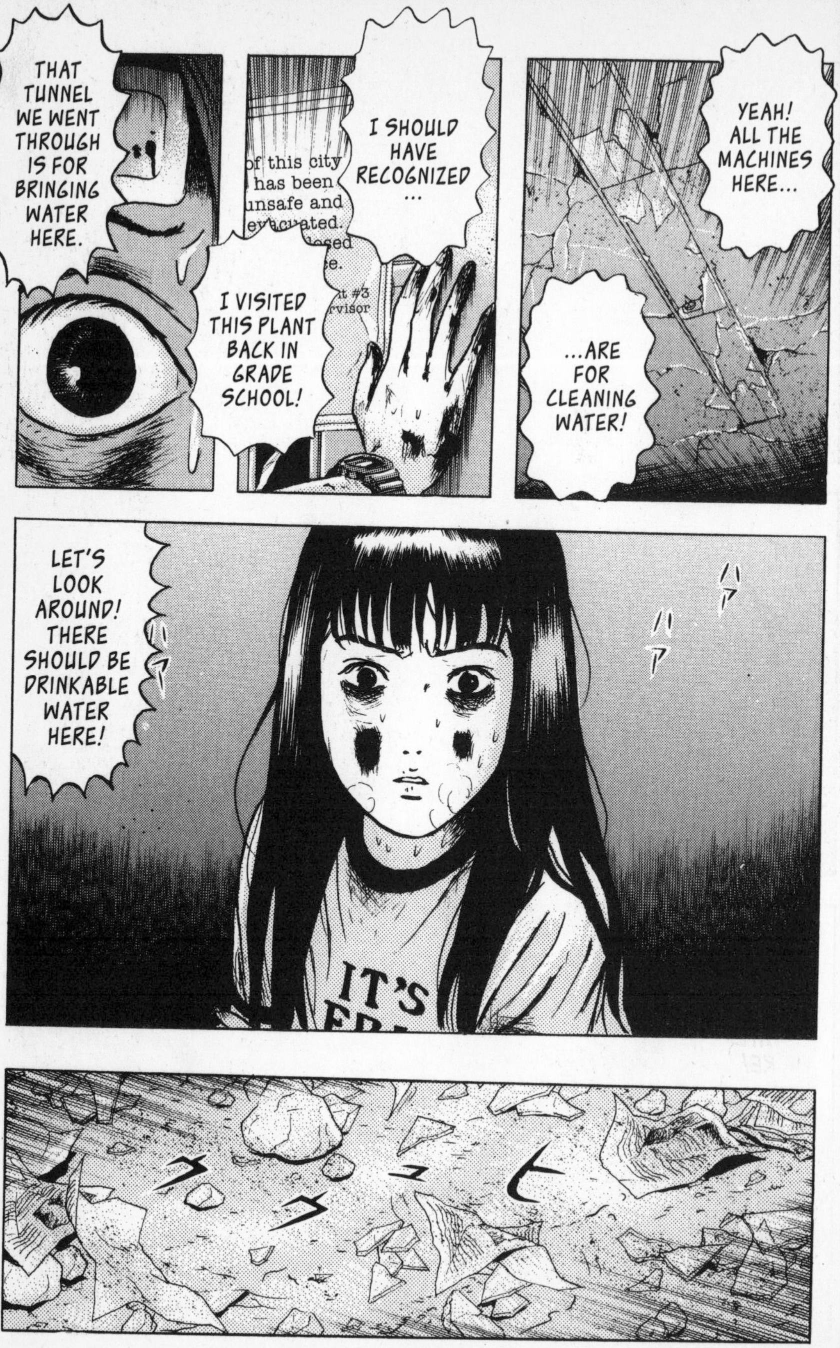
YEAH! ALL THE MACHINES HERE...
...ARE FOR CLEANING WATER!
I SHOULD HAVE RECOGNIZED...
I VISITED THIS PLANT BACK IN GRADE SCHOOL!
THAT TUNNEL WE WENT THROUGH IS FOR BRINGING WATER HERE.
ハァ
ハァ
LET'S LOOK AROUND! THERE SHOULD BE DRINKABLE WATER HERE!
ハァ

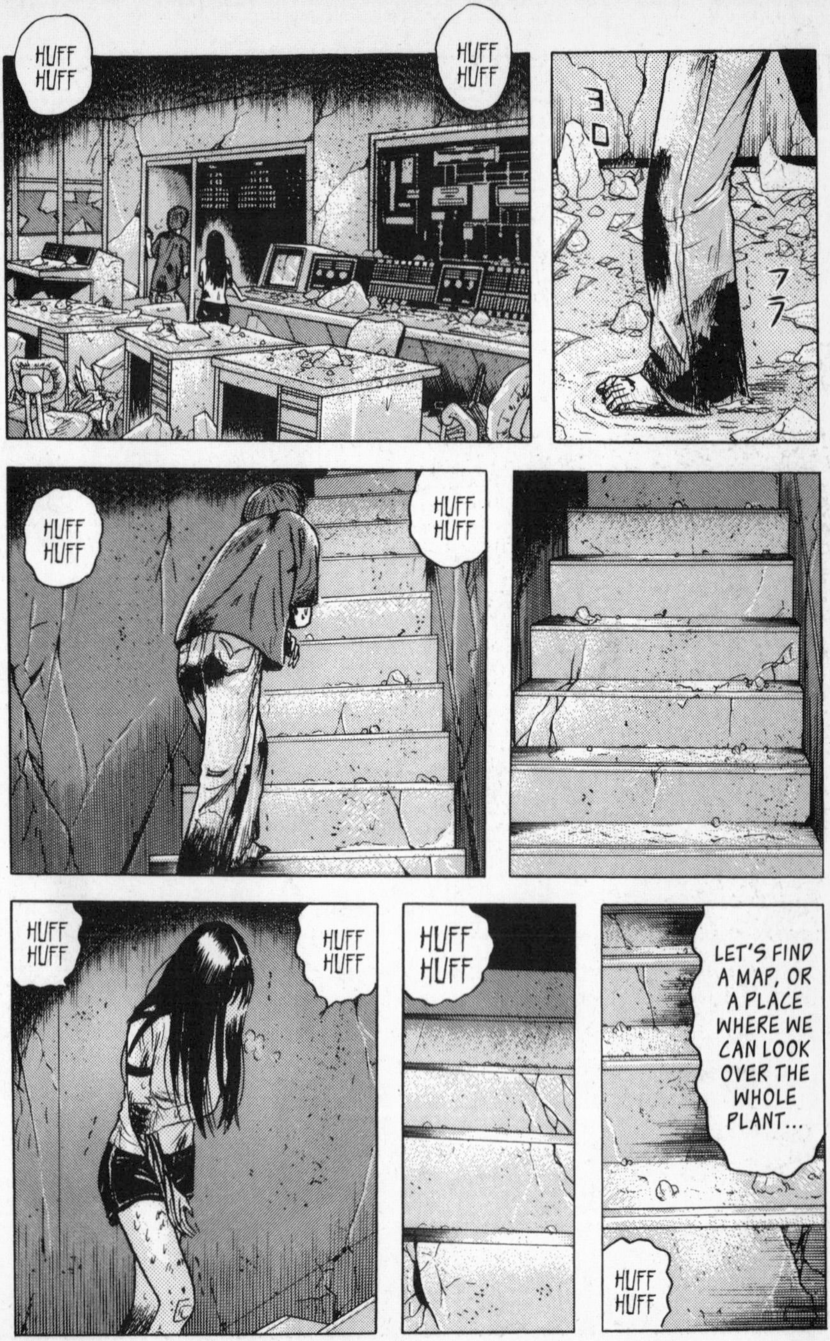
ヨロ
フラ
HUFF HUFF
HUFF HUFF
HUFF HUFF
HUFF HUFF
LET'S FIND A MAP, OR A PLACE WHERE WE CAN LOOK OVER THE WHOLE PLANT...
HUFF HUFF
HUFF HUFF
HUFF HUFF
HUFF HUFF

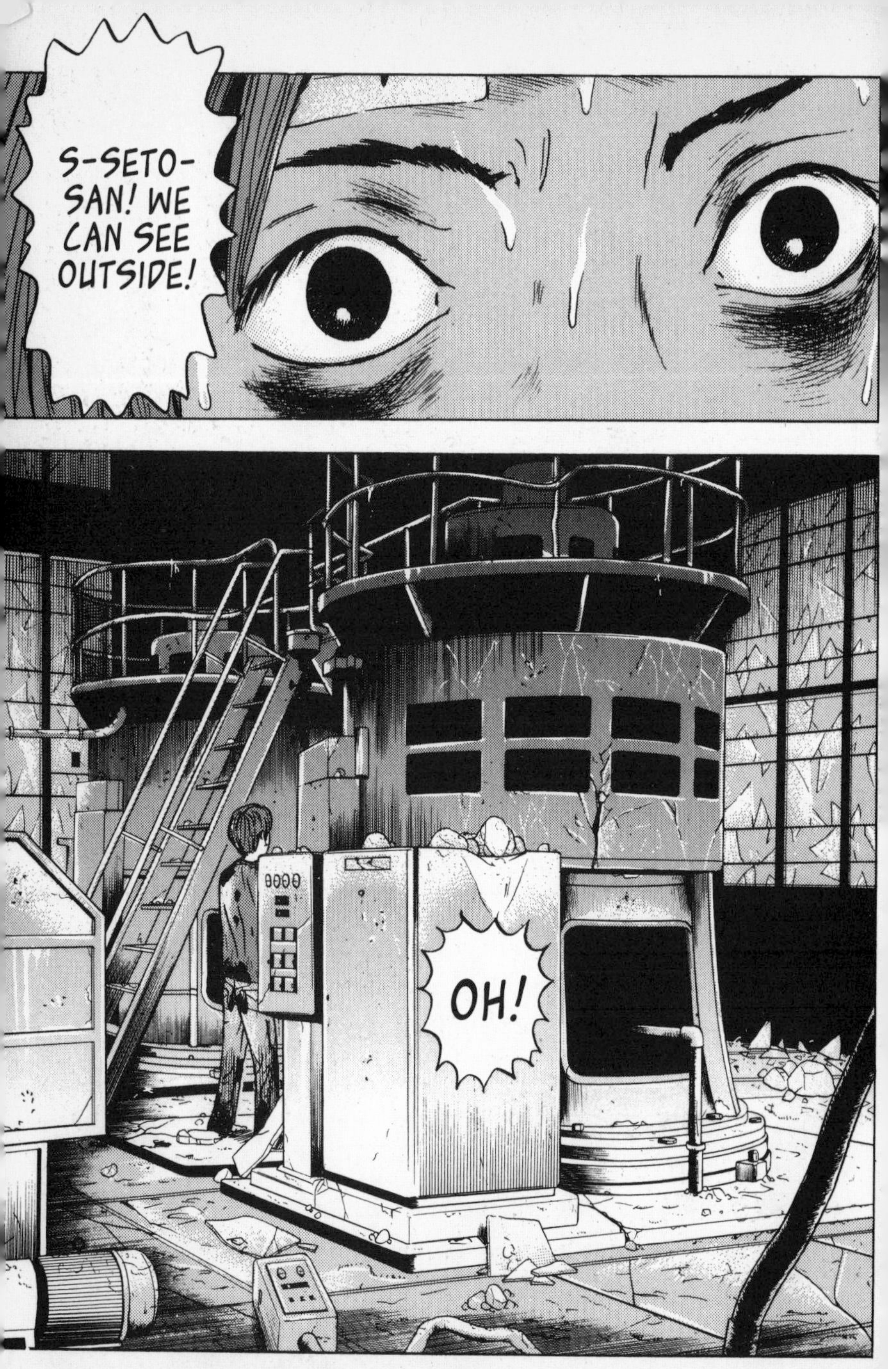
S-SETO-SAN! WE CAN SEE OUTSIDE!
OH!

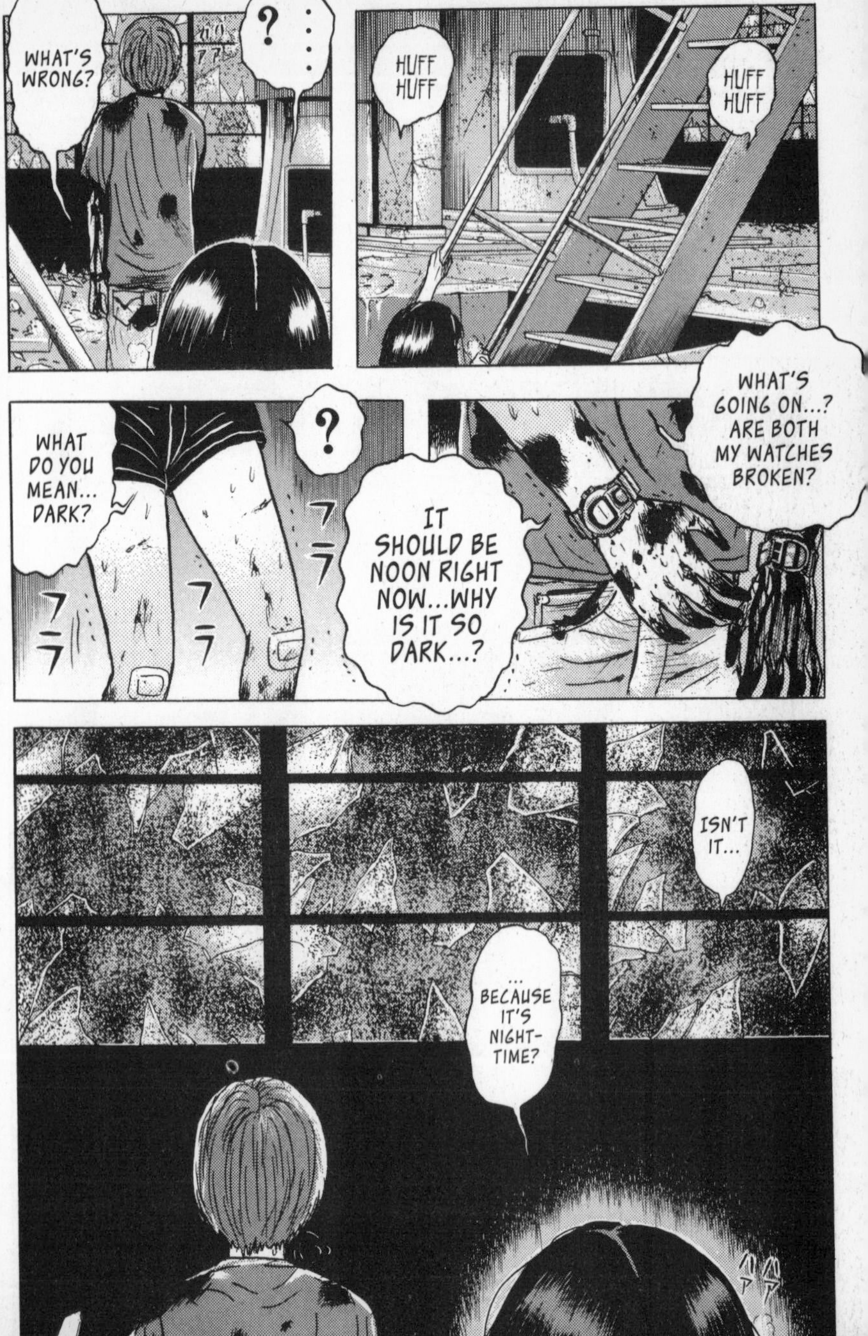
HUFF HUFF
HUFF HUFF
? ...
WHAT'S WRONG?
WHAT'S GOING ON...? ARE BOTH MY WATCHES BROKEN?
IT SHOULD BE NOON RIGHT NOW...WHY IS IT SO DARK...?
?
WHAT DO YOU MEAN... DARK?
ISN'T IT...
...BECAUSE IT'S NIGHT-TIME?

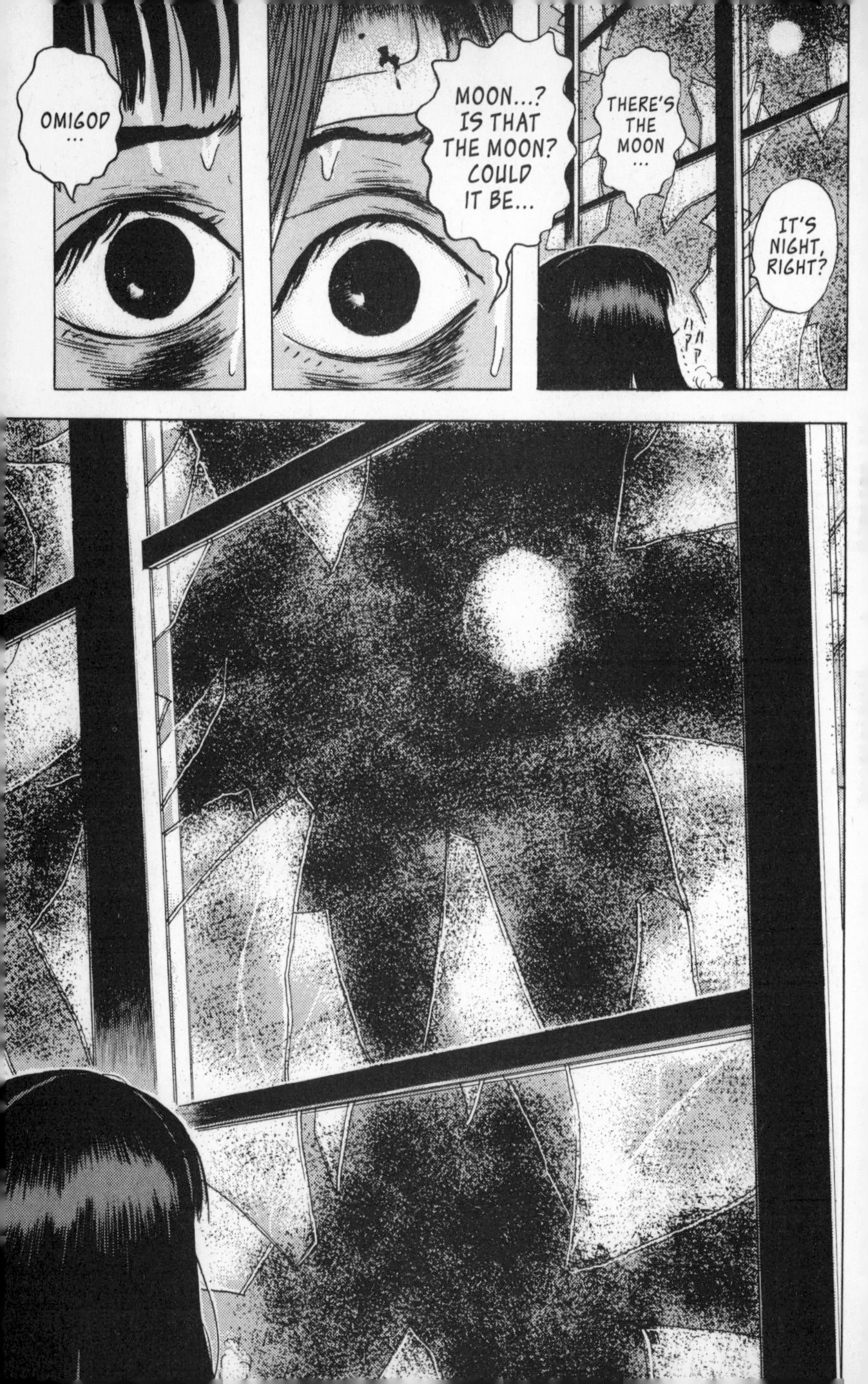
THERE'S THE MOON ...
IT'S NIGHT, RIGHT?
MOON...? IS THAT THE MOON? COULD IT BE...
OMIGOD ...

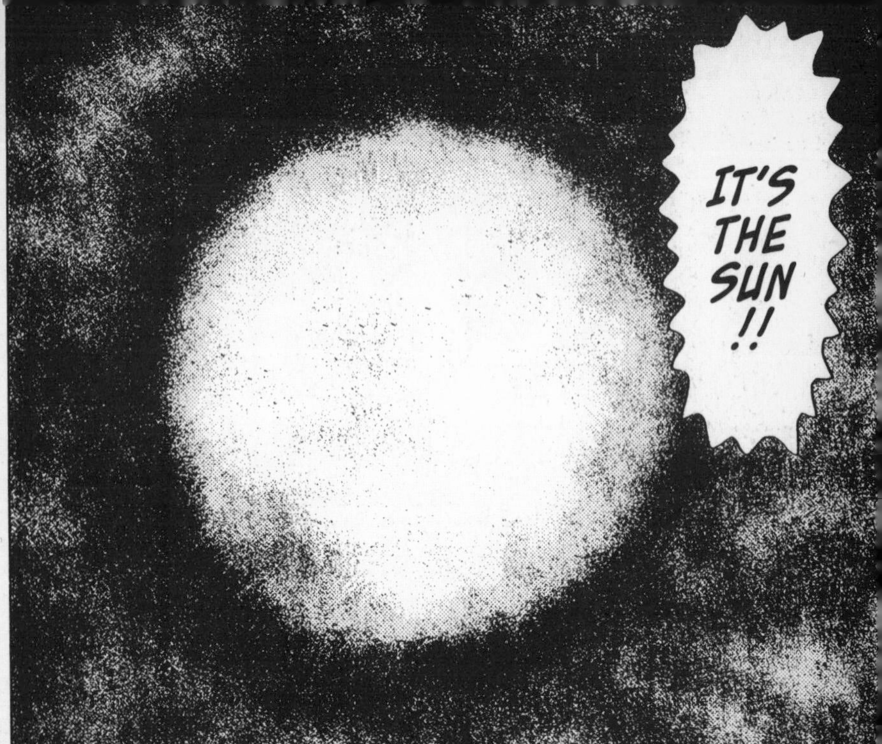
IT'S THE SUN!!
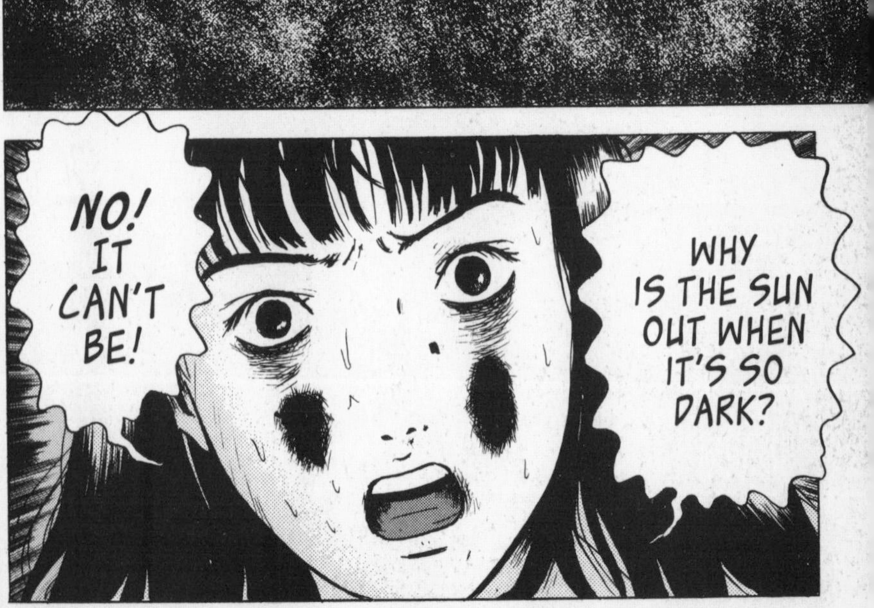
WHY IS THE SUN OUT WHEN IT'S SO DARK?
NO! IT CAN'T BE!

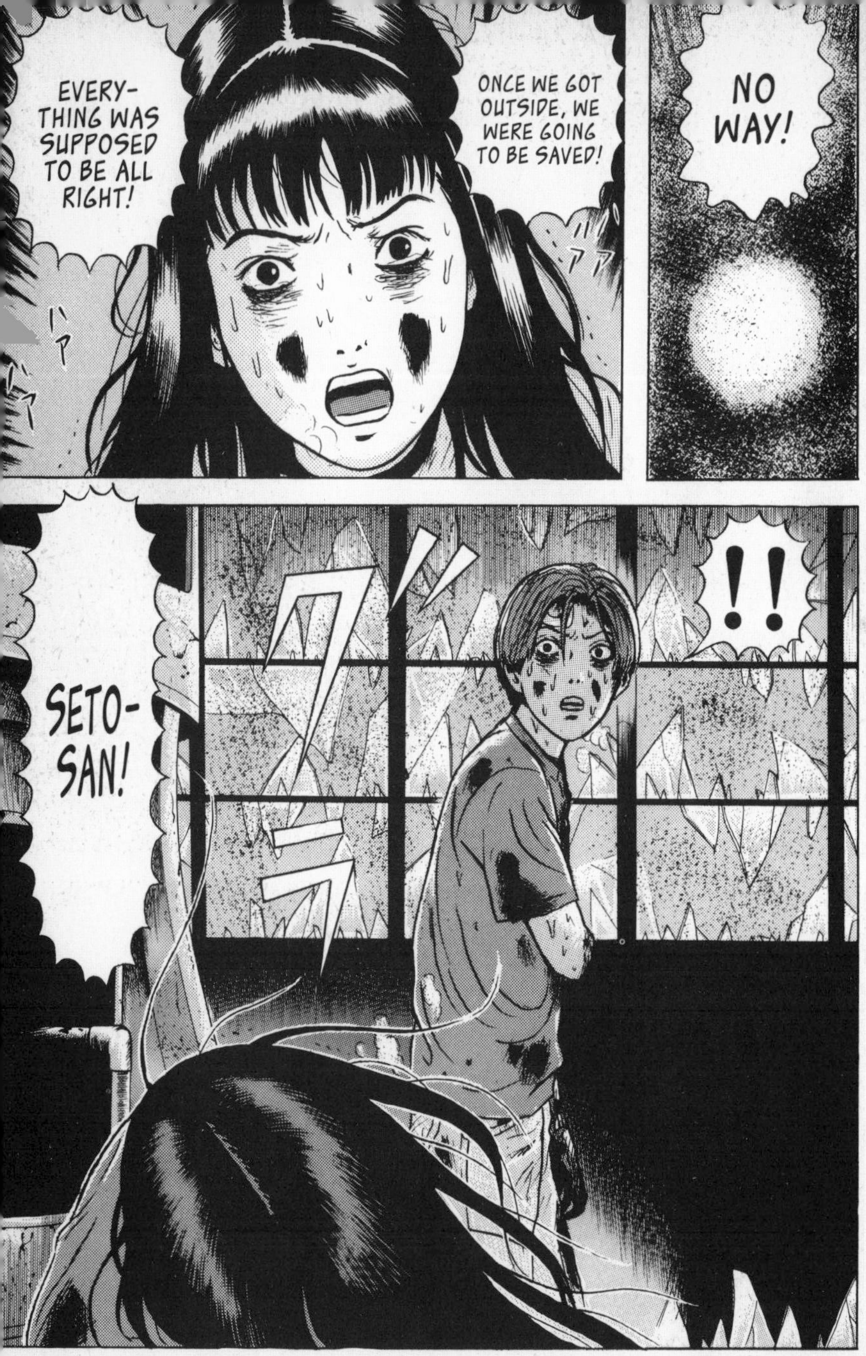

NO WAY!
ONCE WE GOT OUTSIDE, WE WERE GOING TO BE SAVED!
EVERY-THING WAS SUPPOSED TO BE ALL RIGHT!
!!
SETO-SAN!

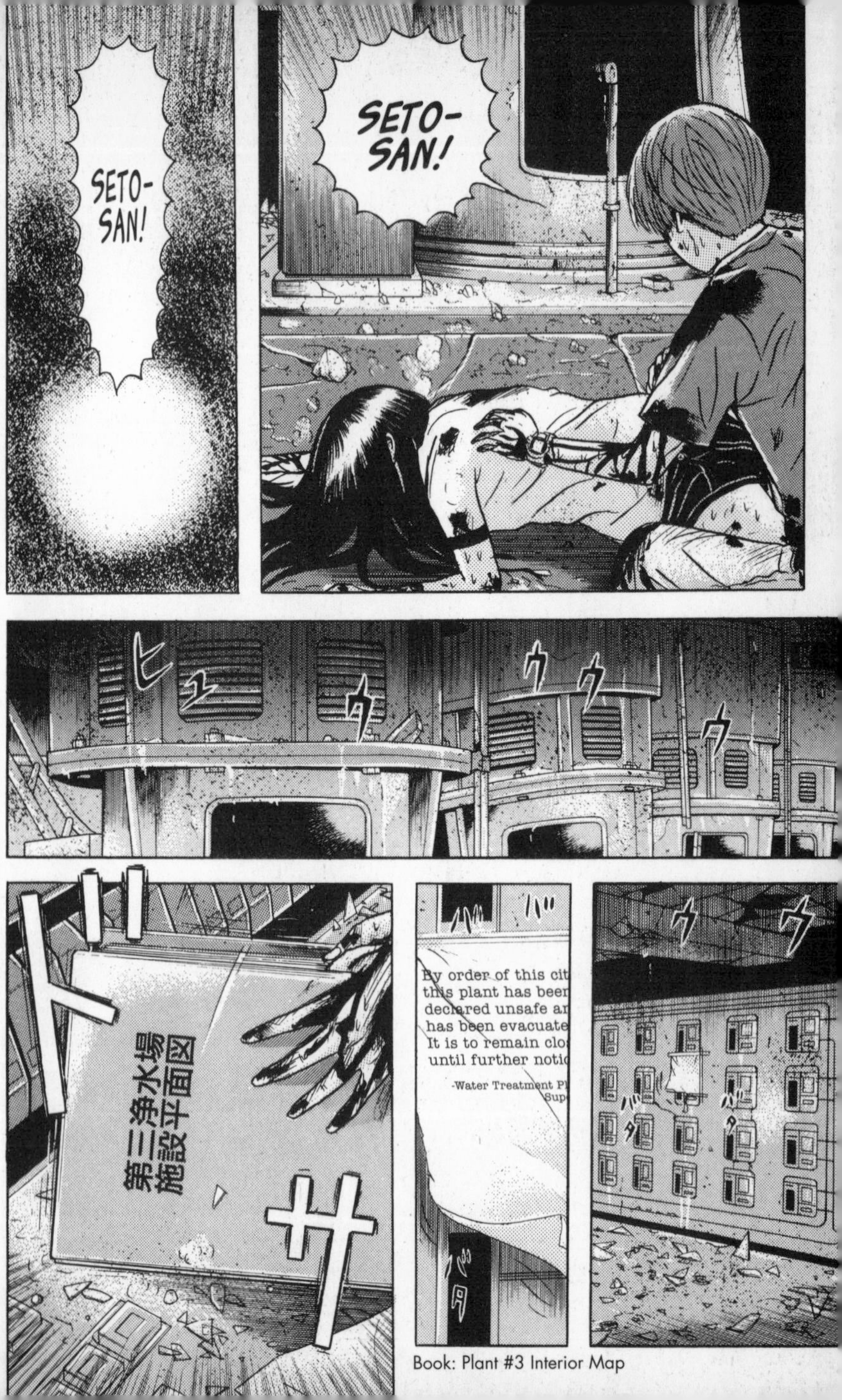
SETO-SAN!
SETO-SAN!
ヒュ
ウ
ウ
ウ
ウ
ウ
ウ
バタ
バタ
バ
バ
By order of this cit
this plant has been
declared unsafe ar
has been evacuate
It is to remain clos
until further notic
-Water Treatment Pl
Sup
ドサ
第三浄水場
施設平面図

Book: Plant #3 Interior Map

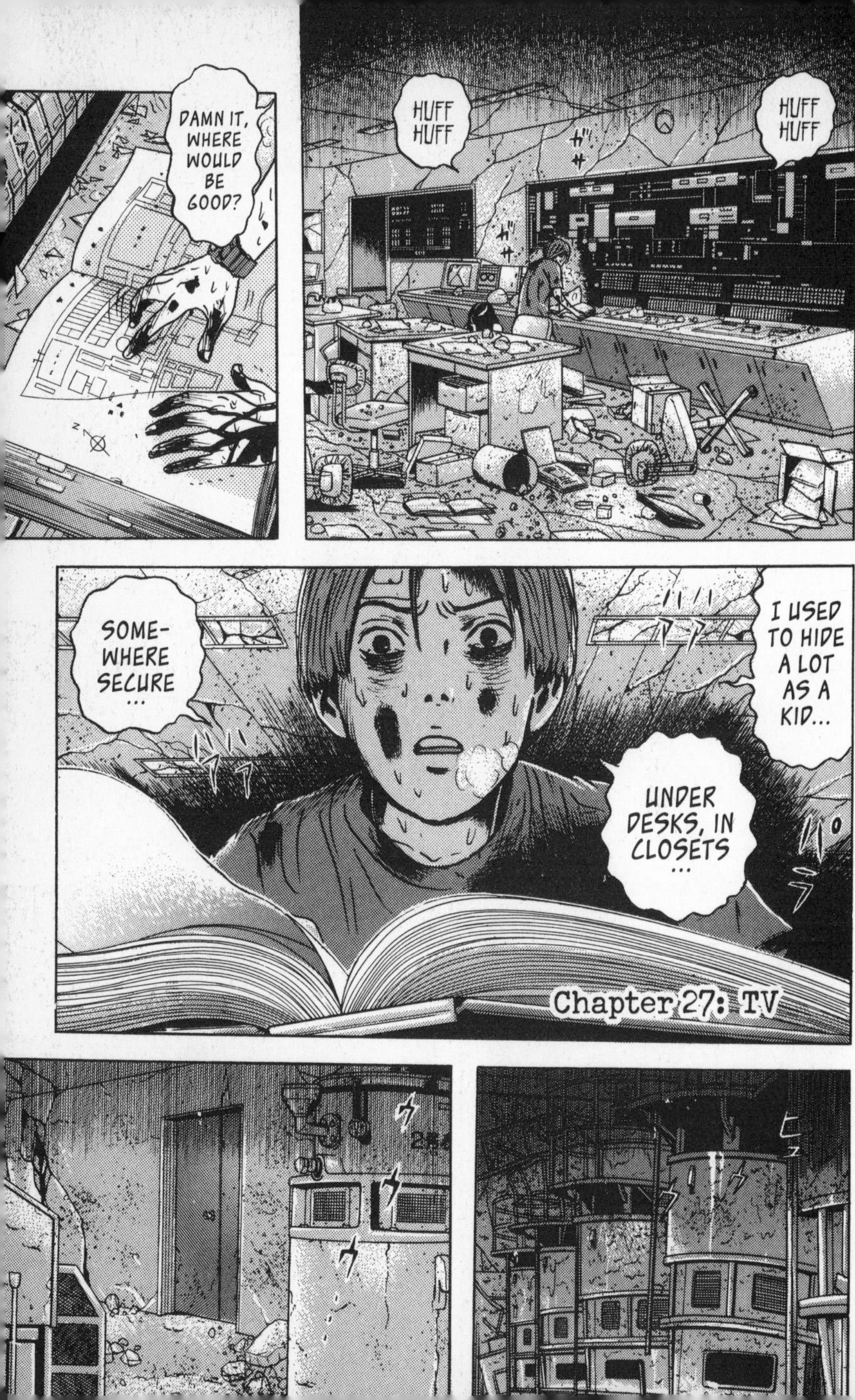
HUFF HUFF
HUFF HUFF
DAMN IT, WHERE WOULD BE GOOD?
I USED TO HIDE A LOT AS A KID...
SOME-WHERE SECURE...
UNDER DESKS, IN CLOSETS...
Chapter 27: TV

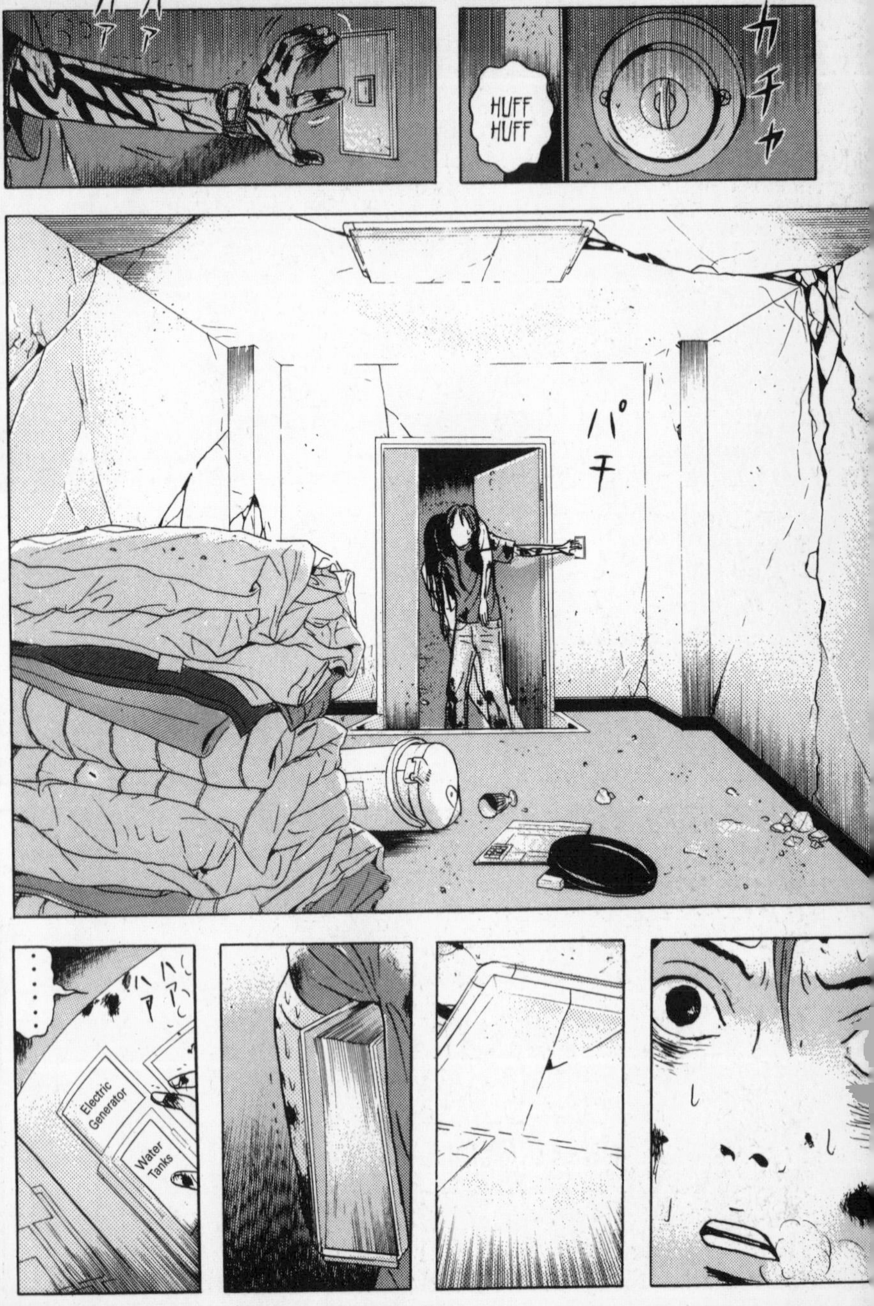

ガチャ
HUFF HUFF
ハァ ハァ
パチ
ハァ ハァ
……
Electric Generator
Water Tanks

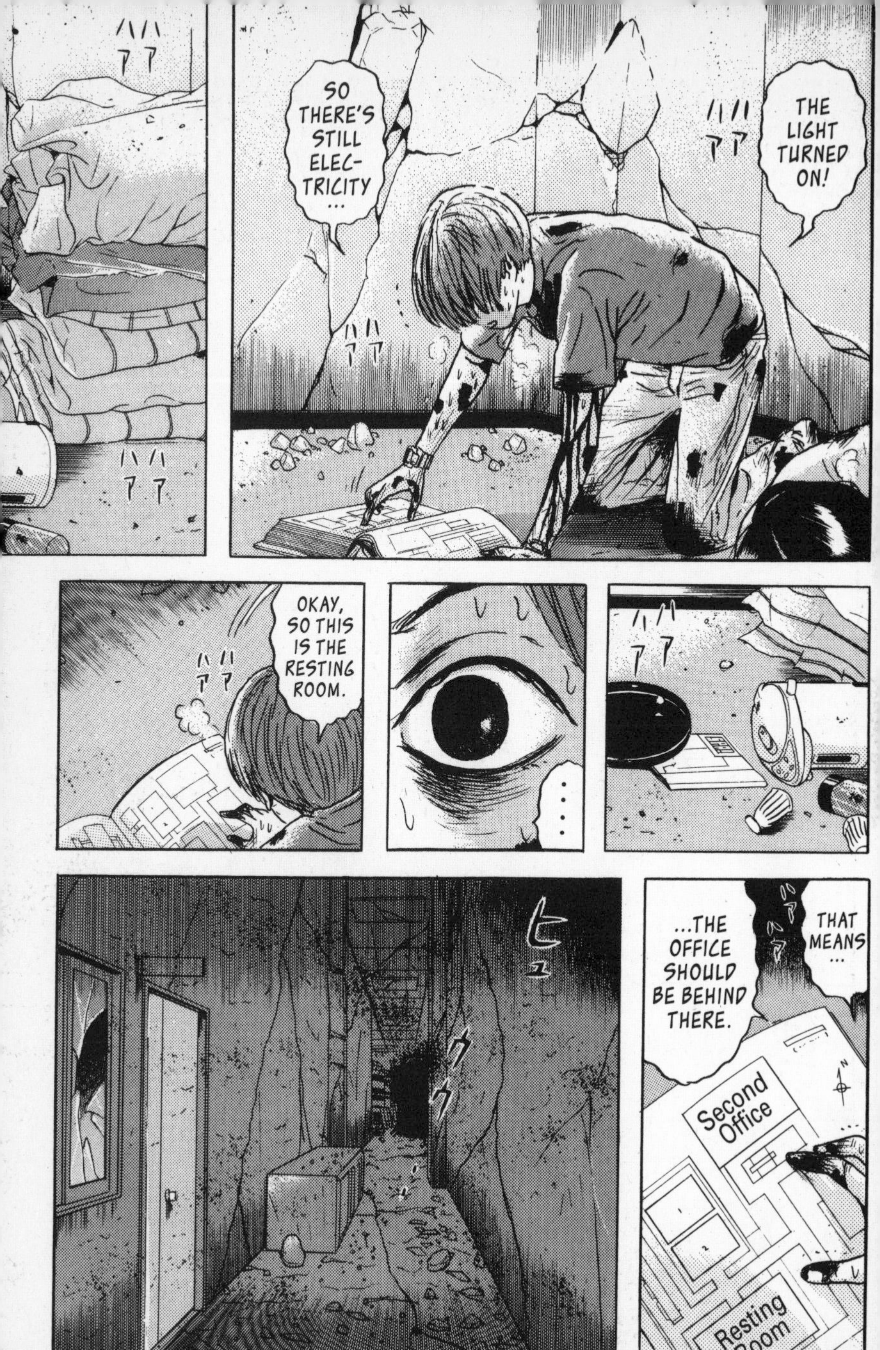
THE LIGHT TURNED ON!
SO THERE'S STILL ELECTRICITY...
....
OKAY, SO THIS IS THE RESTING ROOM.
THAT MEANS...
...THE OFFICE SHOULD BE BEHIND THERE.
Second Office
Resting Room

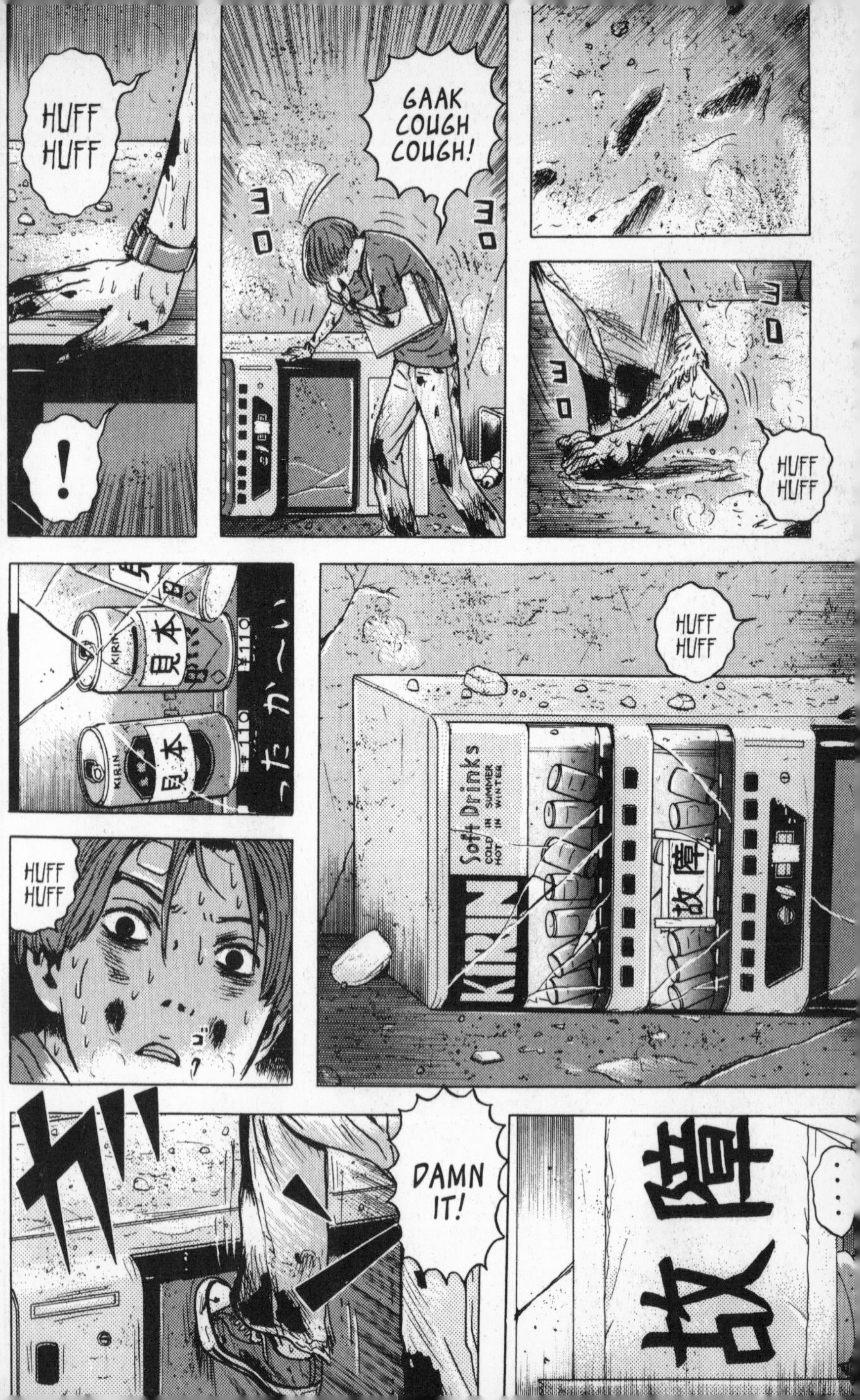
HUFF HUFF
GAAK COUGH COUGH!
HUFF HUFF
!
HUFF HUFF
Soft Drinks
COLD IN SUMMER
HOT IN WINTER
KIRIN
故障
見本
KIRIN
¥110
HUFF HUFF
…
故障
DAMN IT!
ガッ

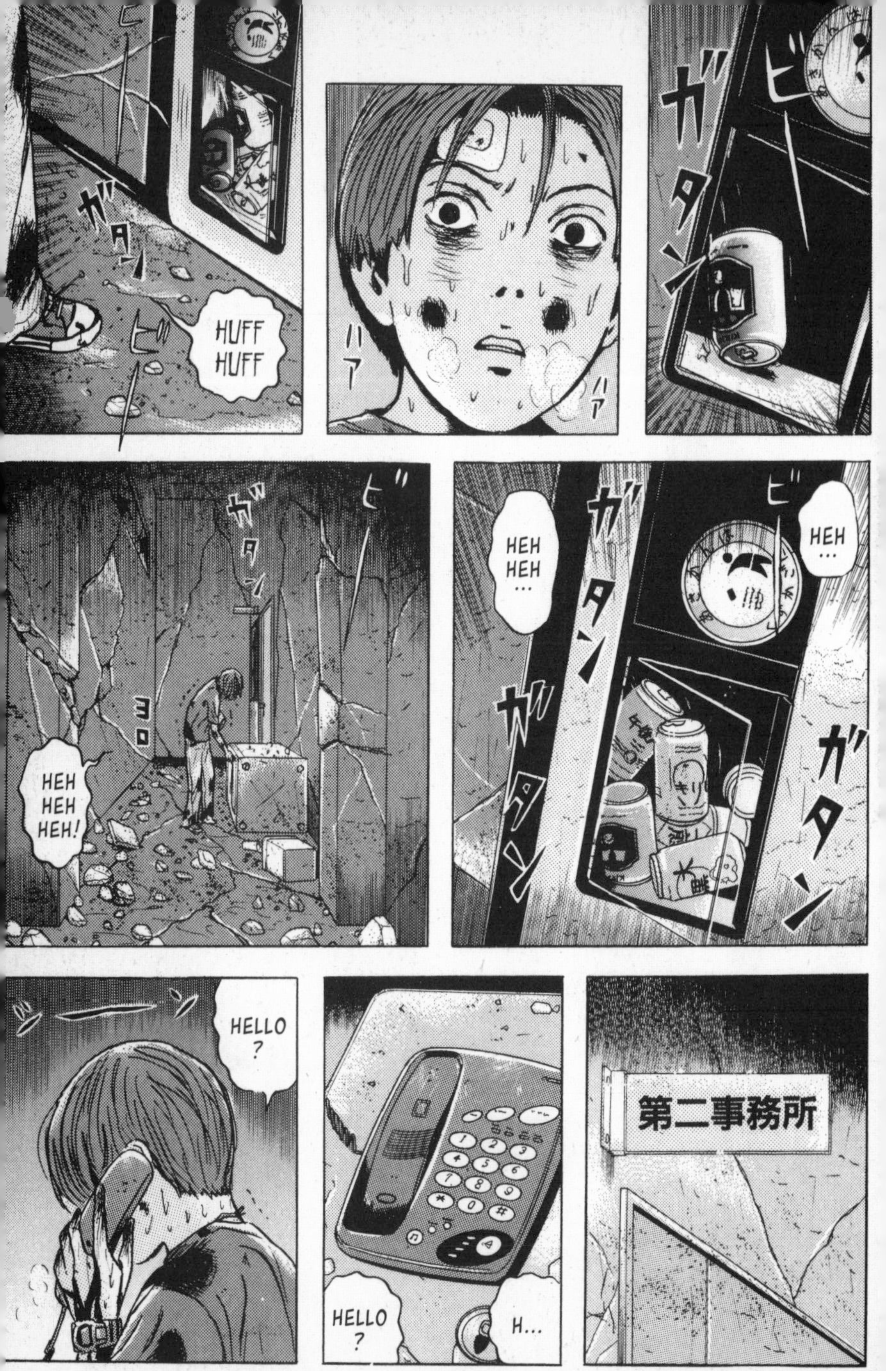
HUFF HUFF
HEH ...
HEH HEH ...
HEH HEH HEH!
第二事務所
H...
HELLO ?
HELLO ?

Sign: Second Office

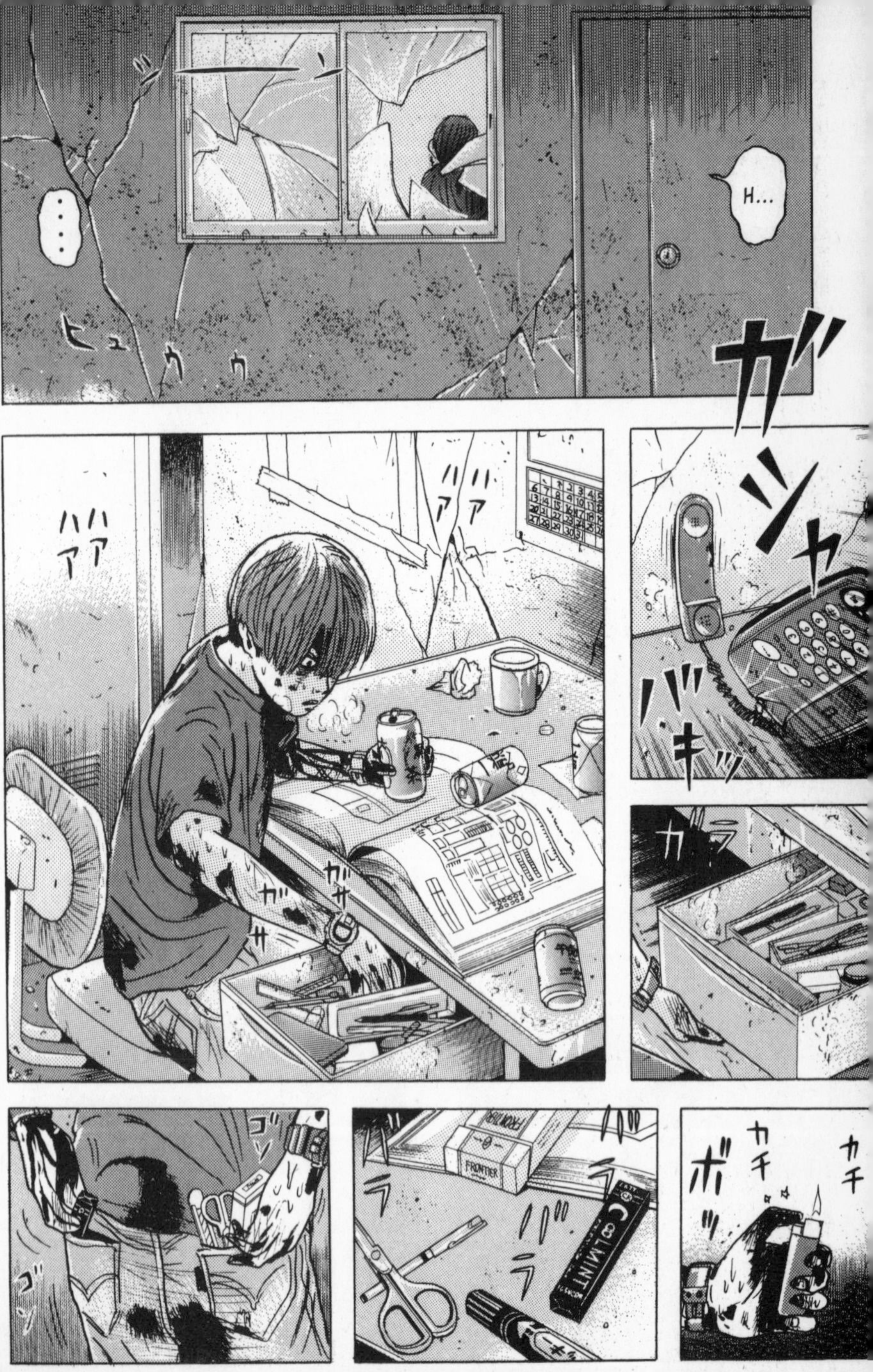

H...
…
ヒュウウウ
ガシャ
バキッ
カラ
ハァハァ
ハァハァ
ガサガサ
カチ
カチ
ボッ
バラバラ
FRONTIER
ゴソゴソ

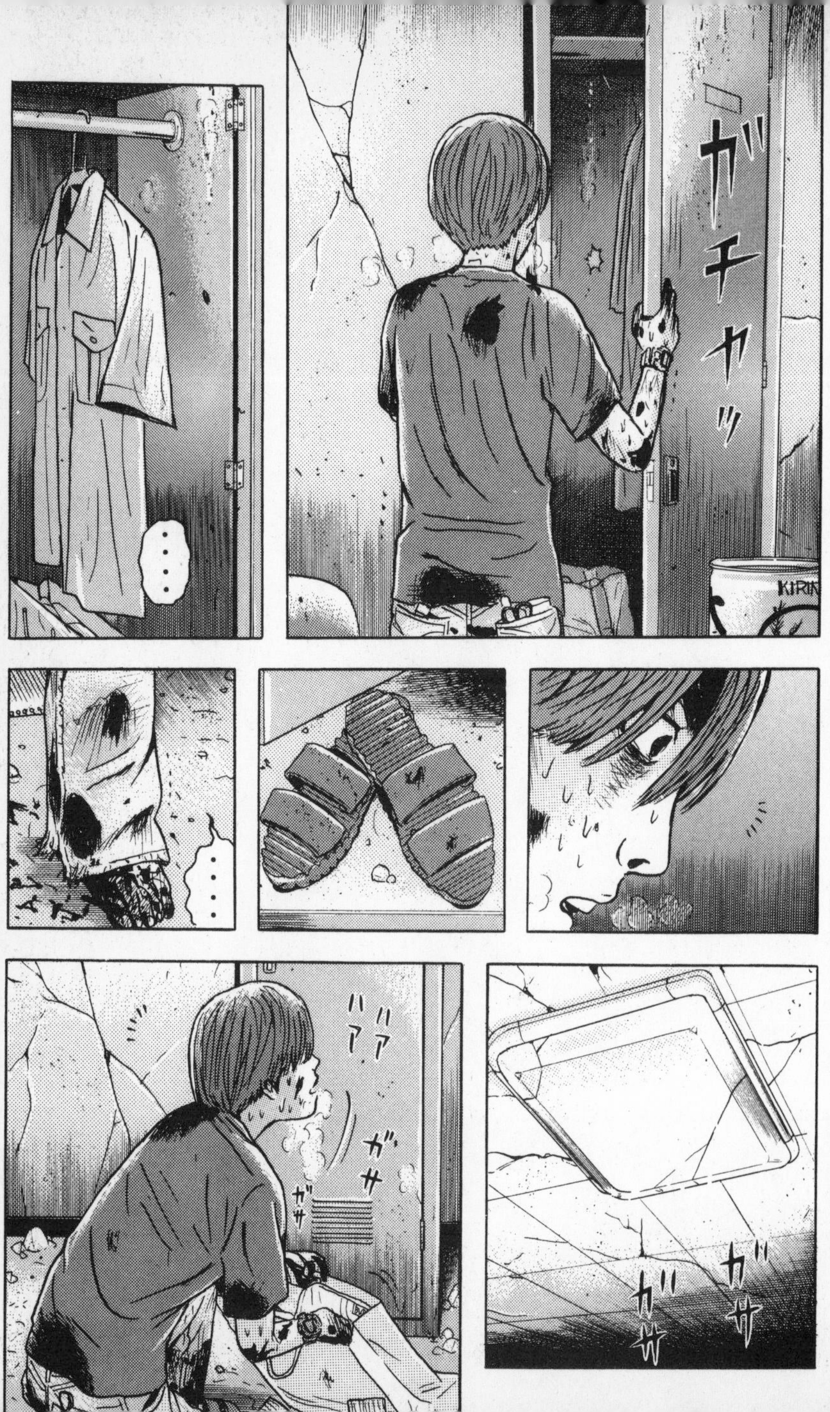
ガチャッ
……
……
ガサ
ガサ
ハア
ハア
ガサ
ガサ

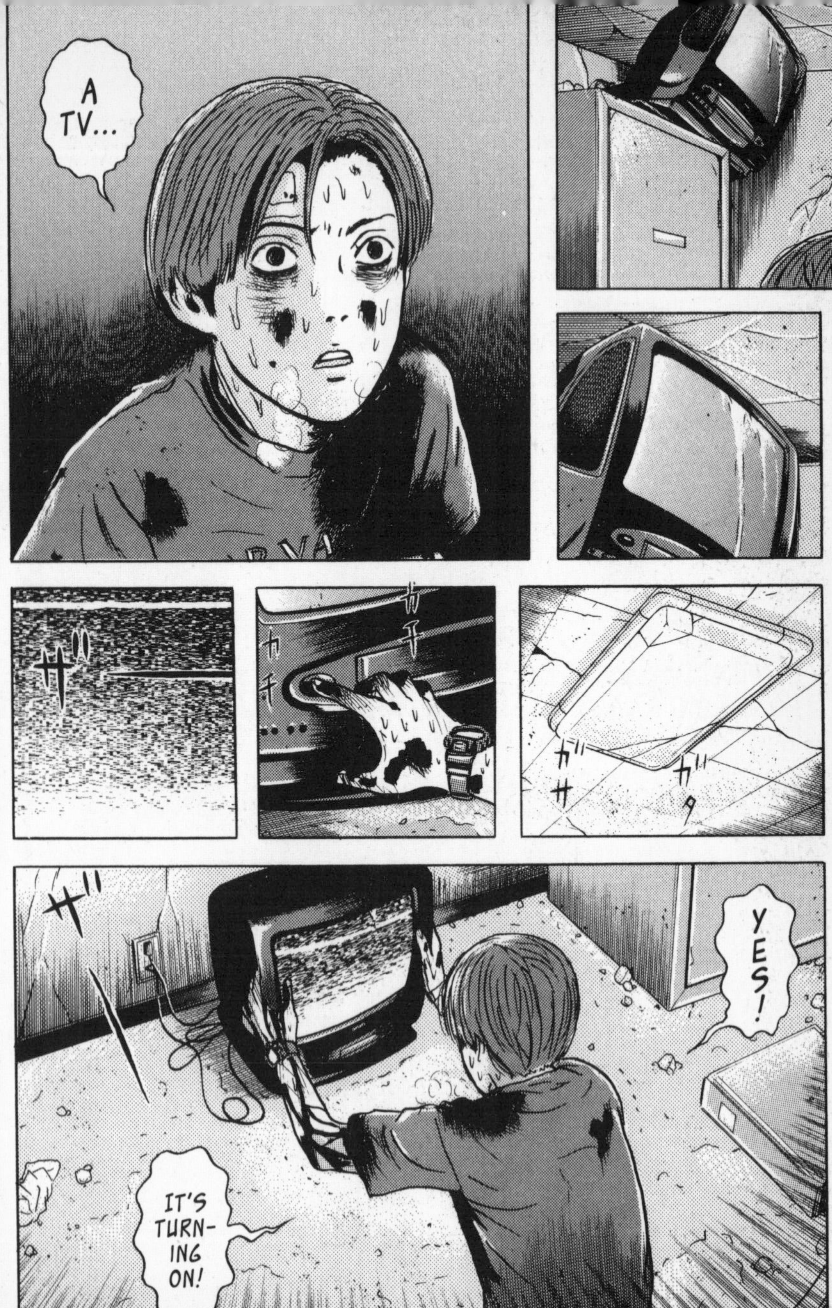
A TV...
ガタ
ガサ
カチ
カチ
ザー
YES!
IT'S TURNING-ING ON!
ザ

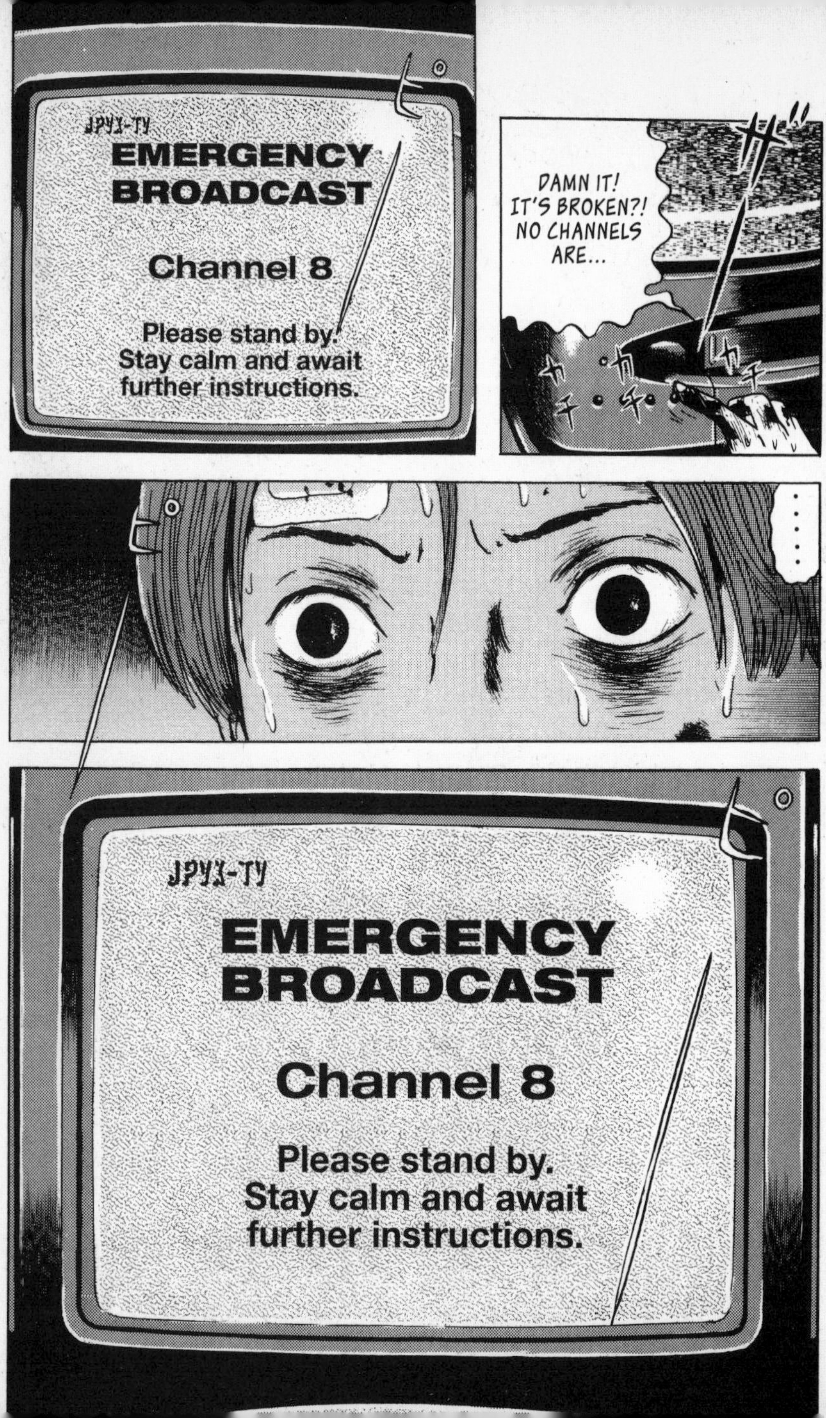
DAMN IT! IT'S BROKEN?! NO CHANNELS ARE...
EMERGENCY BROADCAST
Channel 8
Please stand by. Stay calm and await further instructions.
......
EMERGENCY BROADCAST
Channel 8
Please stand by. Stay calm and await further instructions.

ピ
ヒュウウ
Soft Drinks
KIRIN
故障

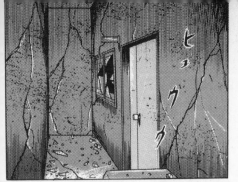

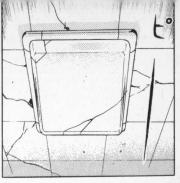

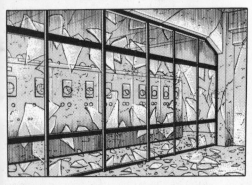

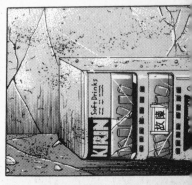

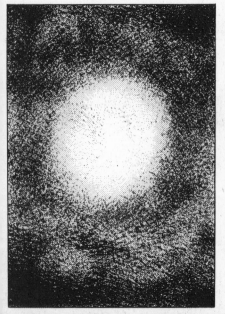

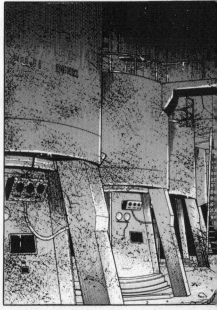

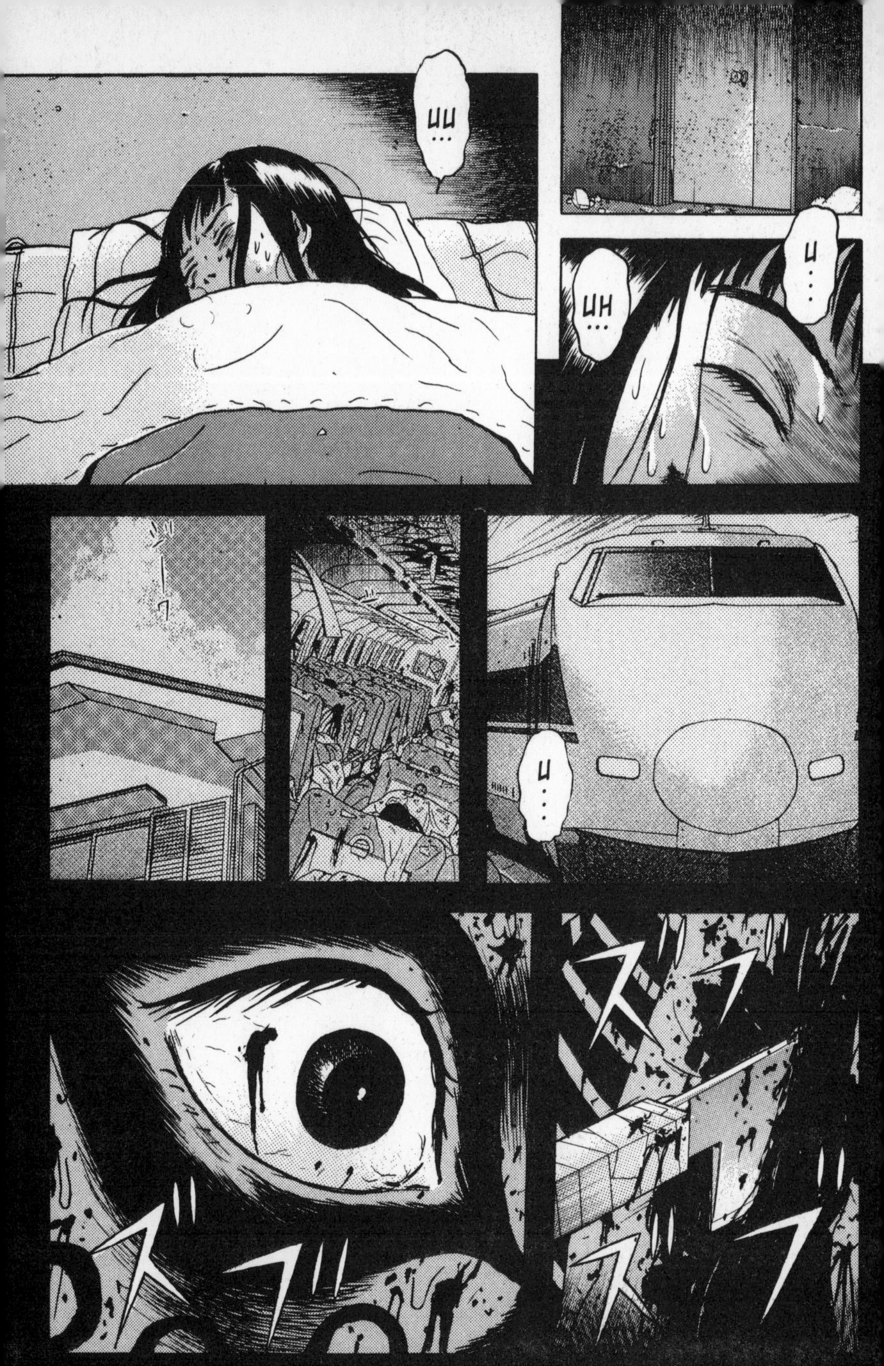
U...
UH...
UU...
U...

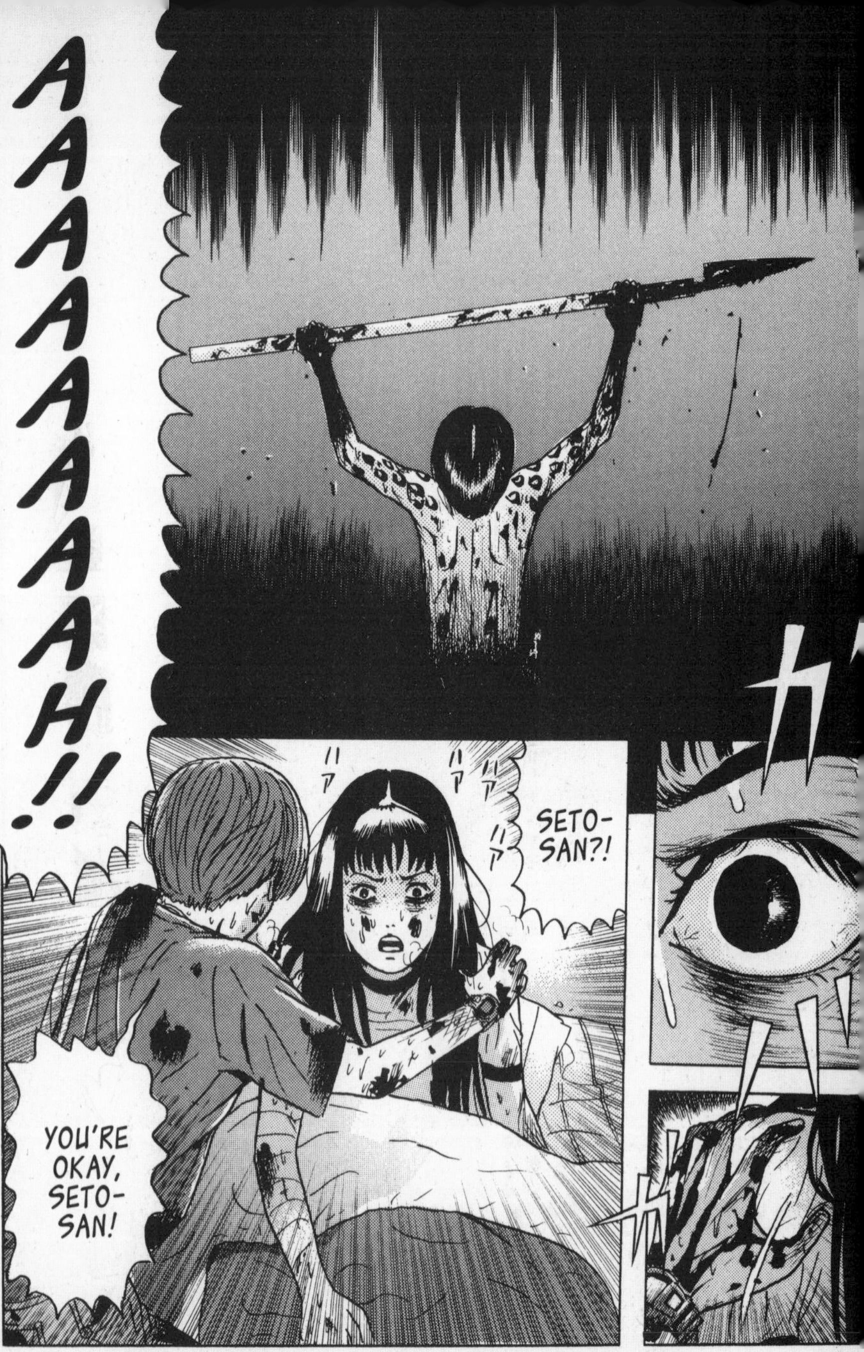
AAAAAAAAH!!
カ
SETO-SAN?!
YOU'RE OKAY, SETO-SAN!

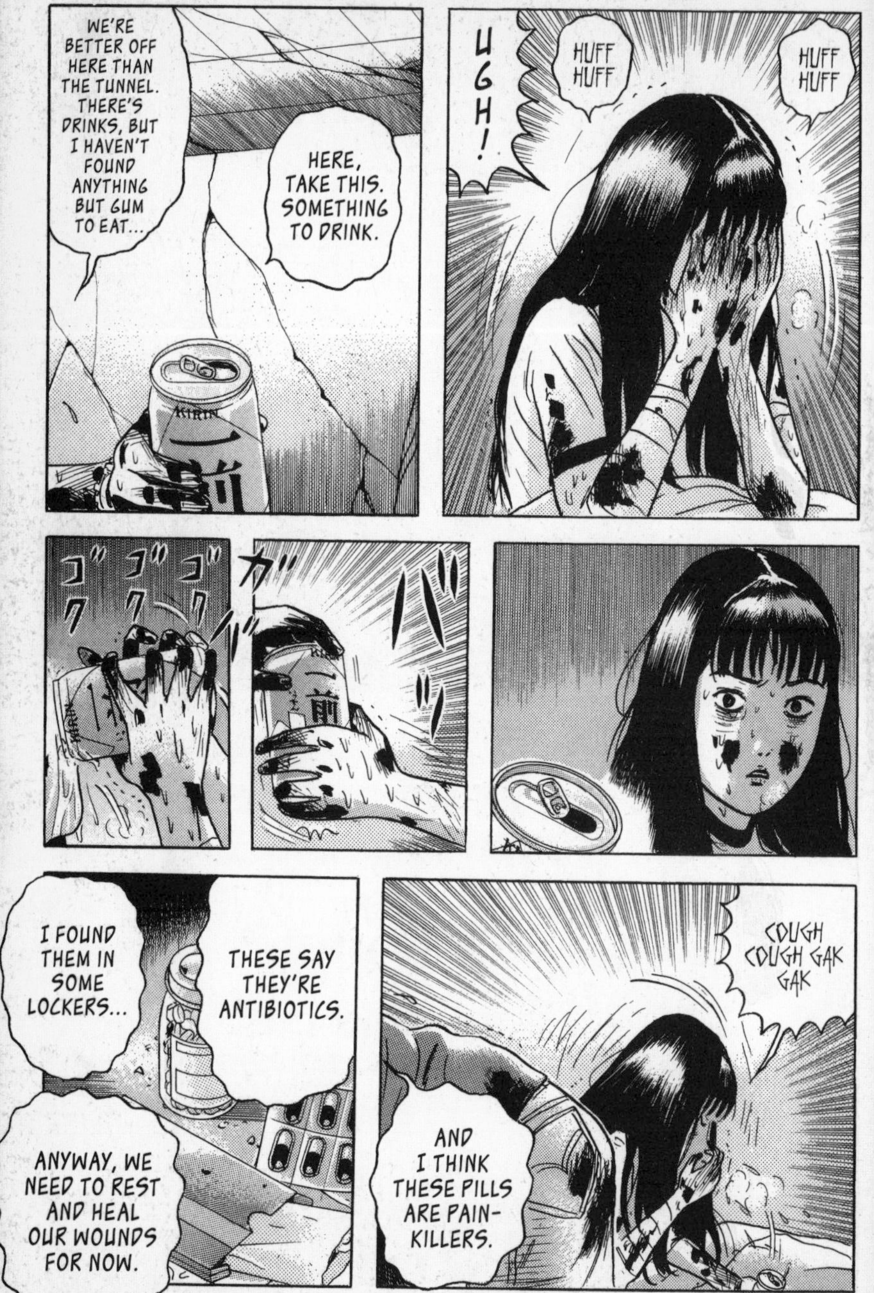
HUFF HUFF
HUFF HUFF
UGH!
WE'RE BETTER OFF HERE THAN THE TUNNEL. THERE'S DRINKS, BUT I HAVEN'T FOUND ANYTHING BUT GUM TO EAT...
HERE, TAKE THIS. SOMETHING TO DRINK.
バ
ガ
ゴクゴクゴク
COUGH COUGH GAK GAK
AND I THINK THESE PILLS ARE PAIN-KILLERS.
THESE SAY THEY'RE ANTIBIOTICS.
I FOUND THEM IN SOME LOCKERS...
ANYWAY, WE NEED TO REST AND HEAL OUR WOUNDS FOR NOW.

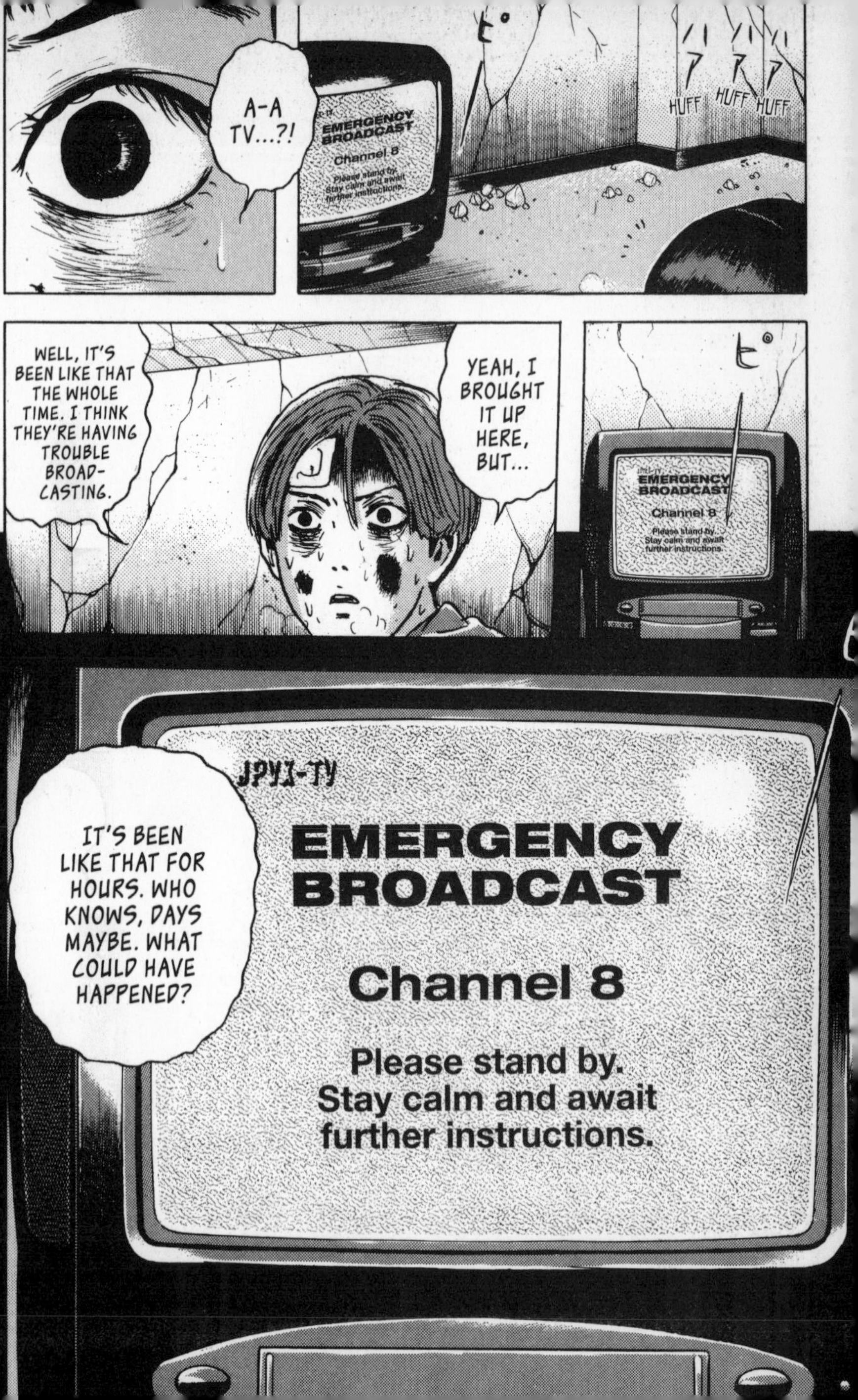
HUFF HUFF HUFF
EMERGENCY BROADCAST
Channel 8
Please stand by. Stay calm and await further instructions.
A-A TV...?!
EMERGENCY BROADCAST
Channel 8
Please stand by. Stay calm and await further instructions.
YEAH, I BROUGHT IT UP HERE, BUT...
WELL, IT'S BEEN LIKE THAT THE WHOLE TIME. I THINK THEY'RE HAVING TROUBLE BROAD-CASTING.
JPYJ-TY
EMERGENCY BROADCAST
Channel 8
Please stand by. Stay calm and await further instructions.
IT'S BEEN LIKE THAT FOR HOURS. WHO KNOWS, DAYS MAYBE. WHAT COULD HAVE HAPPENED?

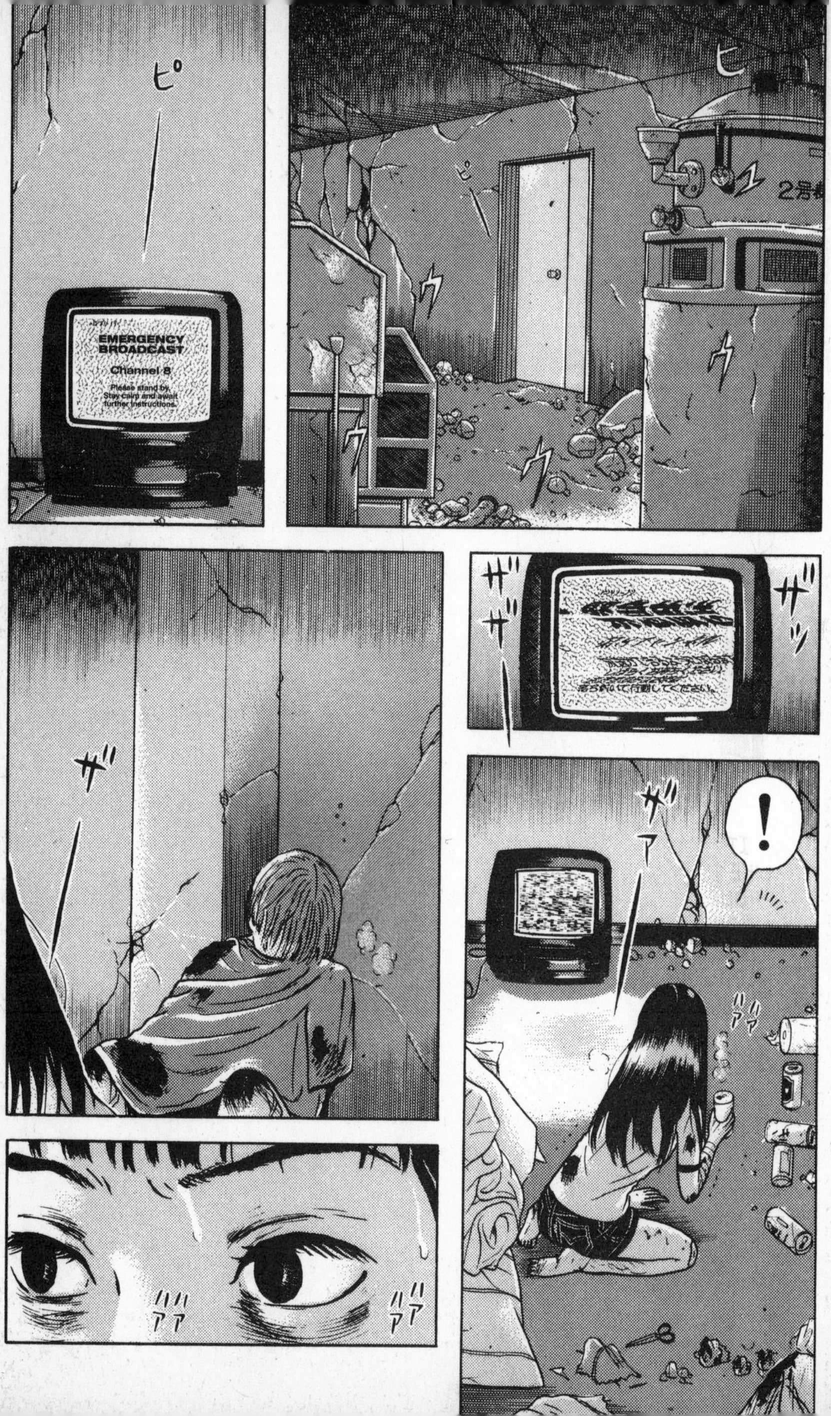
ピ
ピ
ウ
ウ
ウ
ウ
ウ
2号
ピ
EMERGENCY BROADCAST
Channel 8
Please stand by. Stay calm and await further instructions.
ザッ
ザザ
ザア
!
ハァ ハァ
ザ
ハァ ハァ
ハァ ハァ

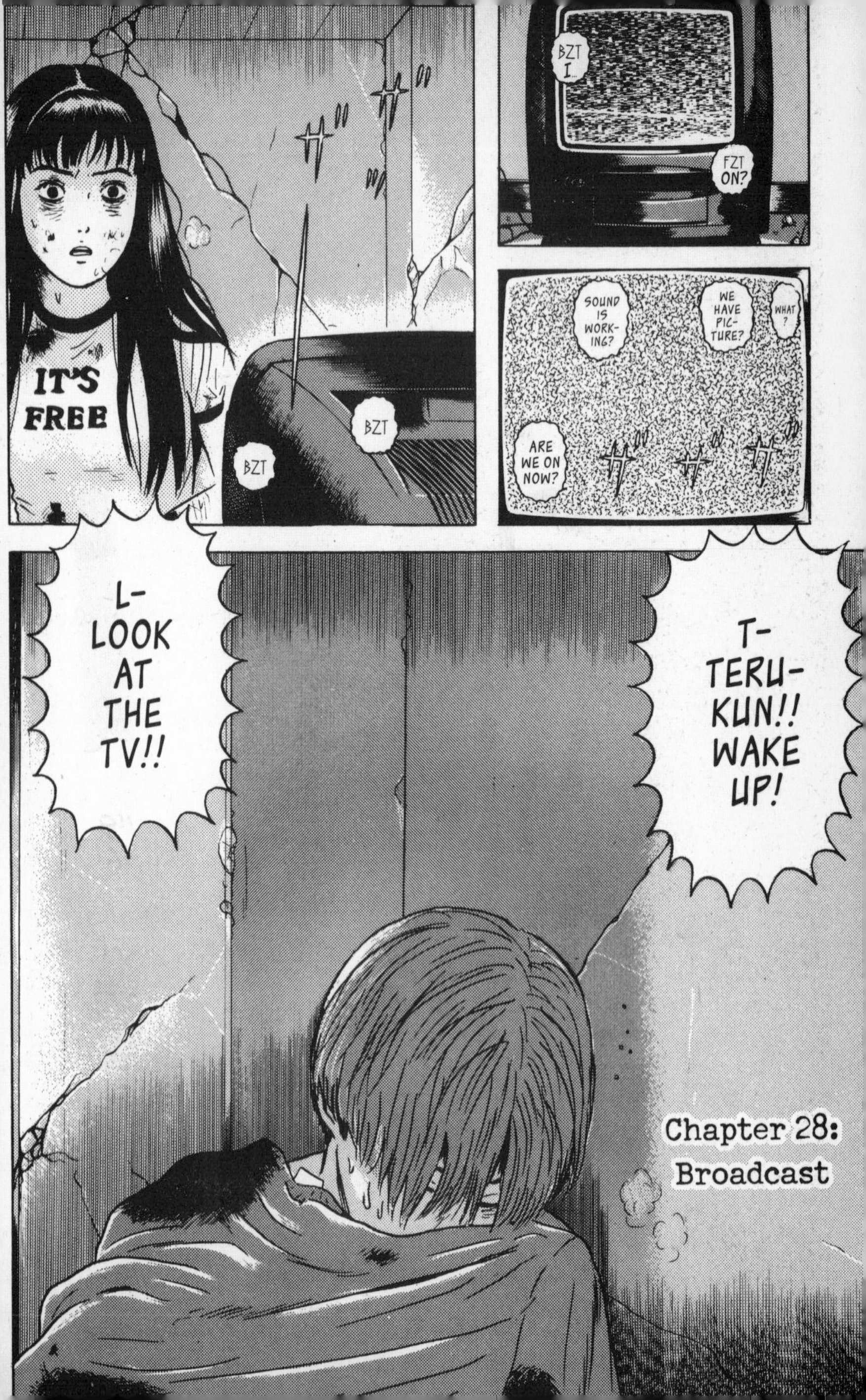
BZT I...
FZT ON?
WHAT?
WE HAVE PICTURE?
SOUND IS WORKING?
ARE WE ON NOW?
IT'S FREE
BZT
BZT
T-TERU-KUN!! WAKE UP!
L-LOOK AT THE TV!!
Chapter 28: Broadcast

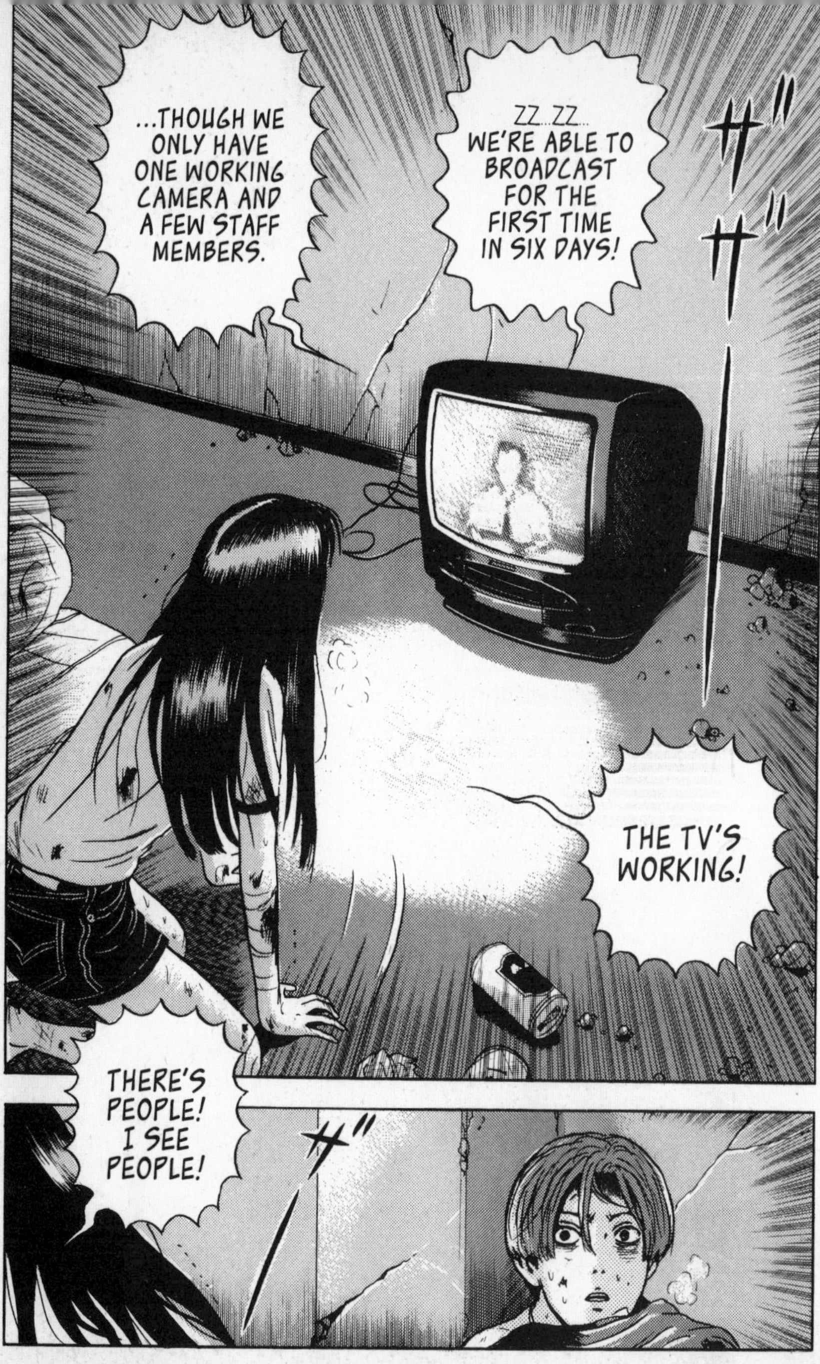
ZZ...ZZ... WE'RE ABLE TO BROADCAST FOR THE FIRST TIME IN SIX DAYS!
...THOUGH WE ONLY HAVE ONE WORKING CAMERA AND A FEW STAFF MEMBERS.
THE TV'S WORKING!
THERE'S PEOPLE! I SEE PEOPLE!

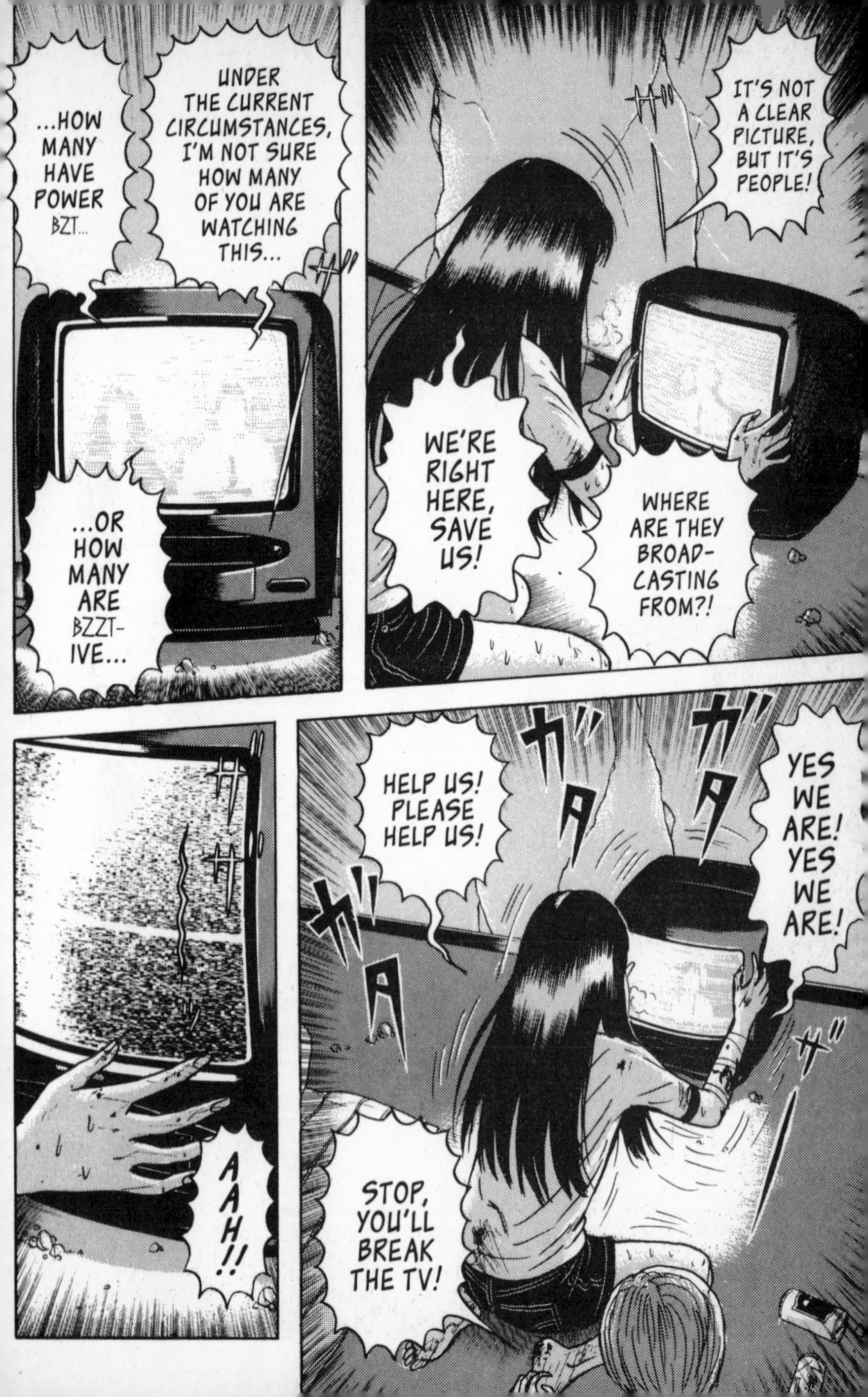
IT'S NOT A CLEAR PICTURE, BUT IT'S PEOPLE!
WHERE ARE THEY BROAD-CASTING FROM?!
WE'RE RIGHT HERE, SAVE US!
UNDER THE CURRENT CIRCUMSTANCES, I'M NOT SURE HOW MANY OF YOU ARE WATCHING THIS...
...HOW MANY HAVE POWER BZT...
...OR HOW MANY ARE BZZT-IVE...
YES WE ARE! YES WE ARE!
HELP US! PLEASE HELP US!
STOP, YOU'LL BREAK THE TV!
AAAH!!

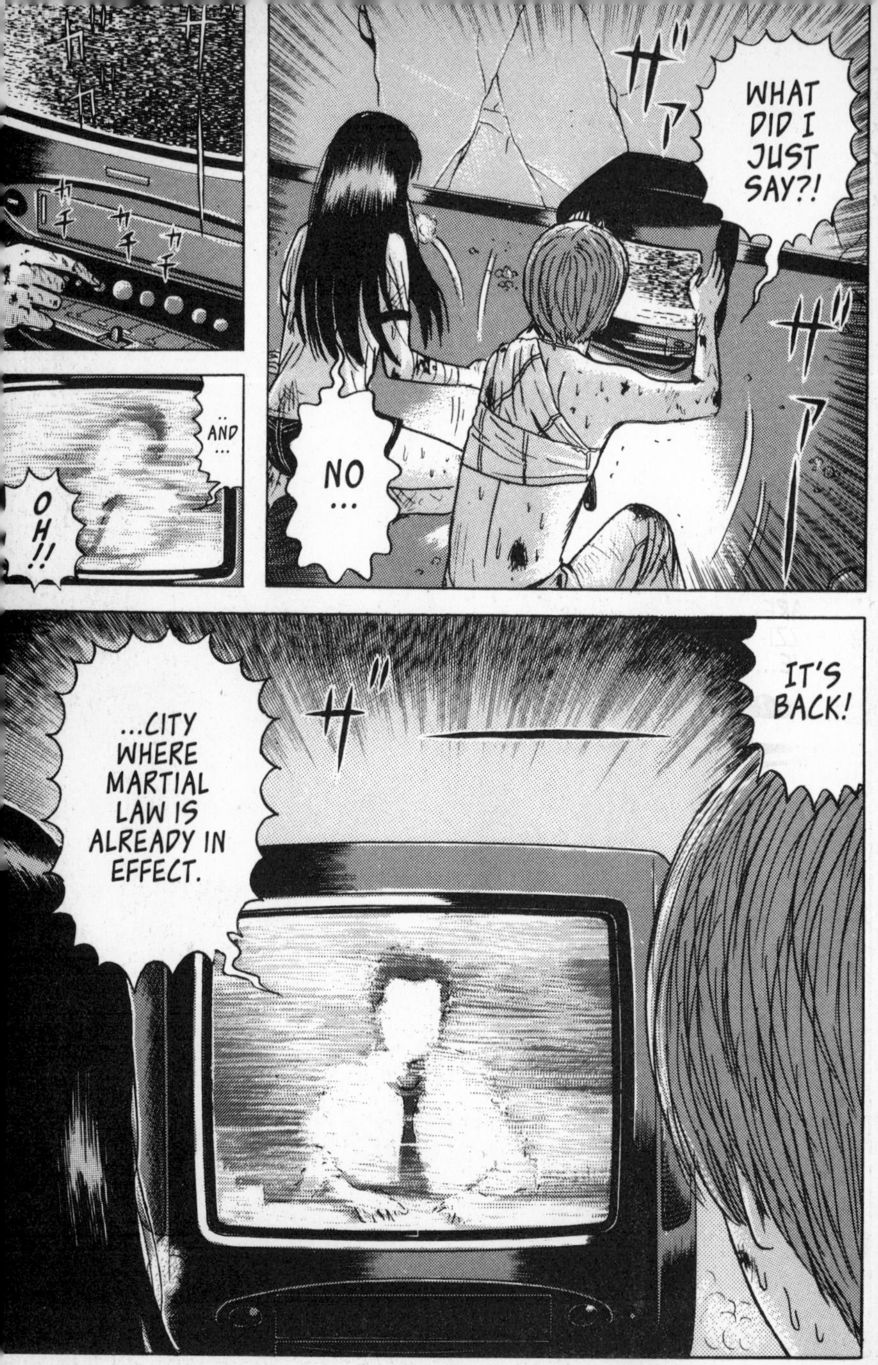
WHAT DID I JUST SAY?!
NO ...
.. AND ...
OH!!
IT'S BACK!
...CITY WHERE MARTIAL LAW IS ALREADY IN EFFECT.

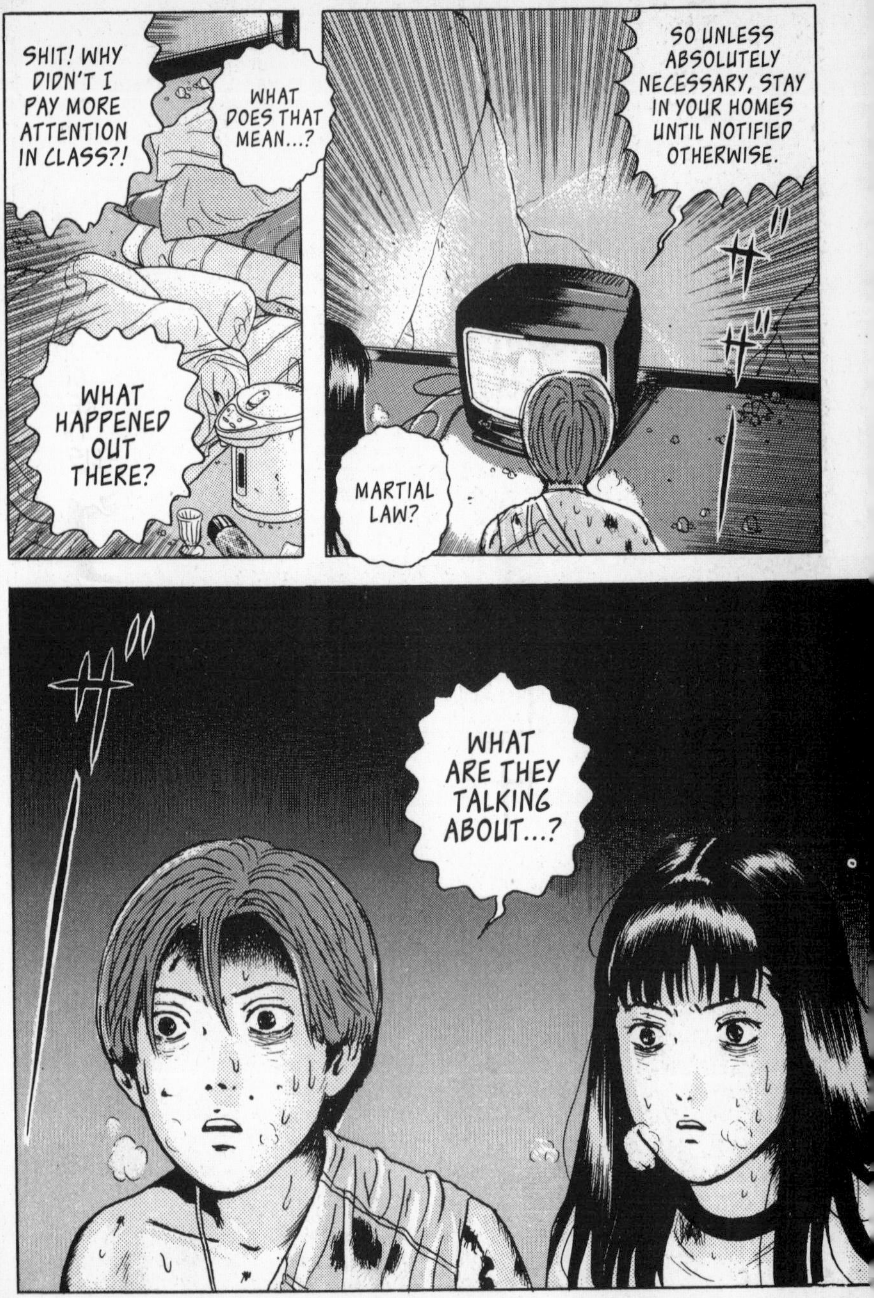
SO UNLESS ABSOLUTELY NECESSARY, STAY IN YOUR HOMES UNTIL NOTIFIED OTHERWISE.
MARTIAL LAW?
WHAT DOES THAT MEAN...?
SHIT! WHY DIDN'T I PAY MORE ATTENTION IN CLASS?!
WHAT HAPPENED OUT THERE?
WHAT ARE THEY TALKING ABOUT...?

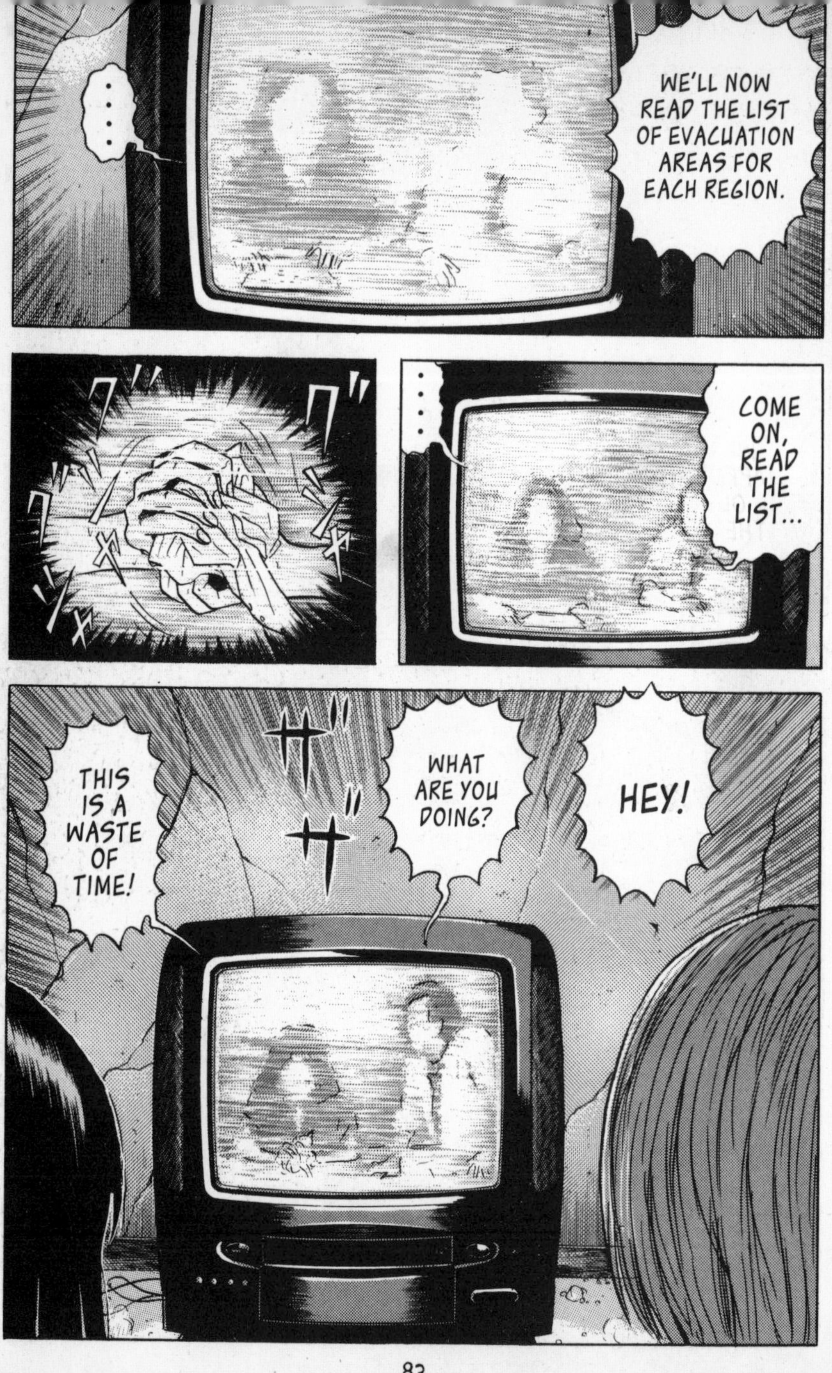
WE'LL NOW READ THE LIST OF EVACUATION AREAS FOR EACH REGION.
....
COME ON, READ THE LIST...
....
HEY!
WHAT ARE YOU DOING?
THIS IS A WASTE OF TIME!

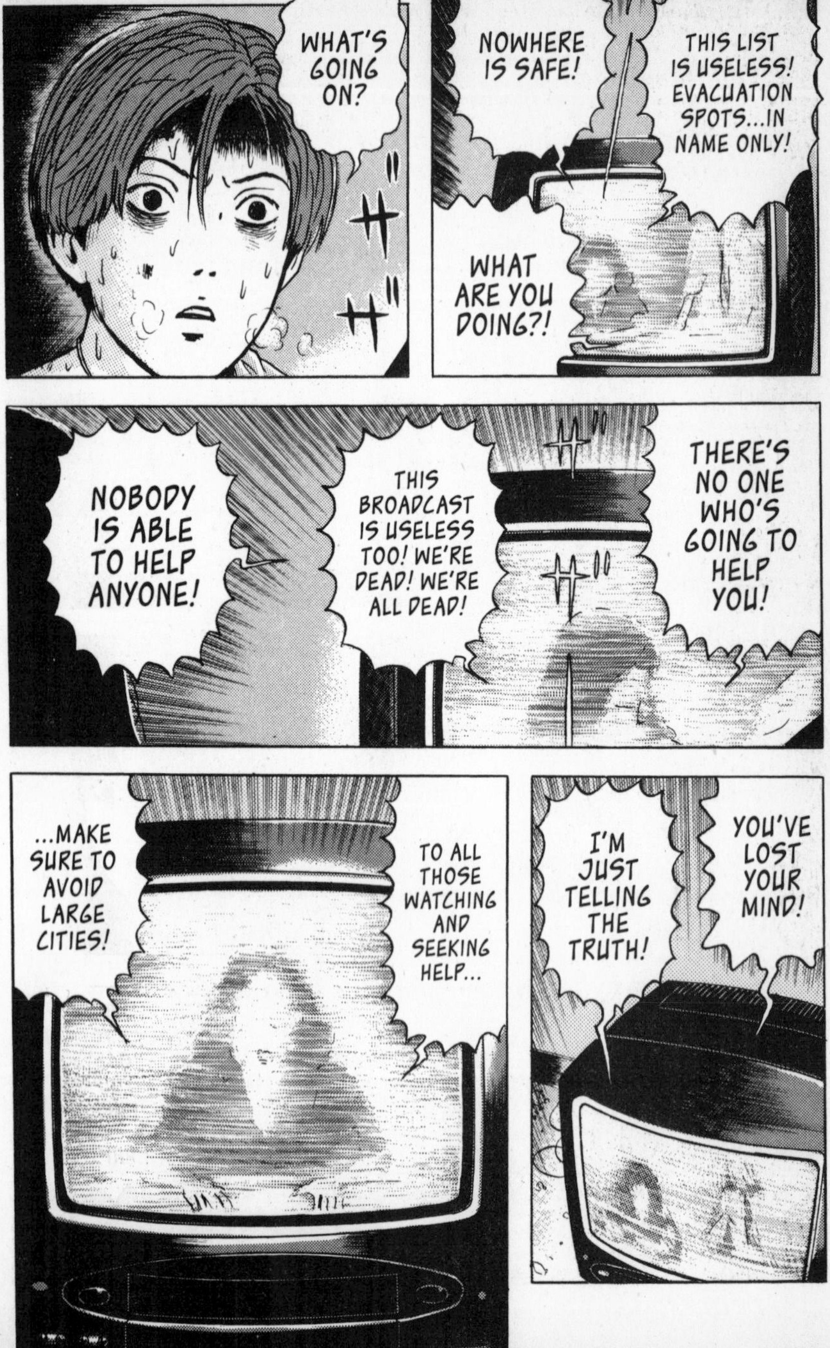
THIS LIST IS USELESS! EVACUATION SPOTS...IN NAME ONLY!
NOWHERE IS SAFE!
WHAT ARE YOU DOING?!
WHAT'S GOING ON?
THERE'S NO ONE WHO'S GOING TO HELP YOU!
THIS BROADCAST IS USELESS TOO! WE'RE DEAD! WE'RE ALL DEAD!
NOBODY IS ABLE TO HELP ANYONE!
YOU'VE LOST YOUR MIND!
I'M JUST TELLING THE TRUTH!
TO ALL THOSE WATCHING AND SEEKING HELP...
...MAKE SURE TO AVOID LARGE CITIES!

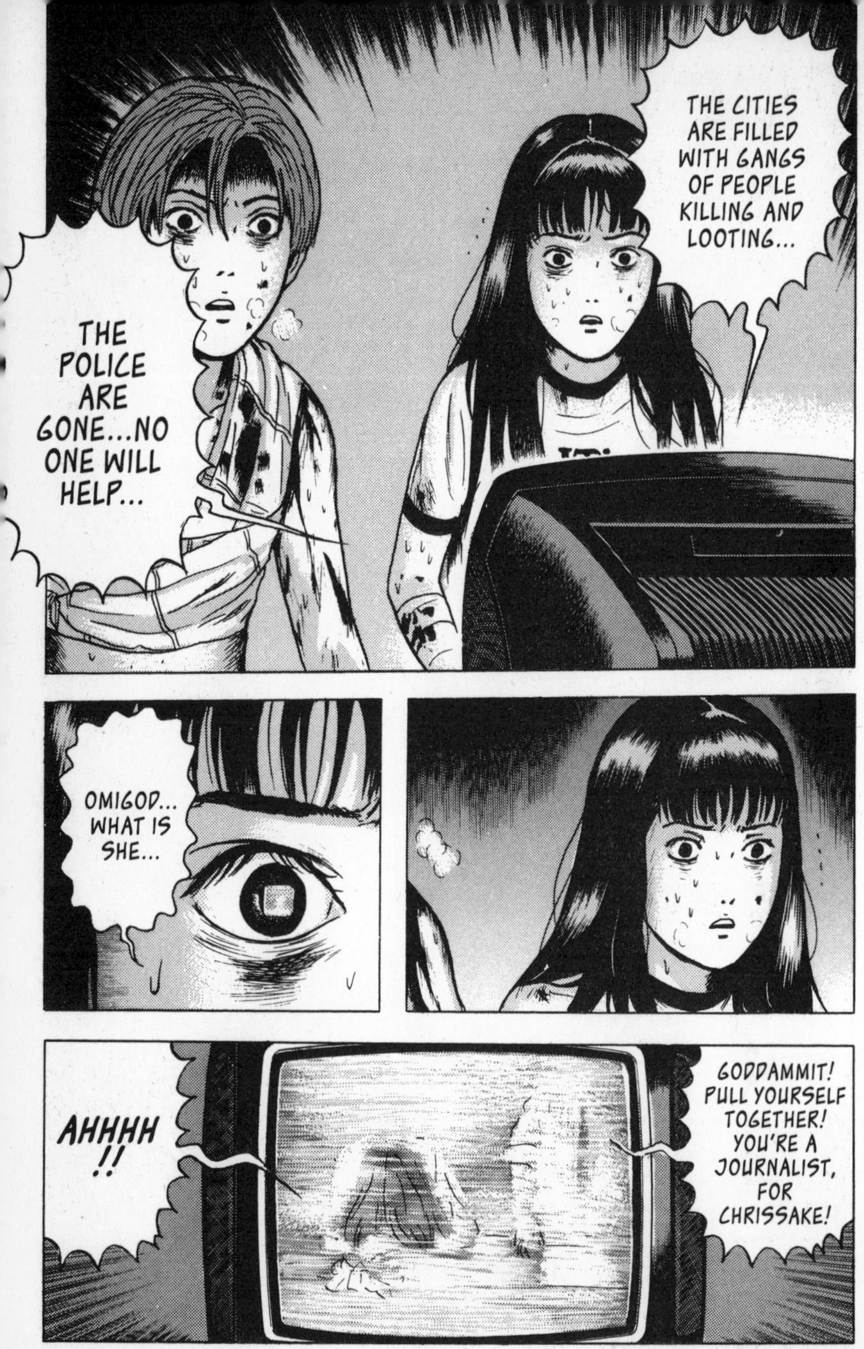
THE CITIES ARE FILLED WITH GANGS OF PEOPLE KILLING AND LOOTING...
THE POLICE ARE GONE...NO ONE WILL HELP...
OMIGOD... WHAT IS SHE...
GODDAMMIT! PULL YOURSELF TOGETHER! YOU'RE A JOURNALIST, FOR CHRISSAKE!
AHHHH !!

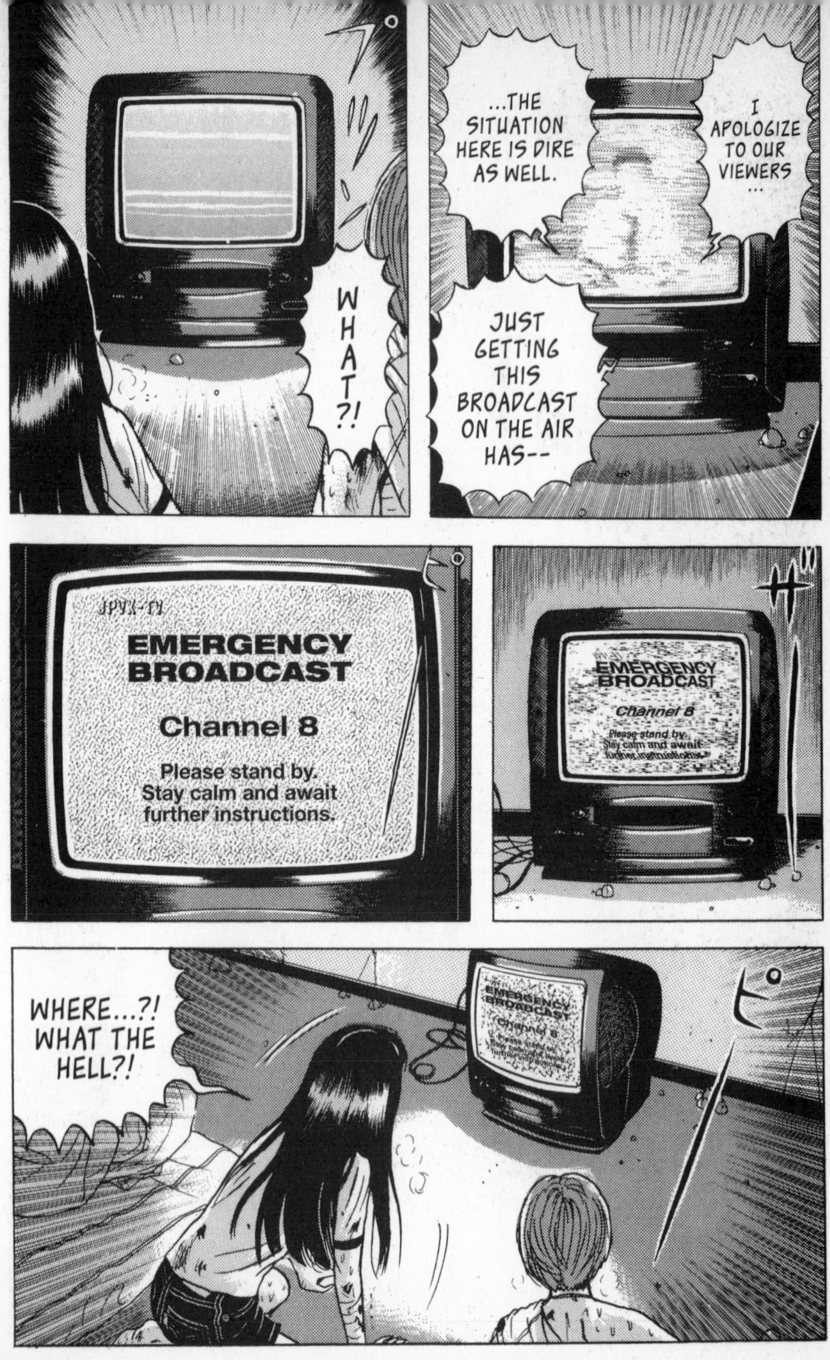
I APOLOGIZE TO OUR VIEWERS...
...THE SITUATION HERE IS DIRE AS WELL.
JUST GETTING THIS BROADCAST ON THE AIR HAS--
WHAT?!
EMERGENCY BROADCAST
Channel 8
Please stand by.
Stay calm and await
EMERGENCY BROADCAST
Channel 8
Please stand by.
Stay calm and await
further instructions.
WHERE...?! WHAT THE HELL?!

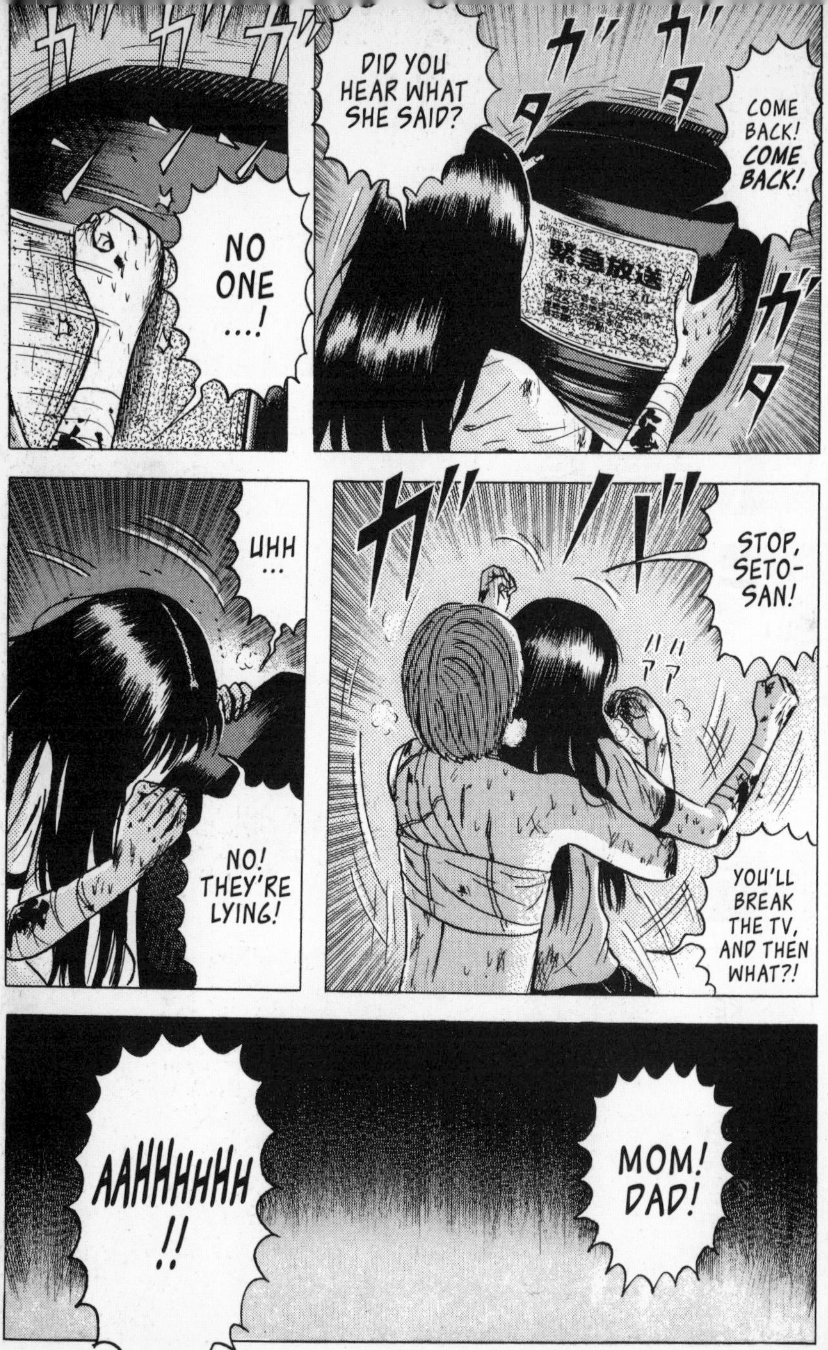
DID YOU HEAR WHAT SHE SAID?
COME BACK! COME BACK!
ガタ ガタ
緊急放送
ガタ
NO ONE ...!
STOP, SETO-SAN!
ハァ ハァ
YOU'LL BREAK THE TV, AND THEN WHAT?!
UHH ...
NO! THEY'RE LYING!
MOM! DAD!
AAHHHHHH !!

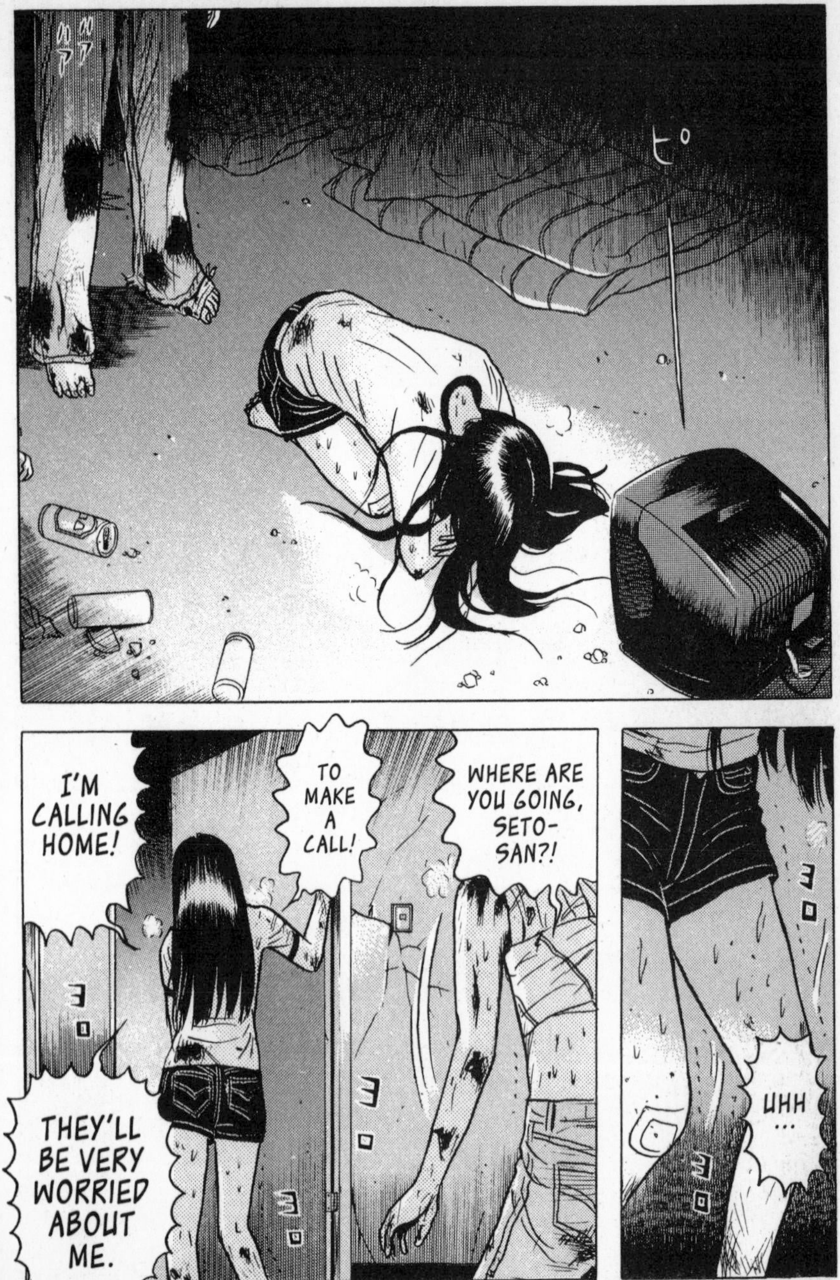
ピ
UHH ...
WHERE ARE YOU GOING, SETO-SAN?!
TO MAKE A CALL!
I'M CALLING HOME!
THEY'LL BE VERY WORRIED ABOUT ME.

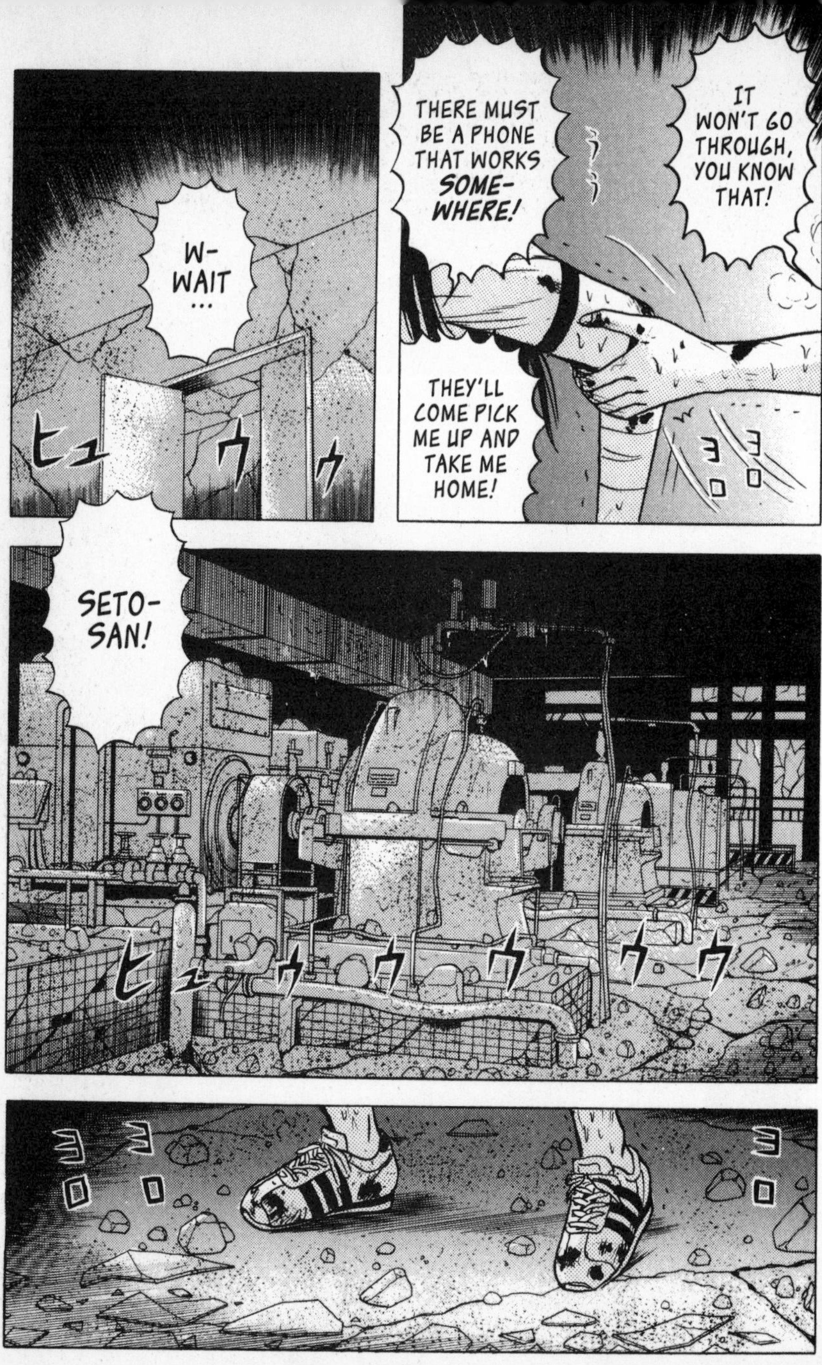
IT WON'T GO THROUGH, YOU KNOW THAT!
THERE MUST BE A PHONE THAT WORKS SOME-WHERE!
THEY'LL COME PICK ME UP AND TAKE ME HOME!
ヨロ ヨロ
W-WAIT ...
ヒュウゥ
SETO-SAN!
ヒュウウウウウ
ヨロ ヨロ ヨロ

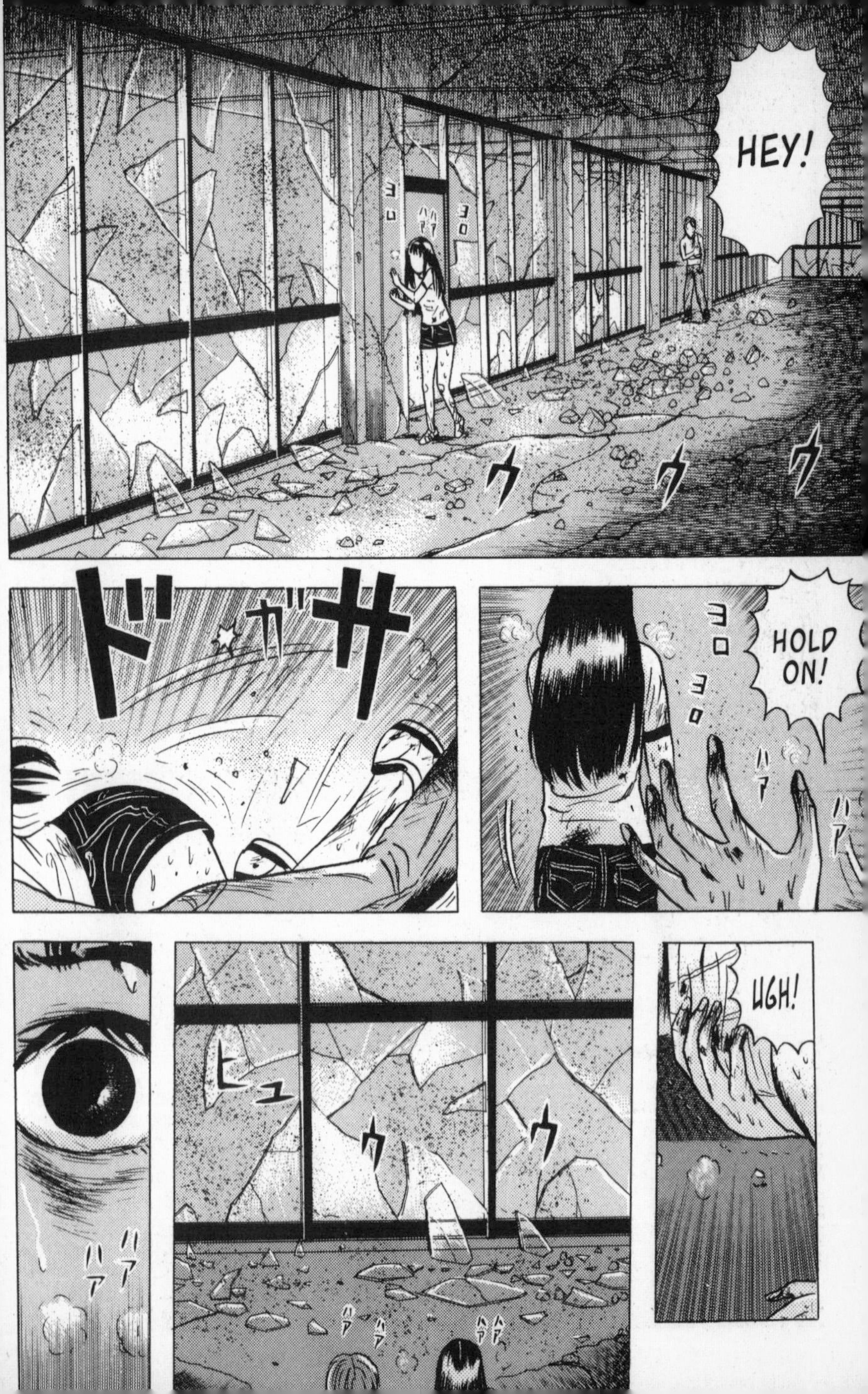
HEY!
HOLD ON!
UGH!

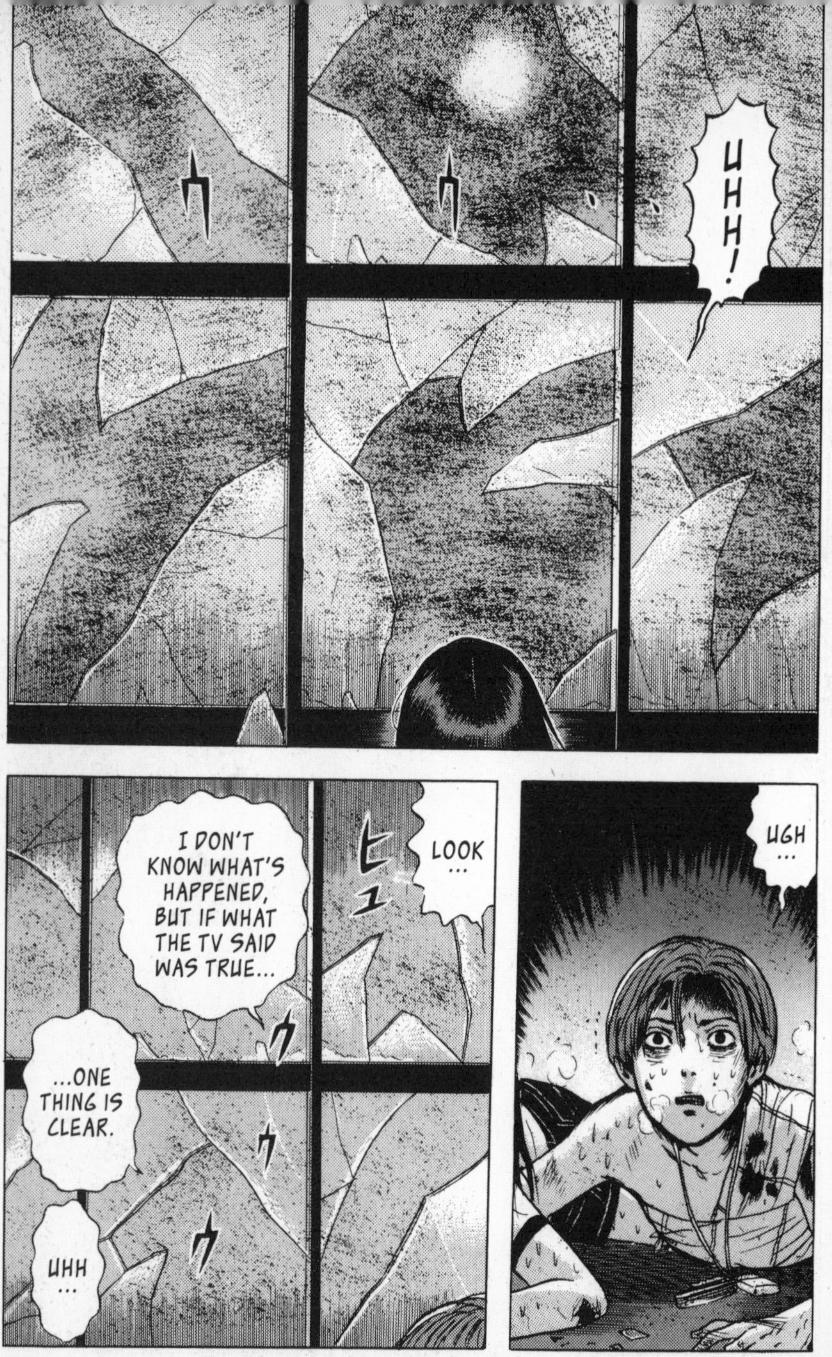
UHHH!
UGH ...
LOOK ...
I DON'T KNOW WHAT'S HAPPENED, BUT IF WHAT THE TV SAID WAS TRUE...
...ONE THING IS CLEAR.
UHH ...

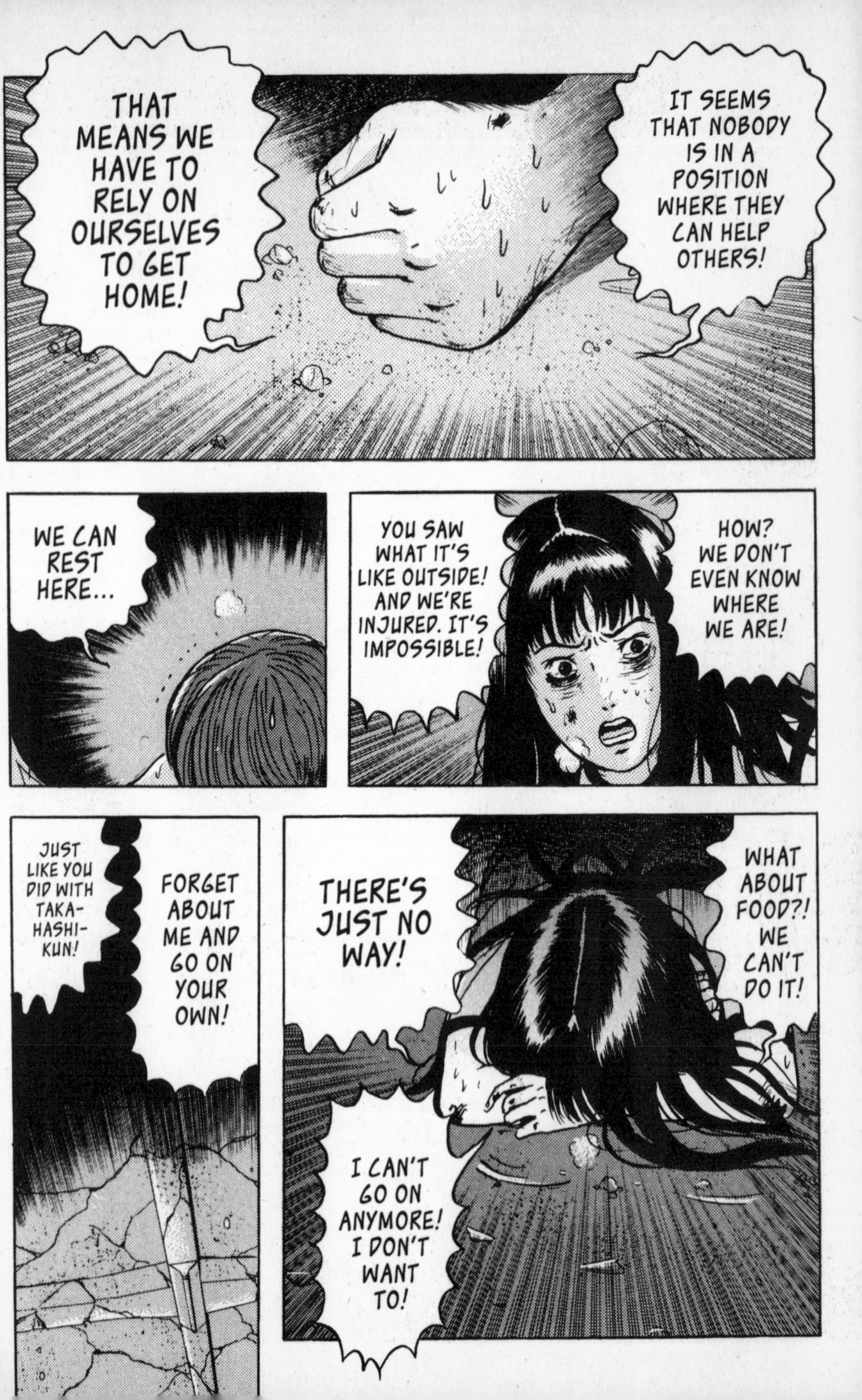
IT SEEMS THAT NOBODY IS IN A POSITION WHERE THEY CAN HELP OTHERS!
THAT MEANS WE HAVE TO RELY ON OURSELVES TO GET HOME!
HOW? WE DON'T EVEN KNOW WHERE WE ARE!
YOU SAW WHAT IT'S LIKE OUTSIDE! AND WE'RE INJURED. IT'S IMPOSSIBLE!
WE CAN REST HERE...
WHAT ABOUT FOOD?! WE CAN'T DO IT!
THERE'S JUST NO WAY!
I CAN'T GO ON ANYMORE! I DON'T WANT TO!
FORGET ABOUT ME AND GO ON YOUR OWN!
JUST LIKE YOU DID WITH TAKA-HASHI-KUN!

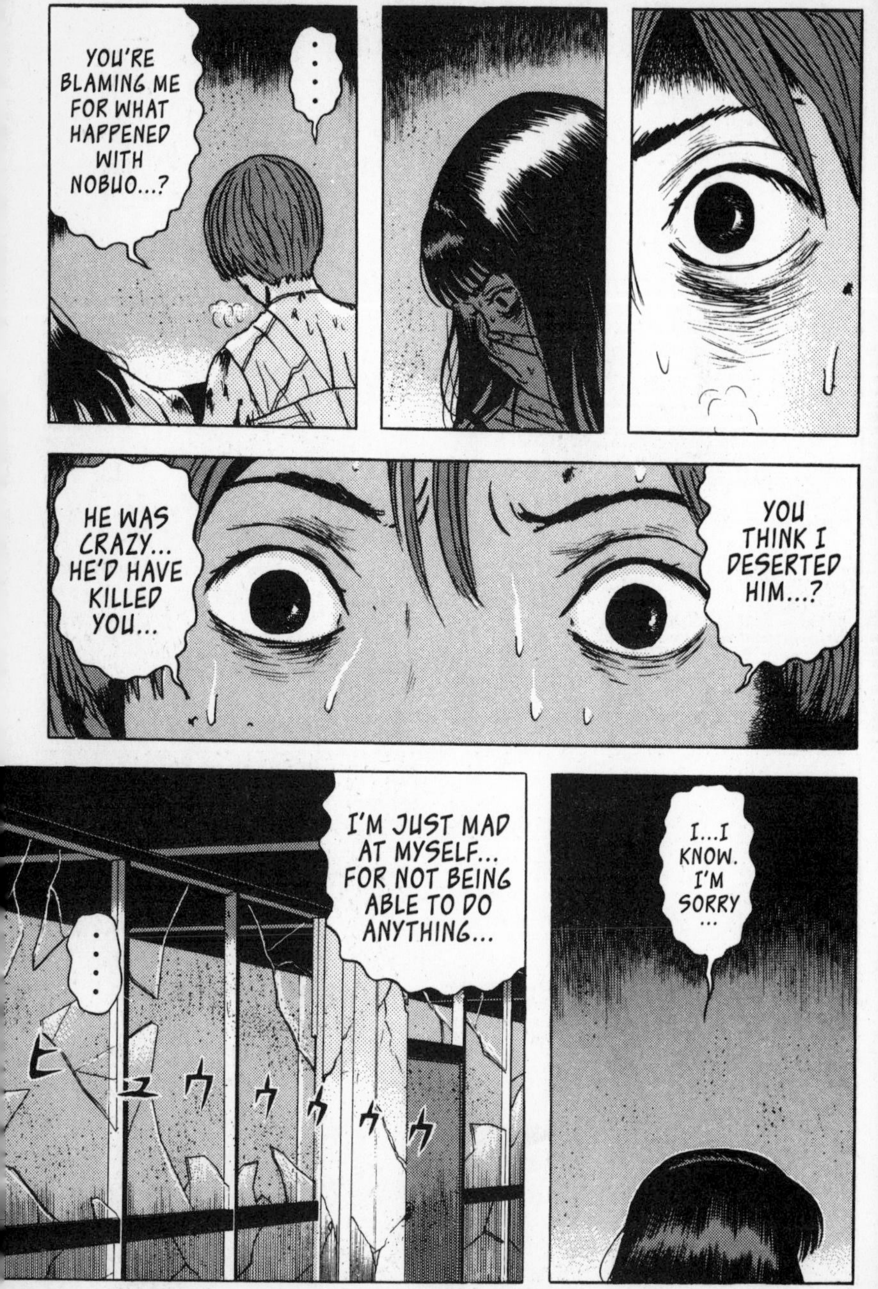
....
YOU'RE BLAMING ME FOR WHAT HAPPENED WITH NOBUO...?
YOU THINK I DESERTED HIM...?
HE WAS CRAZY... HE'D HAVE KILLED YOU...
I...I KNOW. I'M SORRY...
I'M JUST MAD AT MYSELF... FOR NOT BEING ABLE TO DO ANYTHING...
....
ヒュウウウウウ

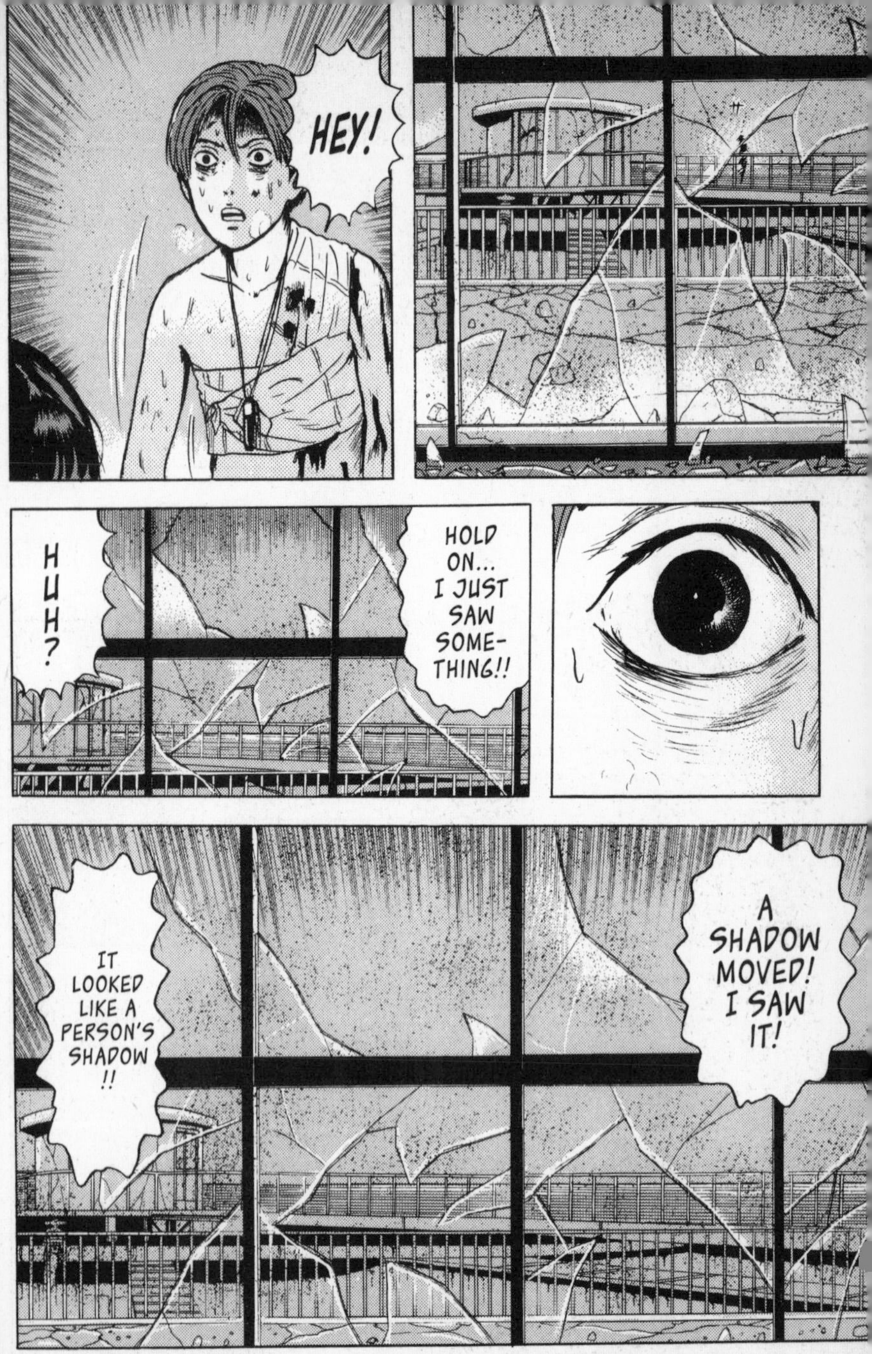
HEY!
HOLD ON... I JUST SAW SOMETHING!!
HUH?
A SHADOW MOVED! I SAW IT!
IT LOOKED LIKE A PERSON'S SHADOW!!

ヒュウウウ
Chapter 29: World of Death
ウウウ
ウウ

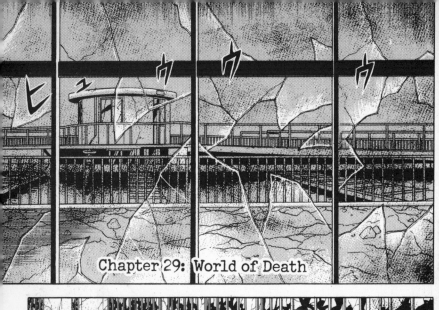

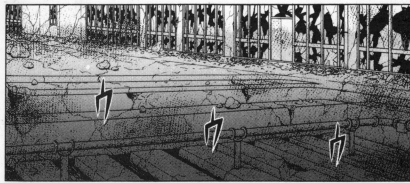

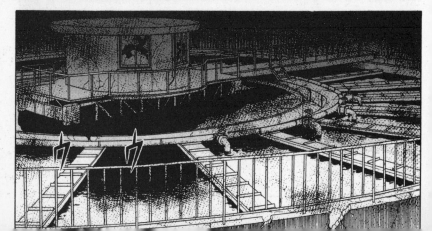

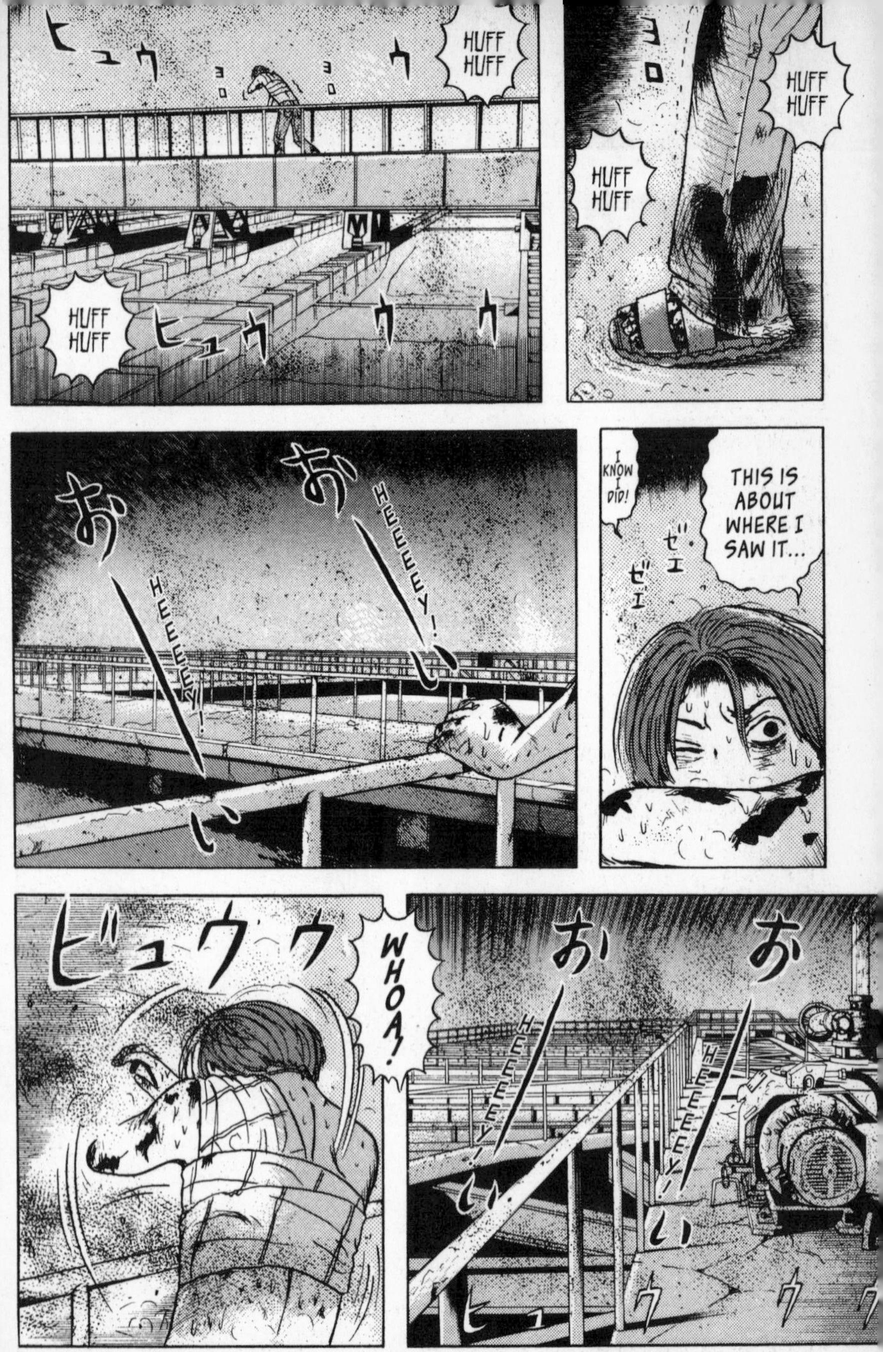

ヨロ
HUFF HUFF
HUFF HUFF
ヒュウウ
ヨロヨロ
HUFF HUFF
ヒュウウウ
HUFF HUFF
THIS IS ABOUT WHERE I SAW IT...
I KNOW I DID!
ゼエゼエ
おーい
HEEEEEY!
おーい
HEEEEEY!
おーい
HEEEEEY!
おーい
HEEEEEY!
ヒュウウ
WHOA!
ビュウウ

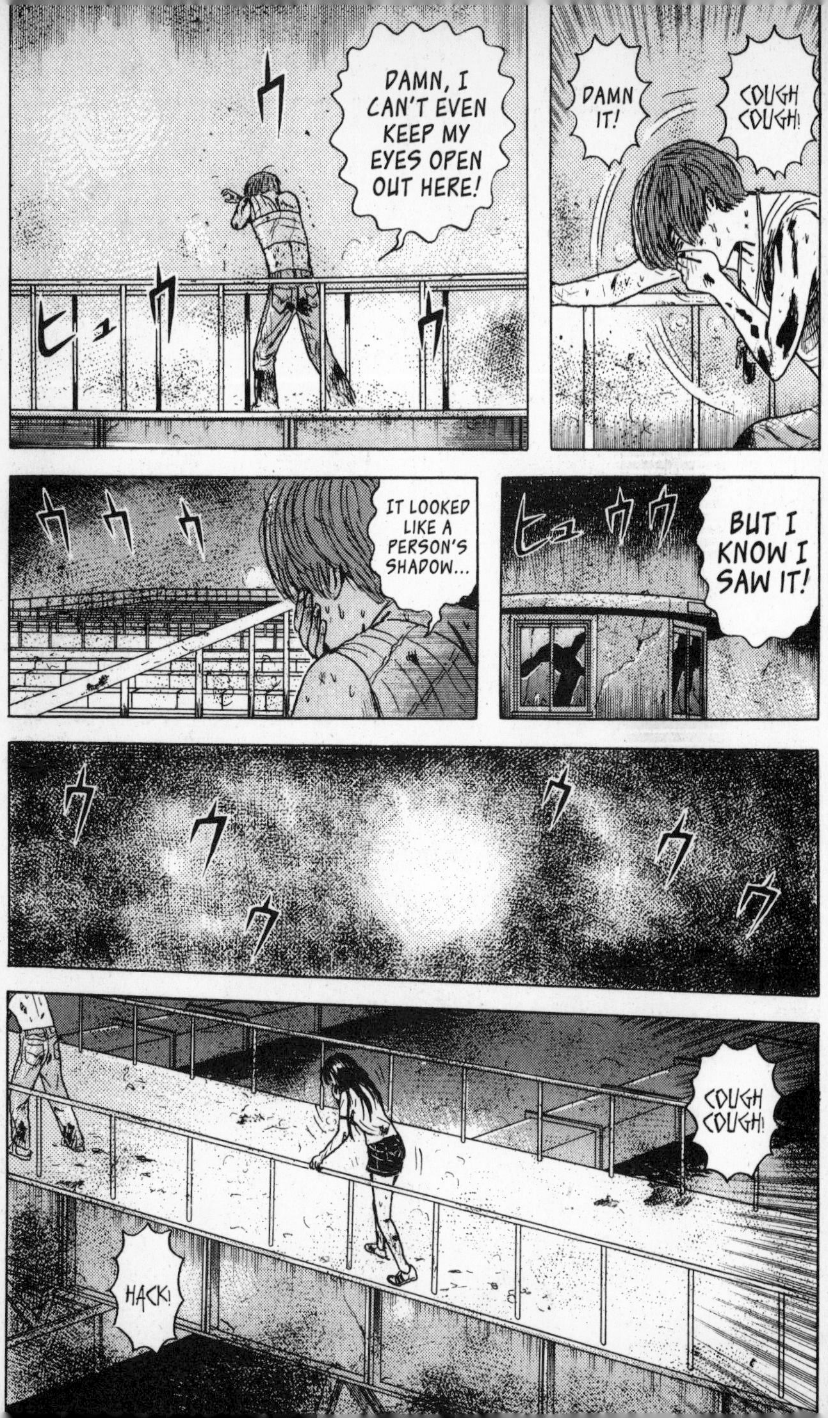
COUGH COUGH!
DAMN IT!
DAMN, I CAN'T EVEN KEEP MY EYES OPEN OUT HERE!
ヒュウ
BUT I KNOW I SAW IT!
ヒュウウ
IT LOOKED LIKE A PERSON'S SHADOW...
COUGH COUGH!
HACK!

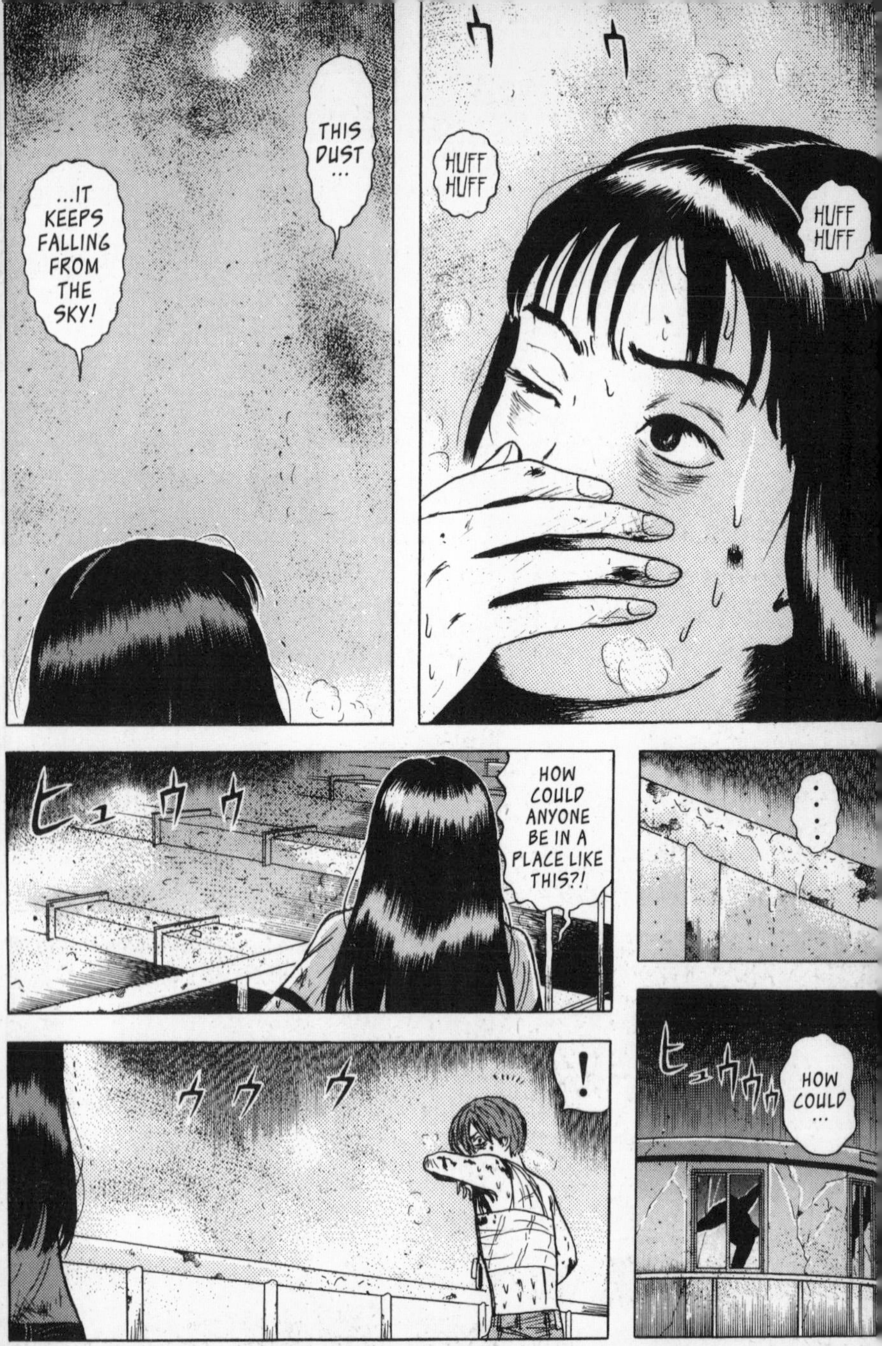
HUFF HUFF
HUFF HUFF
THIS DUST...
...IT KEEPS FALLING FROM THE SKY!
...
ヒュウウ
HOW COULD ANYONE BE IN A PLACE LIKE THIS?!
ヒュウウウ
HOW COULD...
!

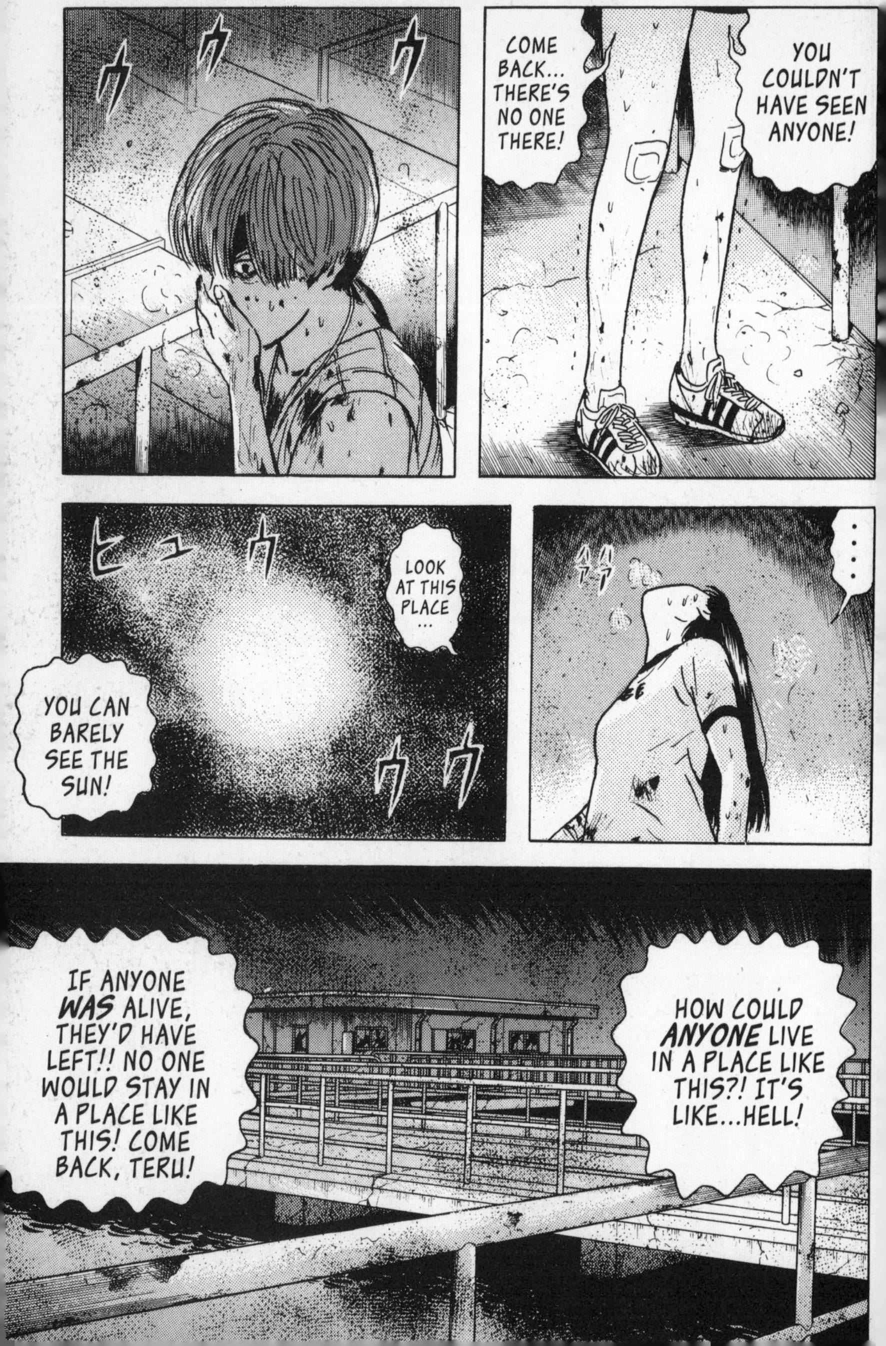
YOU COULDN'T HAVE SEEN ANYONE!
COME BACK... THERE'S NO ONE THERE!
...
LOOK AT THIS PLACE ...
YOU CAN BARELY SEE THE SUN!
HOW COULD ANYONE LIVE IN A PLACE LIKE THIS?! IT'S LIKE...HELL!
IF ANYONE WAS ALIVE, THEY'D HAVE LEFT!! NO ONE WOULD STAY IN A PLACE LIKE THIS! COME BACK, TERU!

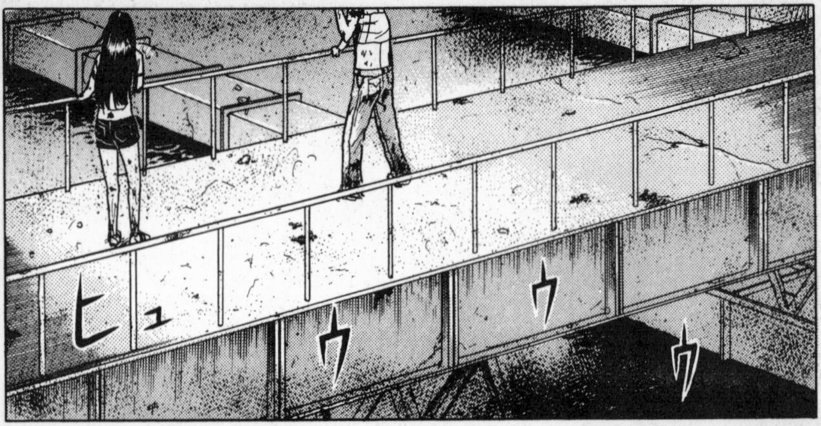
ウ
ウ
ウ
ヒュ
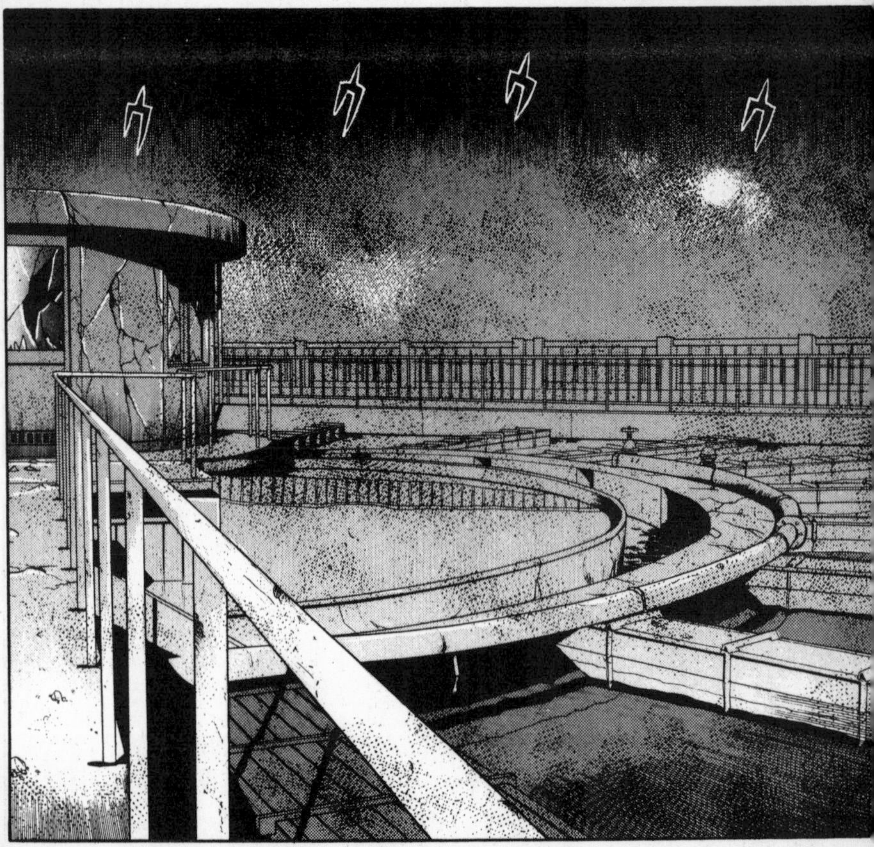
ウ
ウ
ウ
ウ

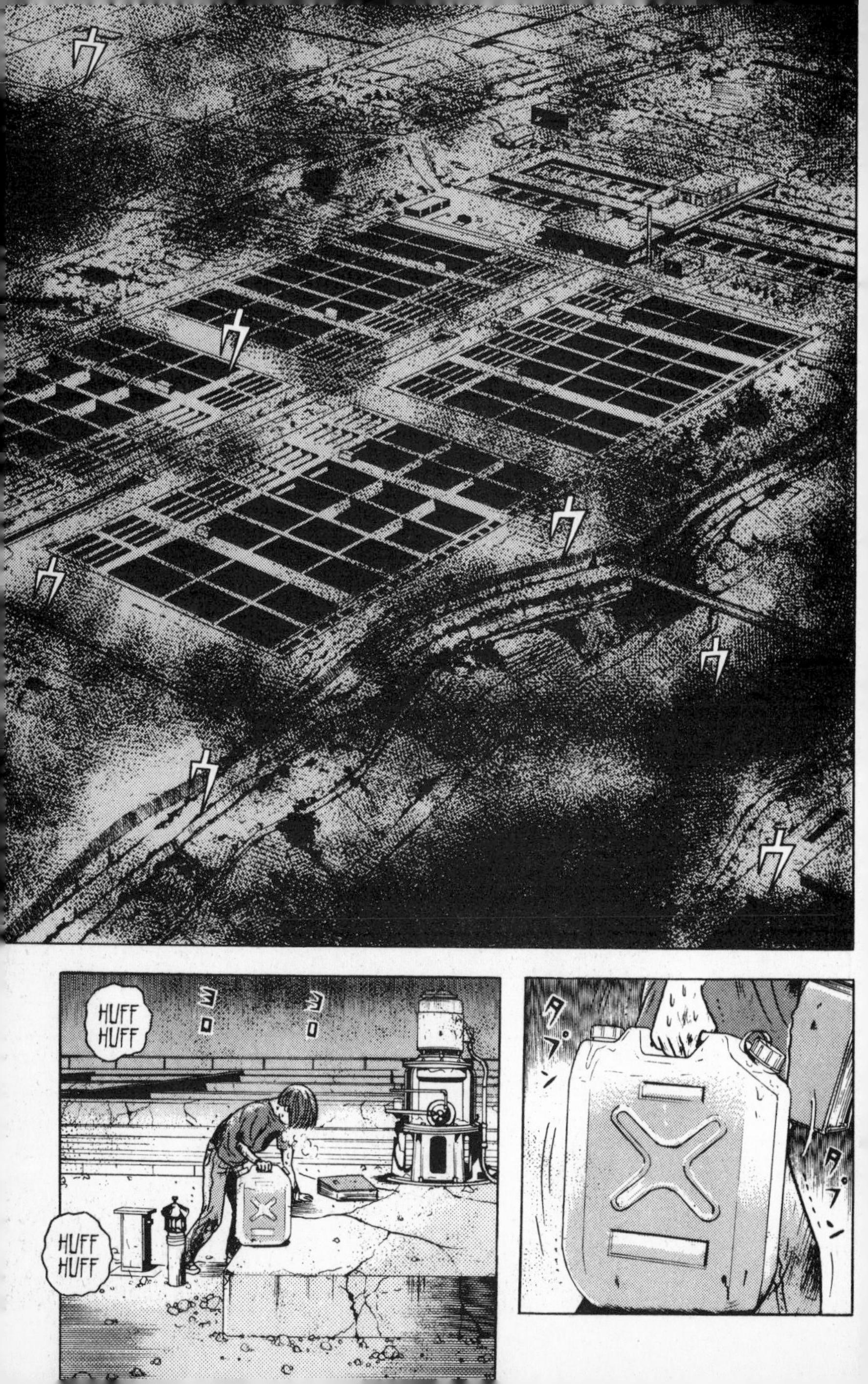
HUFF HUFF
HUFF HUFF

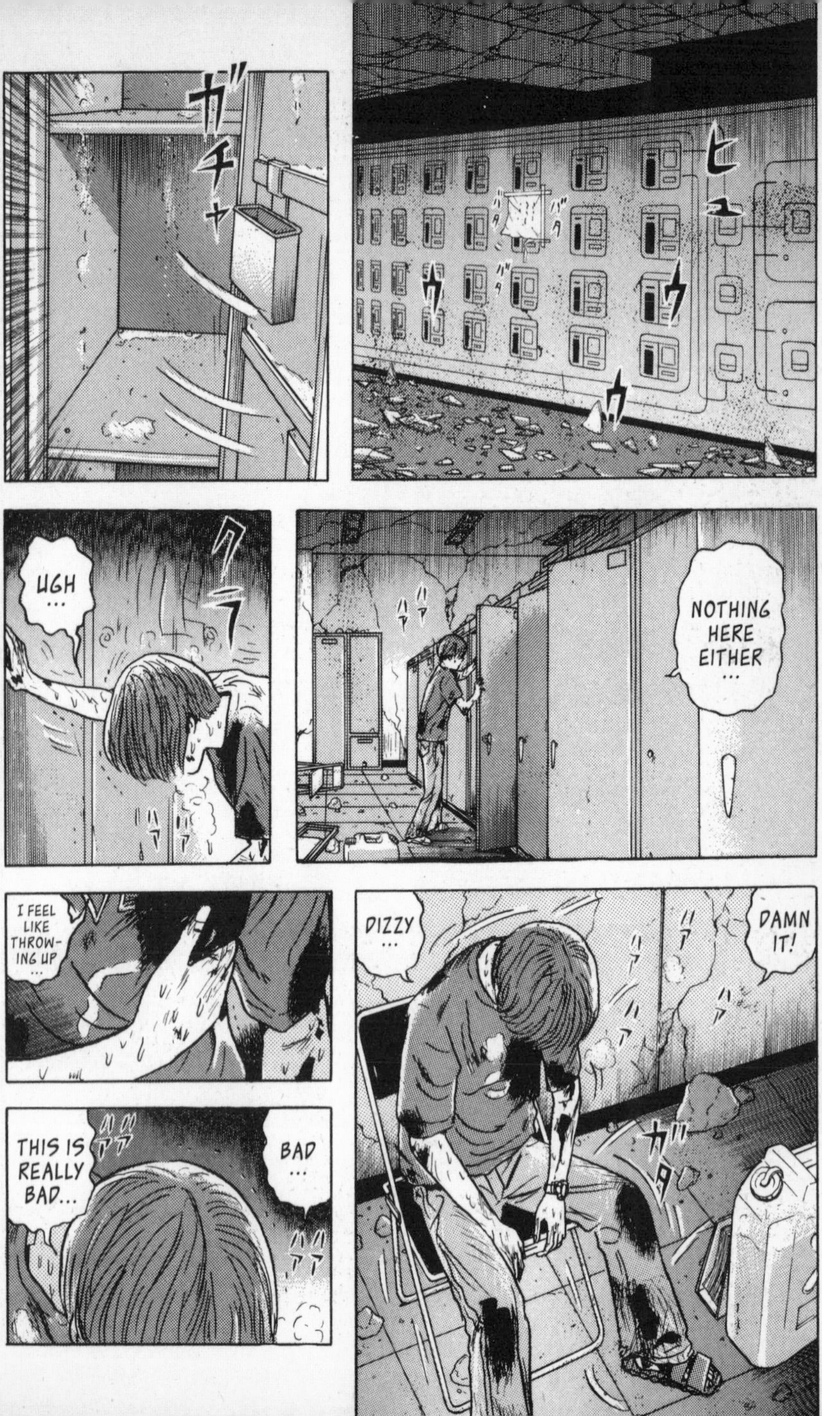
ガチャ
NOTHING HERE EITHER ...
UGH ...
DAMN IT!
DIZZY ...
I FEEL LIKE THROWING UP ...
BAD ...
THIS IS REALLY BAD...

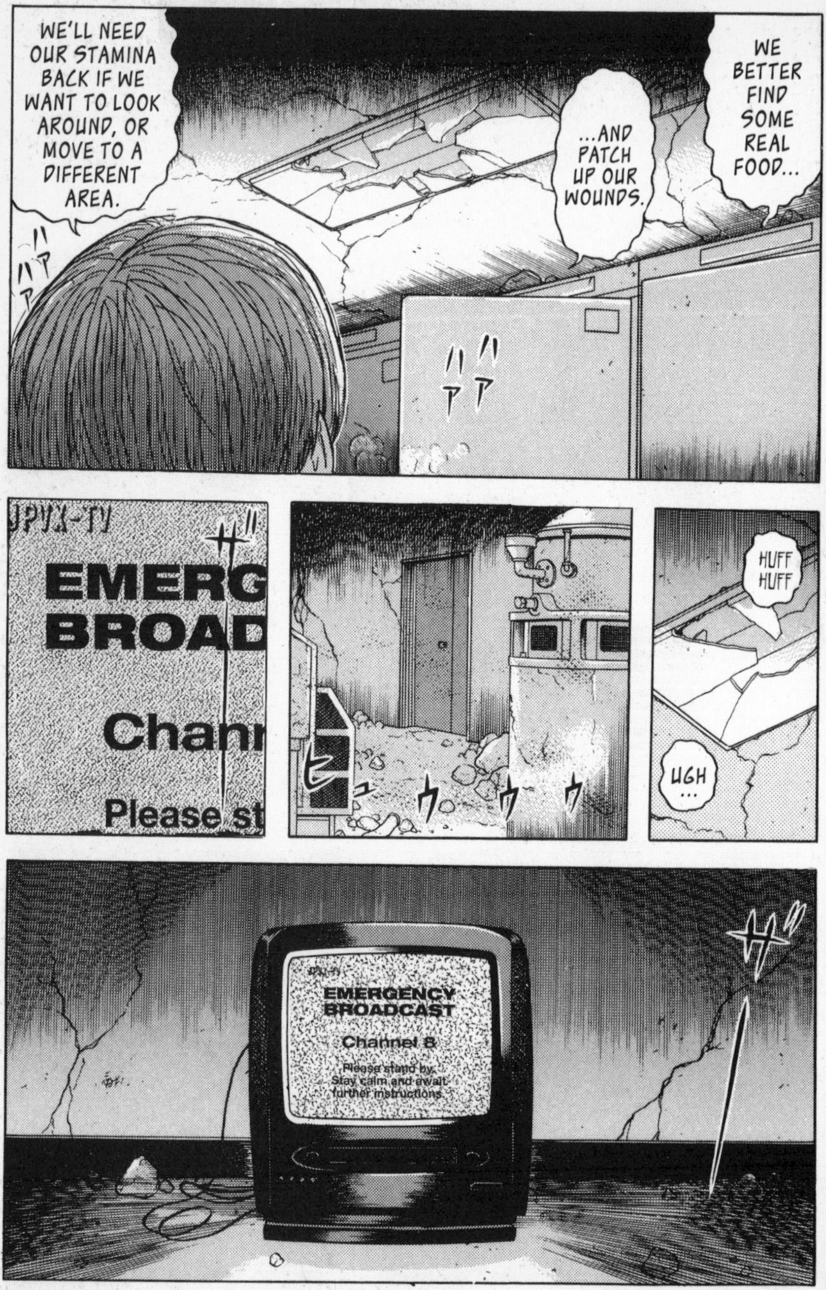
WE BETTER FIND SOME REAL FOOD...
...AND PATCH UP OUR WOUNDS.
WE'LL NEED OUR STAMINA BACK IF WE WANT TO LOOK AROUND, OR MOVE TO A DIFFERENT AREA.
HUFF HUFF
UGH ...
EMERG
BROAD
Chann
Please st
EMERGENCY BROADCAST
Channel 8
Please stand by.
Stay calm and await further instructions.

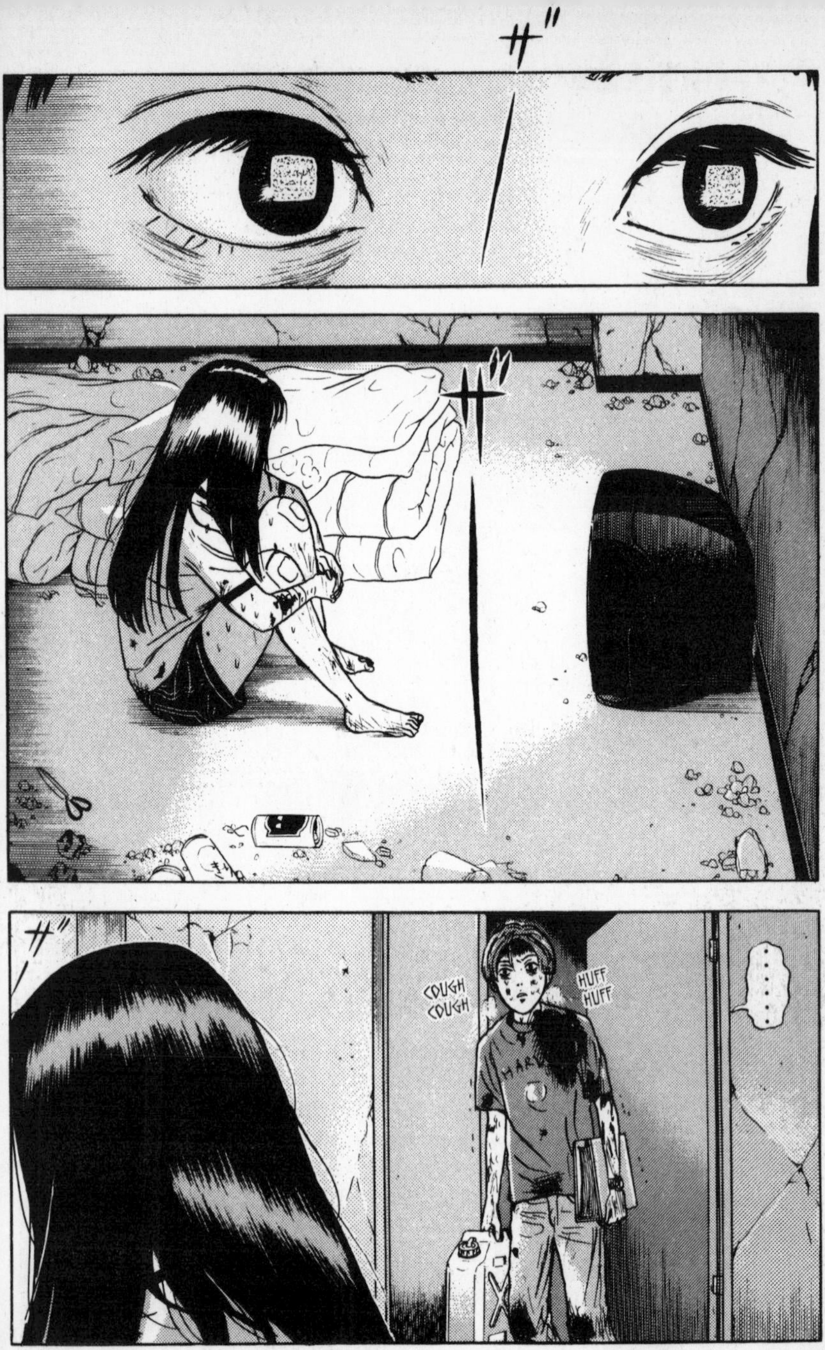
ザ"
ザ"
ザ"
COUGH COUGH
HUFF HUFF
......

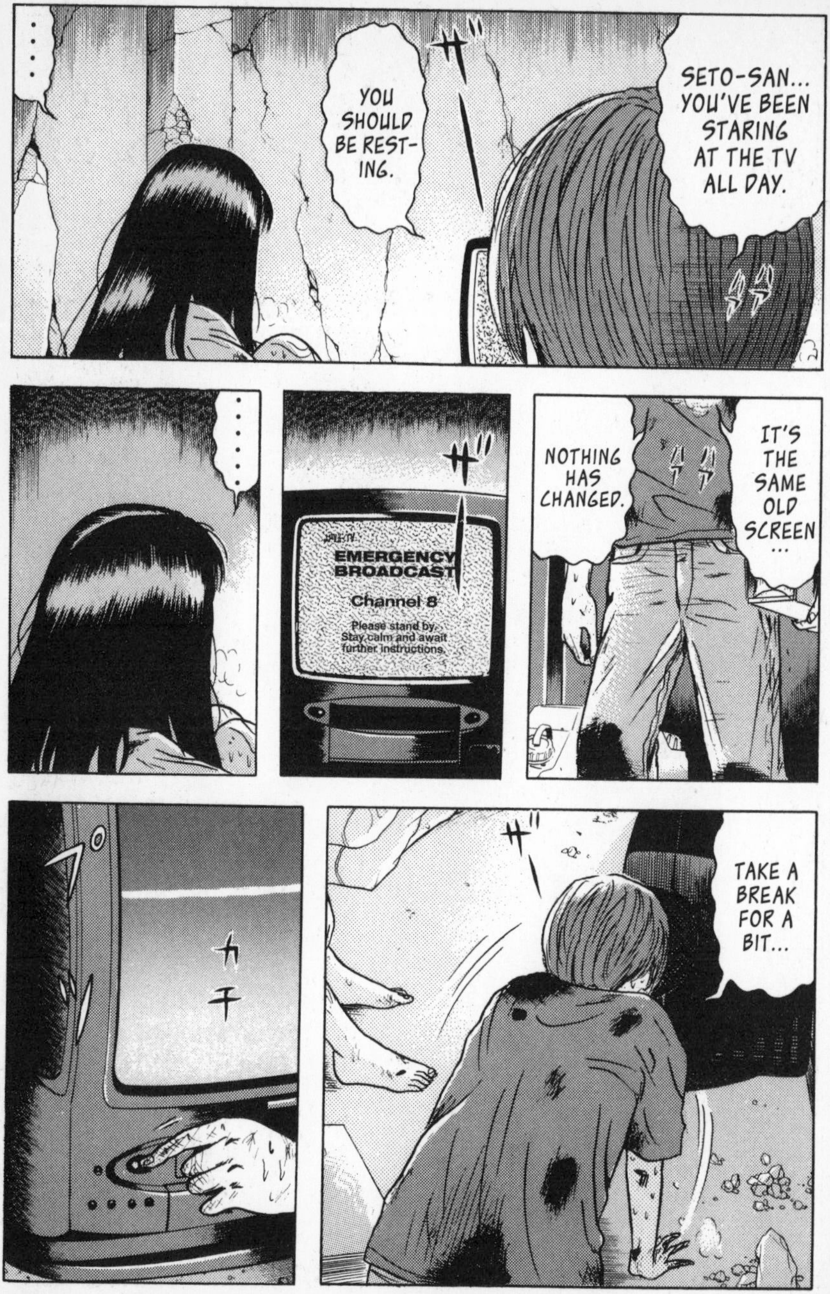
SETO-SAN... YOU'VE BEEN STARING AT THE TV ALL DAY.
YOU SHOULD BE REST-ING.
...
IT'S THE SAME OLD SCREEN...
NOTHING HAS CHANGED.
EMERGENCY BROADCAST
Channel 8
Please stand by. Stay calm and await further instructions.
......
TAKE A BREAK FOR A BIT...

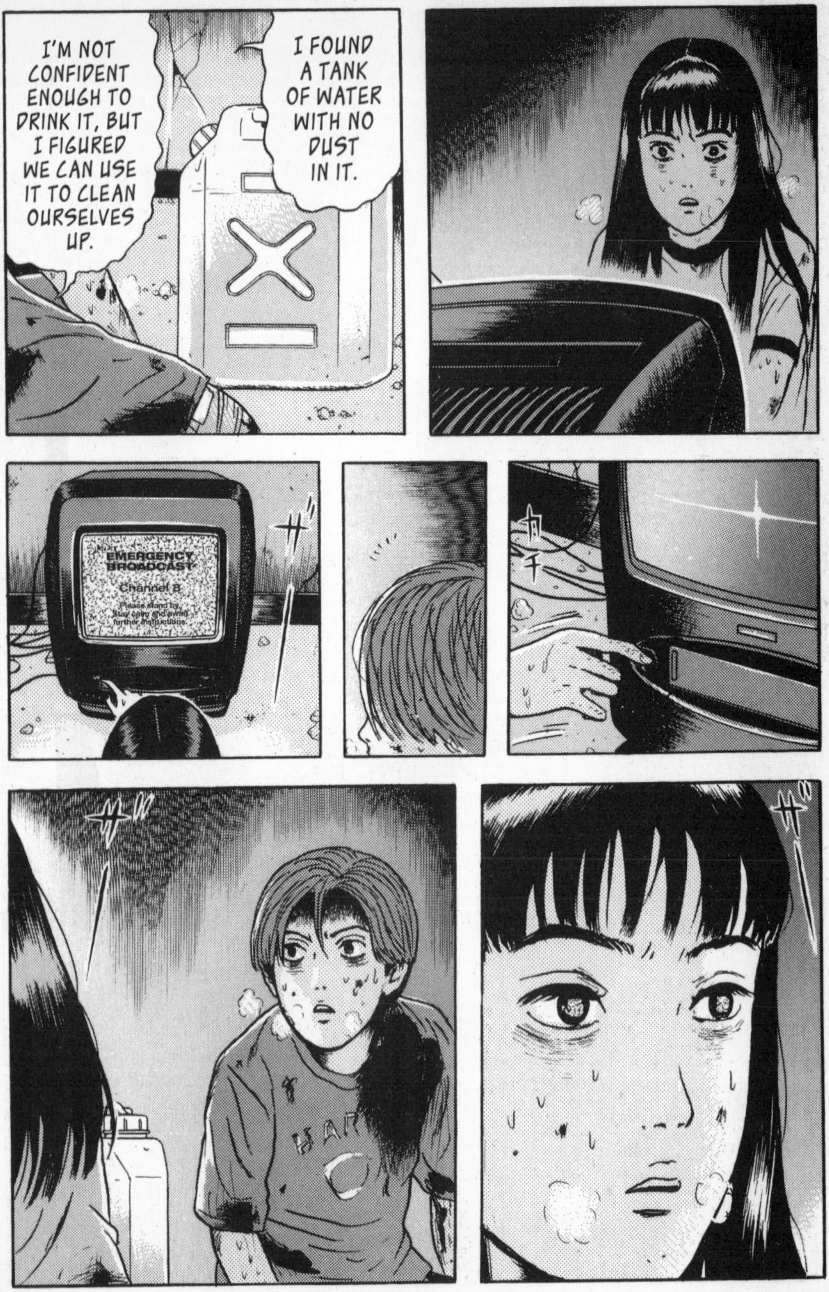
I FOUND A TANK OF WATER WITH NO DUST IN IT.
I'M NOT CONFIDENT ENOUGH TO DRINK IT, BUT I FIGURED WE CAN USE IT TO CLEAN OURSELVES UP.
カチ
ザ
EMERGENCY BROADCAST
Channel 8
Please stand by. Stay calm and await further instructions.
ザ
ザ

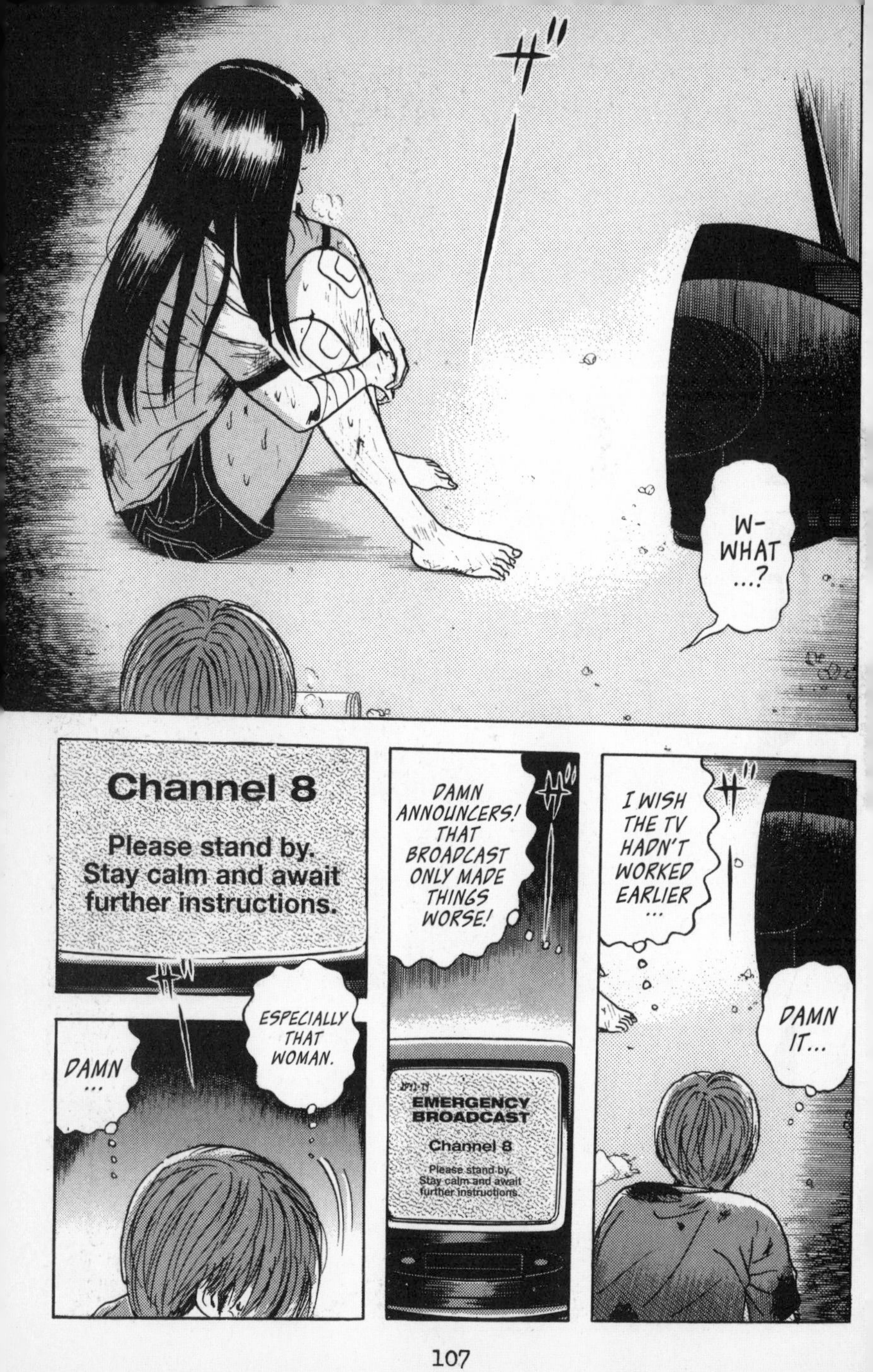
W-WHAT...?
I WISH THE TV HADN'T WORKED EARLIER...
DAMN IT...
DAMN ANNOUNCERS! THAT BROADCAST ONLY MADE THINGS WORSE!
EMERGENCY BROADCAST
Channel 8
Please stand by. Stay calm and await further instructions.
Channel 8
Please stand by. Stay calm and await further instructions.
ESPECIALLY THAT WOMAN.
DAMN...

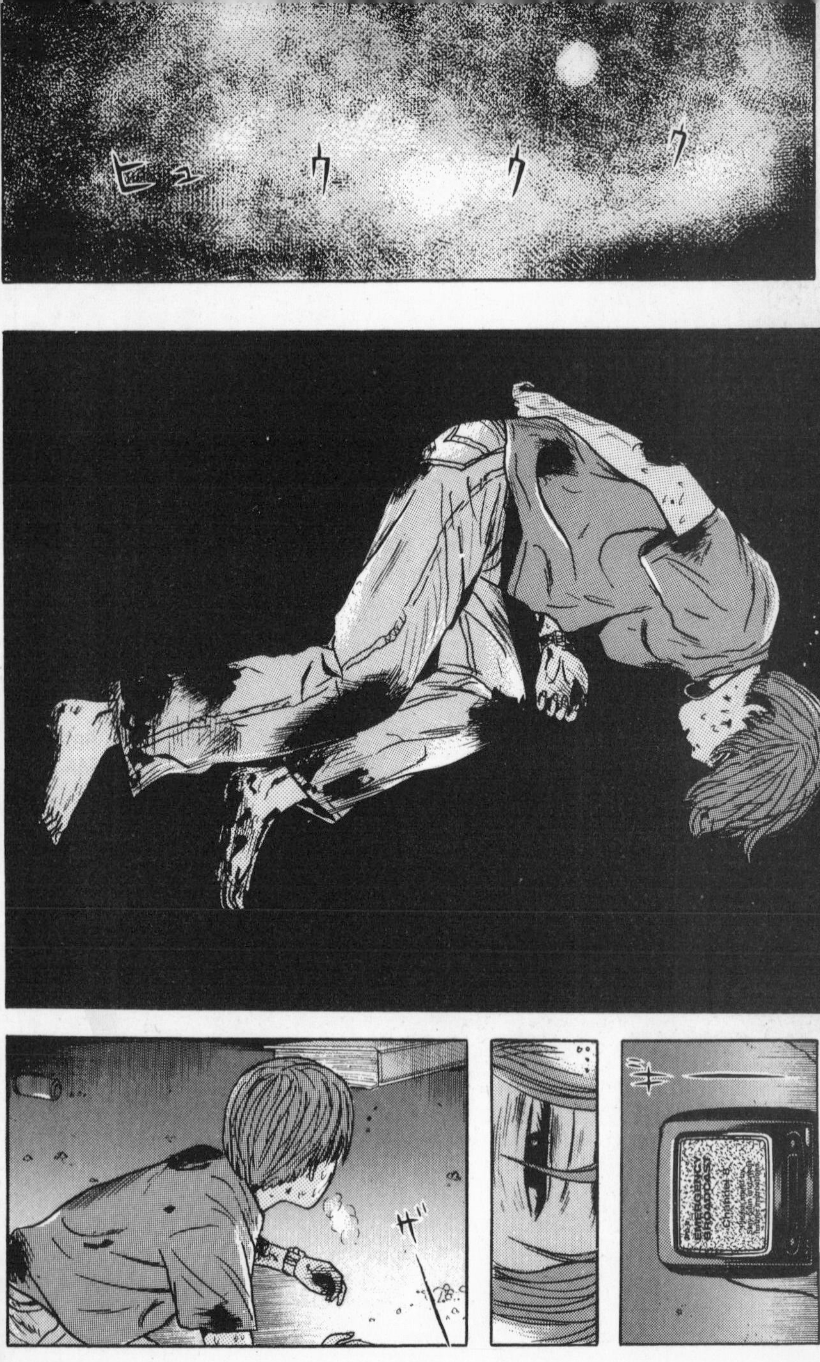
ヒュウウウ
キーン
EMERGENCY BROADCAST
Channel 8
ザ

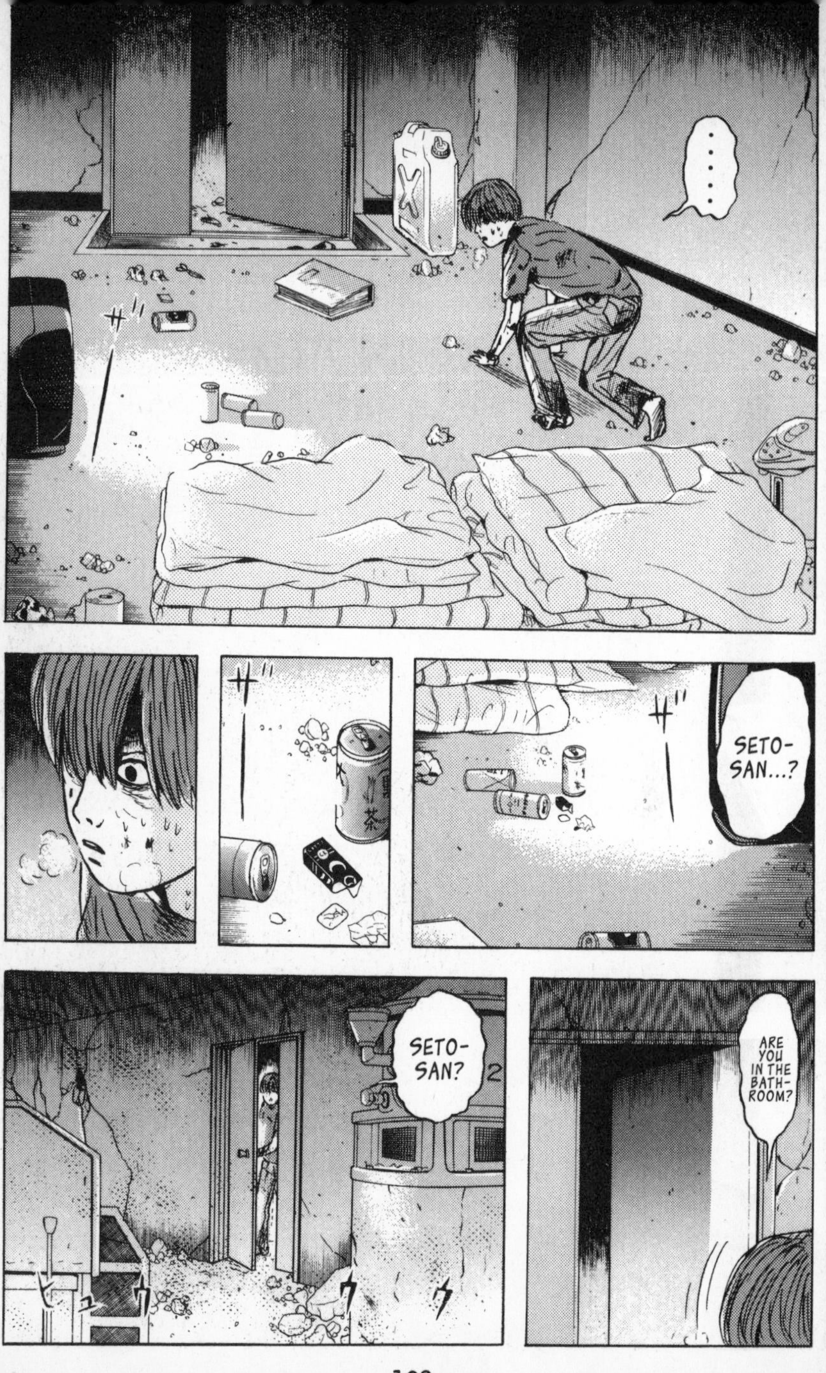
. . . . .
SETO-SAN...?
ARE YOU IN THE BATH-ROOM?
SETO-SAN?

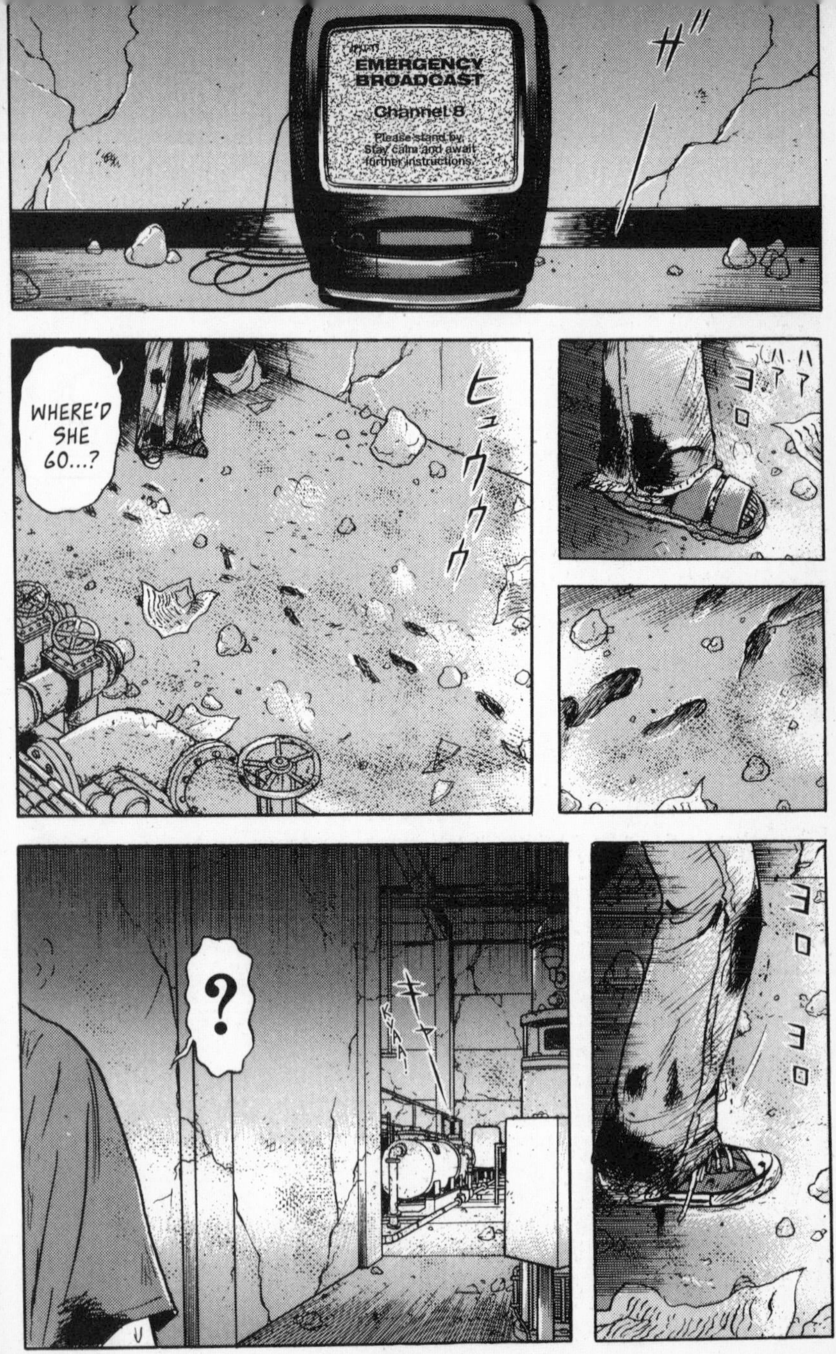
EMERGENCY BROADCAST
Channel 8
Please stand by. Stay calm and await further instructions.
ザ
ハアハア
ヨロ
ヒュウウウウ
WHERE'D SHE GO...?
ヨロヨロ
ヨロ
キャー
KYAA!
?

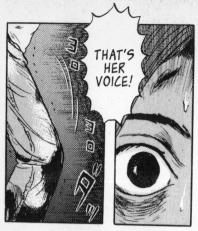

THAT'S HER VOICE!

SETO-SAN!

OH!

38^M

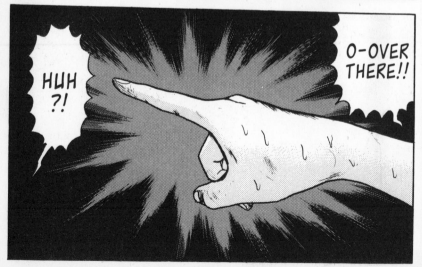

HUH?!

O-OVER THERE!!

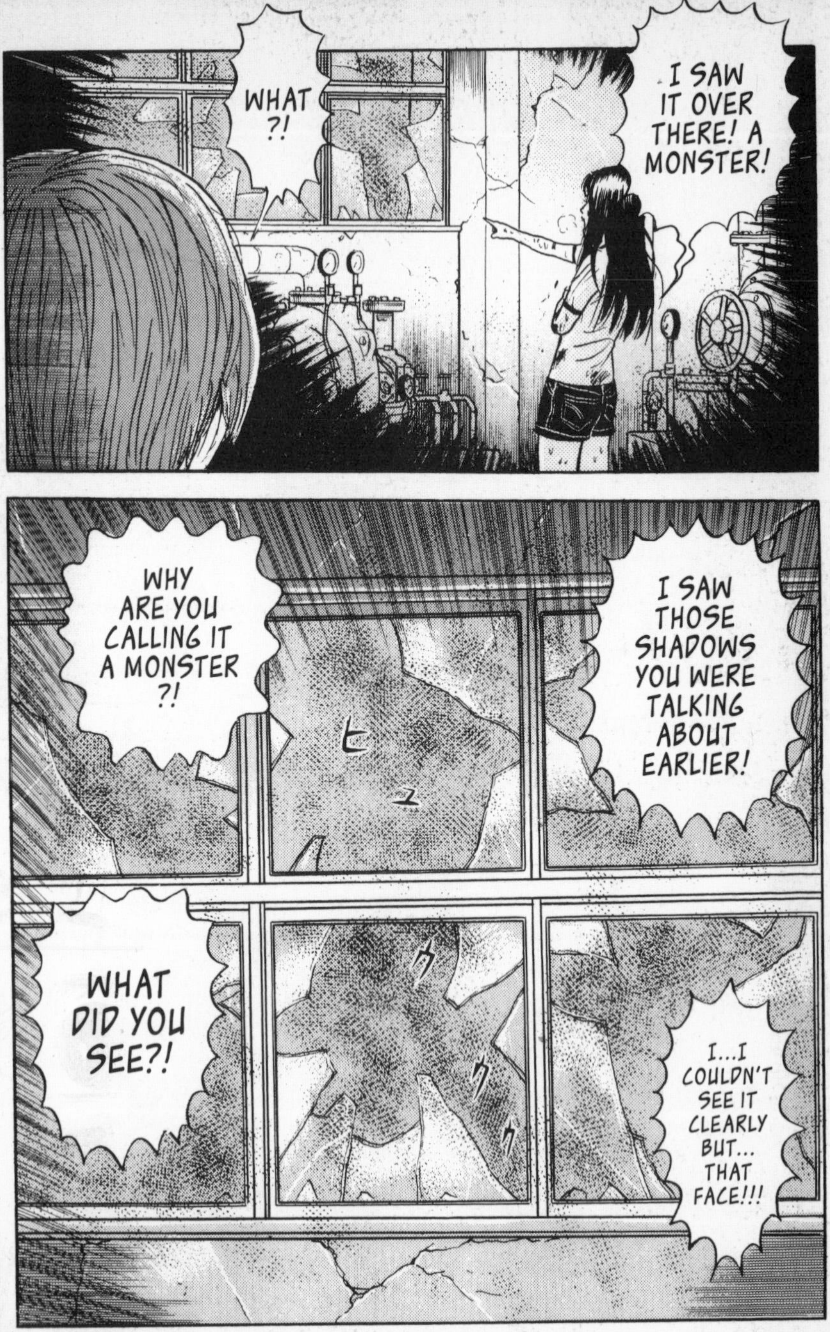
I SAW IT OVER THERE! A MONSTER!
WHAT?!
WHY ARE YOU CALLING IT A MONSTER?!
I SAW THOSE SHADOWS YOU WERE TALKING ABOUT EARLIER!
WHAT DID YOU SEE?!
I...I COULDN'T SEE IT CLEARLY BUT... THAT FACE!!!

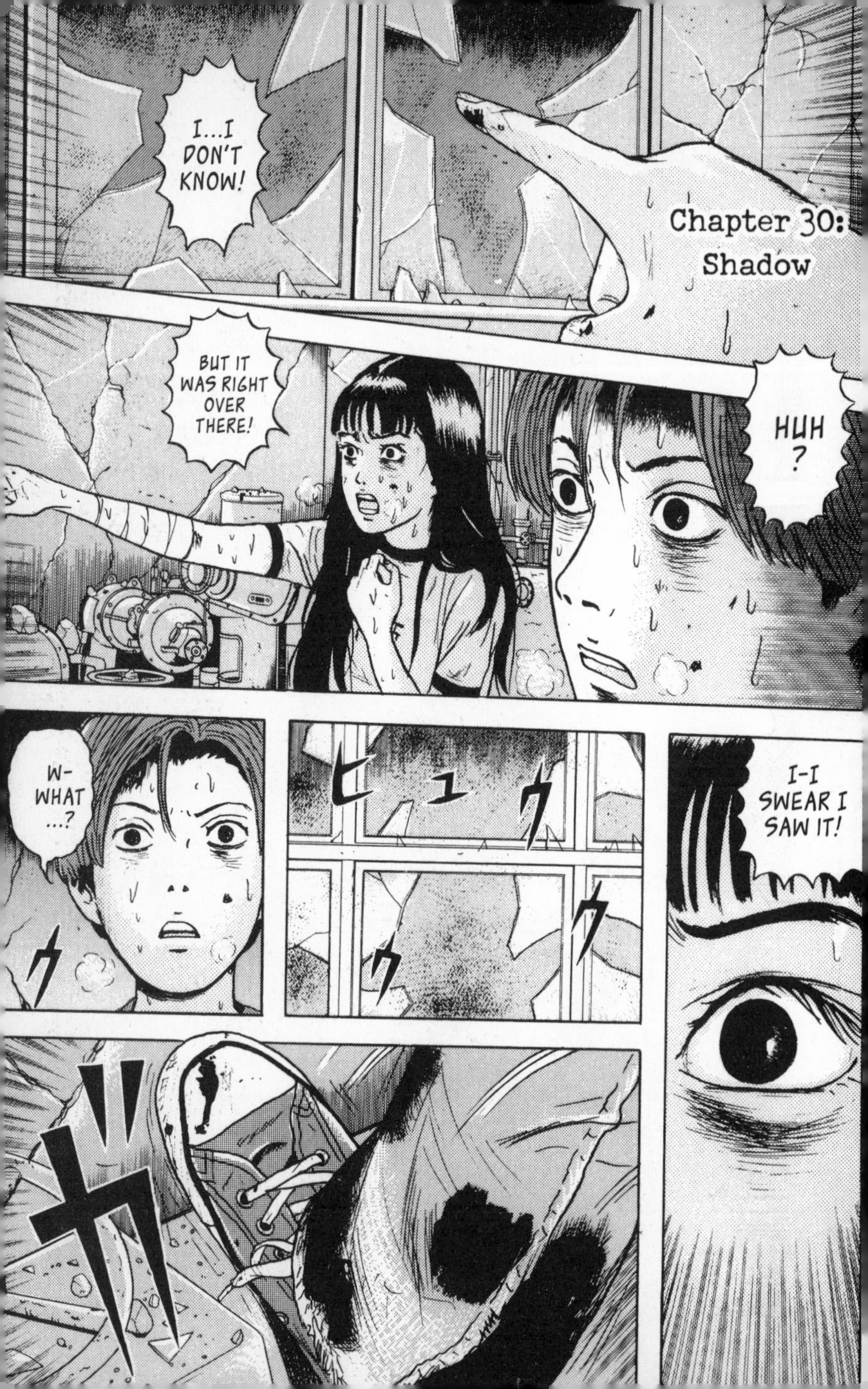
Chapter 30: Shadow
I...I DON'T KNOW!
HUH ?
BUT IT WAS RIGHT OVER THERE!
I-I SWEAR I SAW IT!
ヒュウ
ウ
ウ
W- WHAT ...?
ウ

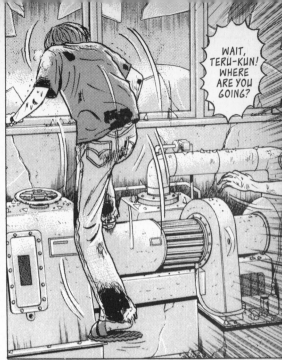

WAIT,
TERU-KUN!
WHERE
ARE YOU
GOING?

OH!!

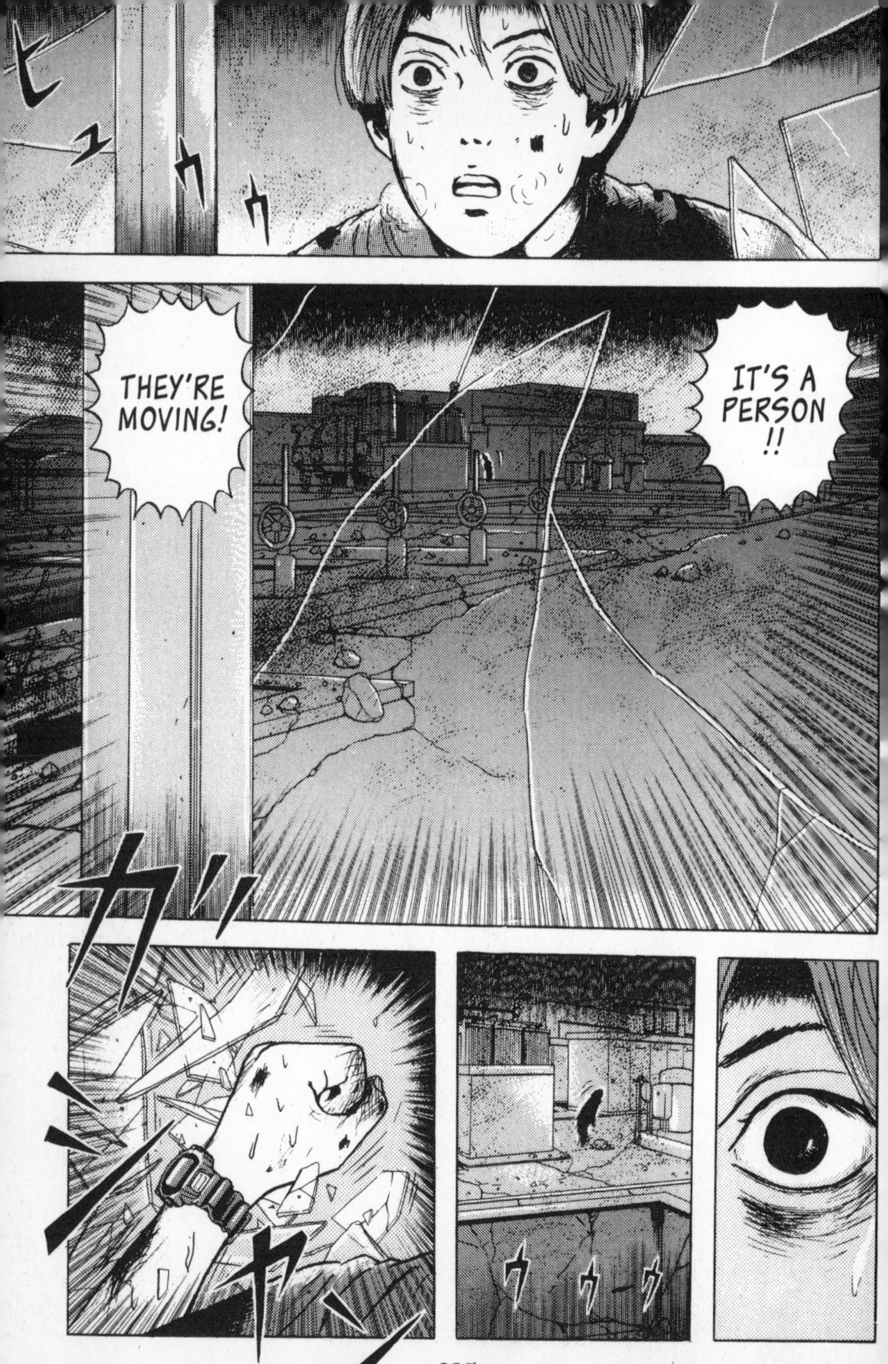
IT'S A PERSON !!
THEY'RE MOVING!

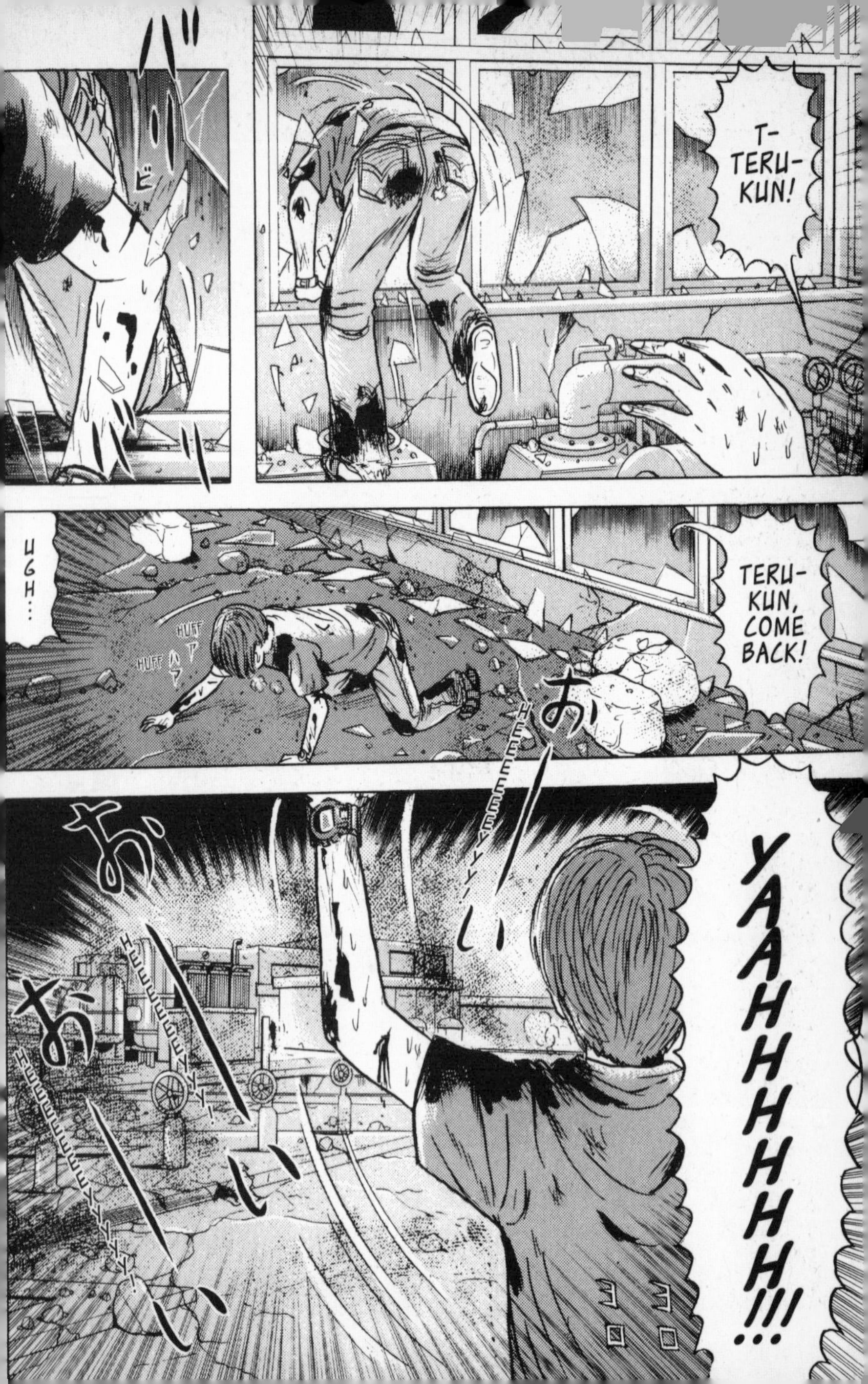

T-TERU-KUN!
バ
ビ
TERU-KUN, COME BACK!
UGH...
HUFF ハァ
HUFF ハァ
お
HEEEEEEEYYY!
い
YAAHHHHHHH!!!
お
HEEEEEEEYYY!
い
お
HEEEEEEEYYYYYY!
い

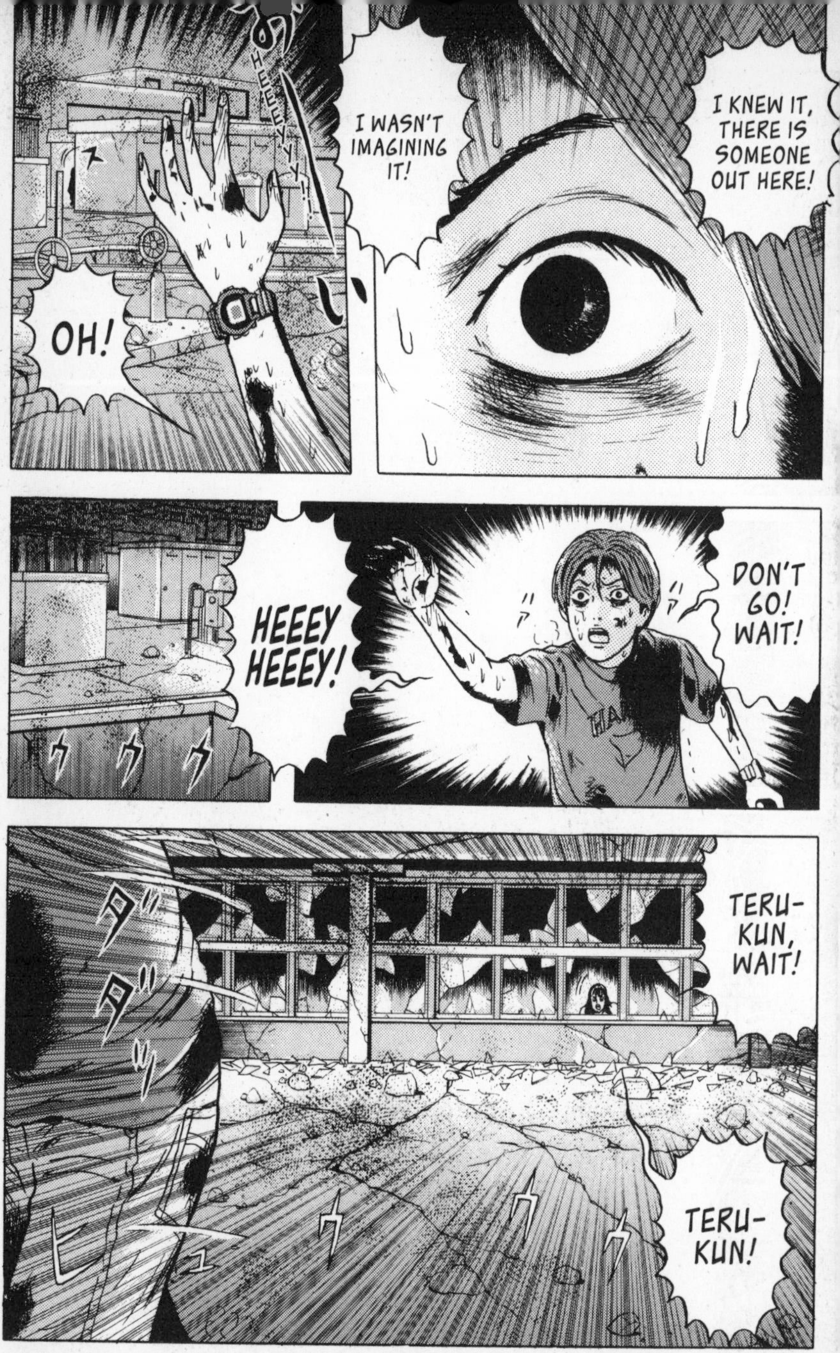
I KNEW IT, THERE IS SOMEONE OUT HERE!
I WASN'T IMAGINING IT!
HEEEYYY!!!
OH!
DON'T GO! WAIT!
HEEEY HEEEY!
TERU-KUN, WAIT!
TERU-KUN!

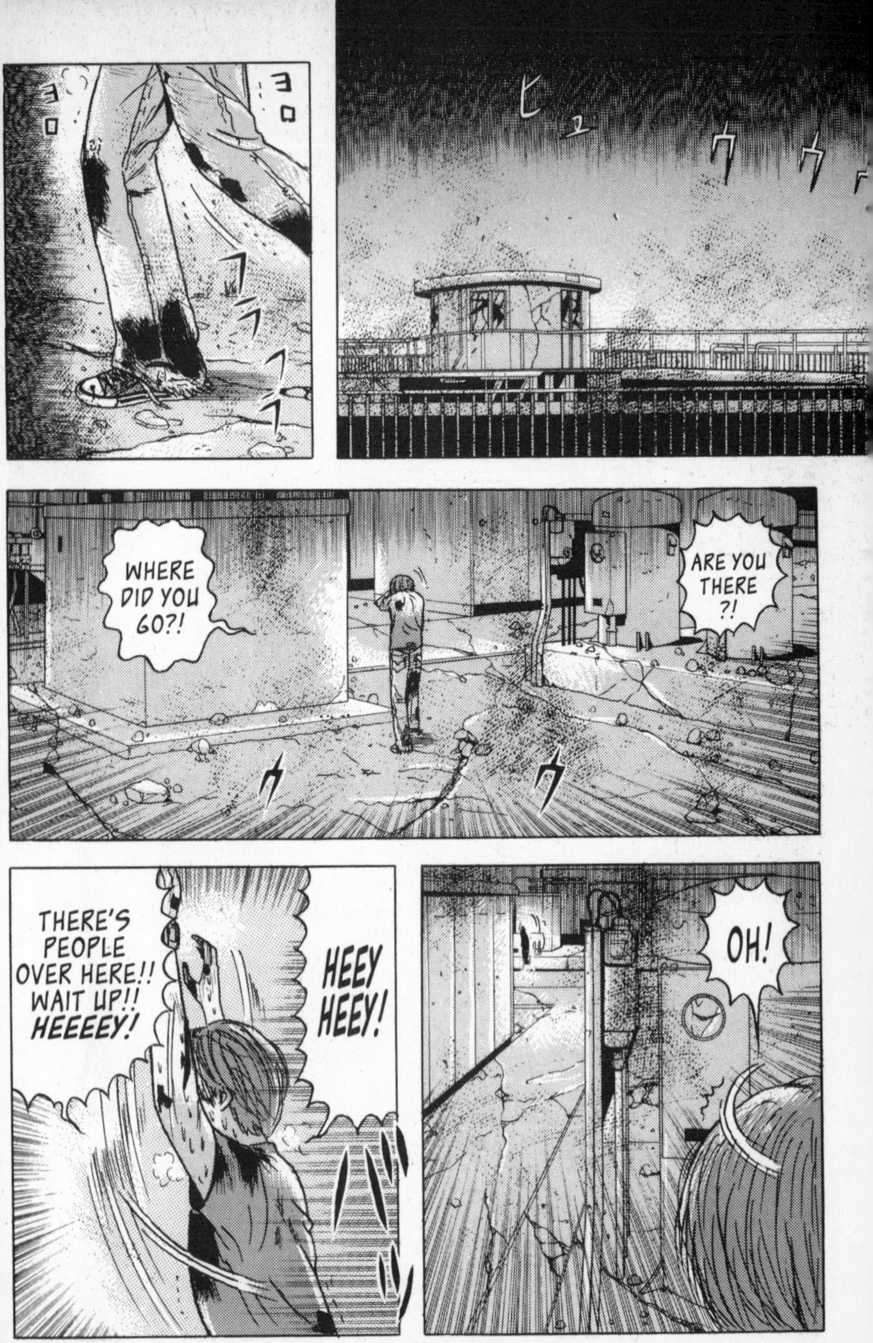
ARE YOU THERE ?!
WHERE DID YOU GO?!
OH!
HEEY HEEY!
THERE'S PEOPLE OVER HERE!! WAIT UP!! HEEEEY!

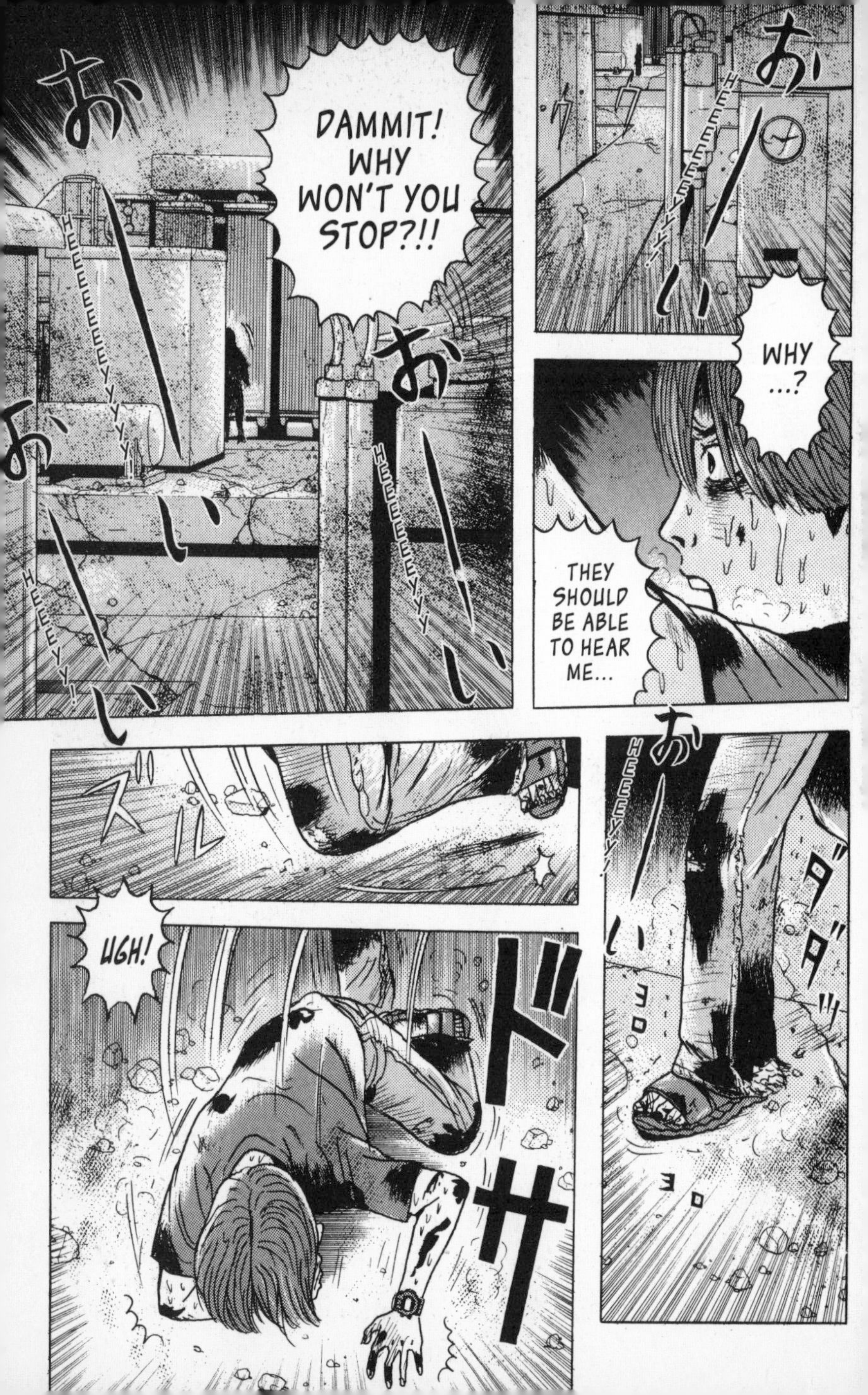
HEEEEEEEYYY!
WHY ...?
THEY SHOULD BE ABLE TO HEAR ME...
DAMMIT! WHY WON'T YOU STOP?!!
HEEEEEEEEYYYYY!!
HEEEEEEEYYY
HEEEYY!
HEEEEYY!
UGH!

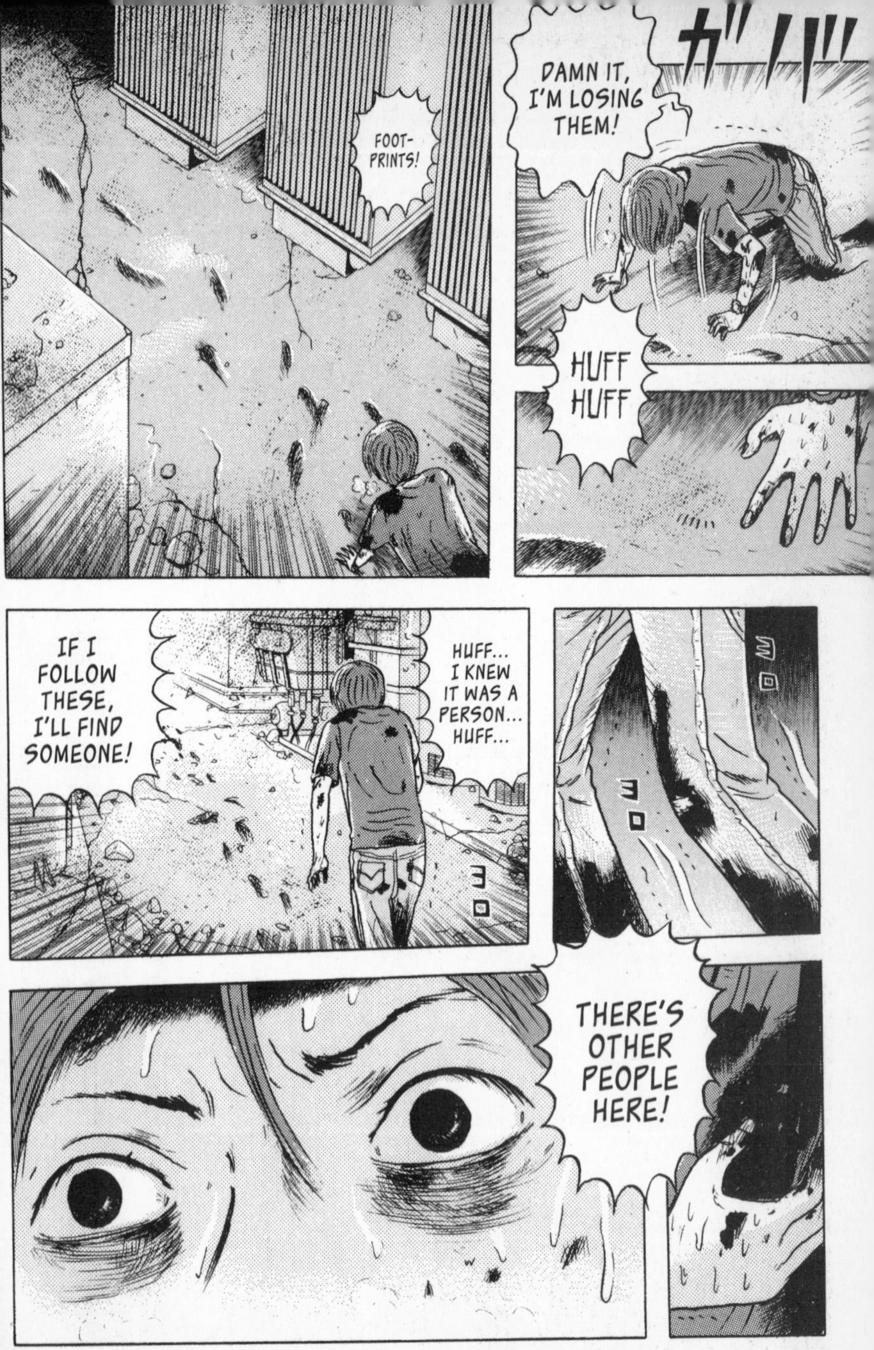
DAMN IT, I'M LOSING THEM!
HUFF HUFF
FOOT-PRINTS!
HUFF... I KNEW IT WAS A PERSON... HUFF...
IF I FOLLOW THESE, I'LL FIND SOMEONE!
THERE'S OTHER PEOPLE HERE!

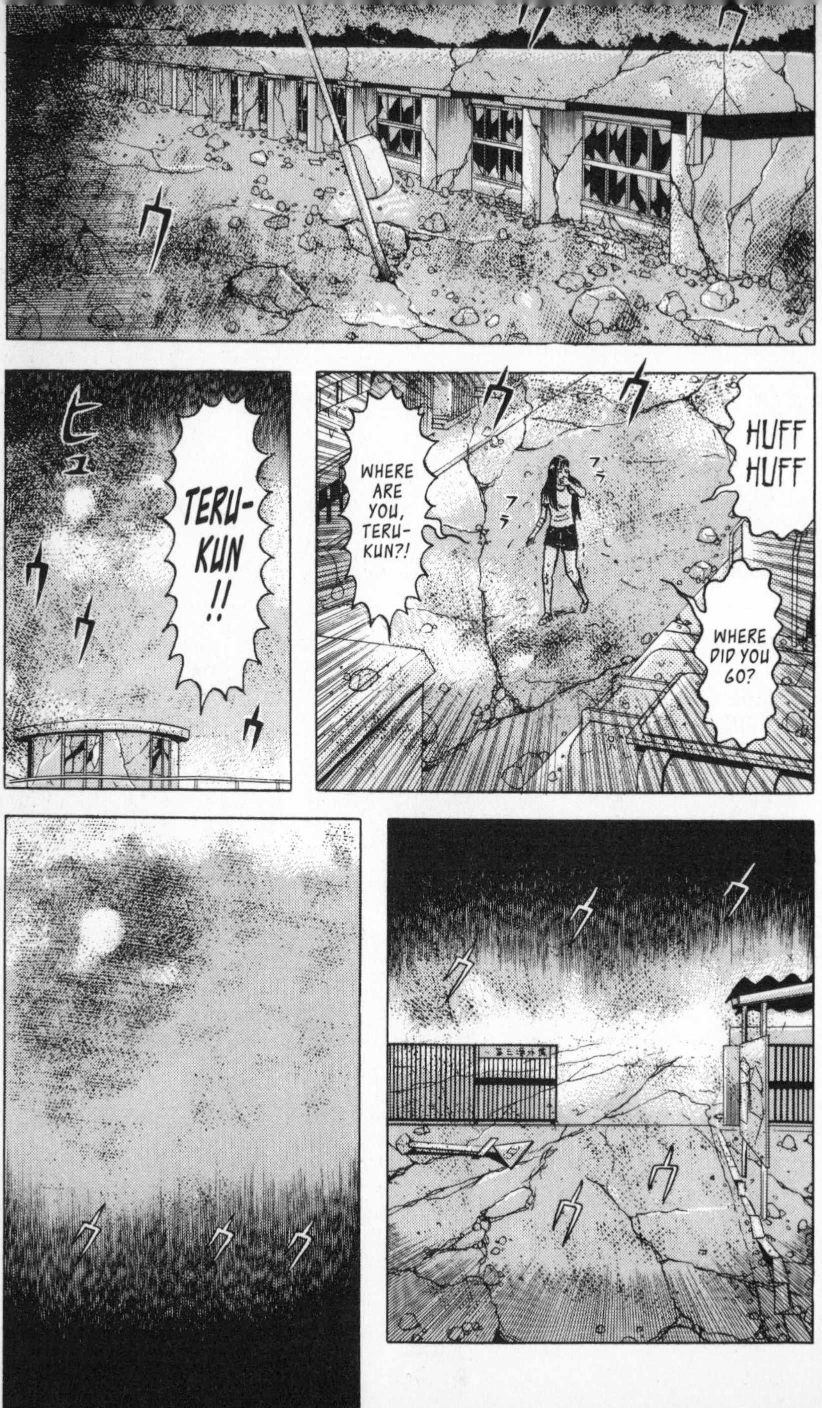
HUFF HUFF
WHERE ARE YOU, TERU-KUN?!
WHERE DID YOU GO?
TERU-KUN!!

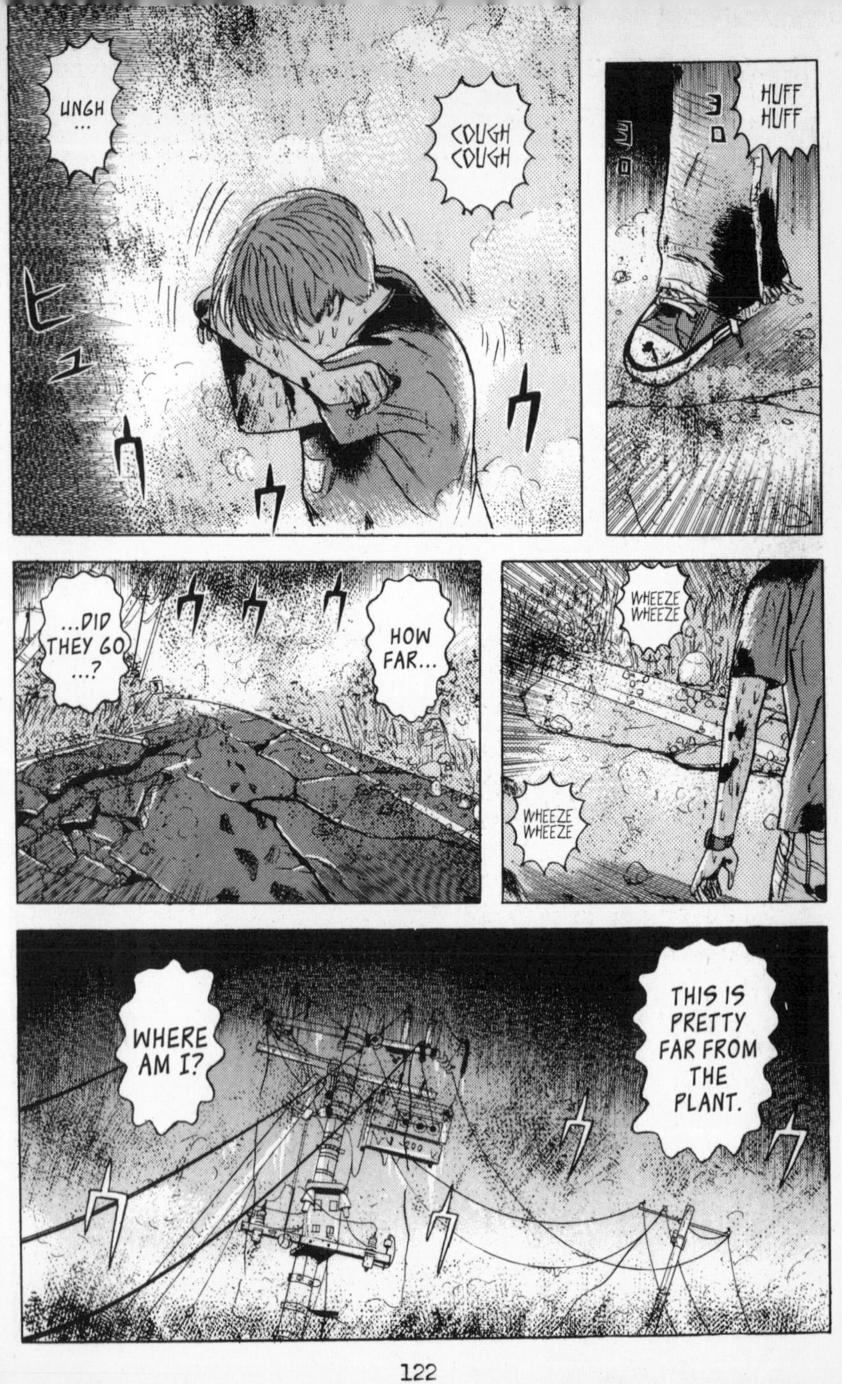
HUFF HUFF
COUGH COUGH
UNGH ...
WHEEZE WHEEZE
WHEEZE WHEEZE
HOW FAR...
...DID THEY GO ...?
THIS IS PRETTY FAR FROM THE PLANT.
WHERE AM I?

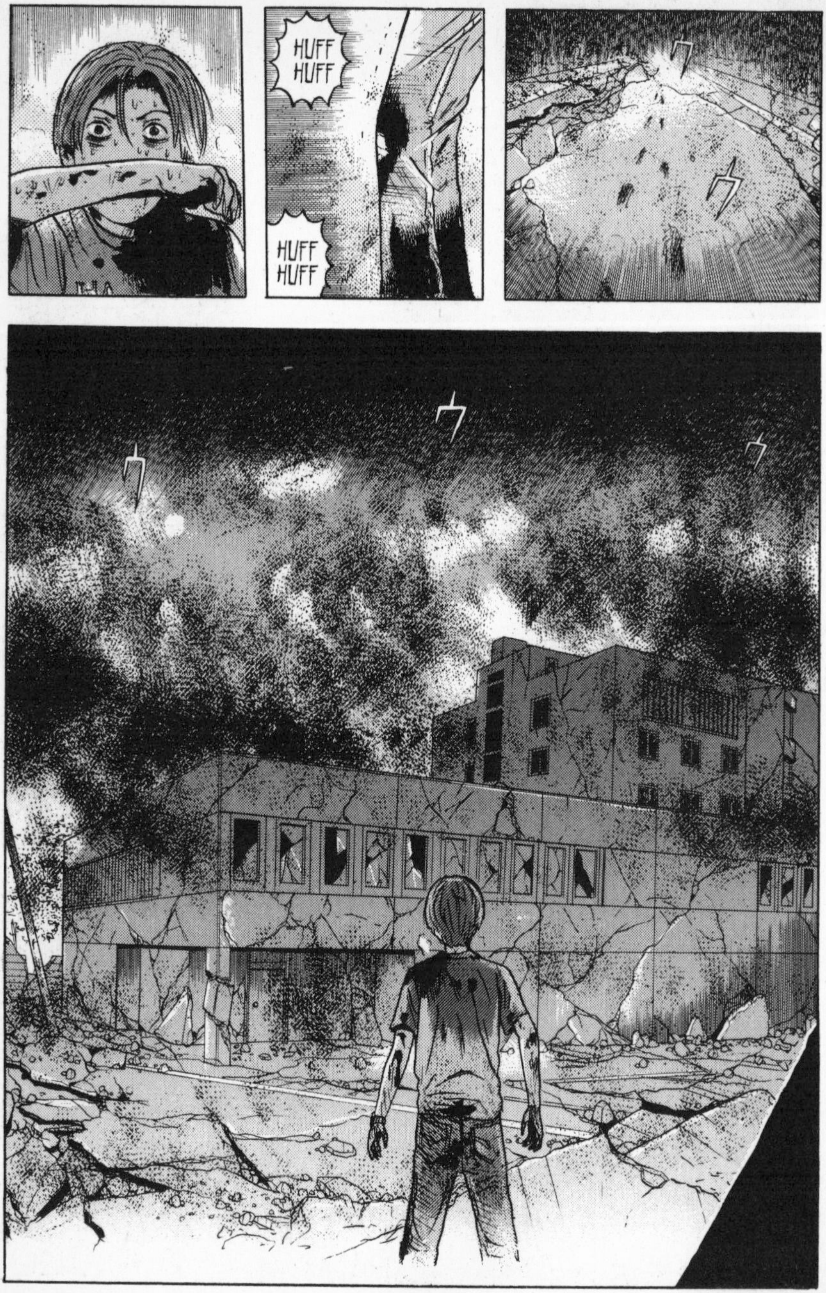
HUFF HUFF
HUFF HUFF

OH!

HEEEY! HEEEY!!

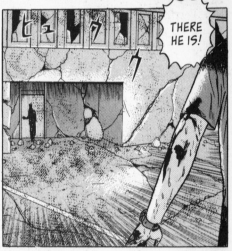

THERE HE IS!

WAIT!

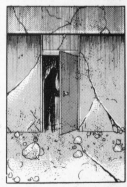

124

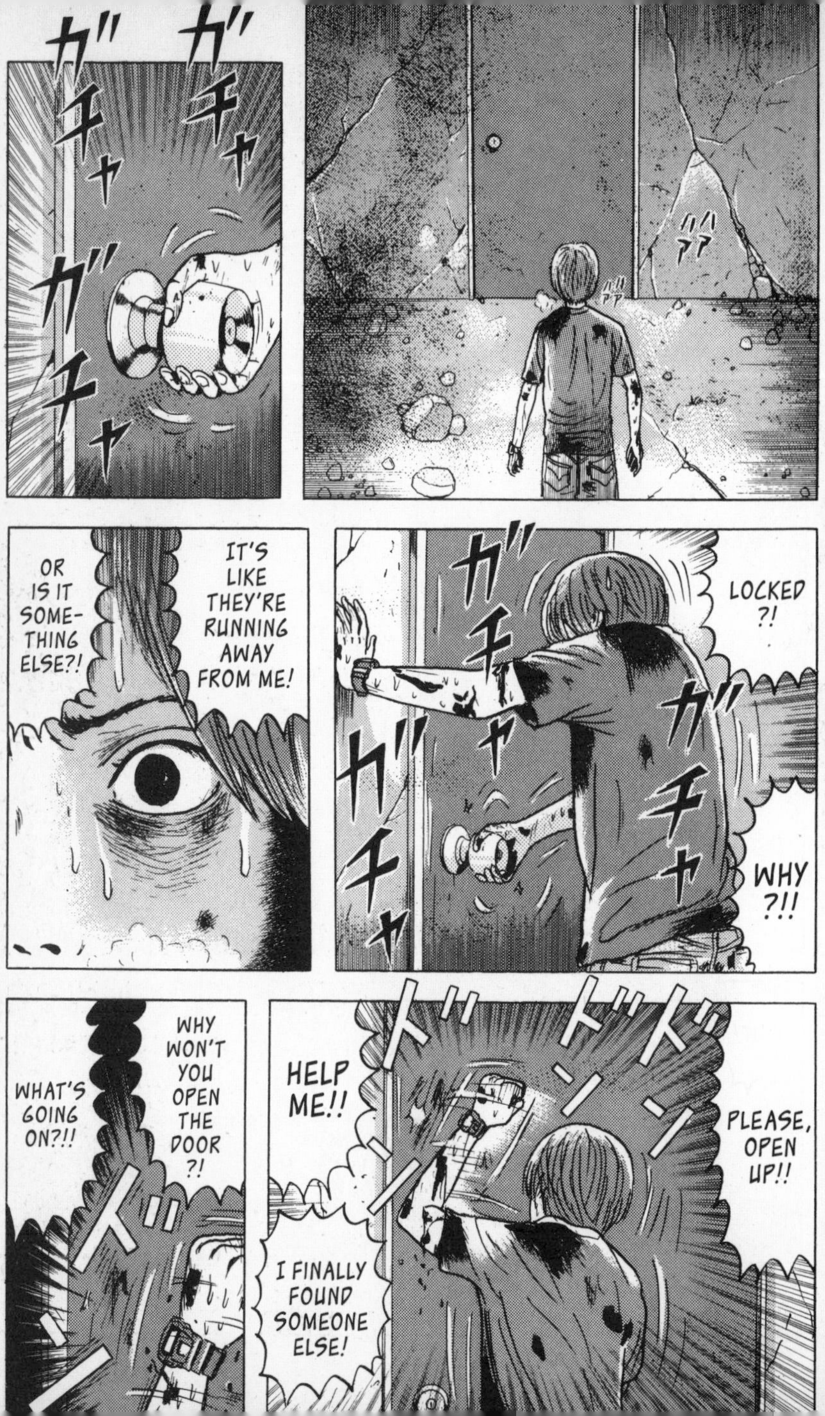
ハァ ハァ
ガチャガチャ ガチャガチャ
LOCKED?!
ガチャガチャ ガチャガチャ
WHY?!!
IT'S LIKE THEY'RE RUNNING AWAY FROM ME!
OR IS IT SOMETHING ELSE?!
PLEASE, OPEN UP!!
HELP ME!!
I FINALLY FOUND SOMEONE ELSE!
WHY WON'T YOU OPEN THE DOOR?!
WHAT'S GOING ON?!!

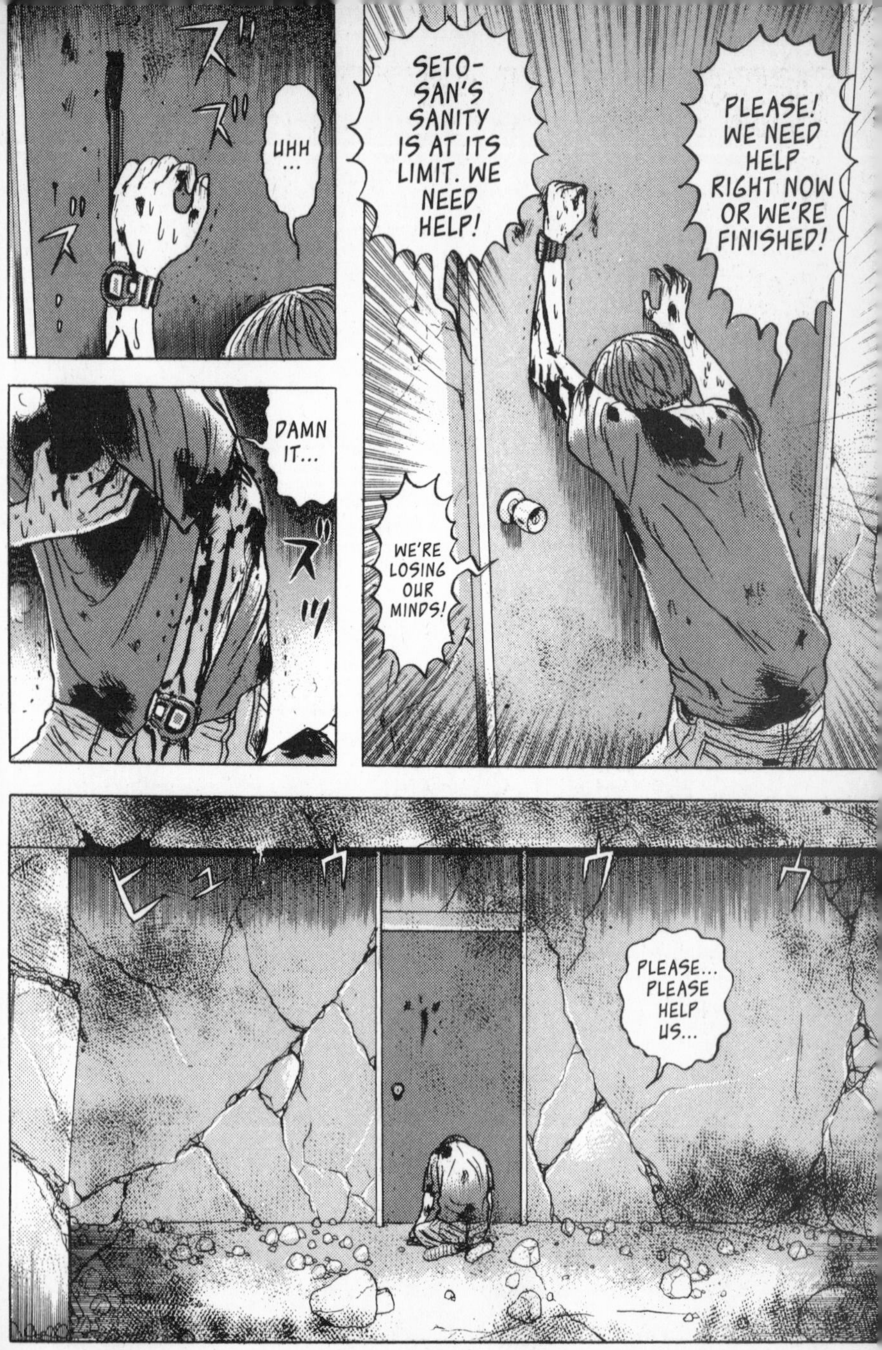
PLEASE! WE NEED HELP RIGHT NOW OR WE'RE FINISHED!
SETO-SAN'S SANITY IS AT ITS LIMIT. WE NEED HELP!
WE'RE LOSING OUR MINDS!
UHH...
DAMN IT...
PLEASE... PLEASE HELP US...

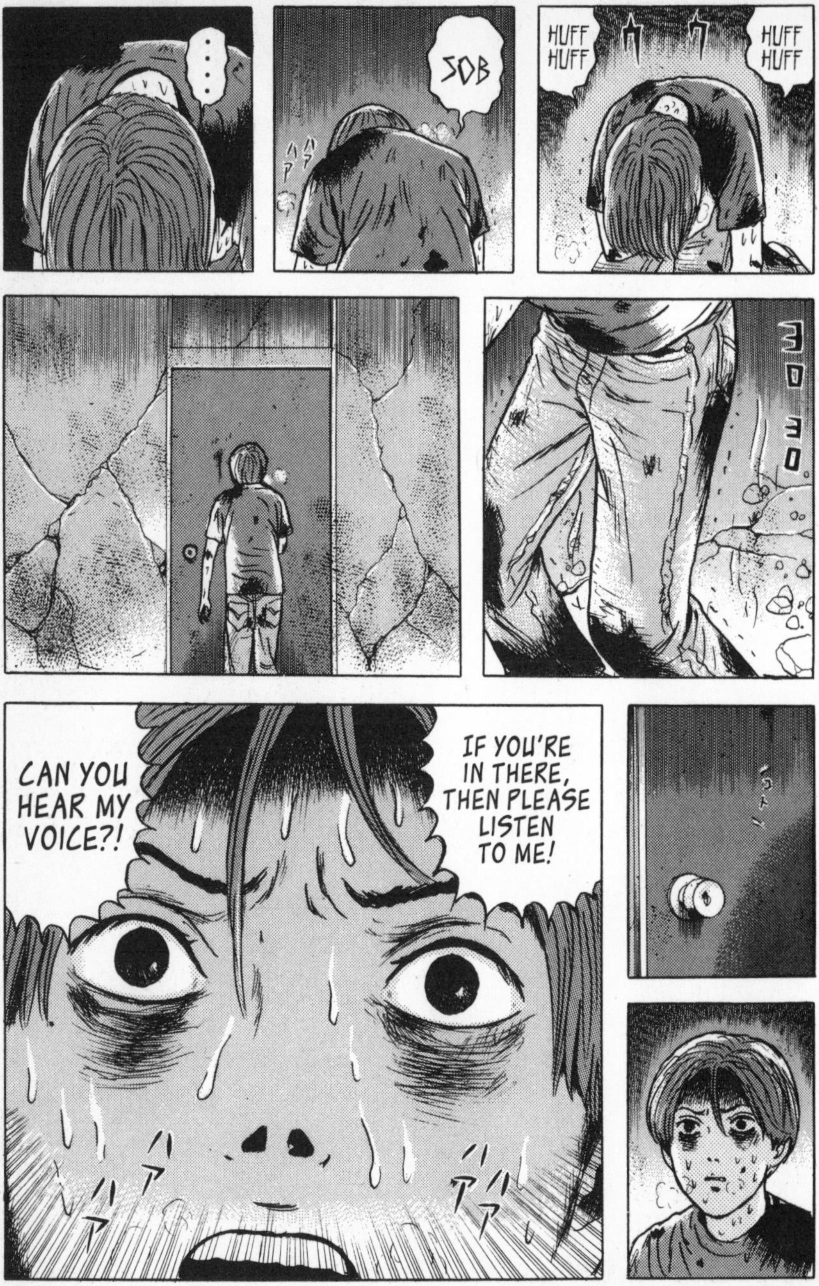
HUFF HUFF
HUFF HUFF
SOB
....
IF YOU'RE IN THERE, THEN PLEASE LISTEN TO ME!
CAN YOU HEAR MY VOICE?!

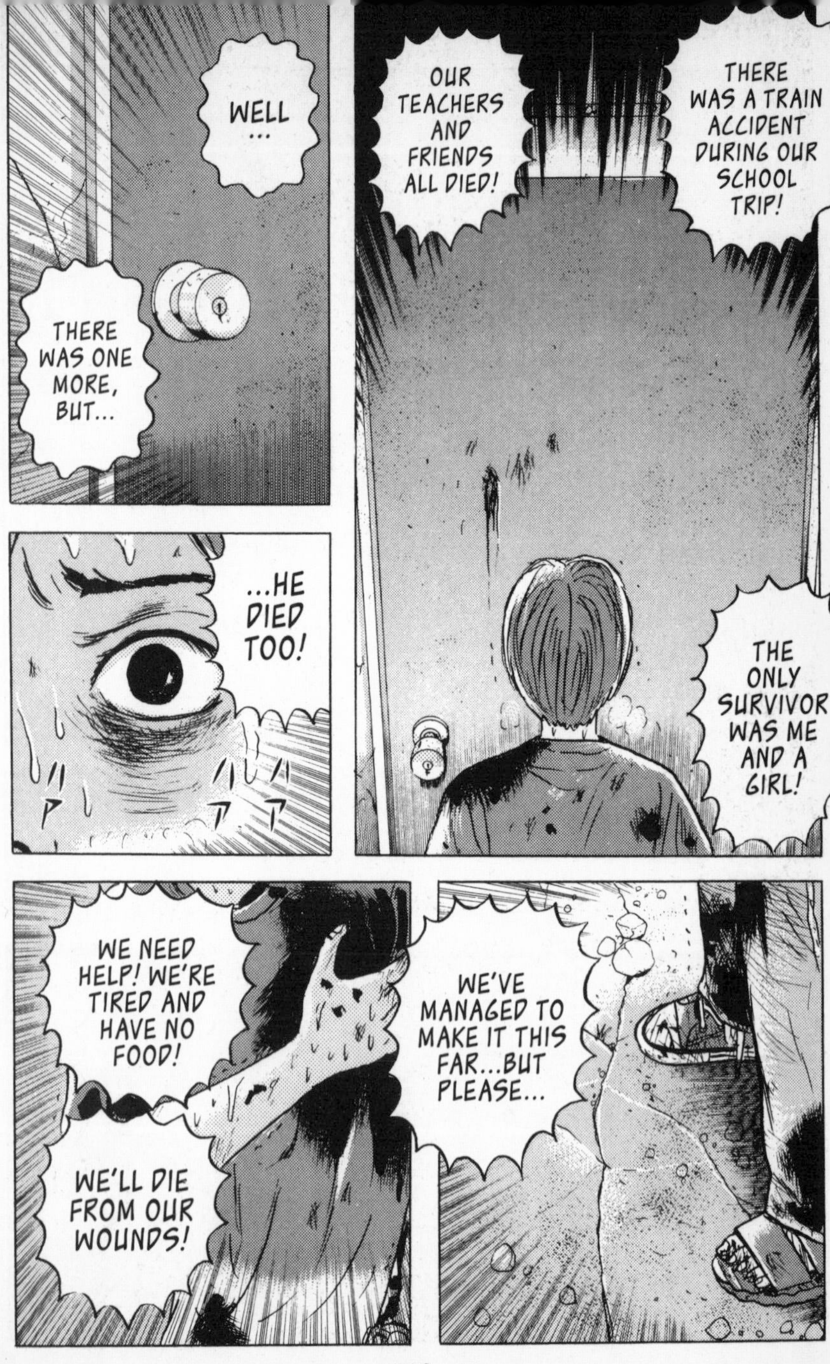
THERE WAS A TRAIN ACCIDENT DURING OUR SCHOOL TRIP!
OUR TEACHERS AND FRIENDS ALL DIED!
THE ONLY SURVIVOR WAS ME AND A GIRL!
WELL...
THERE WAS ONE MORE, BUT...
...HE DIED TOO!
WE'VE MANAGED TO MAKE IT THIS FAR...BUT PLEASE...
WE NEED HELP! WE'RE TIRED AND HAVE NO FOOD!
WE'LL DIE FROM OUR WOUNDS!

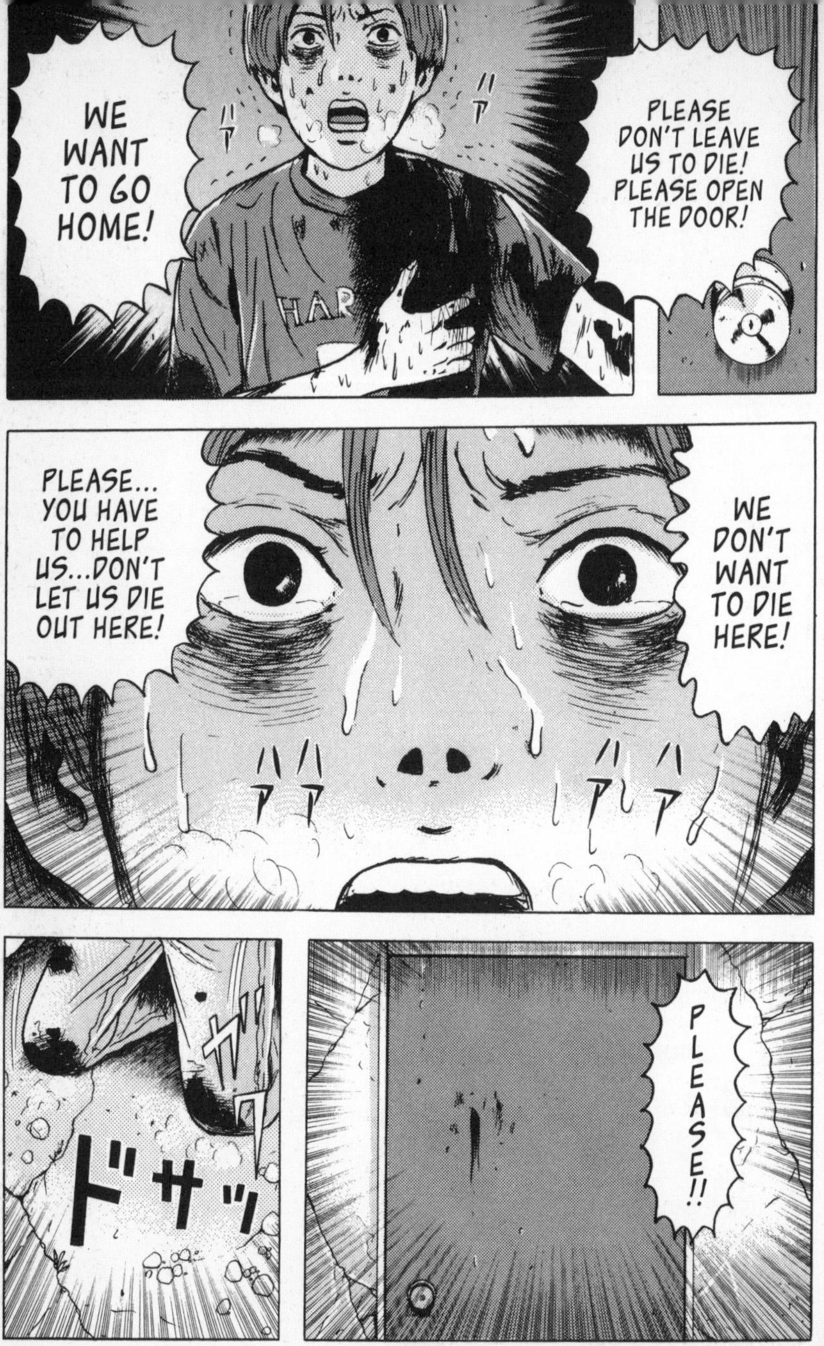
PLEASE DON'T LEAVE US TO DIE! PLEASE OPEN THE DOOR!
WE WANT TO GO HOME!
WE DON'T WANT TO DIE HERE!
PLEASE... YOU HAVE TO HELP US...DON'T LET US DIE OUT HERE!
PLEASE!!
ドサッ

UHH...

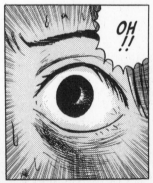

OH!!

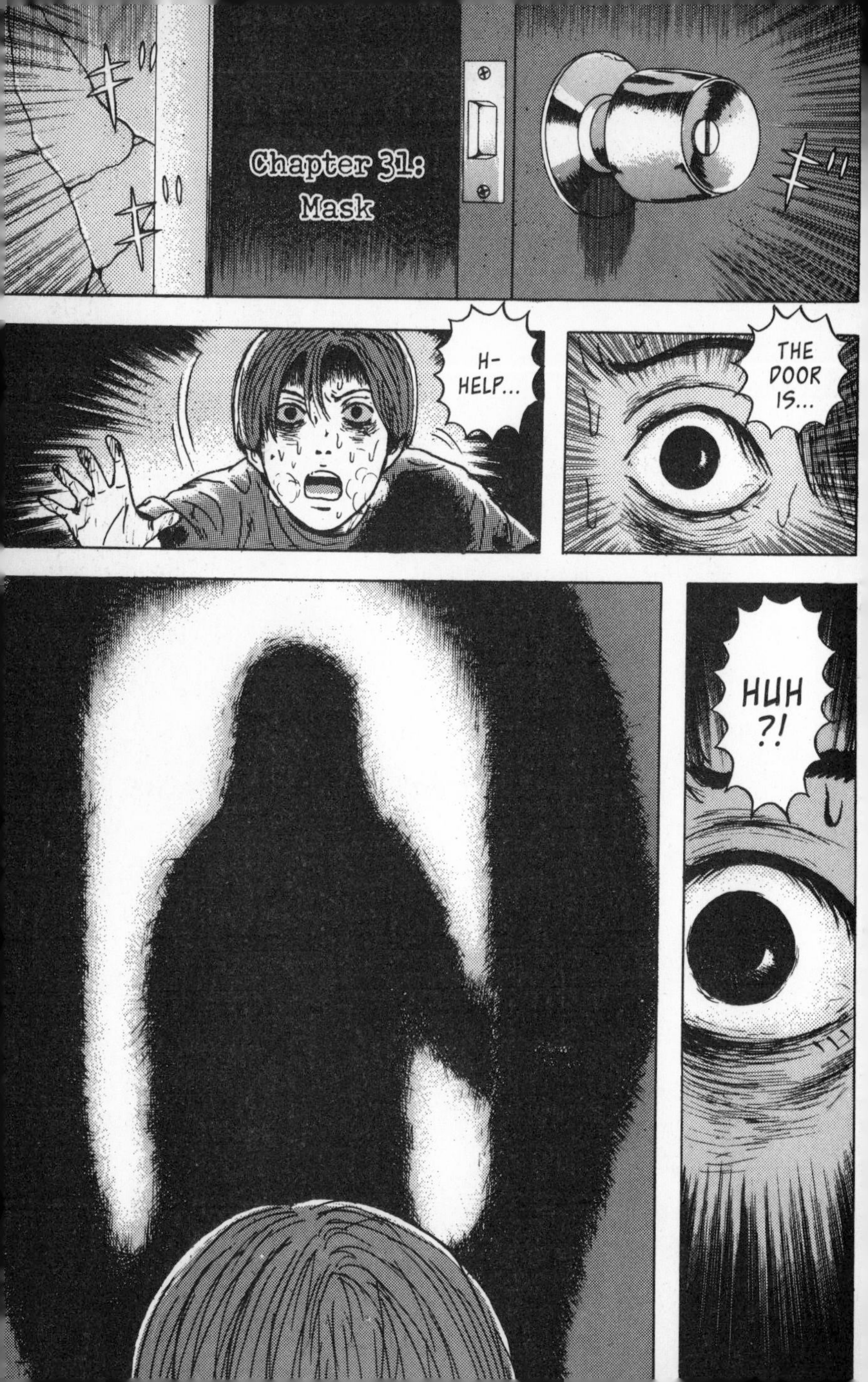
Chapter 31: Mask
THE DOOR IS...
H- HELP...
HUH ?!

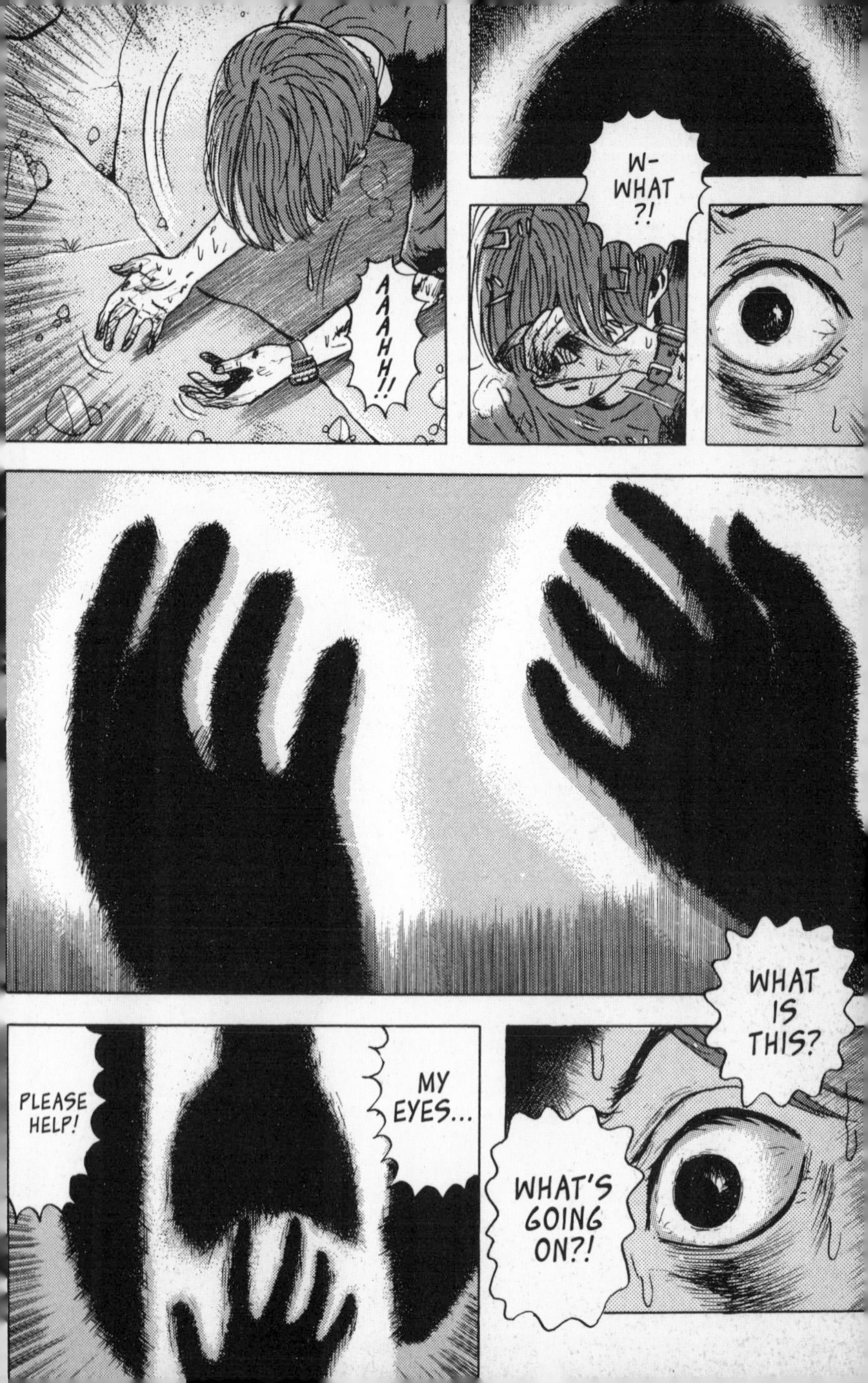

W-WHAT?!
AAAAHH!!
WHAT IS THIS?
WHAT'S GOING ON?!
MY EYES...
PLEASE HELP!

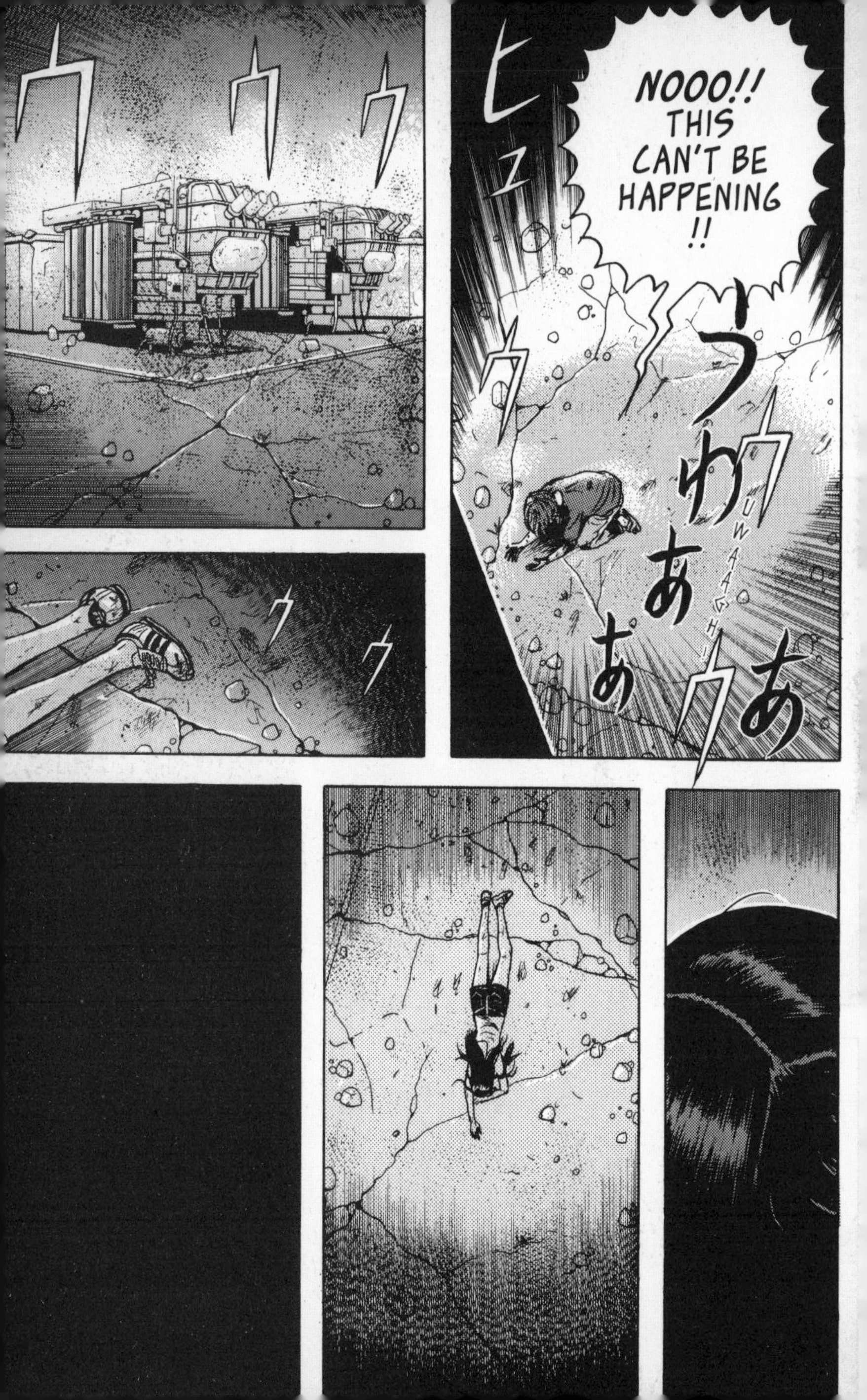
NOOO!! THIS CAN'T BE HAPPENING !!
UWAAGH!!

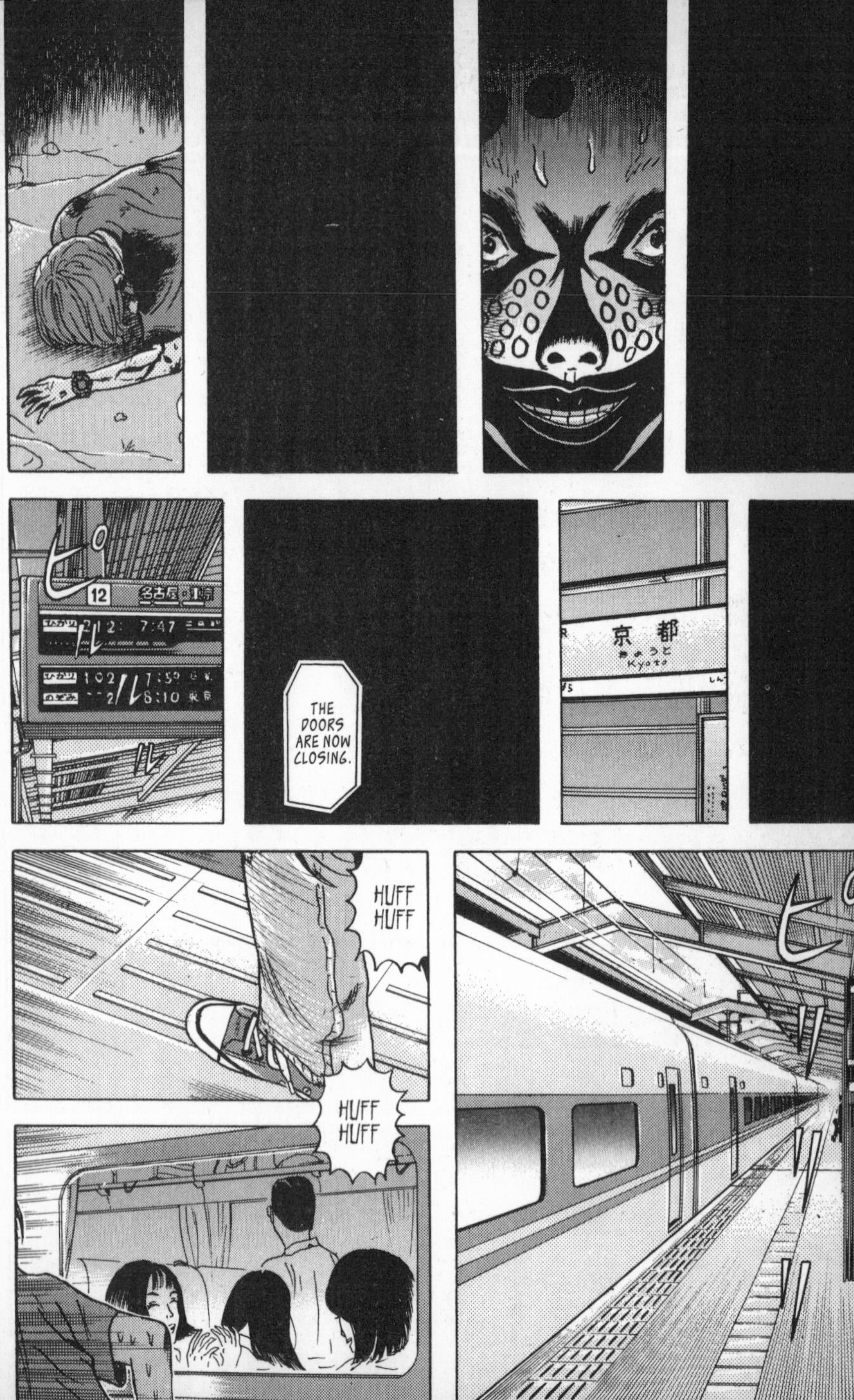
京都
きょうと
Kyoto
THE DOORS ARE NOW CLOSING.
HUFF HUFF
HUFF HUFF

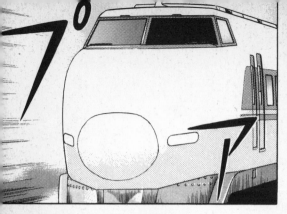

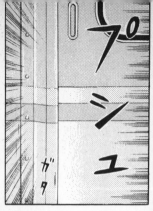

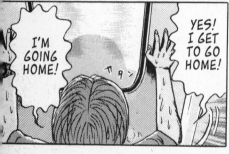

プシュ
ガタ
プア
JUST MADE IT!
PANT PANT
カタン
カタン
YES! I GET TO GO HOME!
カタン
I'M GOING HOME!
HUFF HUFF
GASP!
HUFF HUFF
カタン
カタン
カタン
カタン
JR
UGH...
カタン
OH!!
カタン

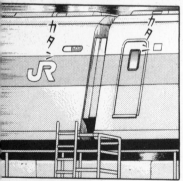

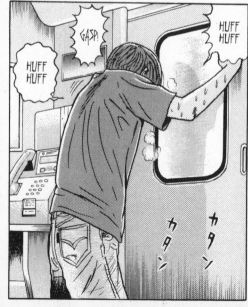

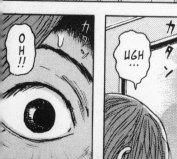

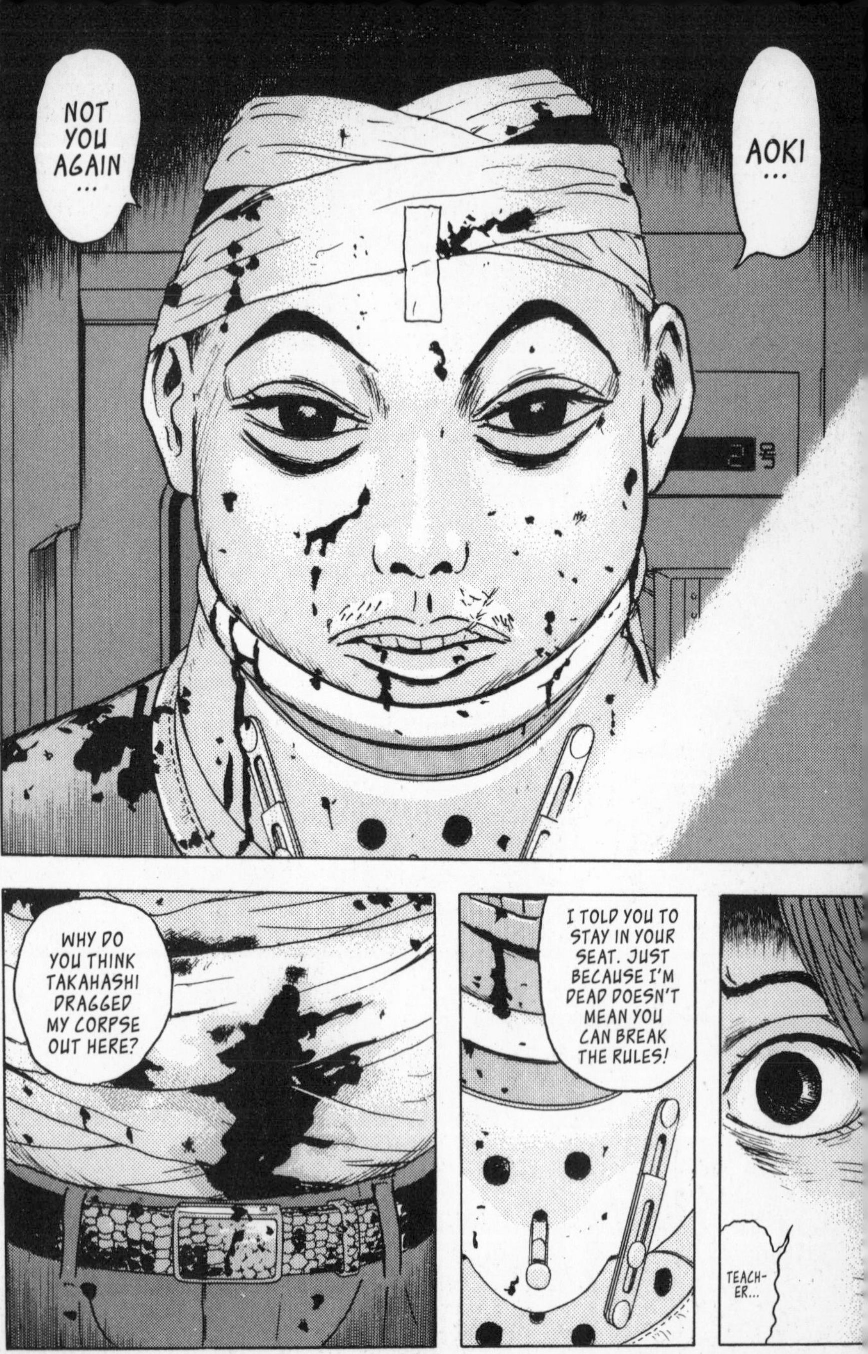
AOKI ...
NOT YOU AGAIN ...
TEACH-ER...
I TOLD YOU TO STAY IN YOUR SEAT. JUST BECAUSE I'M DEAD DOESN'T MEAN YOU CAN BREAK THE RULES!
WHY DO YOU THINK TAKAHASHI DRAGGED MY CORPSE OUT HERE?

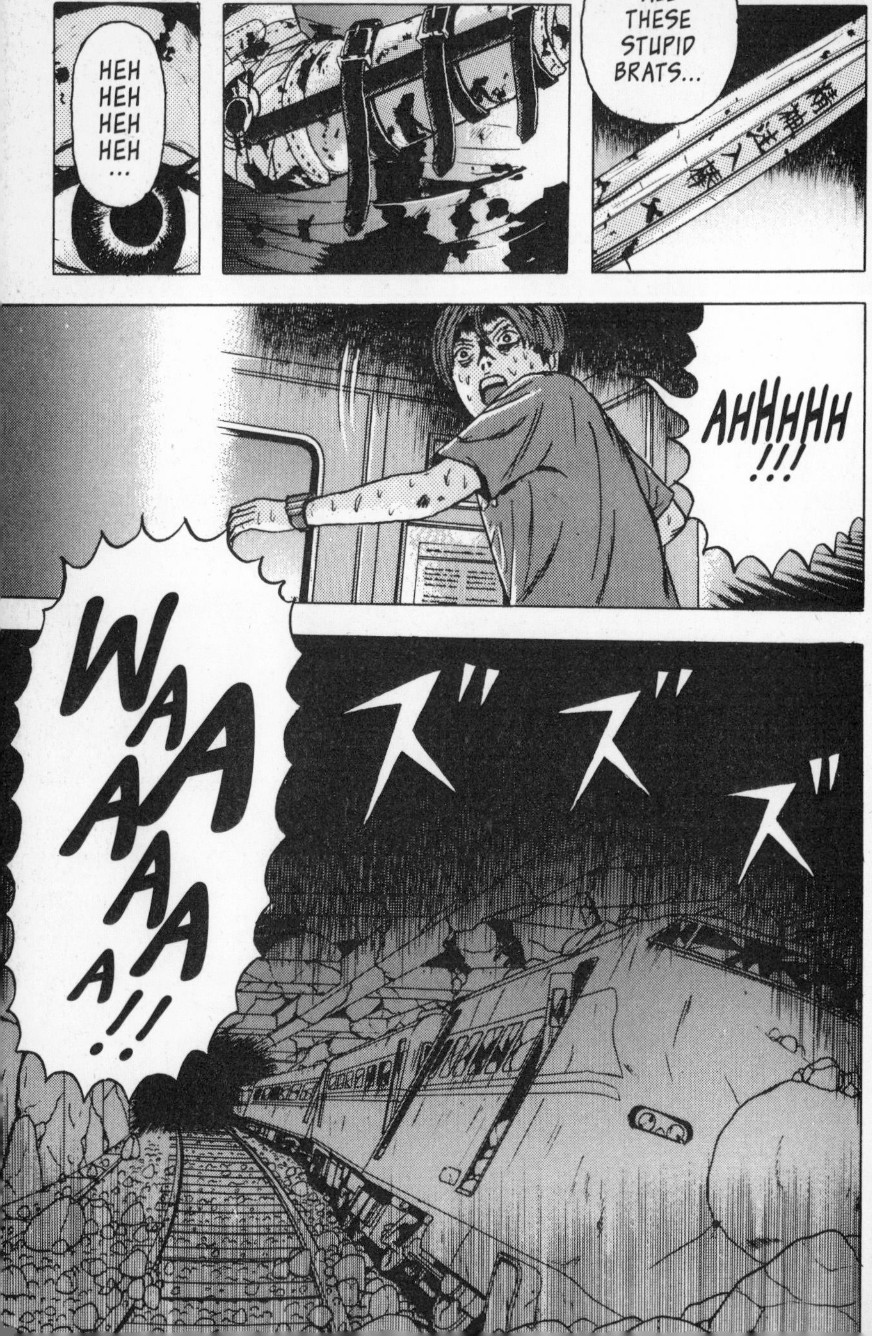
ALL THESE STUPID BRATS...
HEH HEH HEH HEH...
AHHHHHH!!!
WAAAAAAA!!
ズズズ

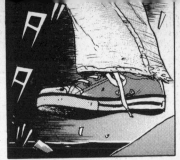

UGH!

UNGH
...

HOW DID
I GET...
BACK
HERE...

DAMN
IT!

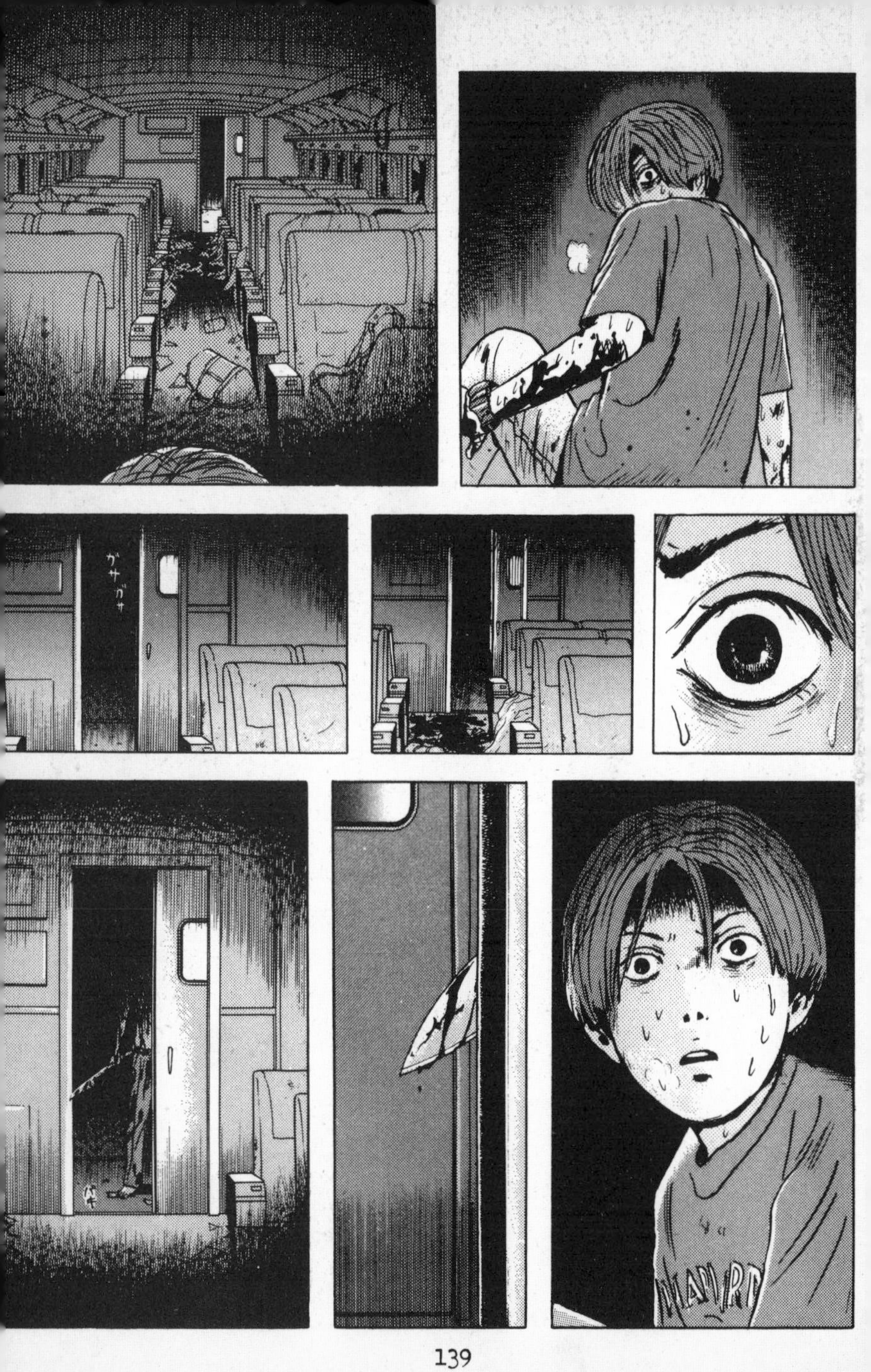
ガサガサ
パキ

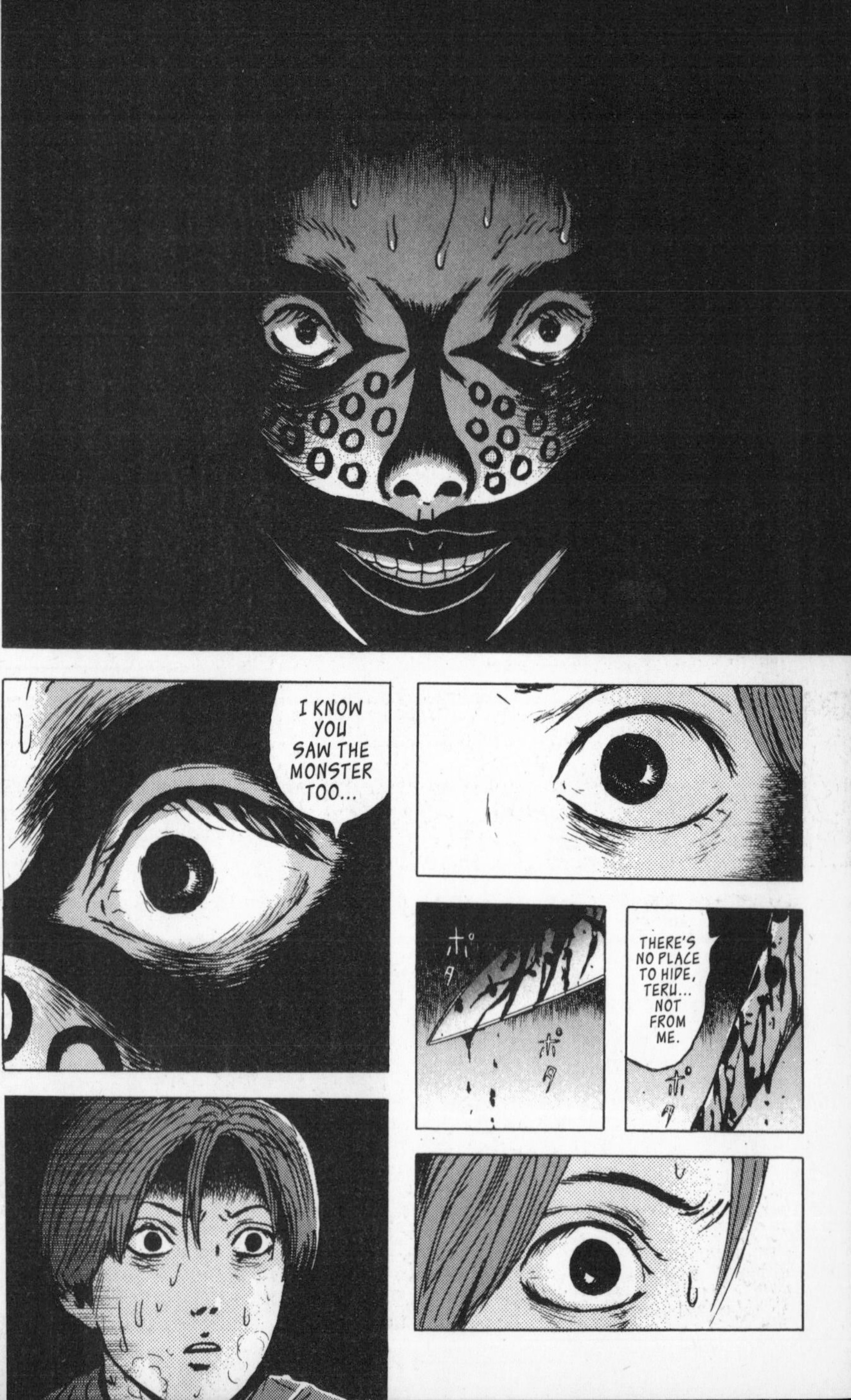
I KNOW YOU SAW THE MONSTER TOO...
THERE'S NO PLACE TO HIDE, TERU... NOT FROM ME.
ポタ
ポタ
ポタ

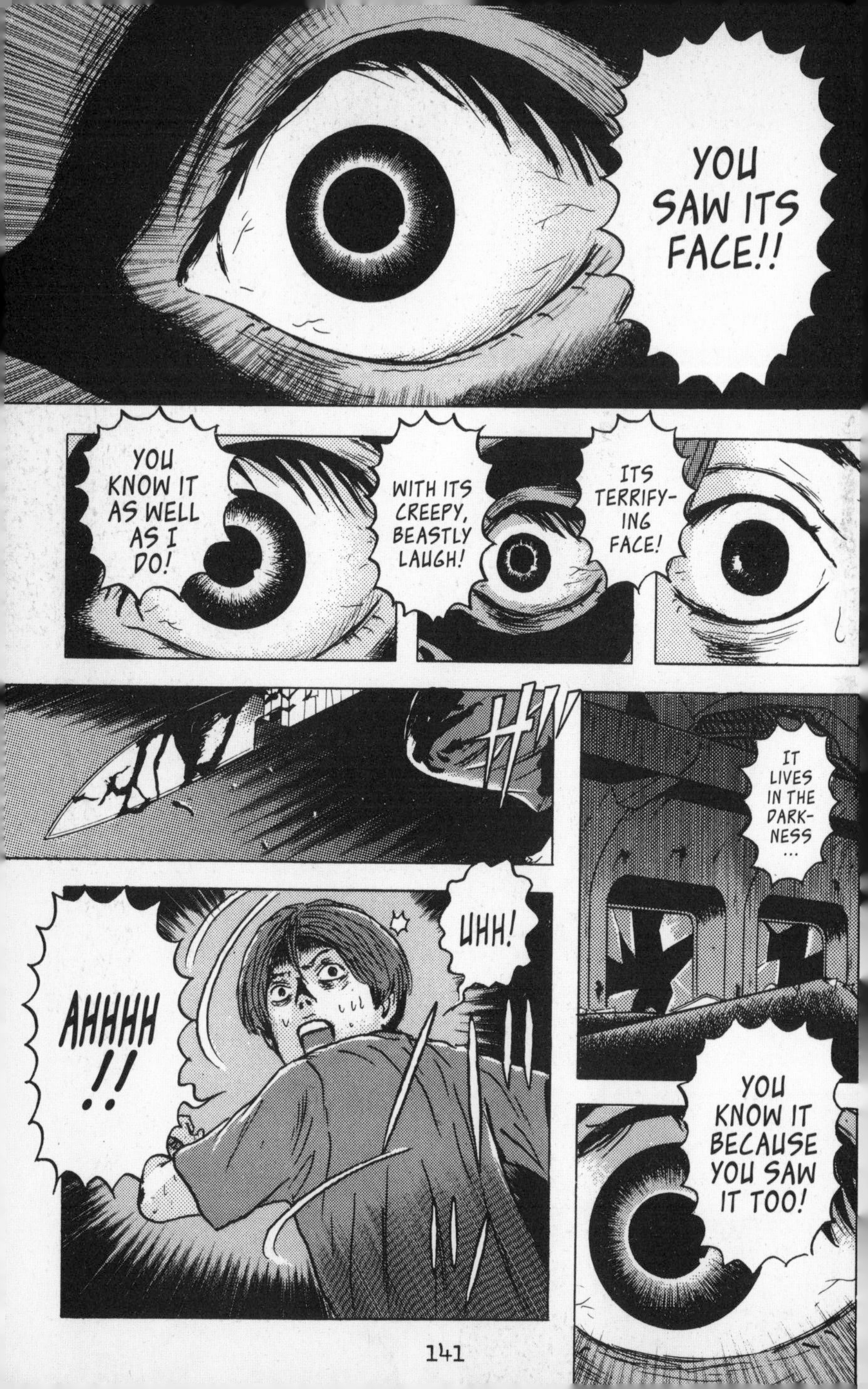
YOU SAW ITS FACE!!
ITS TERRIFY-ING FACE!
WITH ITS CREEPY, BEASTLY LAUGH!
YOU KNOW IT AS WELL AS I DO!
IT LIVES IN THE DARK-NESS ...
YOU KNOW IT BECAUSE YOU SAW IT TOO!
UHH!
AHHHH !!

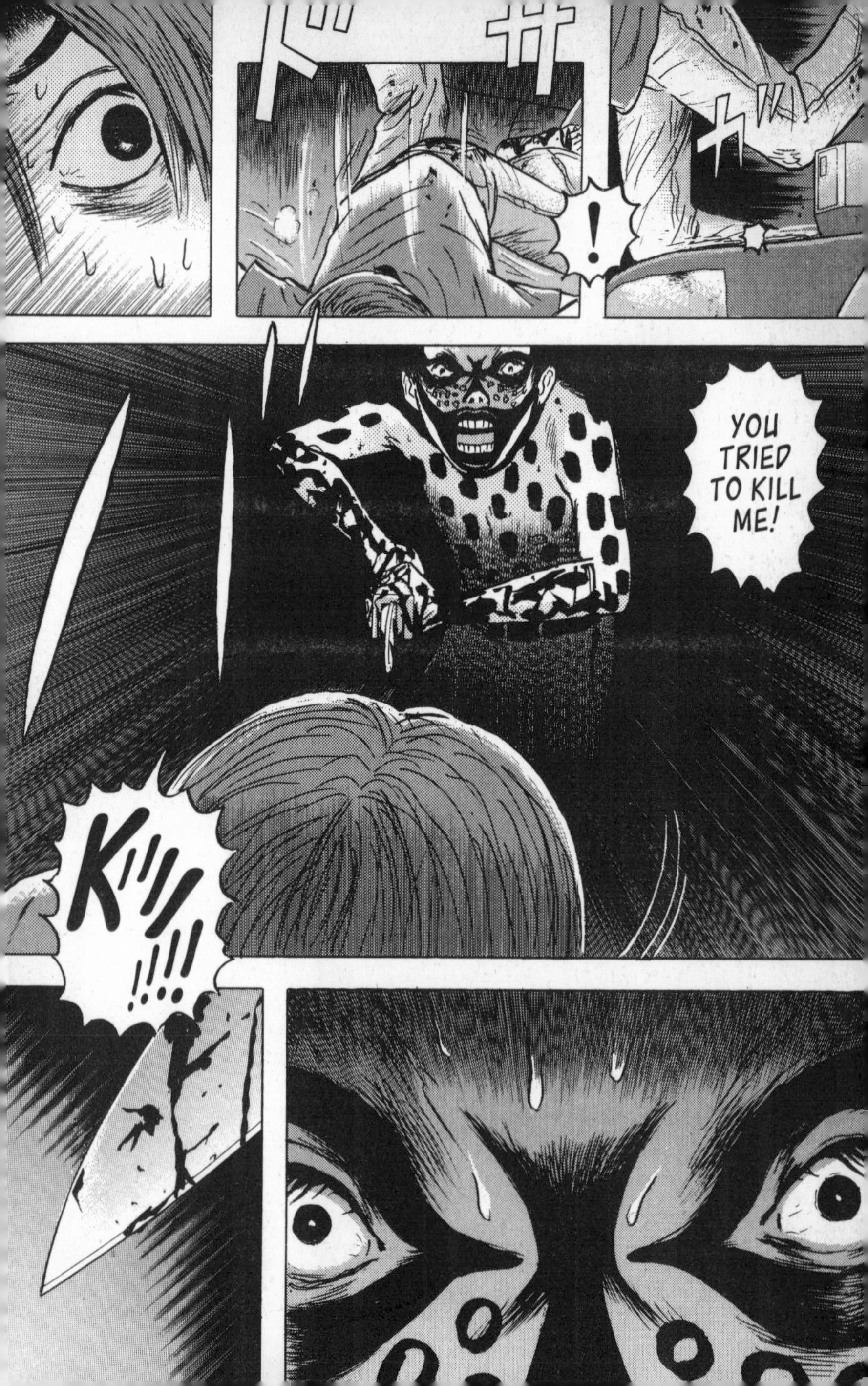
!
YOU TRIED TO KILL ME!
K!!!!!!!

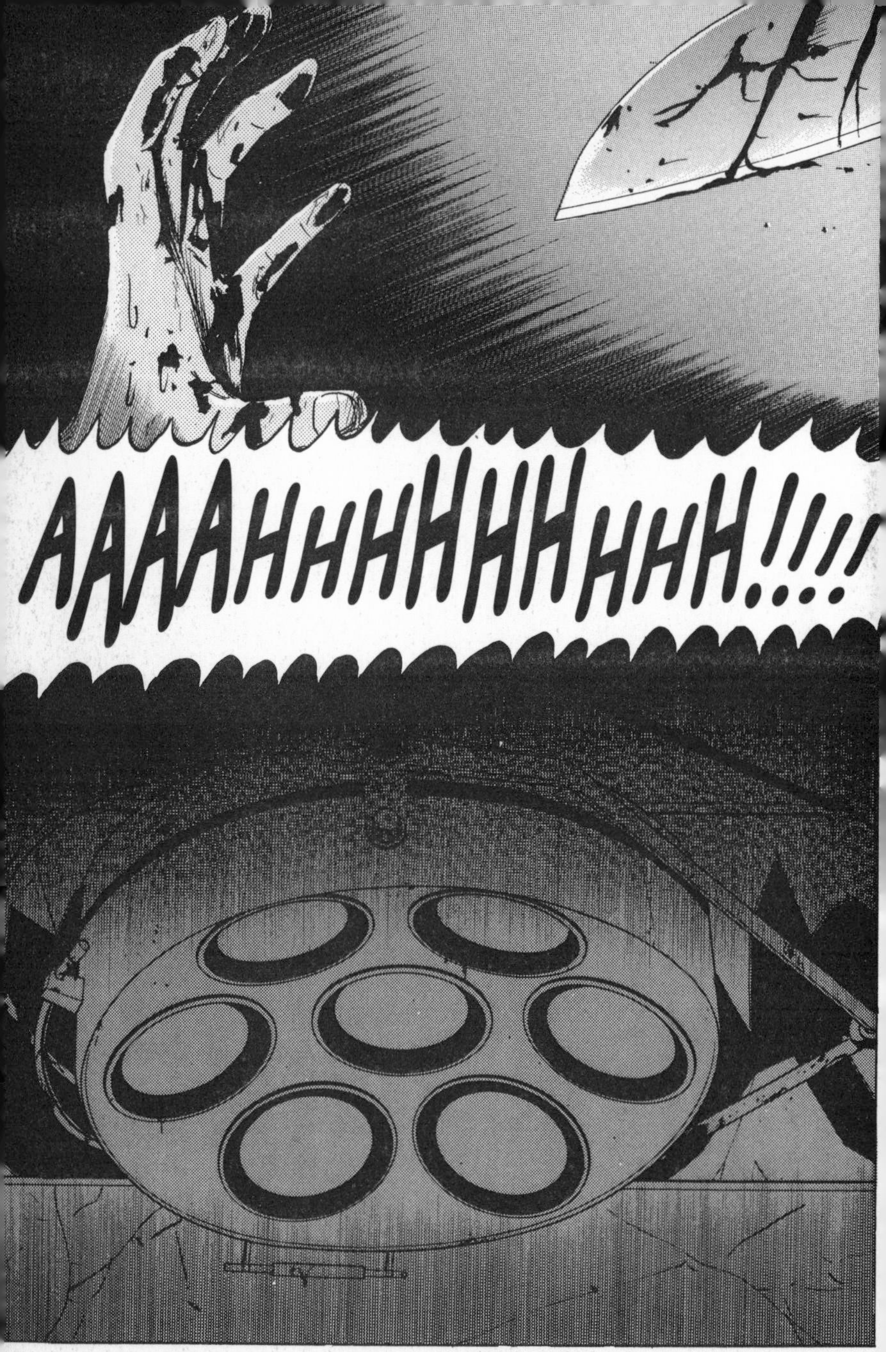
AAAAHHHHHHHHHHHH!!!!

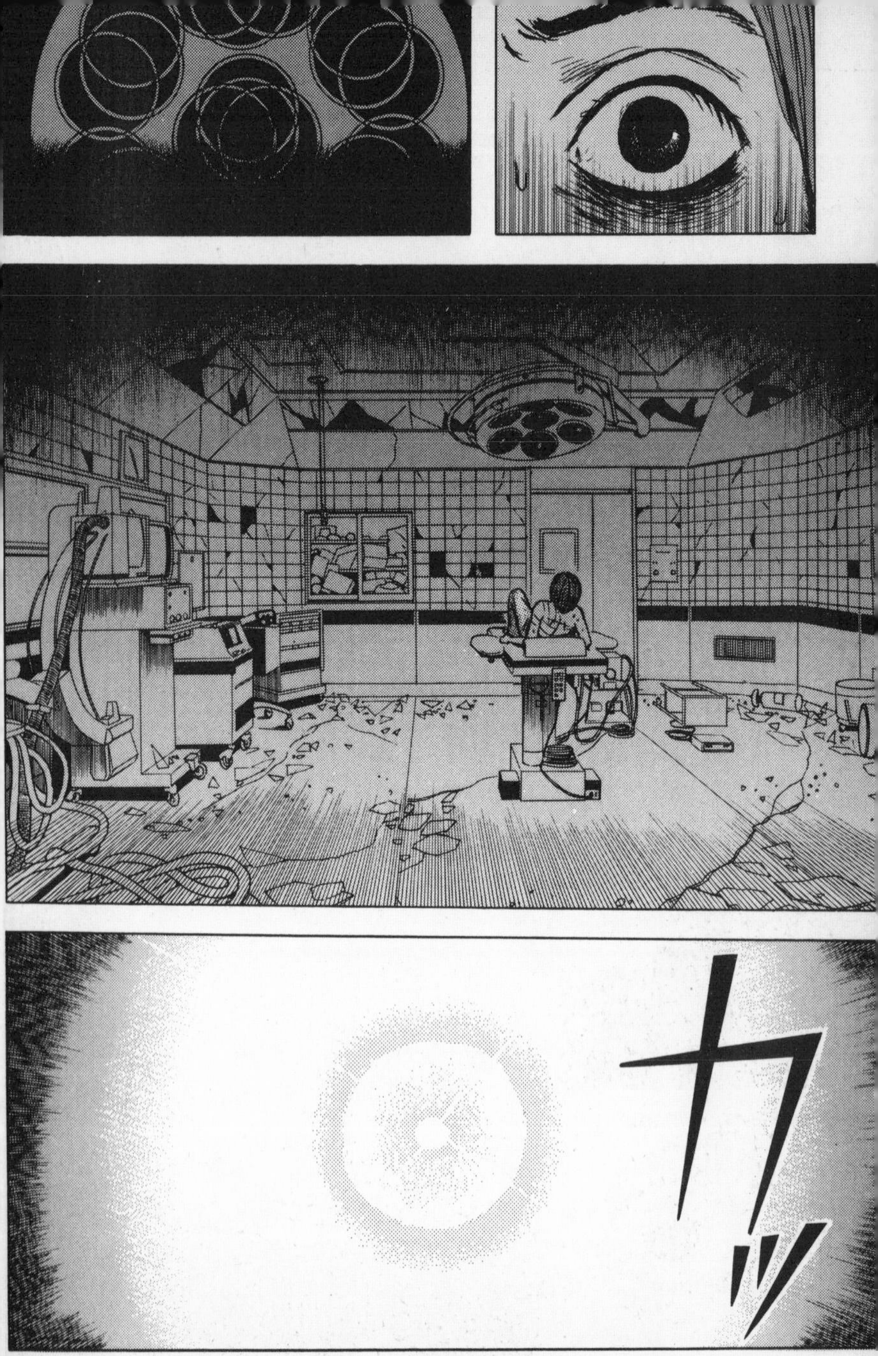
カッ

UHH!

UGH!

WHOA!

WHAT THE HELL ARE YOU DOING HERE?!

?!

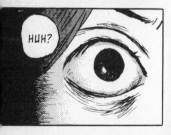

HUH?

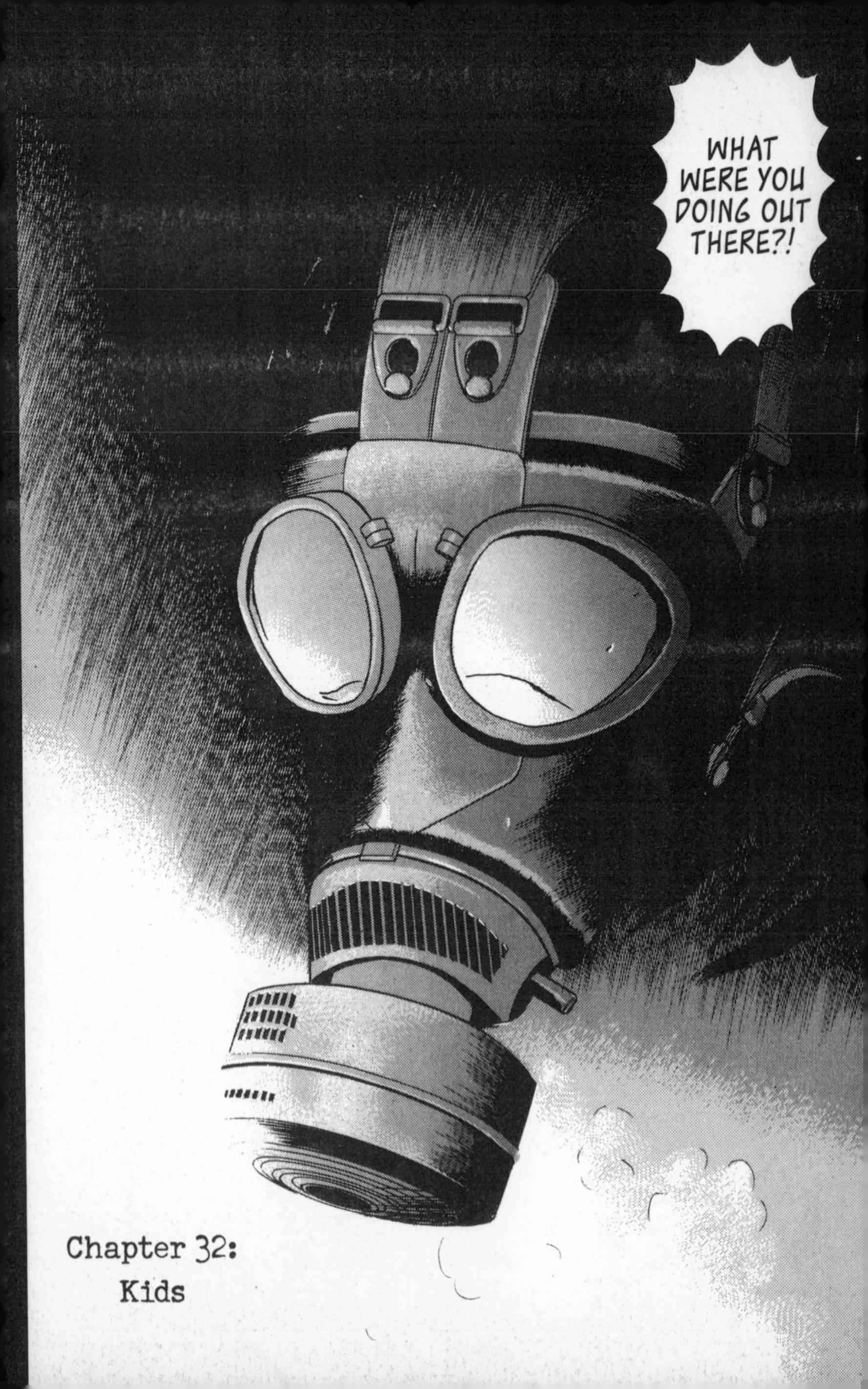
WHAT WERE YOU DOING OUT THERE?!

Chapter 32: Kids

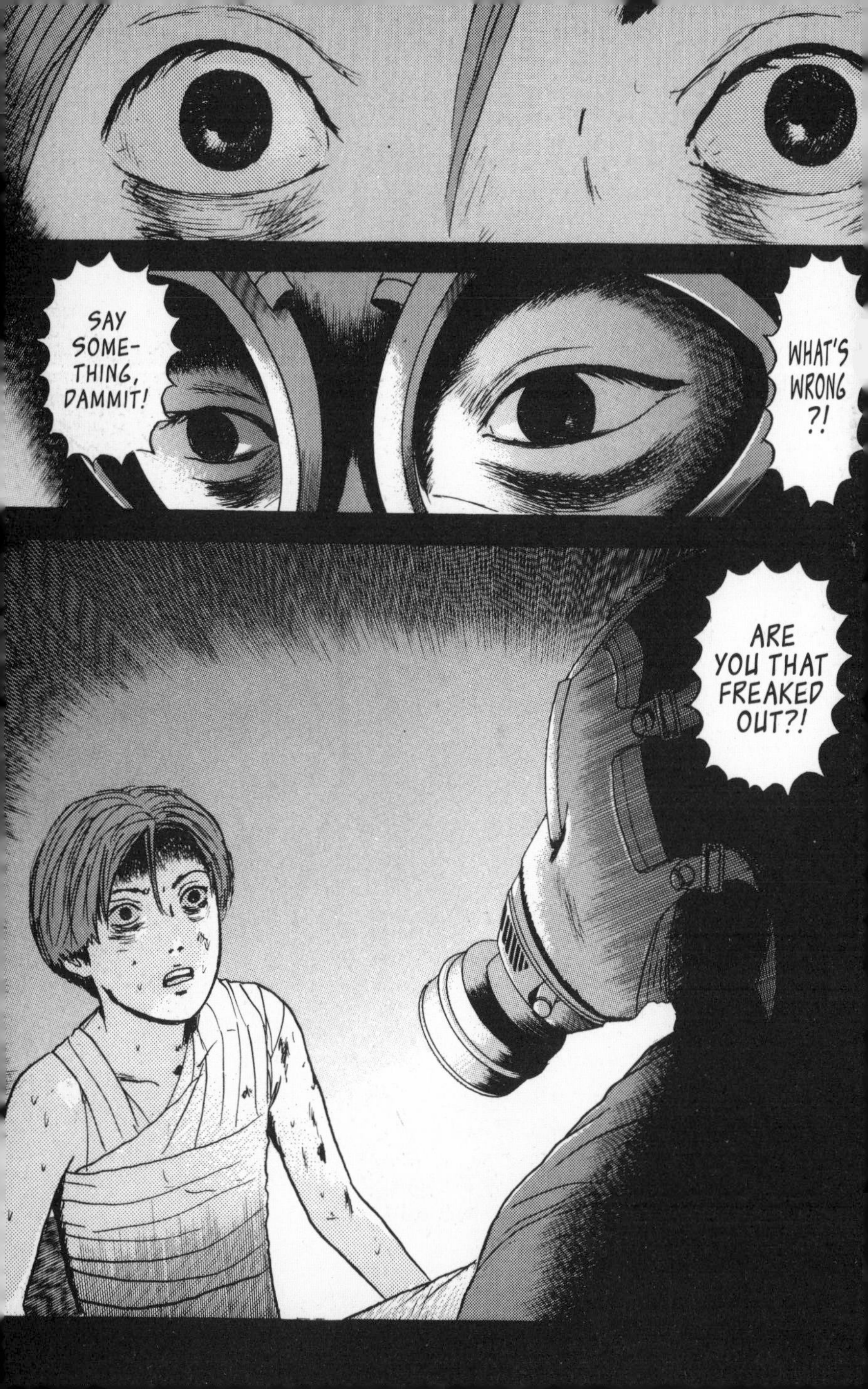
WHAT'S WRONG ?!
SAY SOME-THING, DAMMIT!
ARE YOU THAT FREAKED OUT?!

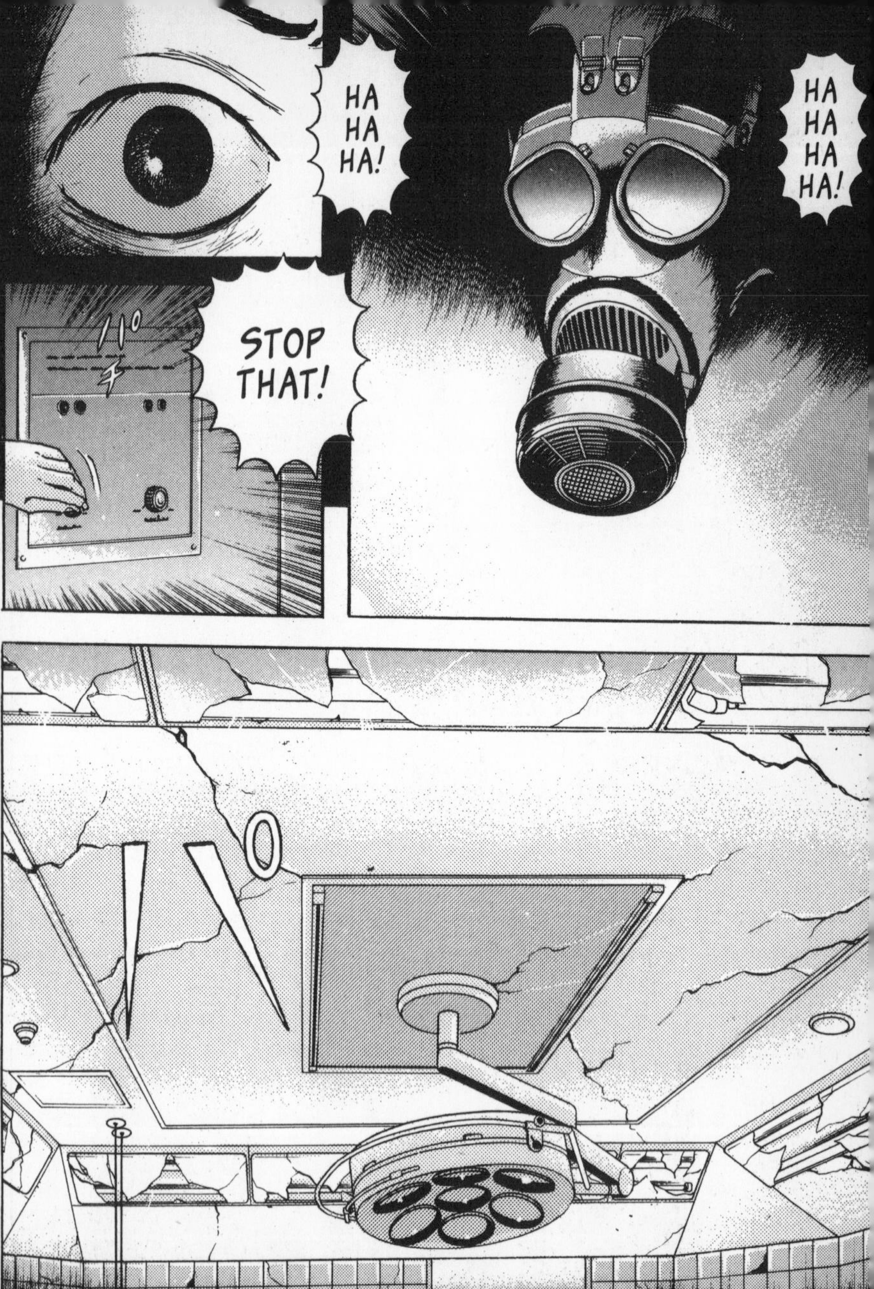
HA HA HA HA!
HA HA HA!
パチ
STOP THAT!

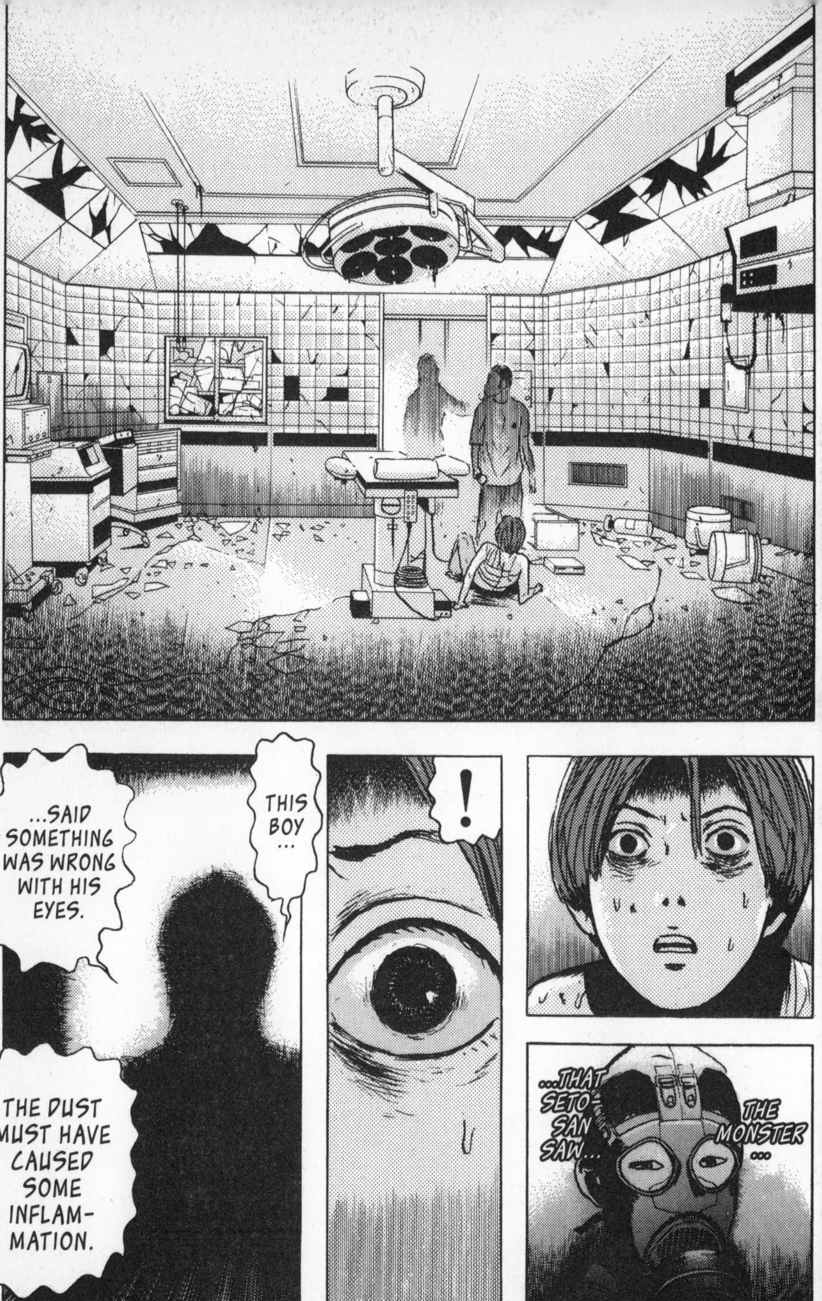
THE MONSTER...
...THAT SETO-SAN SAW...
!
THIS BOY...
...SAID SOMETHING WAS WRONG WITH HIS EYES.
THE DUST MUST HAVE CAUSED SOME INFLAMMATION.

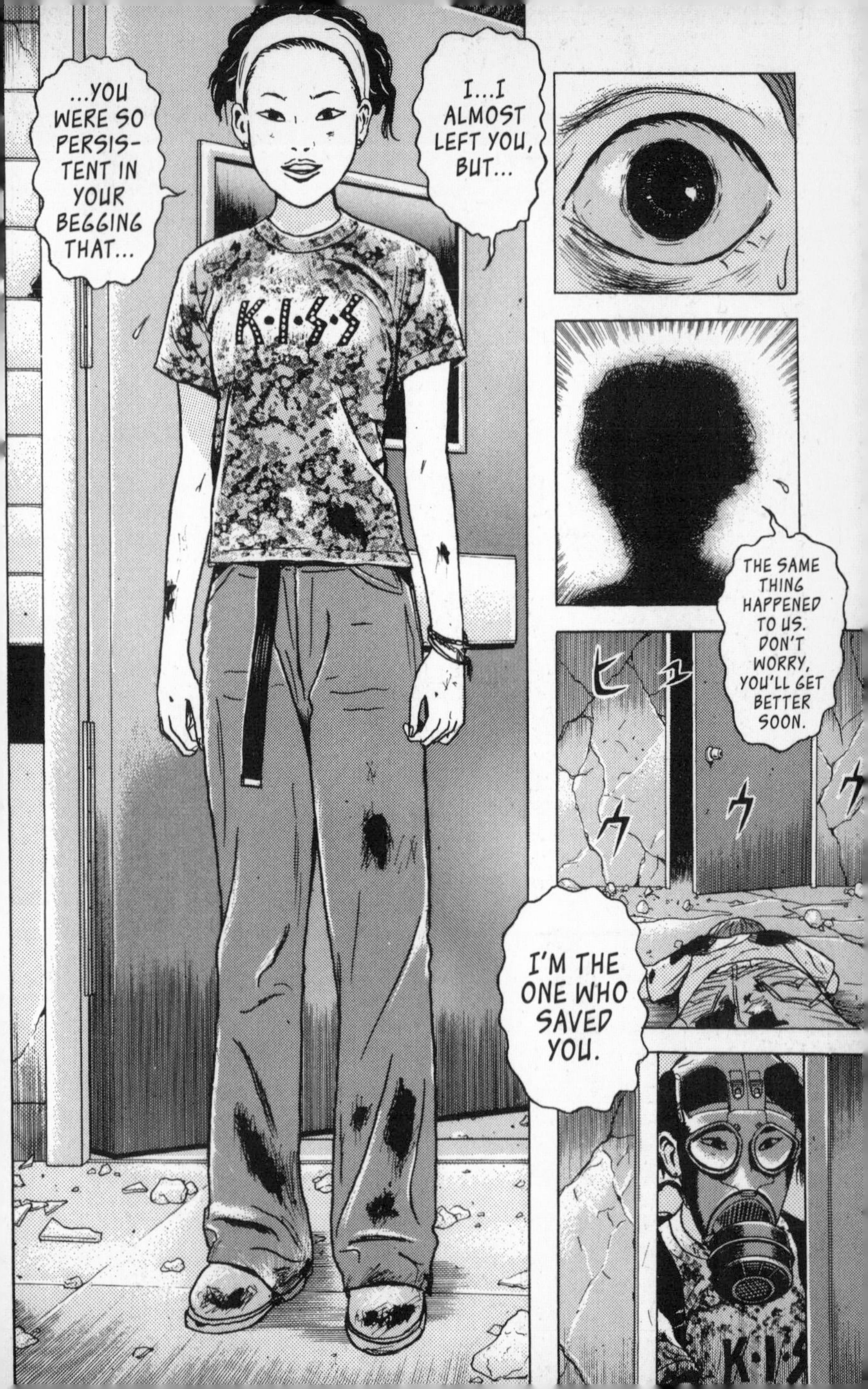
THE SAME THING HAPPENED TO US. DON'T WORRY, YOU'LL GET BETTER SOON.
ヒュ
ウ
ウ
ウ
I'M THE ONE WHO SAVED YOU.
K·I·S
I...I ALMOST LEFT YOU, BUT...
...YOU WERE SO PERSIS-TENT IN YOUR BEGGING THAT...
K·I·S·S

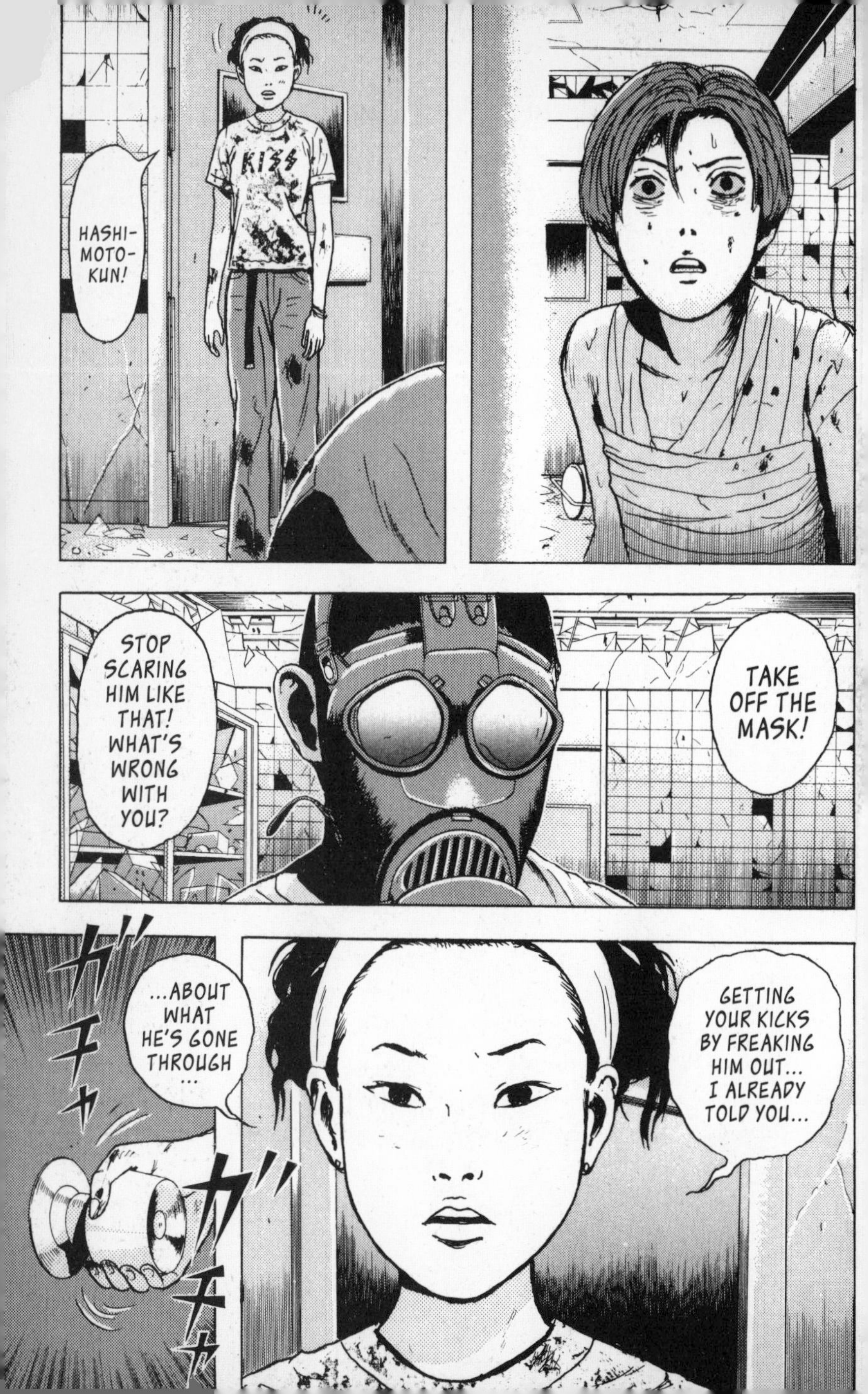
HASHI-MOTO-KUN!
TAKE OFF THE MASK!
STOP SCARING HIM LIKE THAT! WHAT'S WRONG WITH YOU?
GETTING YOUR KICKS BY FREAKING HIM OUT... I ALREADY TOLD YOU...
...ABOUT WHAT HE'S GONE THROUGH...
ガチャ
ガチャ

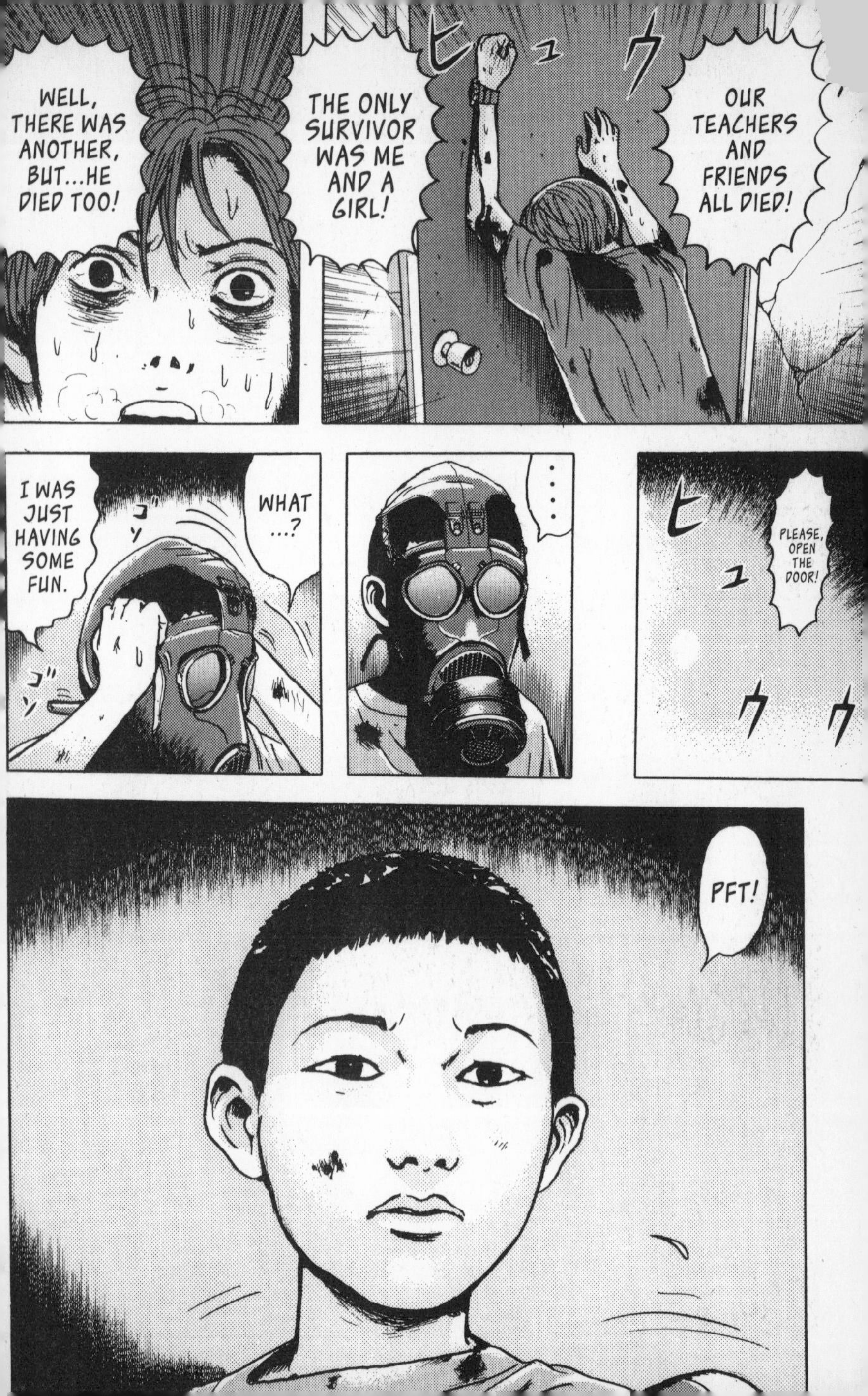
ヒュウ
OUR TEACHERS AND FRIENDS ALL DIED!
THE ONLY SURVIVOR WAS ME AND A GIRL!
WELL, THERE WAS ANOTHER, BUT...HE DIED TOO!
ヒュウウ
PLEASE, OPEN THE DOOR!
....
WHAT ...?
ゴツ
I WAS JUST HAVING SOME FUN.
ゴン
PFT!

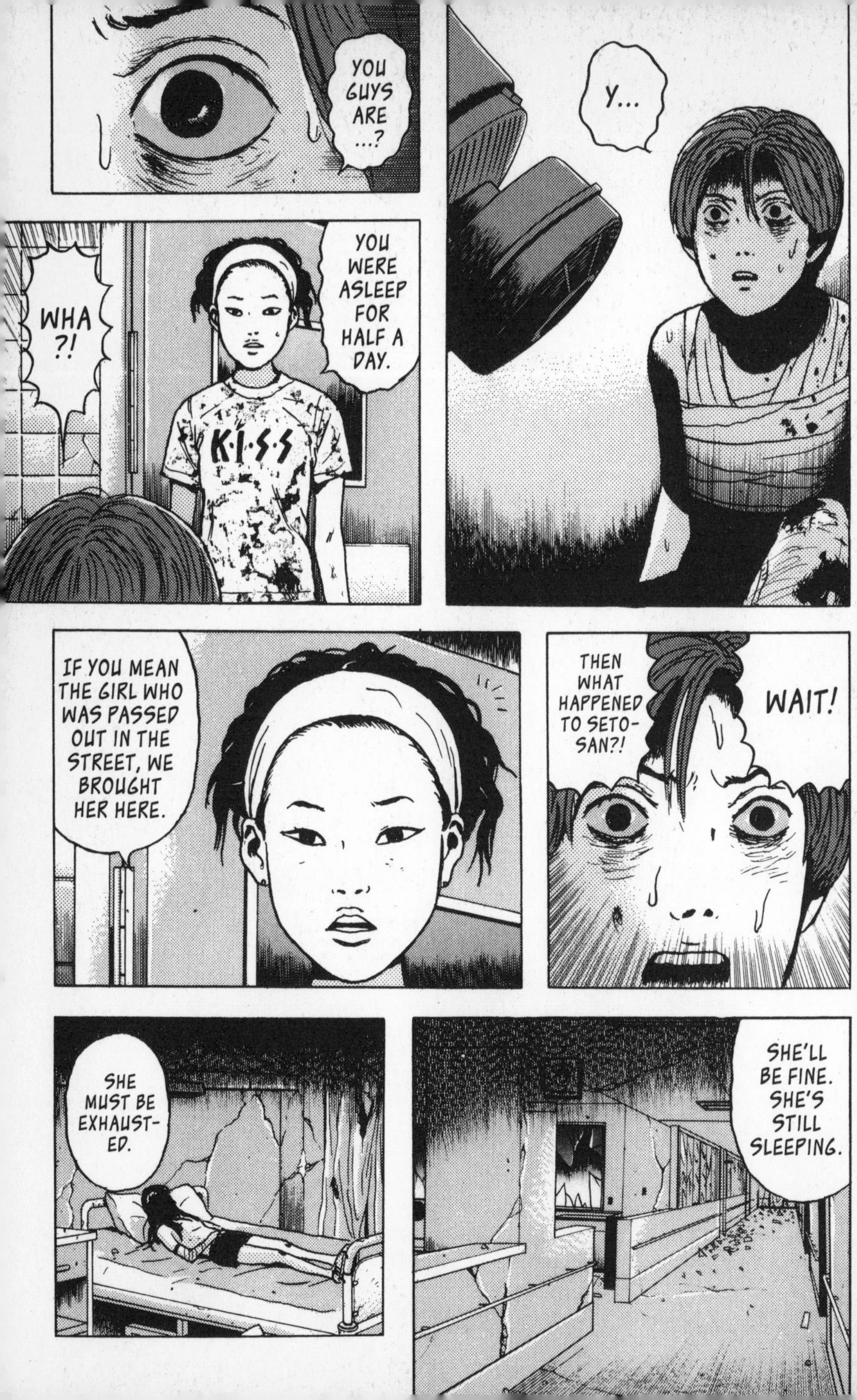
Y...
YOU GUYS ARE ...?
YOU WERE ASLEEP FOR HALF A DAY.
WHA ?!
WAIT!
THEN WHAT HAPPENED TO SETO-SAN?!
IF YOU MEAN THE GIRL WHO WAS PASSED OUT IN THE STREET, WE BROUGHT HER HERE.
SHE'LL BE FINE. SHE'S STILL SLEEPING.
SHE MUST BE EXHAUSTED.

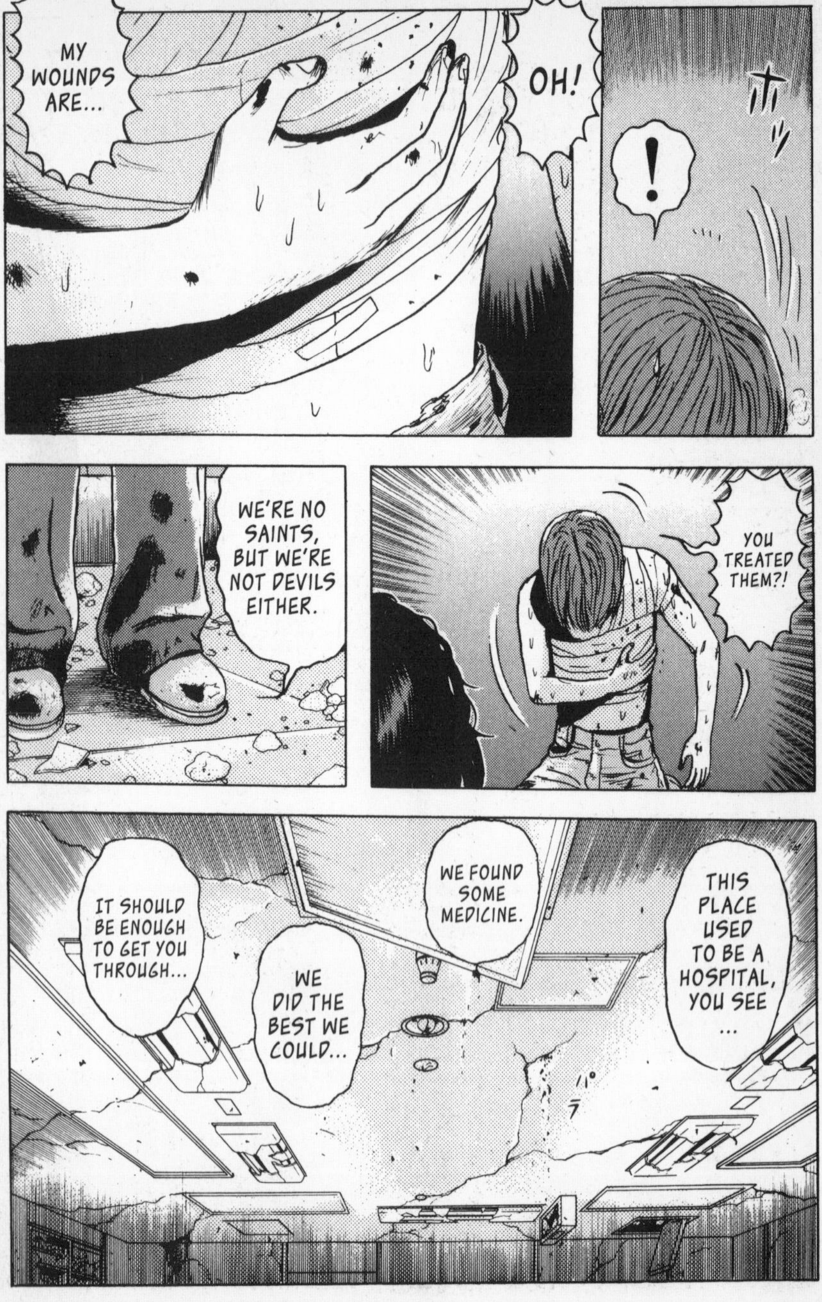
!
OH!
MY WOUNDS ARE...
YOU TREATED THEM?!
WE'RE NO SAINTS, BUT WE'RE NOT DEVILS EITHER.
THIS PLACE USED TO BE A HOSPITAL, YOU SEE ...
WE FOUND SOME MEDICINE.
WE DID THE BEST WE COULD...
IT SHOULD BE ENOUGH TO GET YOU THROUGH...

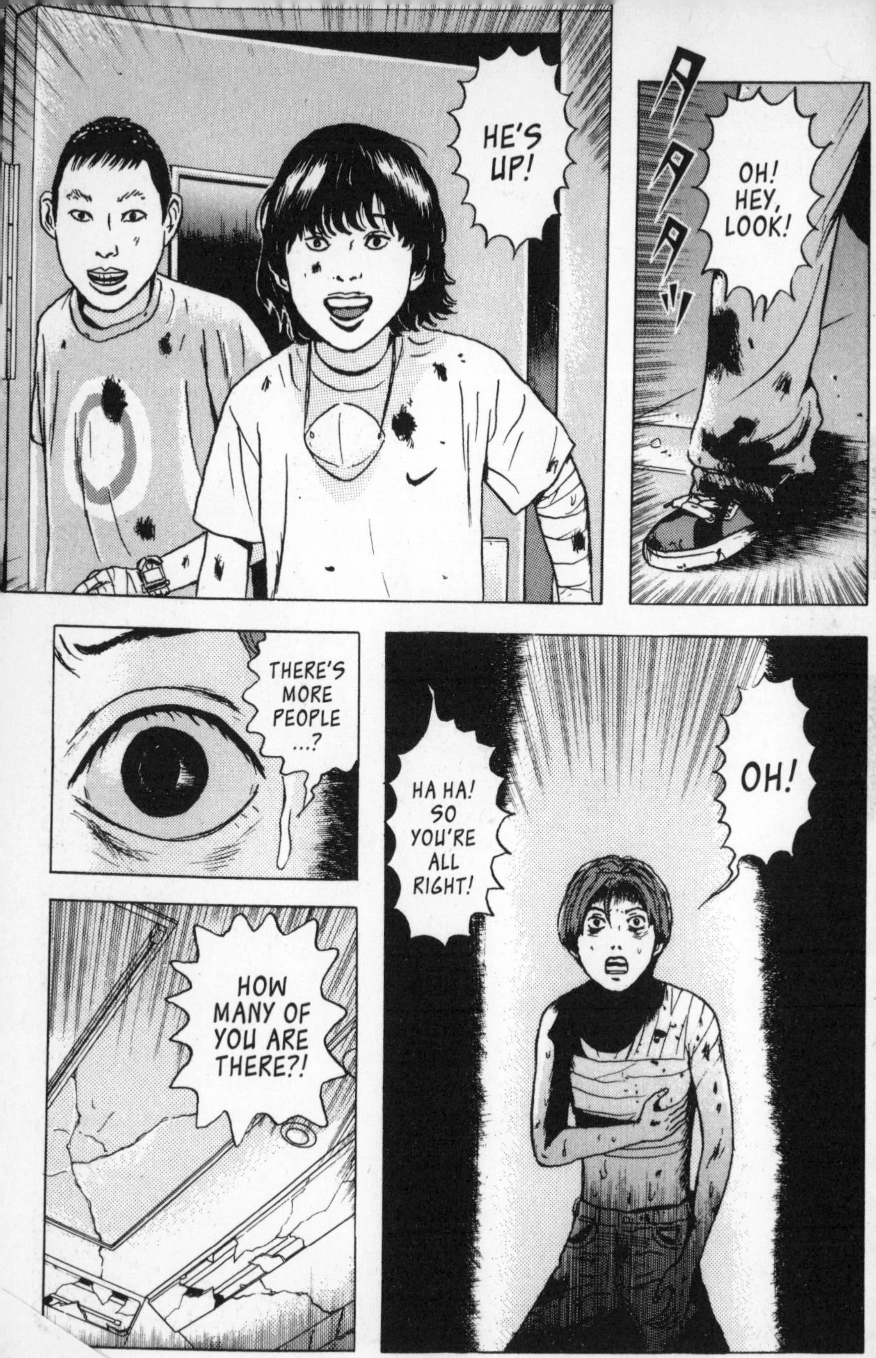
OH! HEY, LOOK!
HE'S UP!
OH!
HA HA! SO YOU'RE ALL RIGHT!
THERE'S MORE PEOPLE ...?
HOW MANY OF YOU ARE THERE?!

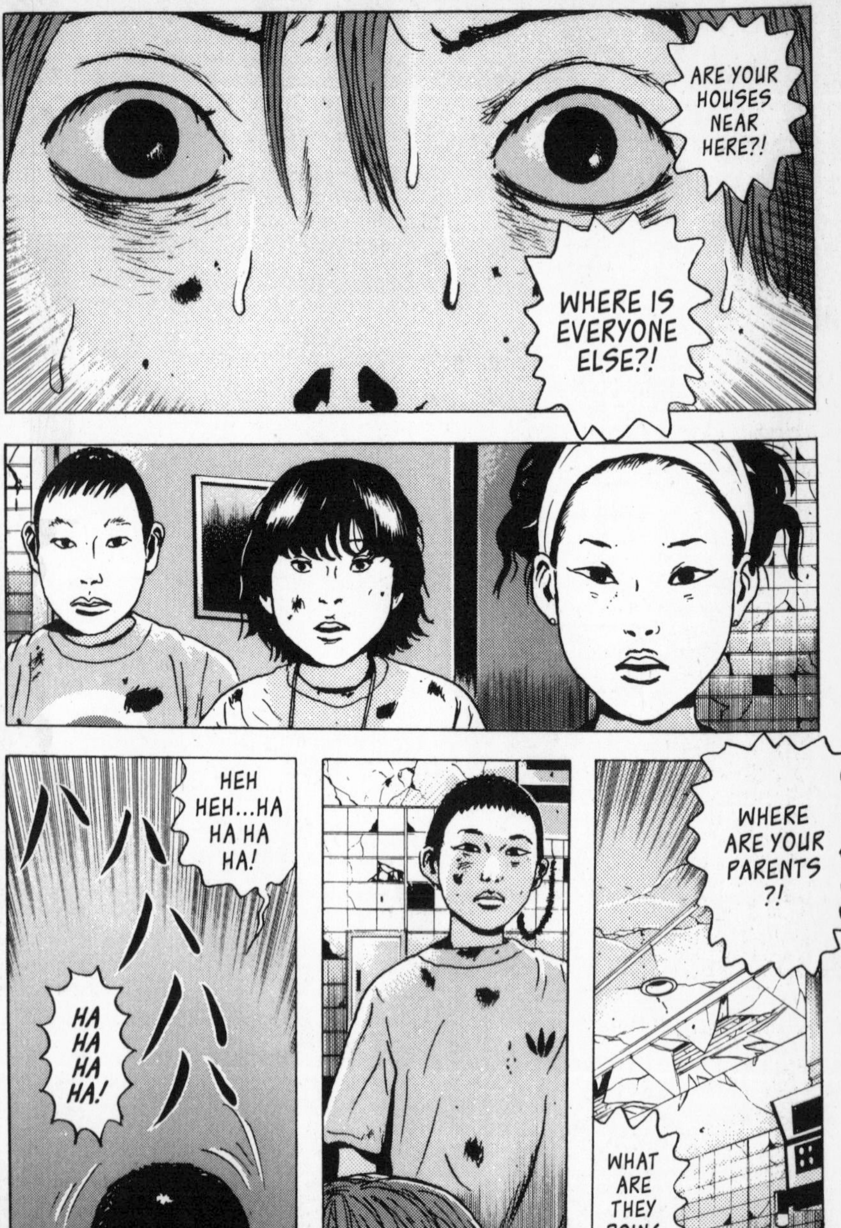
ARE YOUR HOUSES NEAR HERE?!
WHERE IS EVERYONE ELSE?!
WHERE ARE YOUR PARENTS ?!
WHAT ARE THEY DOING ...?!
HEH HEH...HA HA HA HA!
HA HA HA HA!

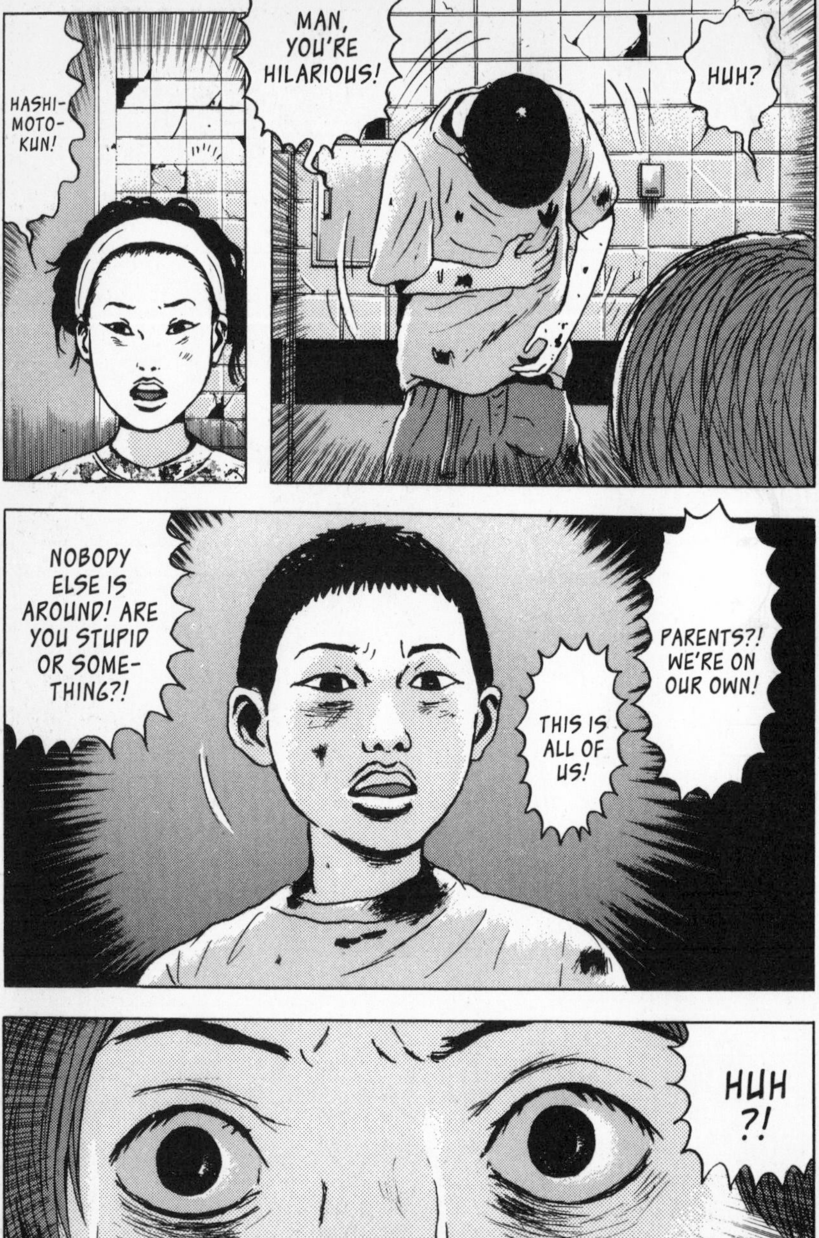
MAN, YOU'RE HILARIOUS!
HUH?
HASHIMOTO-KUN!
PARENTS?! WE'RE ON OUR OWN!
THIS IS ALL OF US!
NOBODY ELSE IS AROUND! ARE YOU STUPID OR SOMETHING?!
HUH ?!

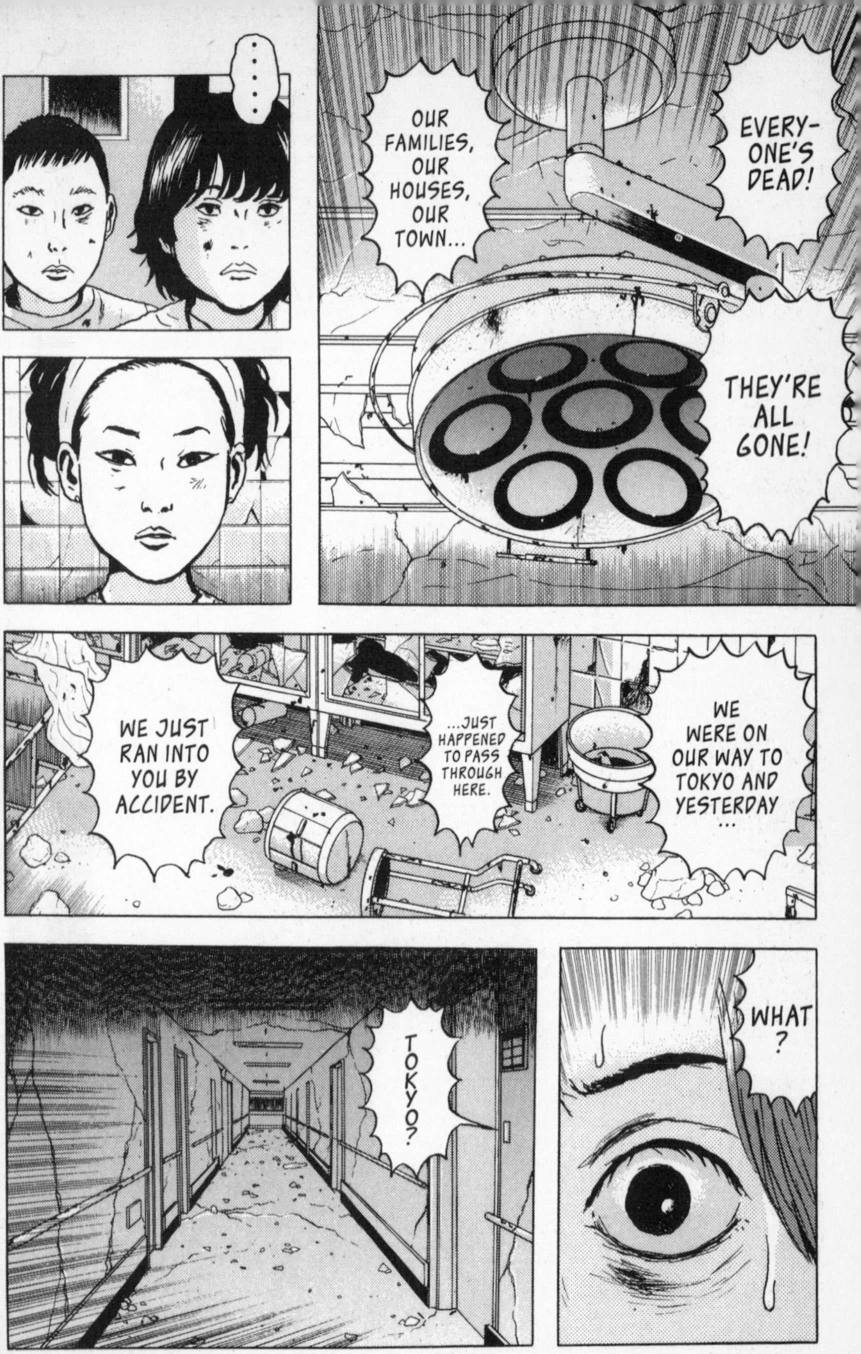
EVERY-ONE'S DEAD!
OUR FAMILIES, OUR HOUSES, OUR TOWN...
THEY'RE ALL GONE!
.....
WE WERE ON OUR WAY TO TOKYO AND YESTERDAY ...
...JUST HAPPENED TO PASS THROUGH HERE.
WE JUST RAN INTO YOU BY ACCIDENT.
WHAT ?
TOKYO?

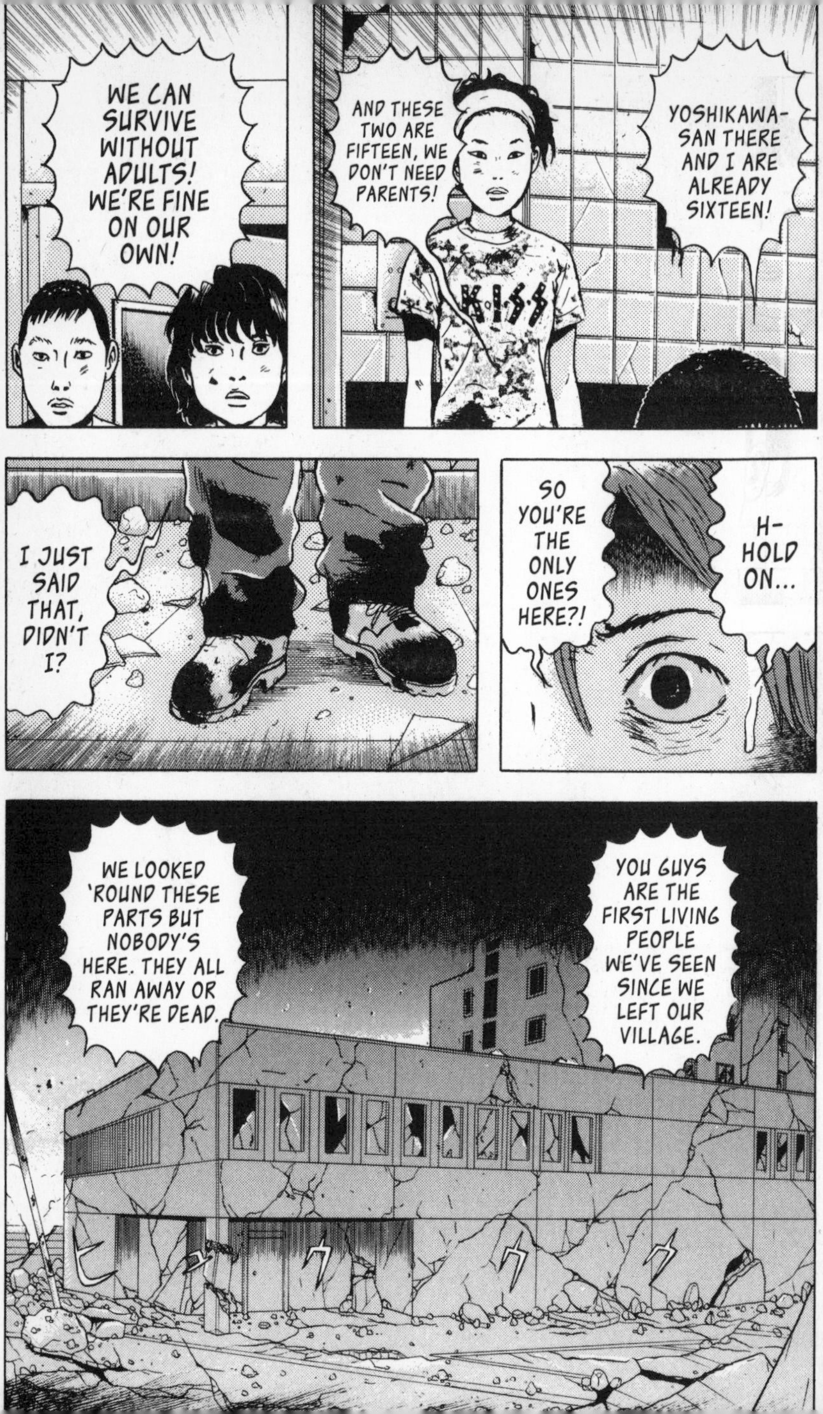
YOSHIKAWA-SAN THERE AND I ARE ALREADY SIXTEEN!
AND THESE TWO ARE FIFTEEN, WE DON'T NEED PARENTS!
WE CAN SURVIVE WITHOUT ADULTS! WE'RE FINE ON OUR OWN!
H-HOLD ON...
SO YOU'RE THE ONLY ONES HERE?!
I JUST SAID THAT, DIDN'T I?
YOU GUYS ARE THE FIRST LIVING PEOPLE WE'VE SEEN SINCE WE LEFT OUR VILLAGE.
WE LOOKED 'ROUND THESE PARTS BUT NOBODY'S HERE. THEY ALL RAN AWAY OR THEY'RE DEAD.

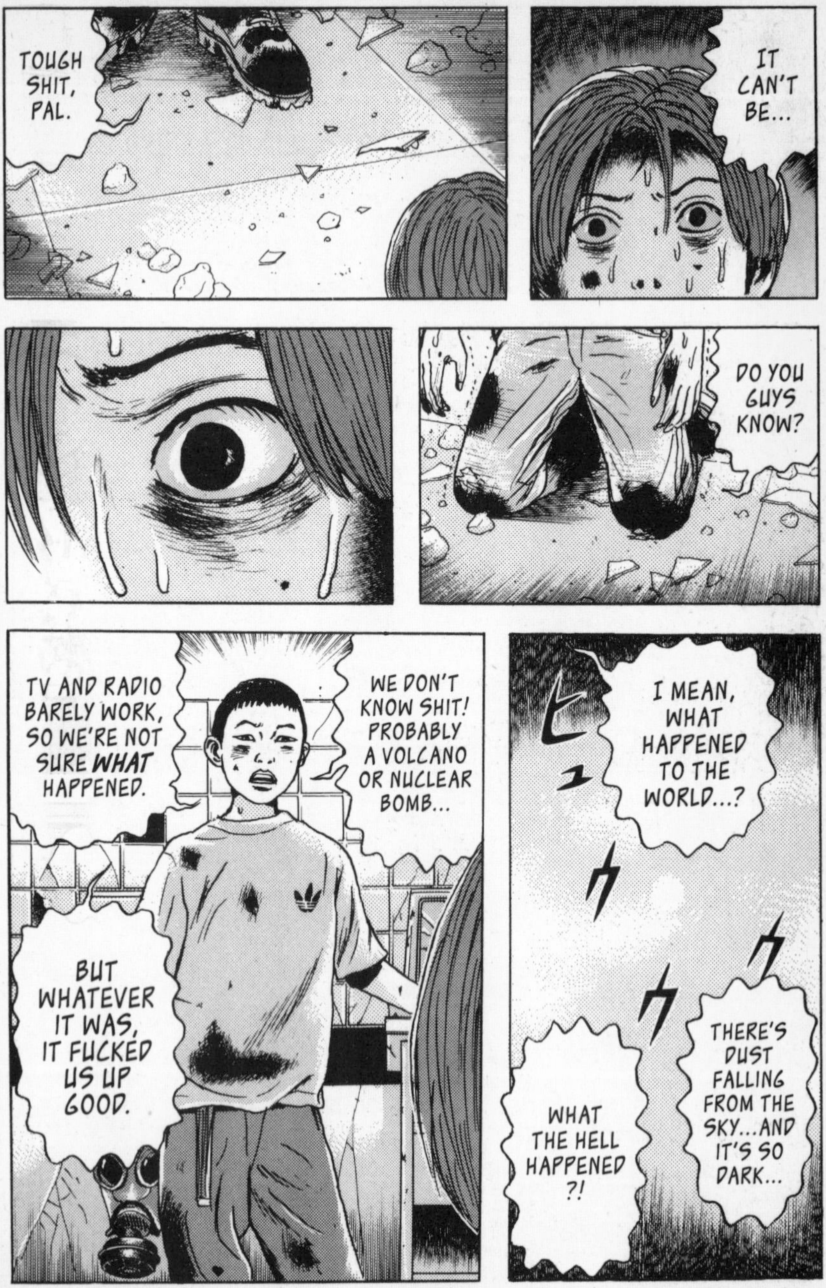
IT CAN'T BE...
TOUGH SHIT, PAL.
DO YOU GUYS KNOW?
I MEAN, WHAT HAPPENED TO THE WORLD...?
ヒュウウウ
THERE'S DUST FALLING FROM THE SKY...AND IT'S SO DARK...
WHAT THE HELL HAPPENED ?!
WE DON'T KNOW SHIT! PROBABLY A VOLCANO OR NUCLEAR BOMB...
TV AND RADIO BARELY WORK, SO WE'RE NOT SURE ***WHAT*** HAPPENED.
BUT WHATEVER IT WAS, IT FUCKED US UP GOOD.

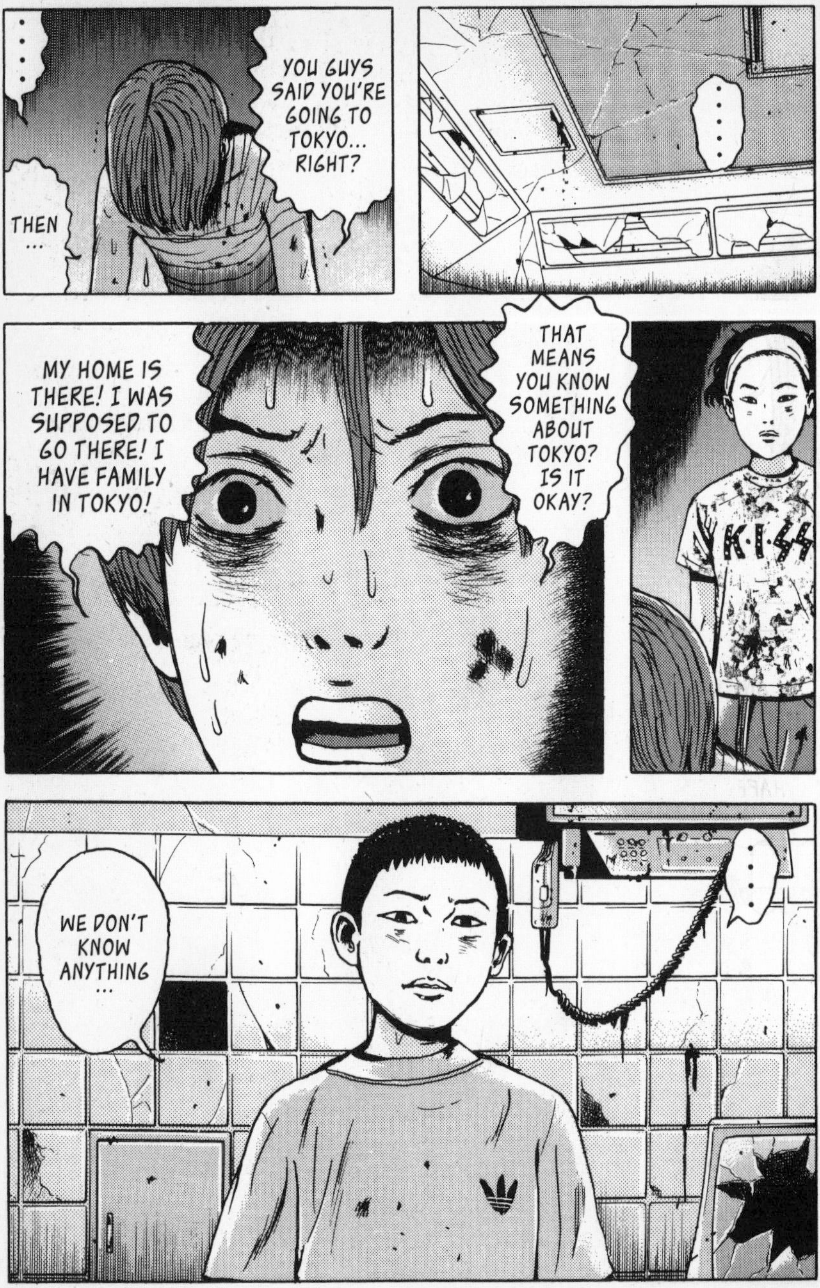
....
....
YOU GUYS SAID YOU'RE GOING TO TOKYO... RIGHT?
THEN ...
THAT MEANS YOU KNOW SOMETHING ABOUT TOKYO? IS IT OKAY?
MY HOME IS THERE! I WAS SUPPOSED TO GO THERE! I HAVE FAMILY IN TOKYO!
....
WE DON'T KNOW ANYTHING ...

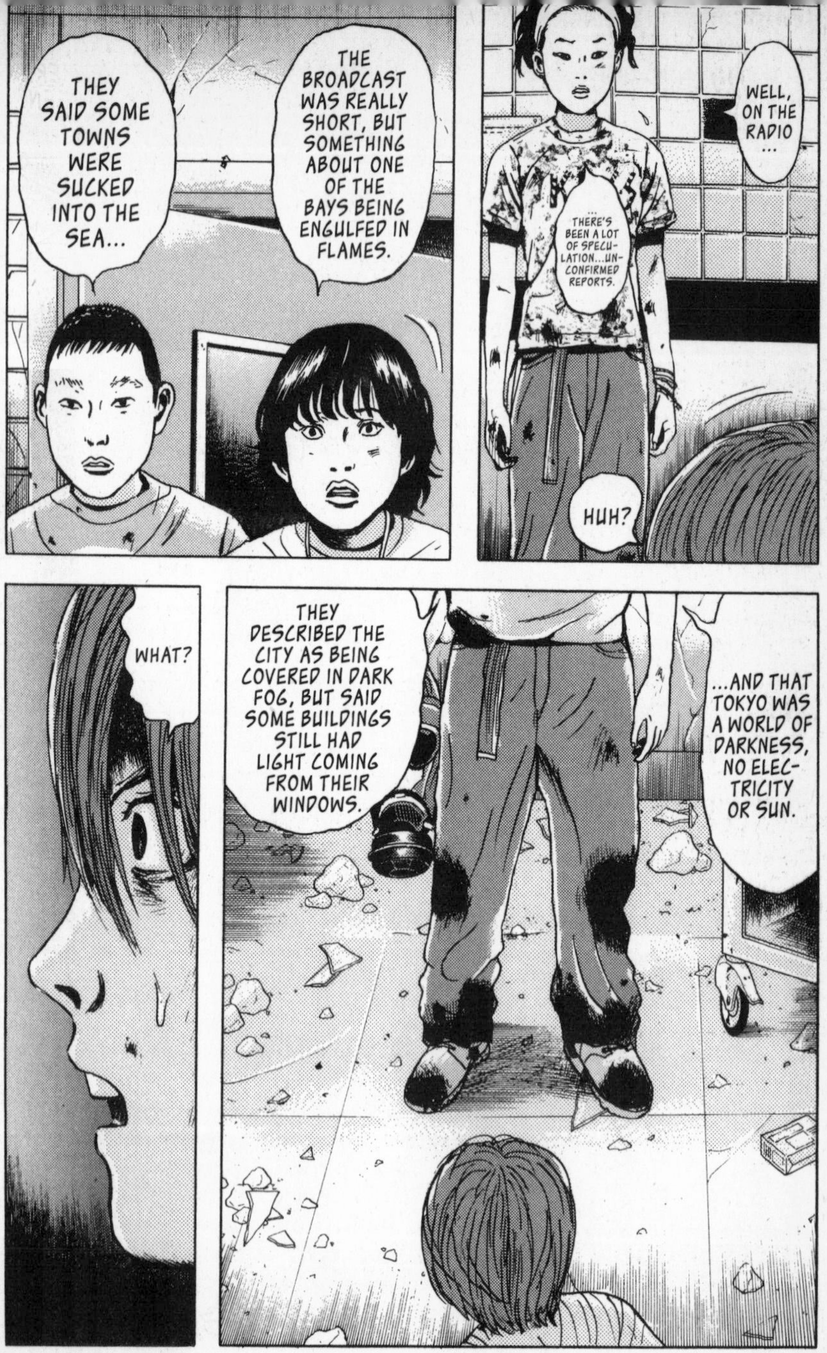
WELL, ON THE RADIO ...
... THERE'S BEEN A LOT OF SPECULATION...UNCONFIRMED REPORTS.
HUH?
THE BROADCAST WAS REALLY SHORT, BUT SOMETHING ABOUT ONE OF THE BAYS BEING ENGULFED IN FLAMES.
THEY SAID SOME TOWNS WERE SUCKED INTO THE SEA...
THEY DESCRIBED THE CITY AS BEING COVERED IN DARK FOG, BUT SAID SOME BUILDINGS STILL HAD LIGHT COMING FROM THEIR WINDOWS.
...AND THAT TOKYO WAS A WORLD OF DARKNESS, NO ELECTRICITY OR SUN.
WHAT?

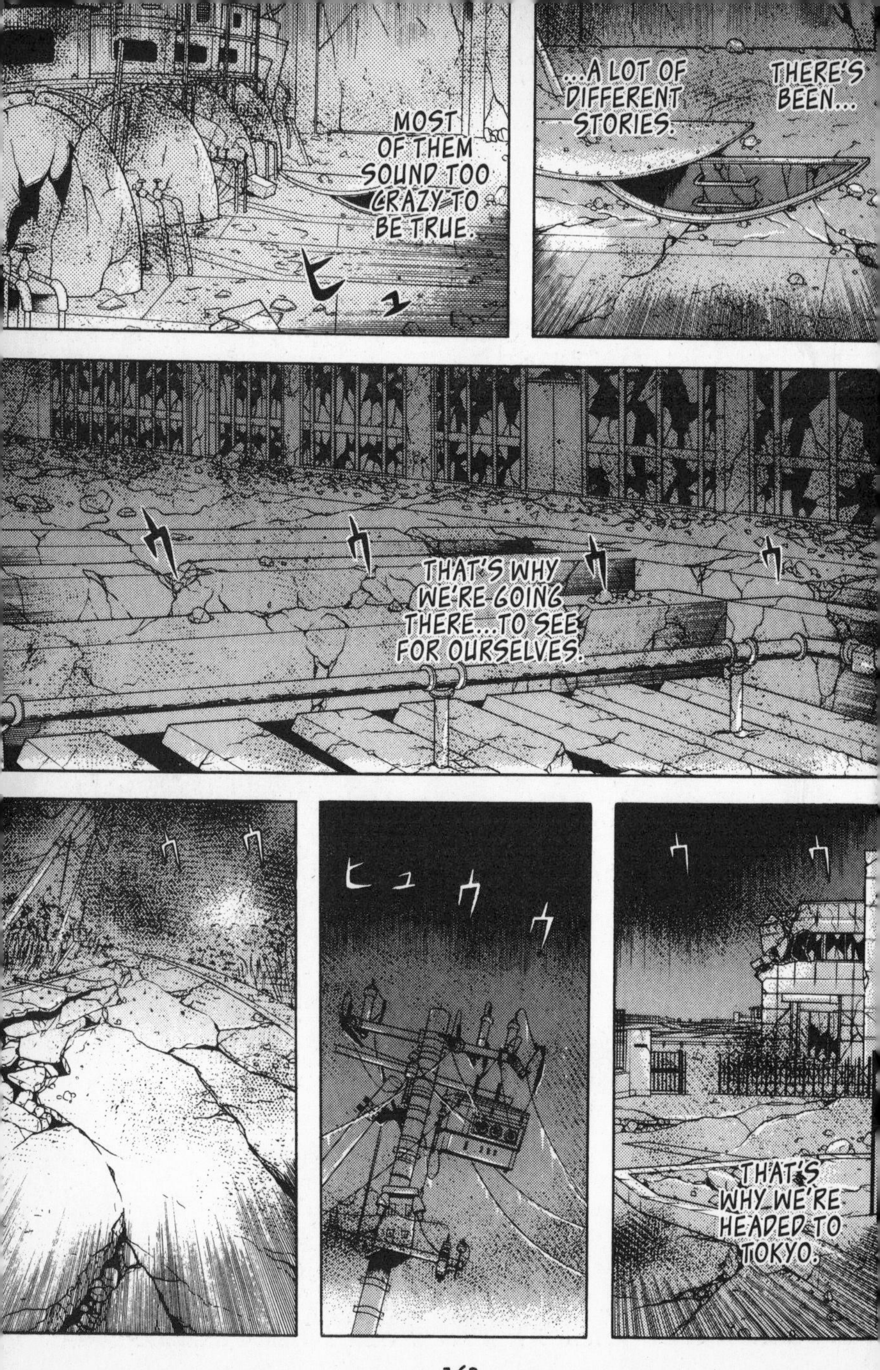
THERE'S BEEN...
...A LOT OF DIFFERENT STORIES.
MOST OF THEM SOUND TOO CRAZY TO BE TRUE.
ヒュ
THAT'S WHY WE'RE GOING THERE...TO SEE FOR OURSELVES.
THAT'S WHY WE'RE HEADED TO TOKYO.
ヒュウウ

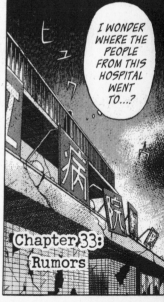

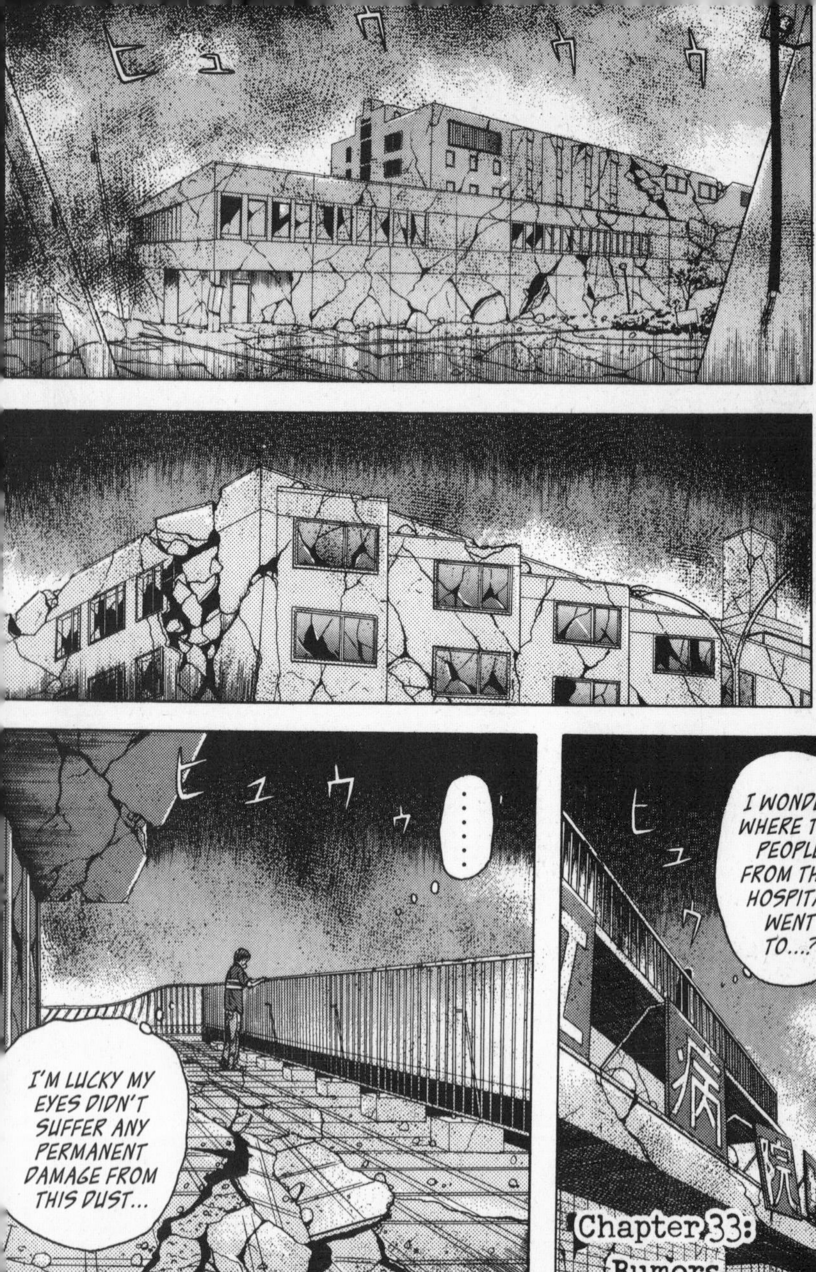
I WONDER WHERE THE PEOPLE FROM THIS HOSPITAL WENT TO...?
病院
Chapter 33: Rumors
......
I'M LUCKY MY EYES DIDN'T SUFFER ANY PERMANENT DAMAGE FROM THIS DUST...

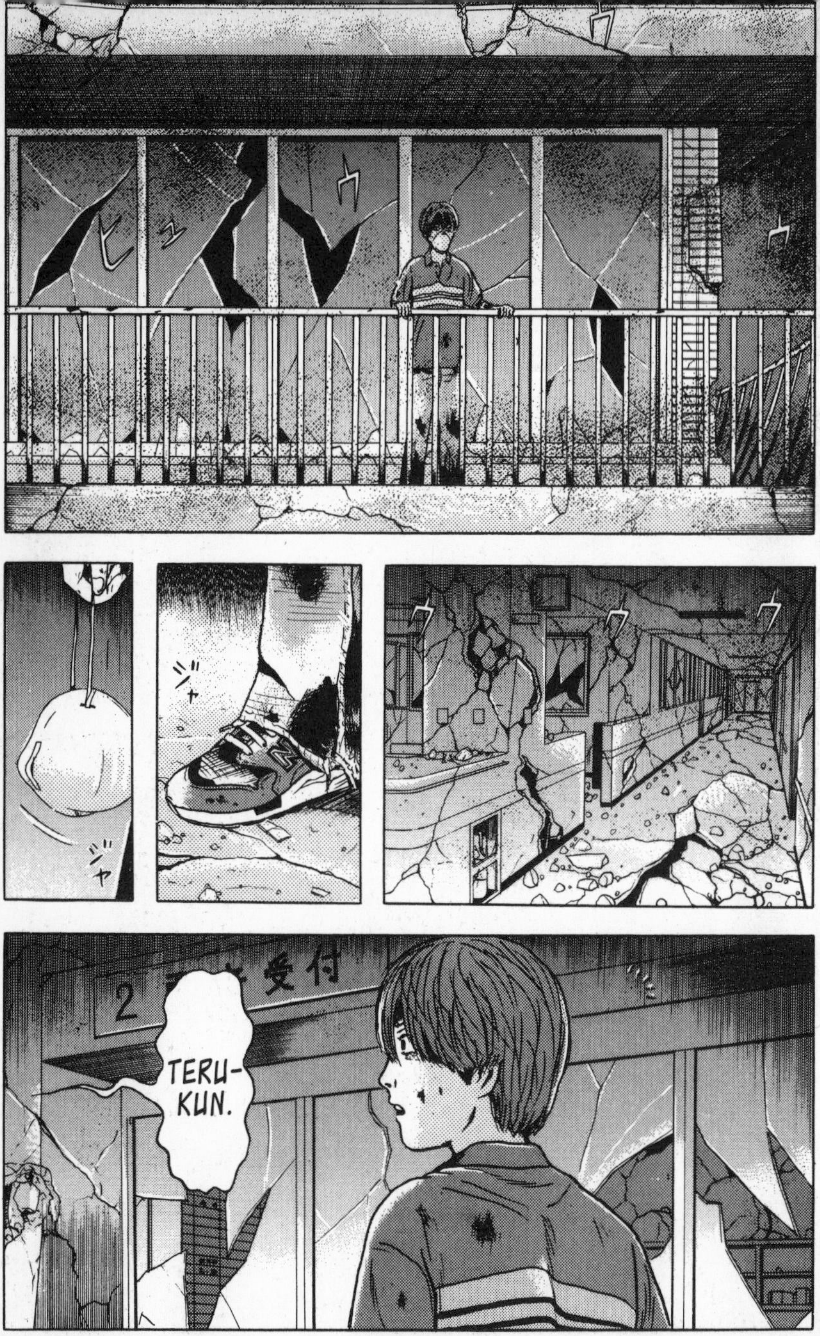
ヒュゥ
ジャ
ジャ
2
受付
TERU-KUN.

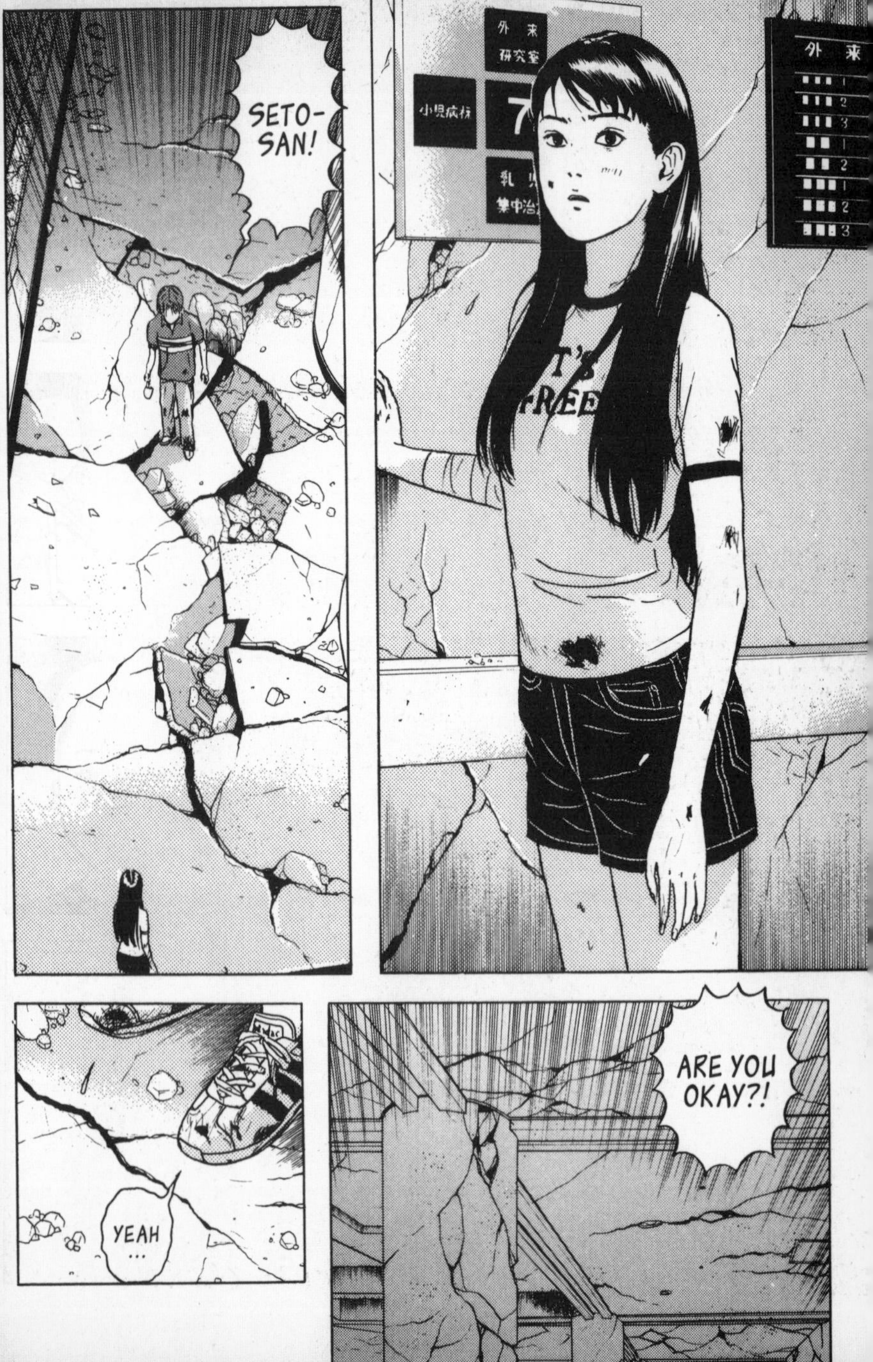
SETO-SAN!
ARE YOU OKAY?!
YEAH ...

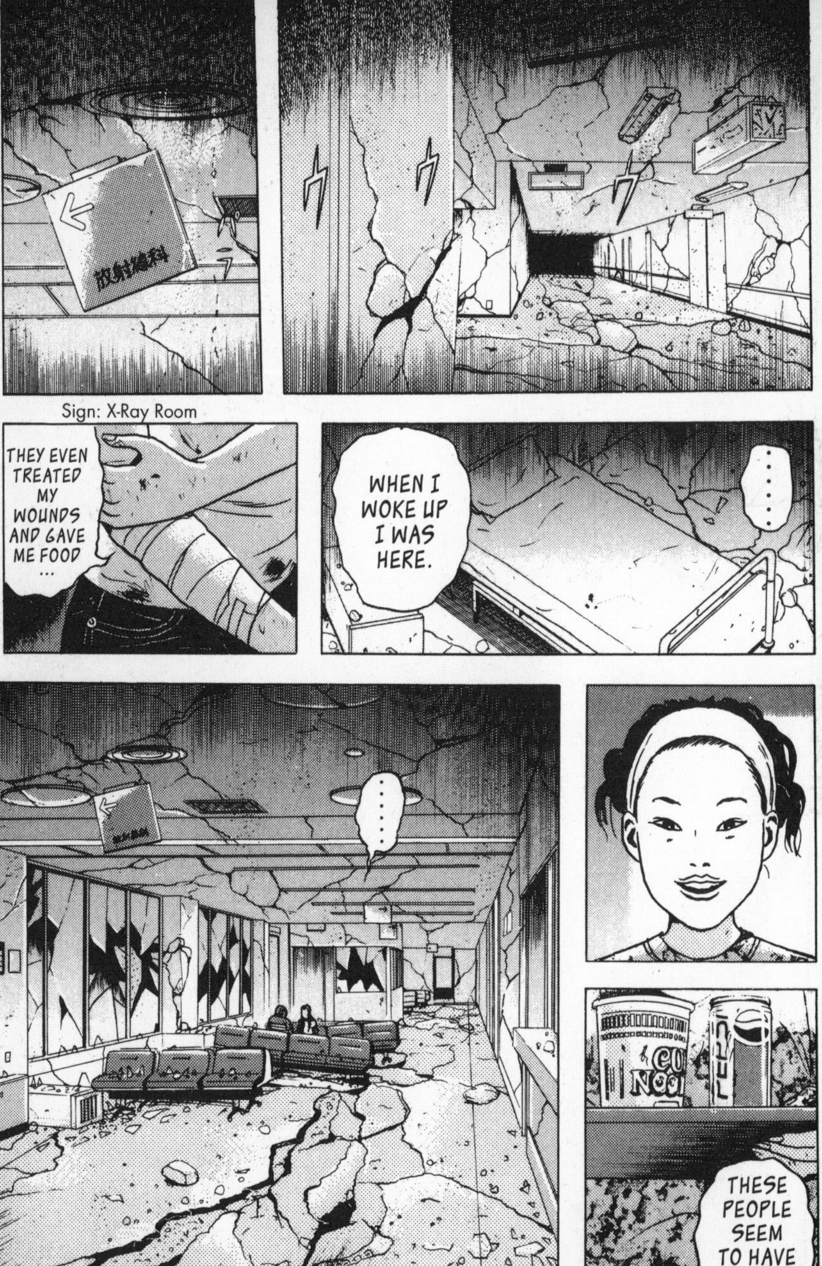
Sign: X-Ray Room
......
WHEN I WOKE UP I WAS HERE.
THEY EVEN TREATED MY WOUNDS AND GAVE ME FOOD ...
THESE PEOPLE SEEM TO HAVE EVERY-THING.
......

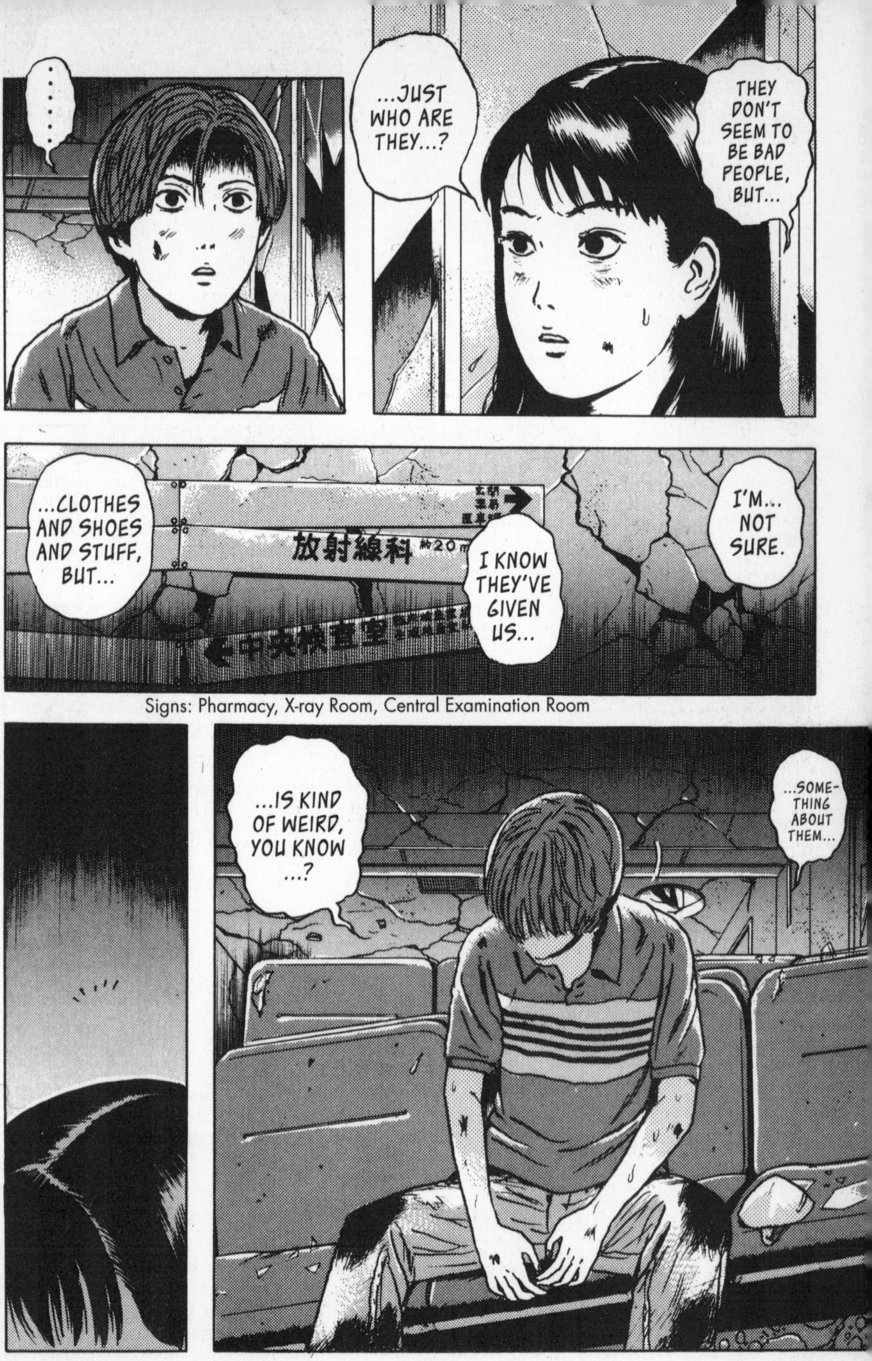
THEY DON'T SEEM TO BE BAD PEOPLE, BUT...
...JUST WHO ARE THEY...?
......
I'M... NOT SURE.
I KNOW THEY'VE GIVEN US...
...CLOTHES AND SHOES AND STUFF, BUT...
放射線科 約20m
中央検査室
...SOMETHING ABOUT THEM...
...IS KIND OF WEIRD, YOU KNOW...?

Signs: Pharmacy, X-ray Room, Central Examination Room

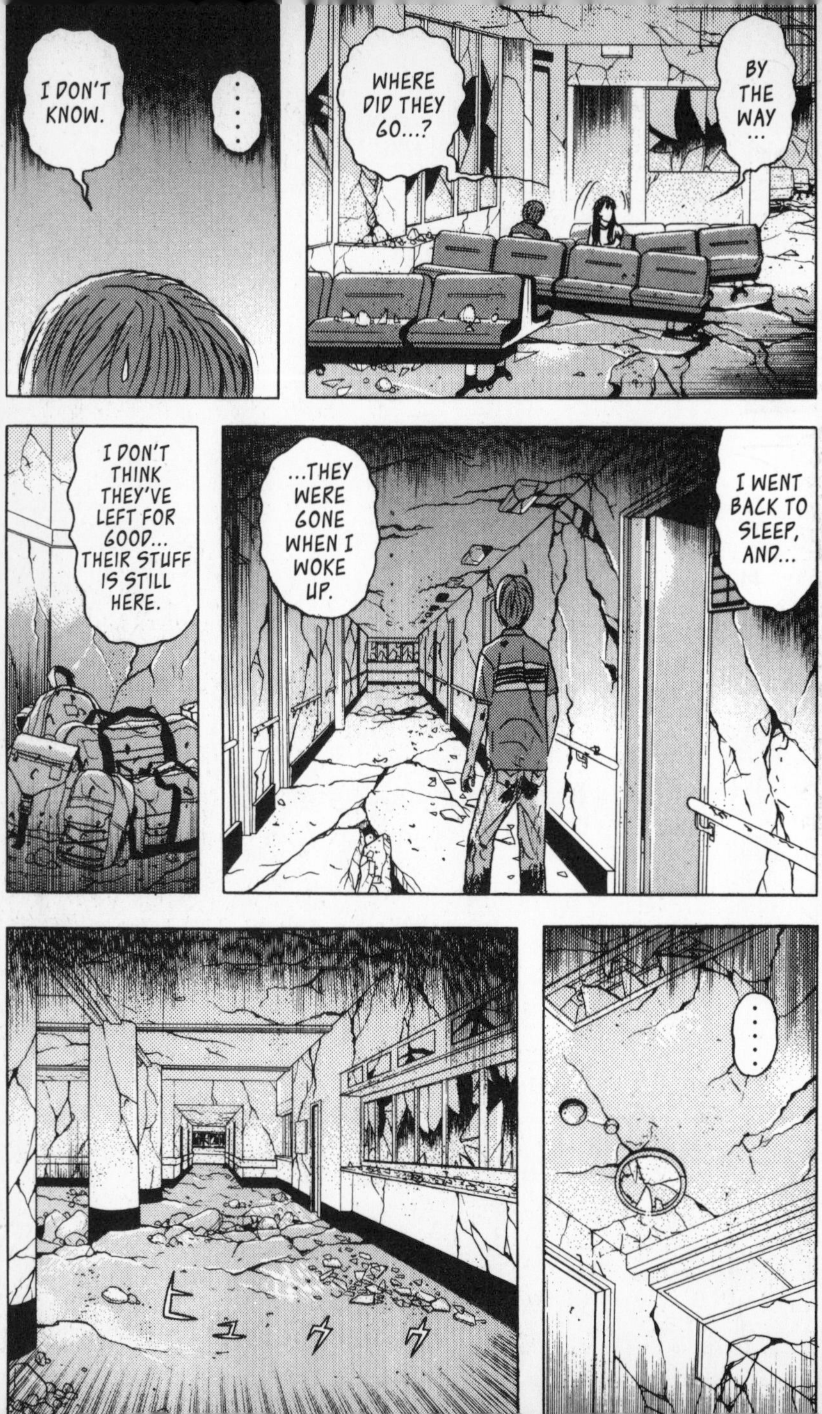
BY THE WAY...
WHERE DID THEY GO...?
.....
I DON'T KNOW.
I WENT BACK TO SLEEP, AND...
...THEY WERE GONE WHEN I WOKE UP.
I DON'T THINK THEY'VE LEFT FOR GOOD... THEIR STUFF IS STILL HERE.
......
ヒュウウ

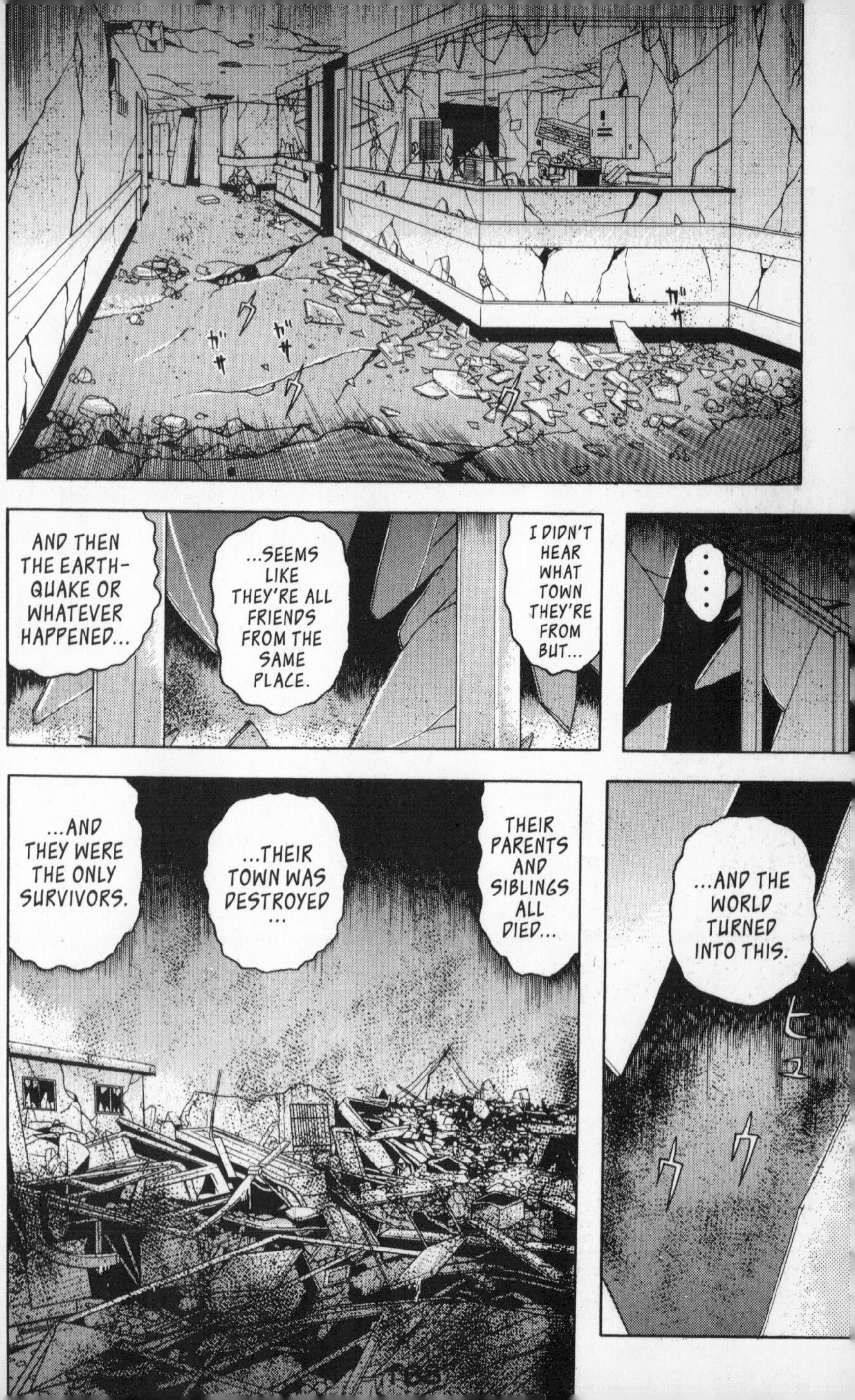

.....
I DIDN'T HEAR WHAT TOWN THEY'RE FROM BUT...
...SEEMS LIKE THEY'RE ALL FRIENDS FROM THE SAME PLACE.
AND THEN THE EARTH-QUAKE OR WHATEVER HAPPENED...
...AND THE WORLD TURNED INTO THIS.
ヒュウ
THEIR PARENTS AND SIBLINGS ALL DIED...
...THEIR TOWN WAS DESTROYED...
...AND THEY WERE THE ONLY SURVIVORS.

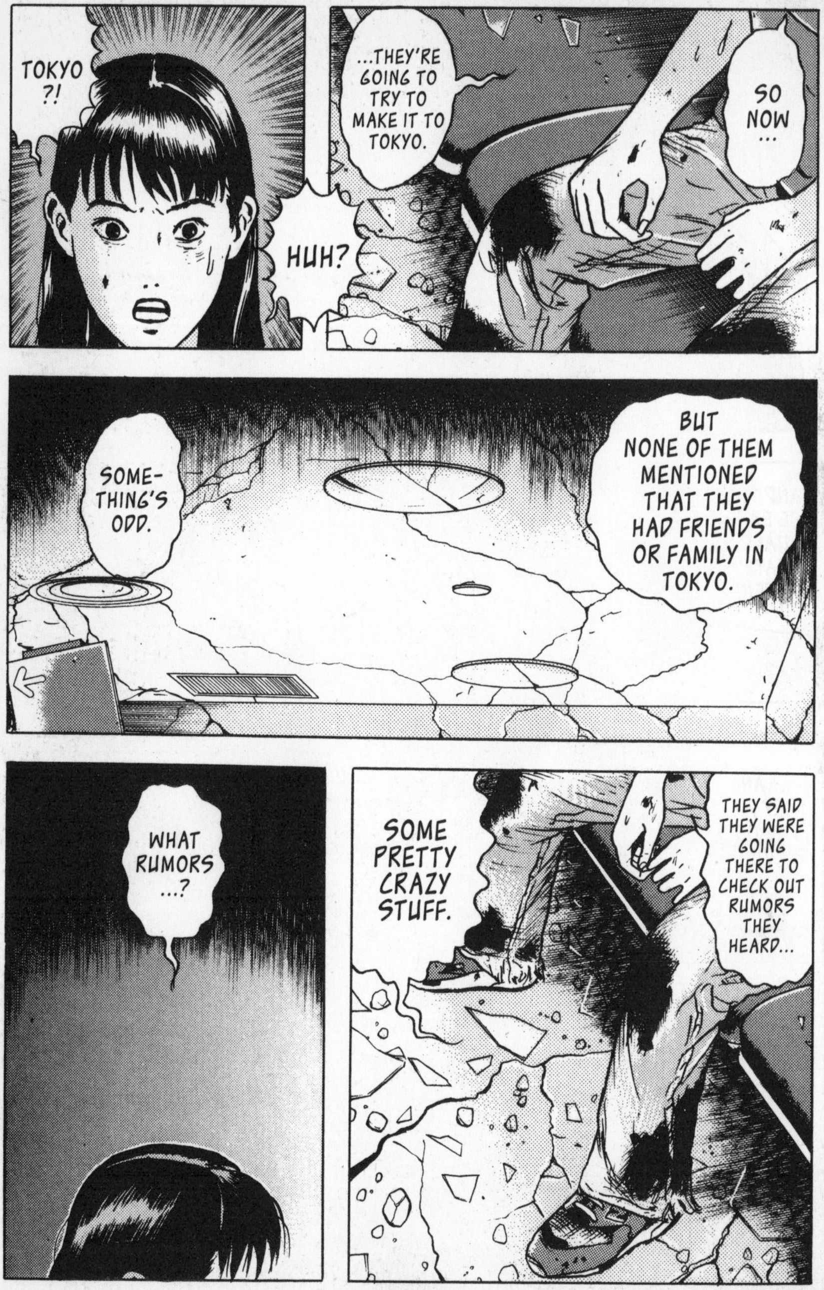
SO NOW ...
...THEY'RE GOING TO TRY TO MAKE IT TO TOKYO.
HUH?
TOKYO ?!
BUT NONE OF THEM MENTIONED THAT THEY HAD FRIENDS OR FAMILY IN TOKYO.
SOME-THING'S ODD.
THEY SAID THEY WERE GOING THERE TO CHECK OUT RUMORS THEY HEARD...
SOME PRETTY CRAZY STUFF.
WHAT RUMORS ...?

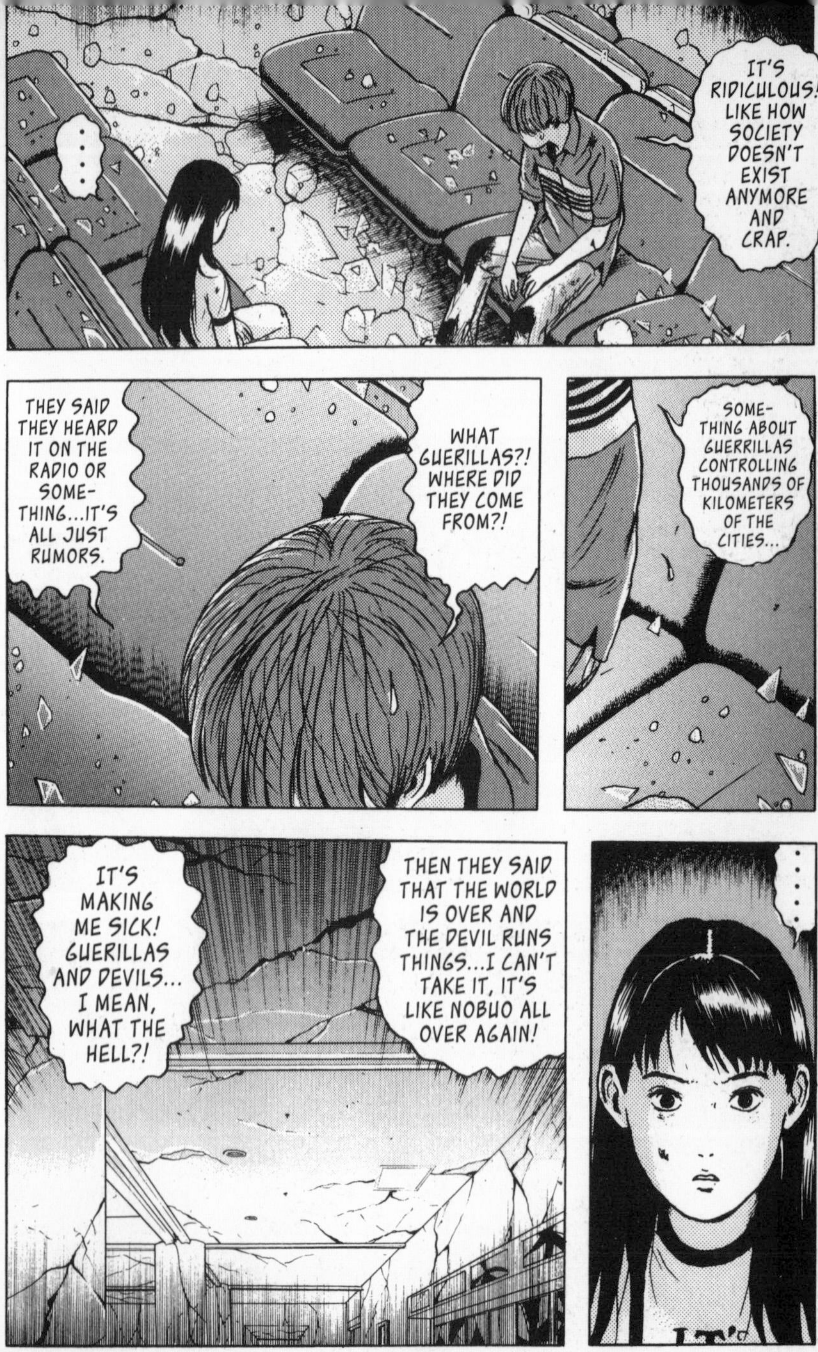
IT'S RIDICULOUS! LIKE HOW SOCIETY DOESN'T EXIST ANYMORE AND CRAP.
.....
SOME-THING ABOUT GUERRILLAS CONTROLLING THOUSANDS OF KILOMETERS OF THE CITIES...
WHAT GUERILLAS?! WHERE DID THEY COME FROM?!
THEY SAID THEY HEARD IT ON THE RADIO OR SOME-THING...IT'S ALL JUST RUMORS.
.....
THEN THEY SAID THAT THE WORLD IS OVER AND THE DEVIL RUNS THINGS...I CAN'T TAKE IT, IT'S LIKE NOBUO ALL OVER AGAIN!
IT'S MAKING ME SICK! GUERILLAS AND DEVILS... I MEAN, WHAT THE HELL?!

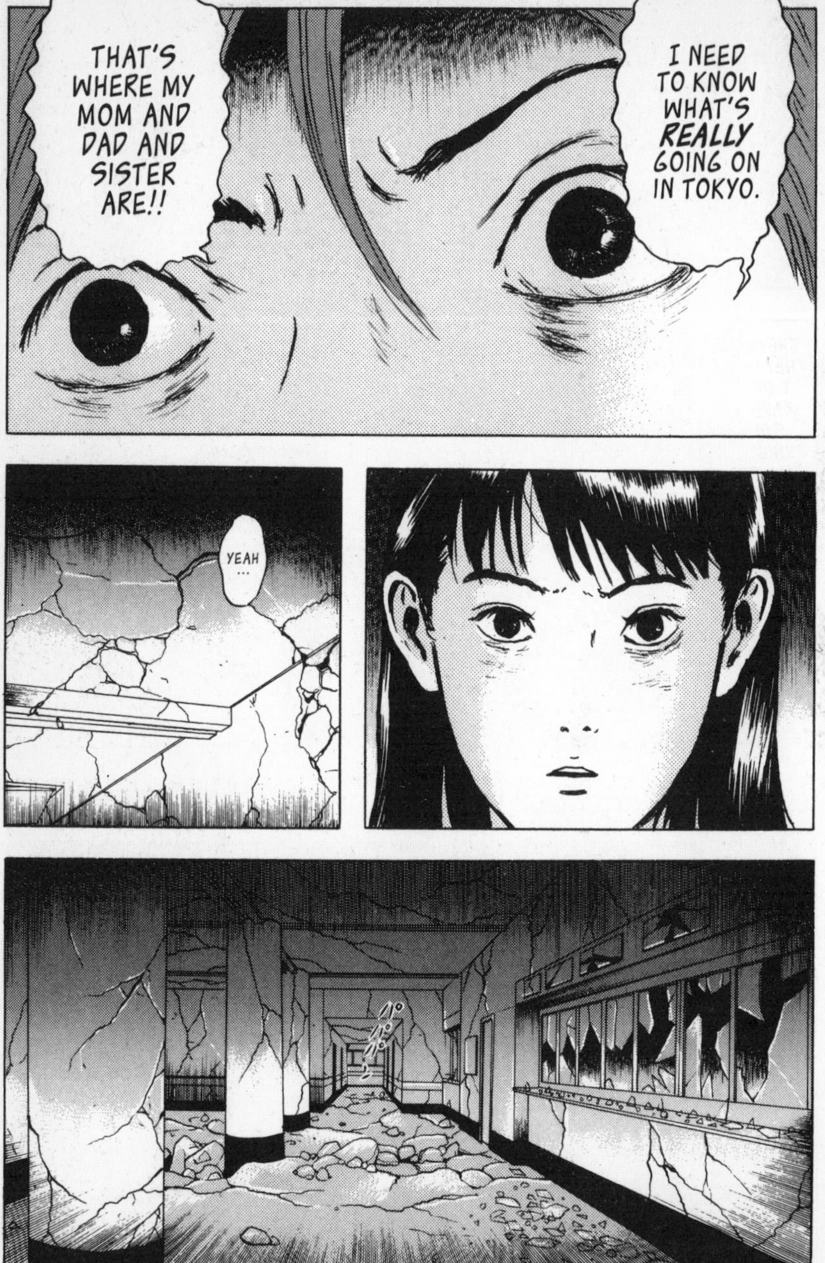
I NEED TO KNOW WHAT'S REALLY GOING ON IN TOKYO.
THAT'S WHERE MY MOM AND DAD AND SISTER ARE!!
YEAH ...

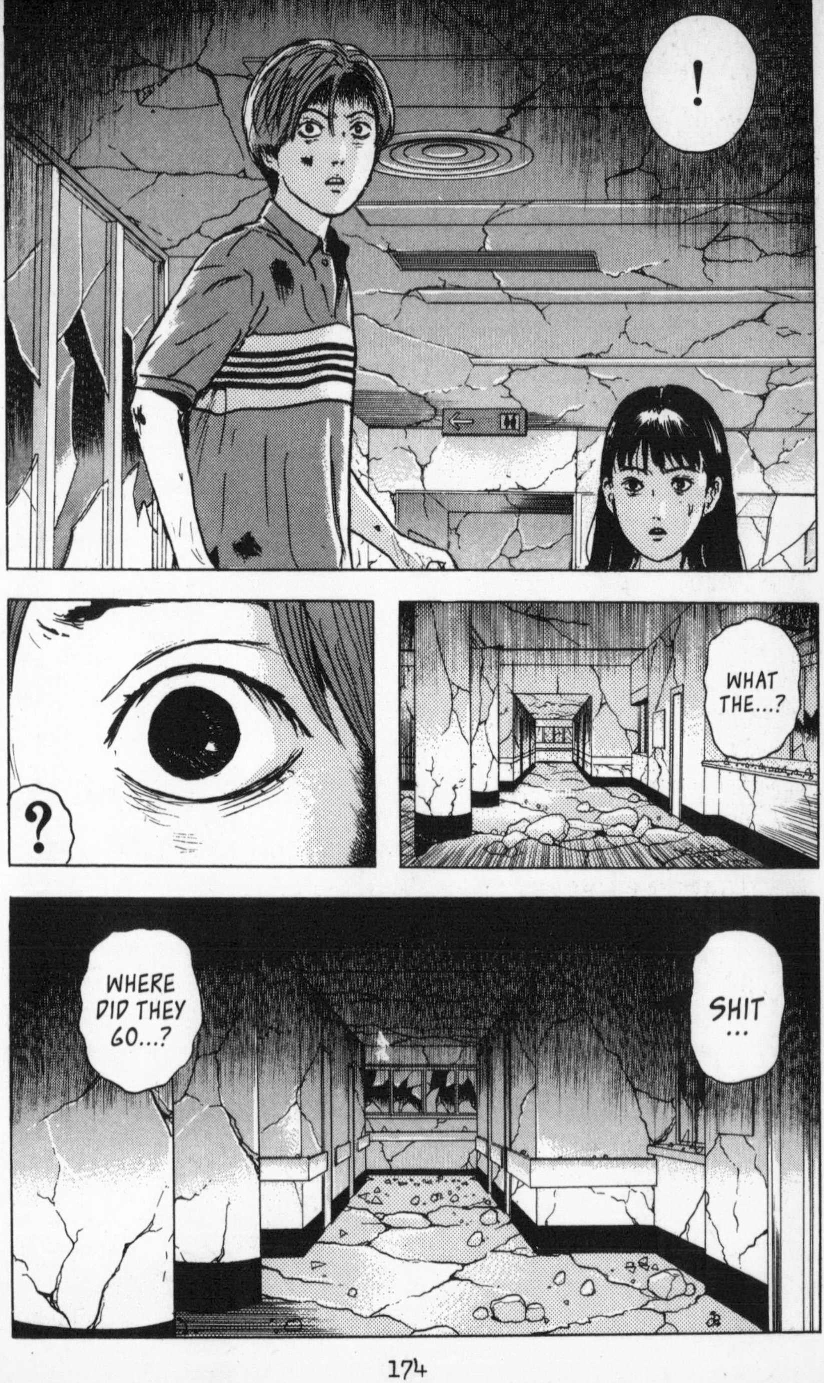
!
WHAT THE...?
?
SHIT ...
WHERE DID THEY GO...?

I HEARD SOMETHING THIS WAY...

THE FLOOR...

YEAH?

TERU-KUN...

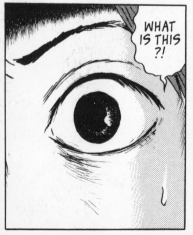

WHAT IS THIS?!

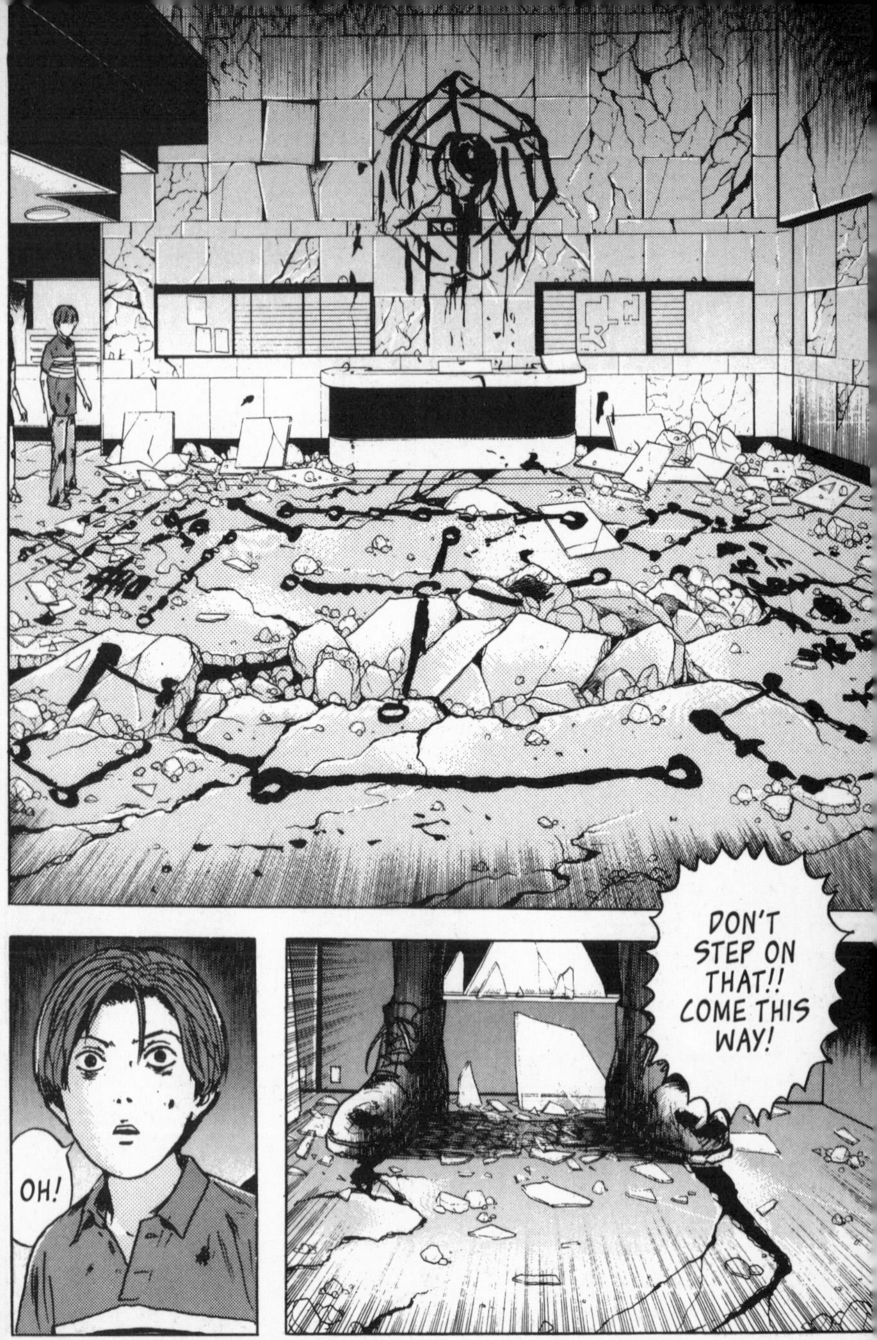
DON'T STEP ON THAT!! COME THIS WAY!
OH!

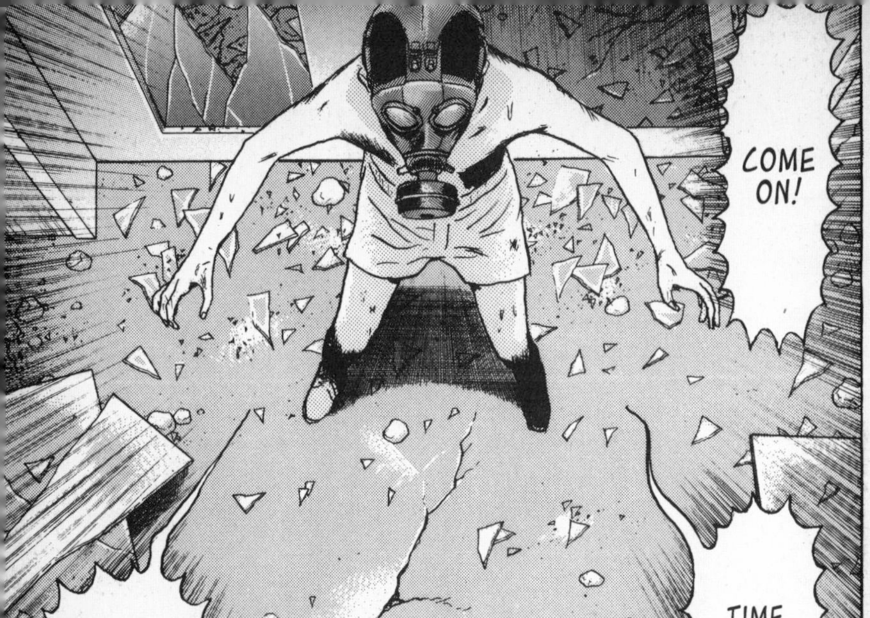
COME ON!
TIME FOR THE ASSEM-BLY!
EVERYONE ASSEMBLE!
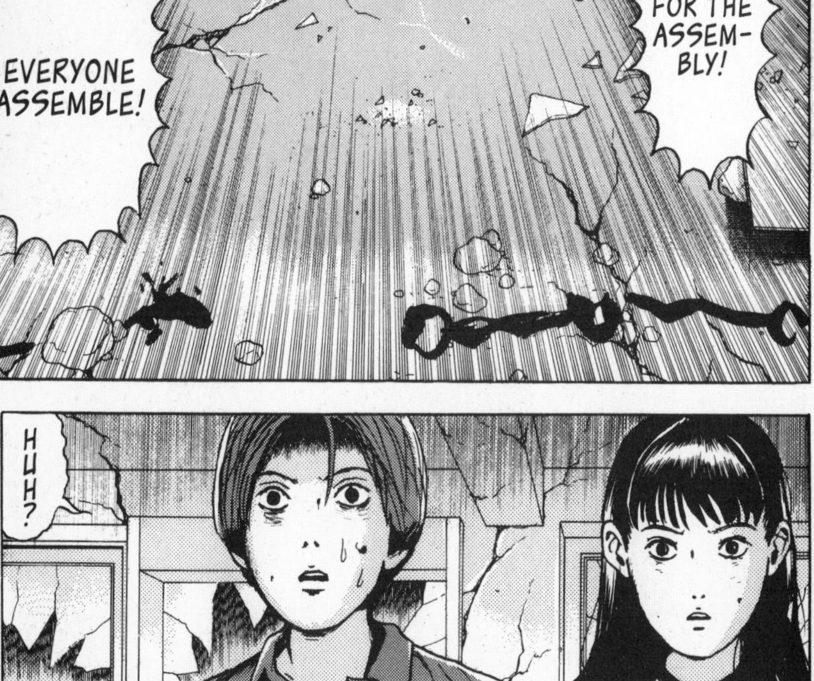
HUH?

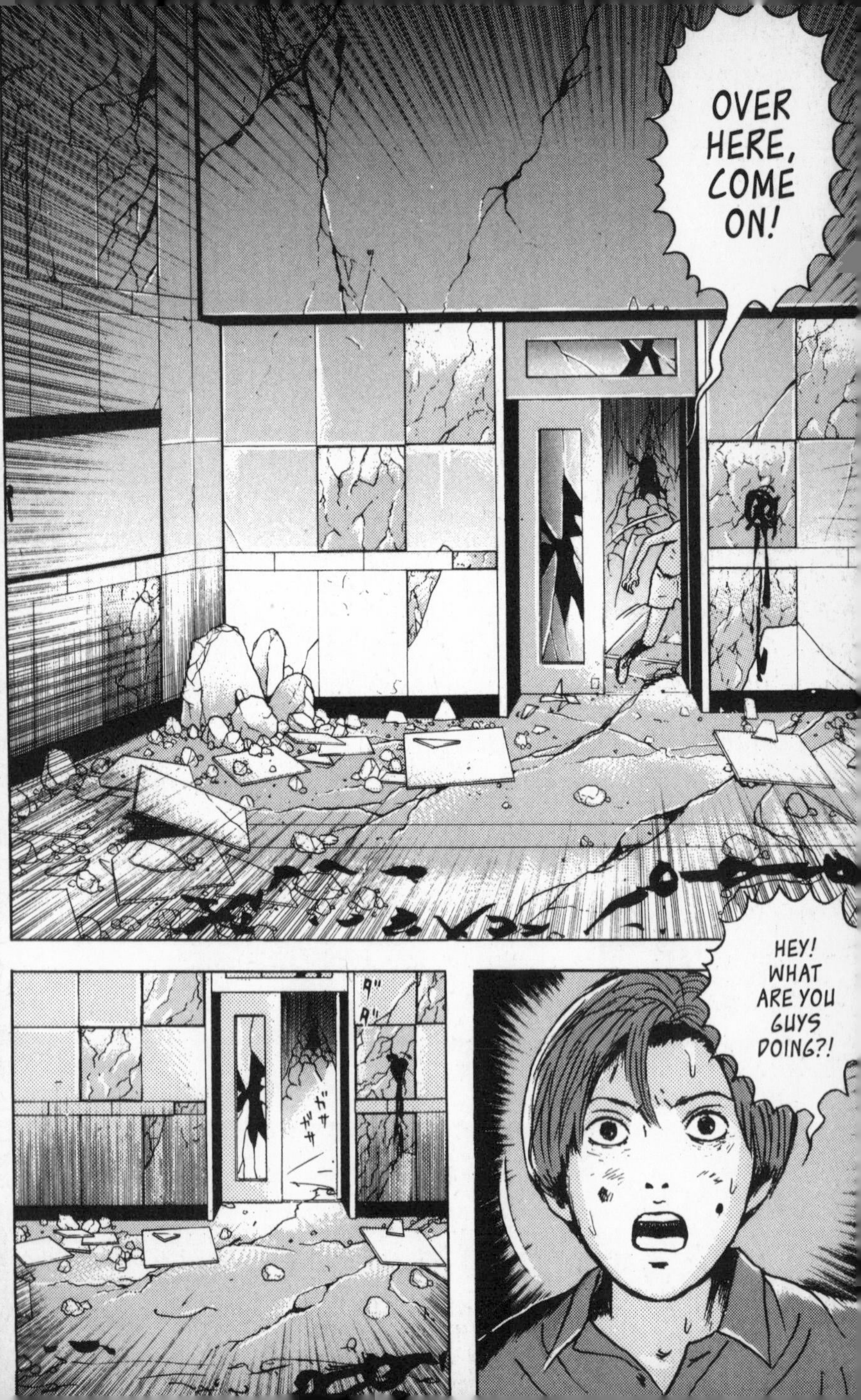
OVER HERE, COME ON!
HEY! WHAT ARE YOU GUYS DOING?!
ガサ ガサ

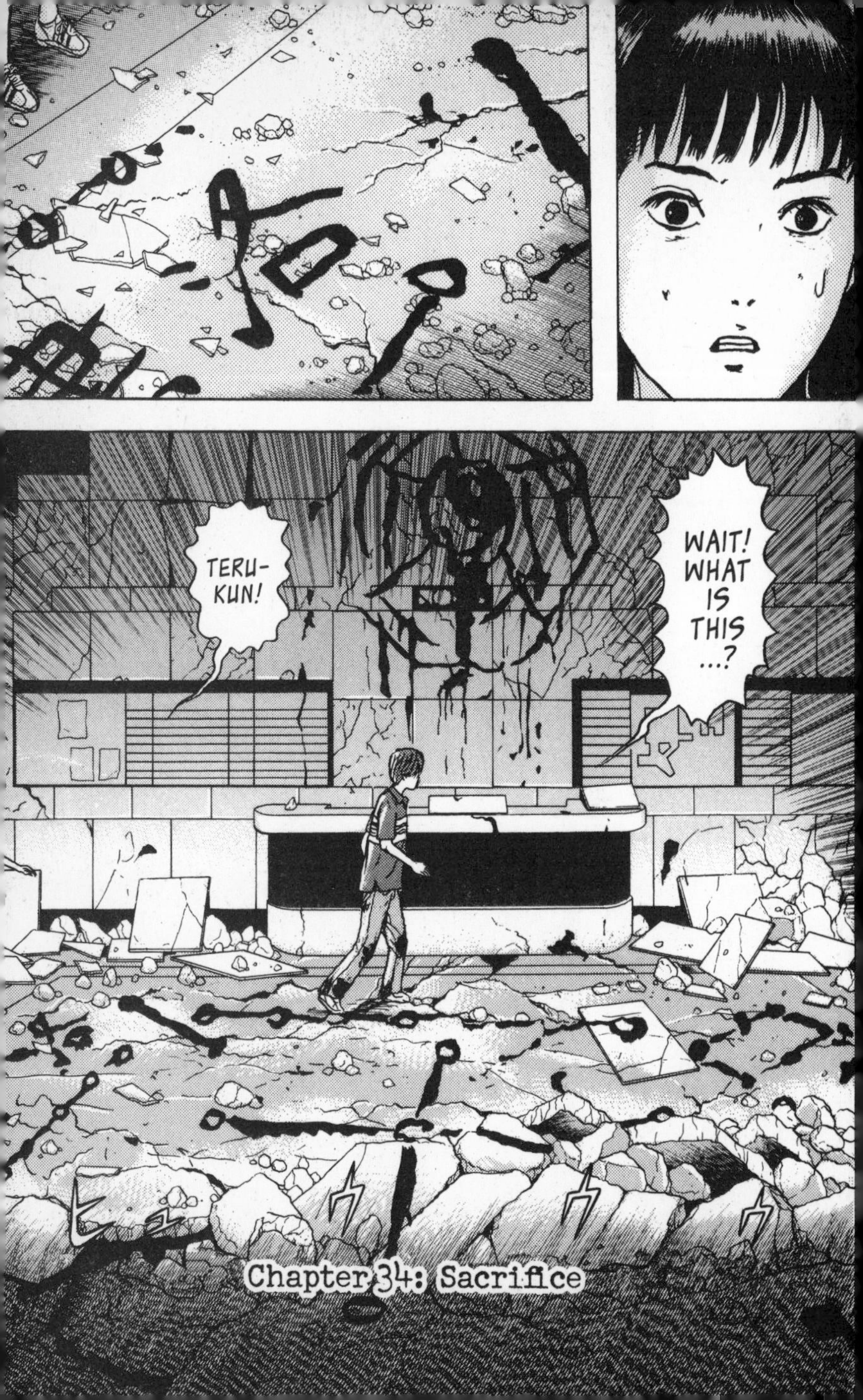
WAIT! WHAT IS THIS ...?
TERU-KUN!
Chapter 34: Sacrifice

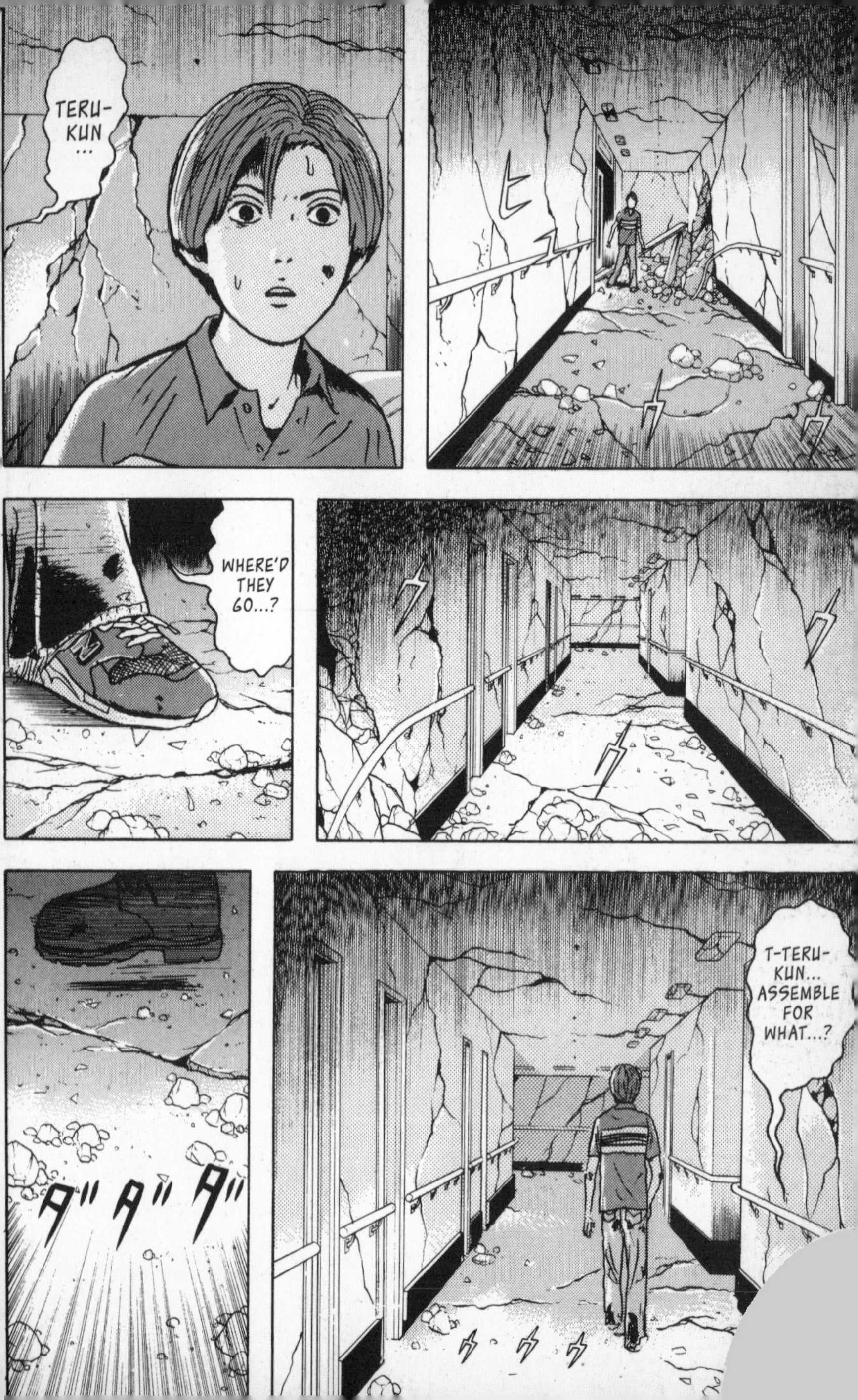
TERU-KUN ...
WHERE'D THEY GO...?
T-TERU-KUN... ASSEMBLE FOR WHAT...?

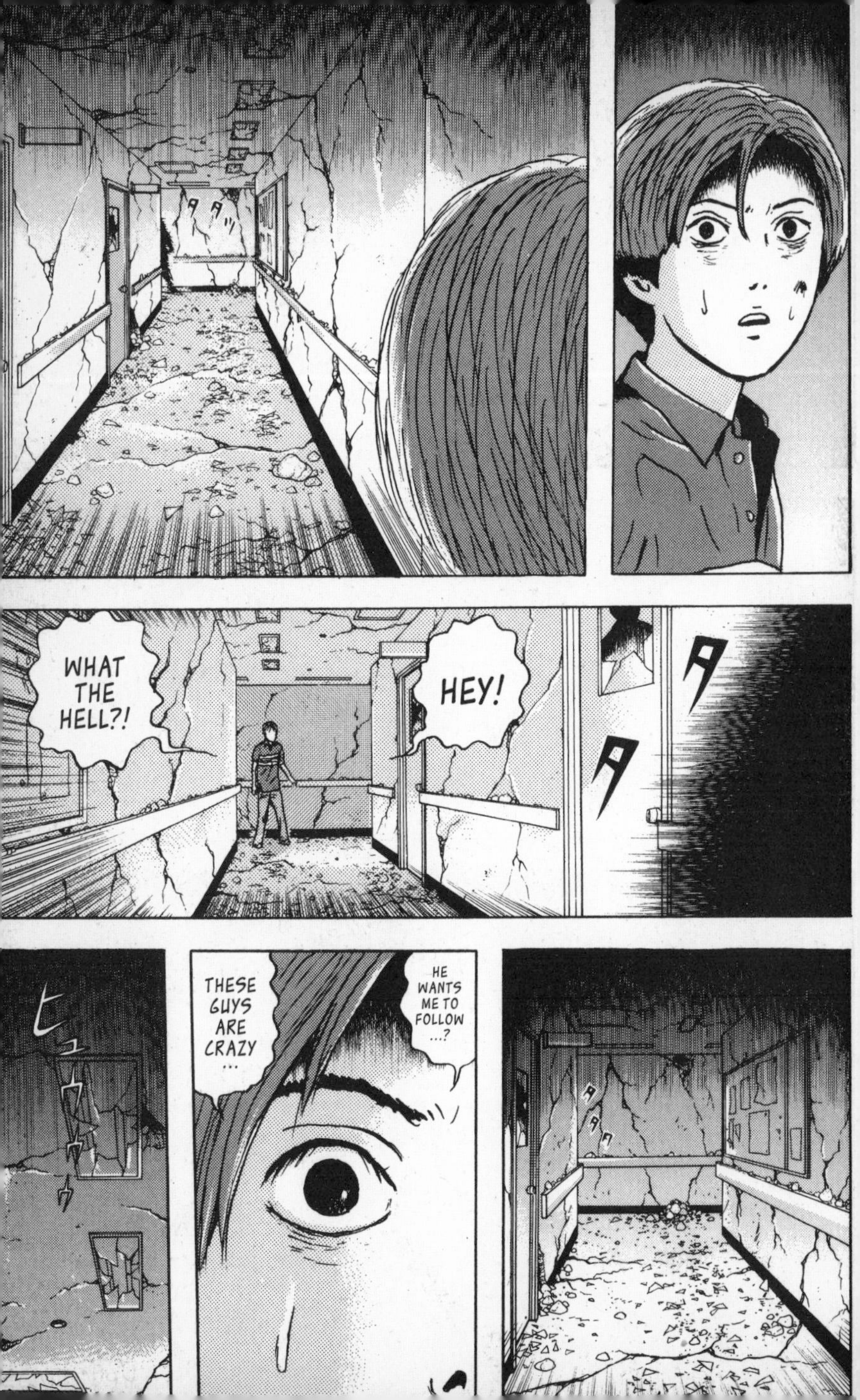
HEY!
WHAT THE HELL?!
HE WANTS ME TO FOLLOW ...?
THESE GUYS ARE CRAZY ...

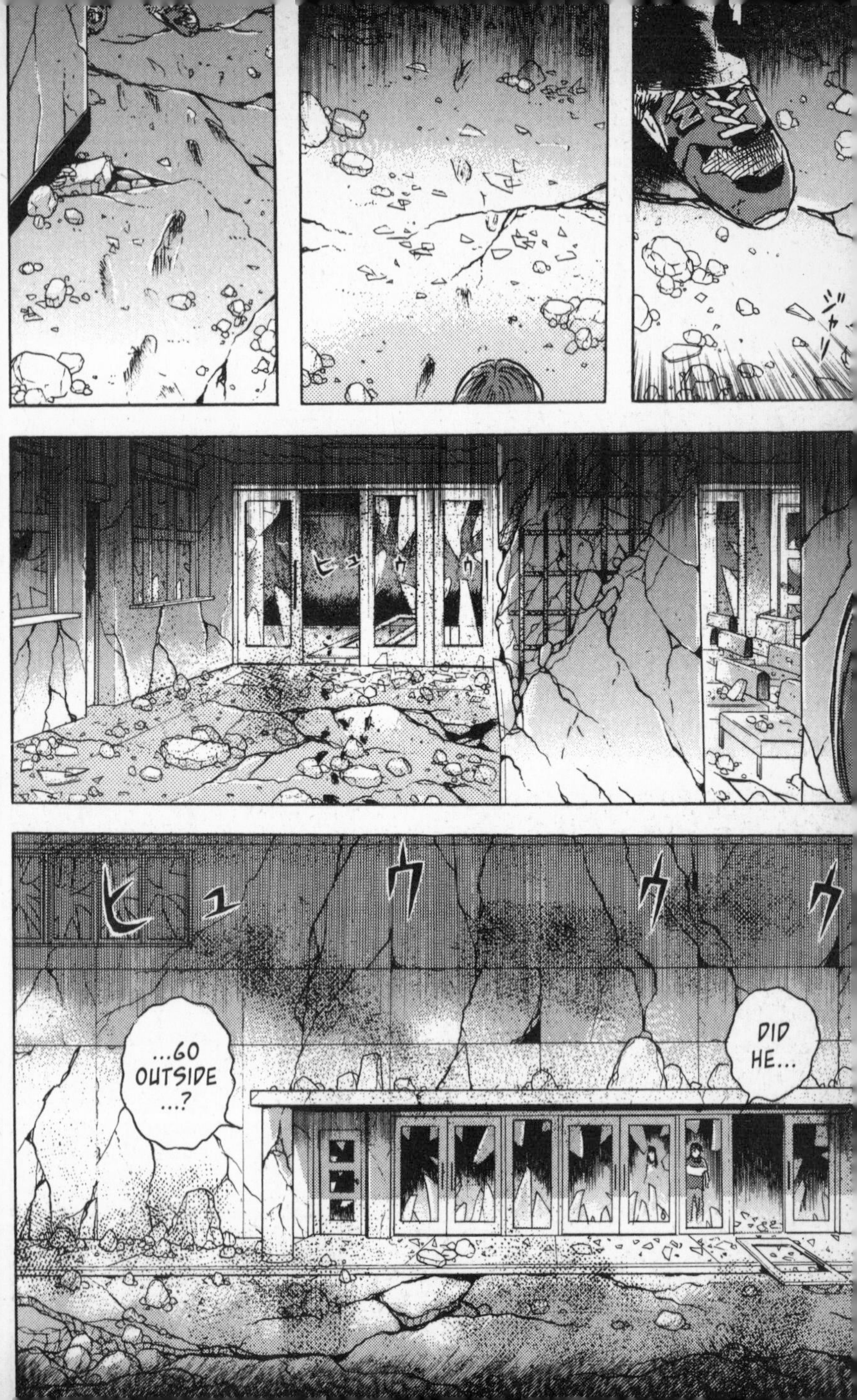
ジャリ
ヒュウウ
ヒュウウウ
DID HE...
...GO OUTSIDE ...?

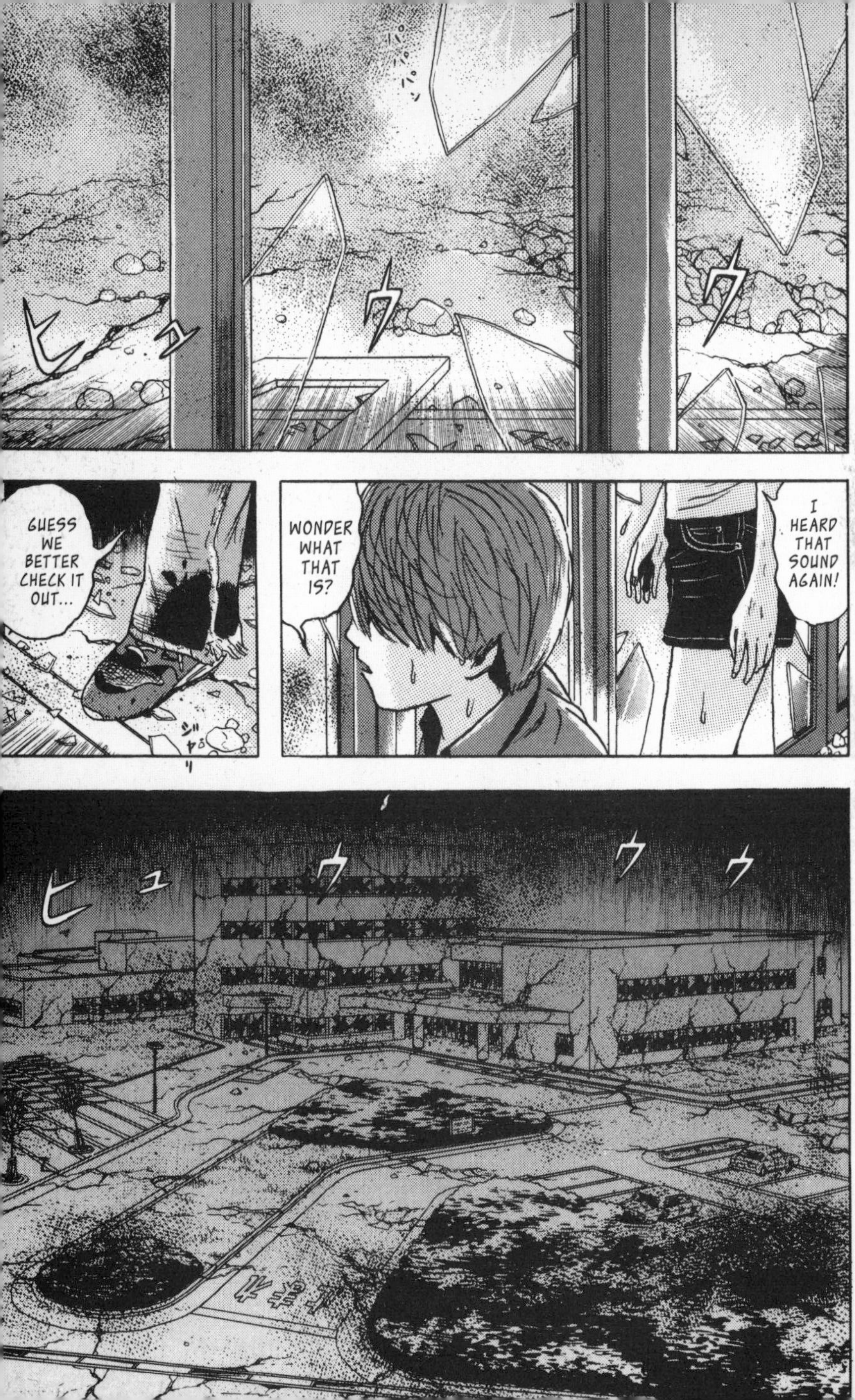
I HEARD THAT SOUND AGAIN!
WONDER WHAT THAT IS?
GUESS WE BETTER CHECK IT OUT...
ヒュウウウ

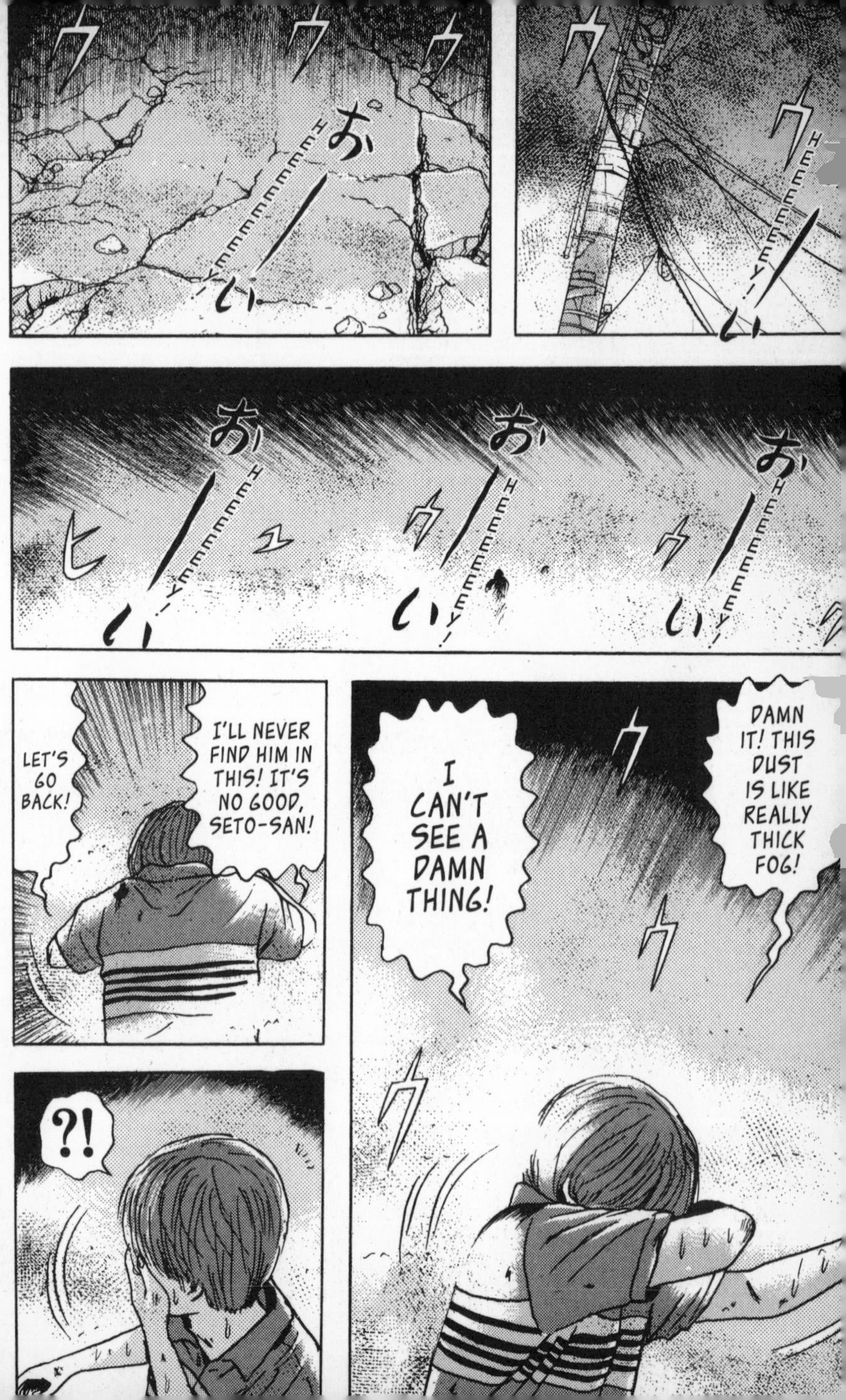
ウ
HEEEEEEY!
い
ウ ウ ウ
お
HEEEEEEEEEEY!
い
お
HEEEEEEEY!
い
ウ
お
HEEEEEEEY!
い
ウ
ヒ
お
HEEEEEEY!
い
DAMN IT! THIS DUST IS LIKE REALLY THICK FOG!
I CAN'T SEE A DAMN THING!
ウ
ウ
ウ
I'LL NEVER FIND HIM IN THIS! IT'S NO GOOD, SETO-SAN!
LET'S GO BACK!
?!

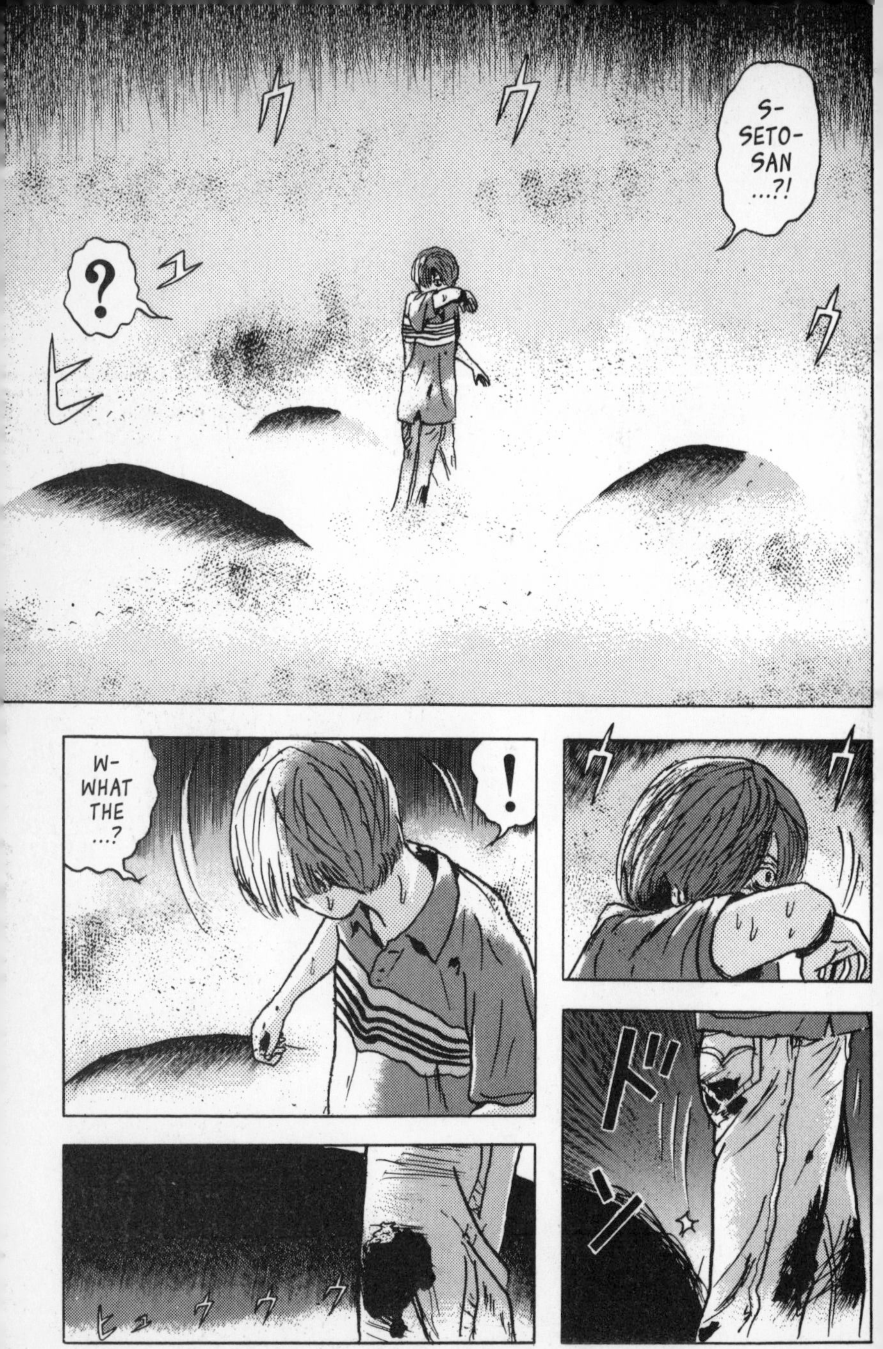

S-SETO-SAN ...?!
ウ
ウ
ウ
?
ヒュ
ウ
ウ
ドン
!
W-WHAT THE ...?
ヒュウウウ

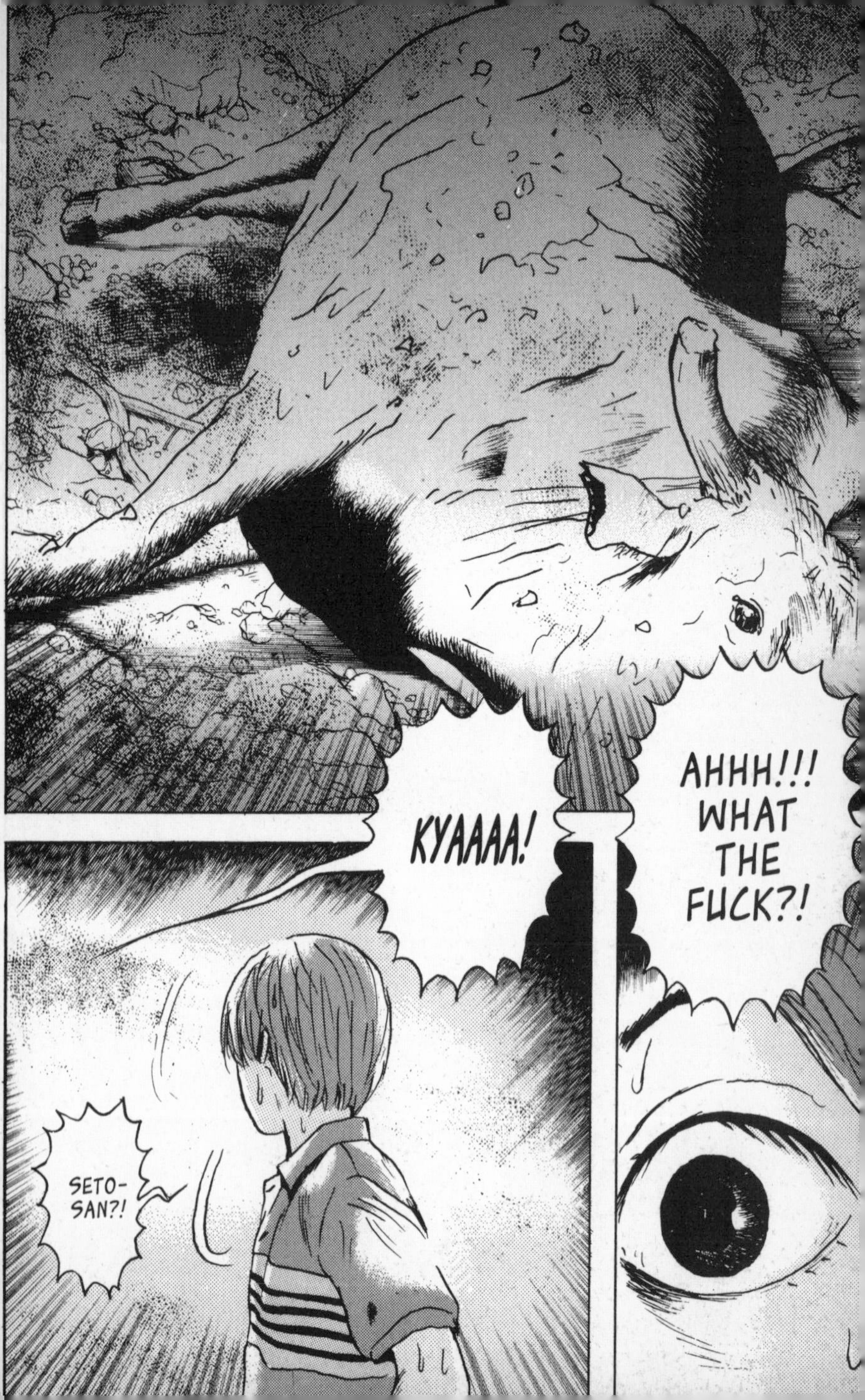
KYAAAA!
AHHH!!! WHAT THE FUCK?!
SETO-SAN?!

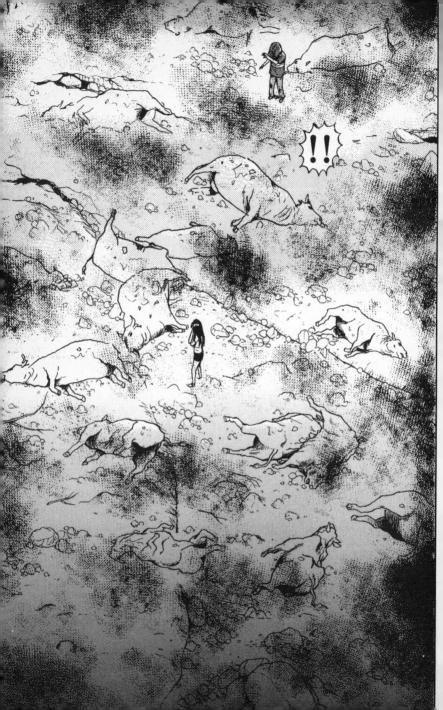

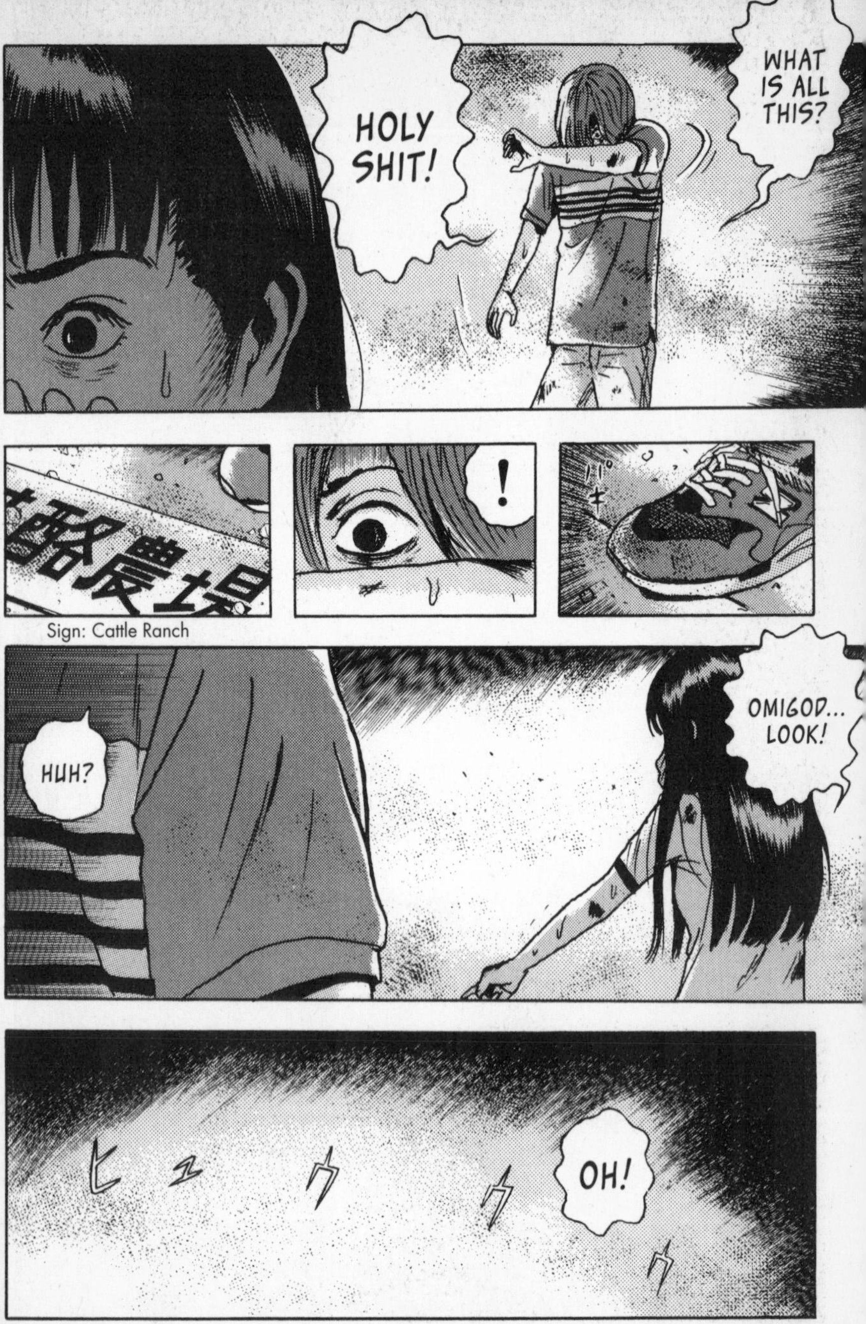
WHAT IS ALL THIS?
HOLY SHIT!
パキ
!
Sign: Cattle Ranch
OMIGOD... LOOK!
HUH?
OH!
ヒュウウウ

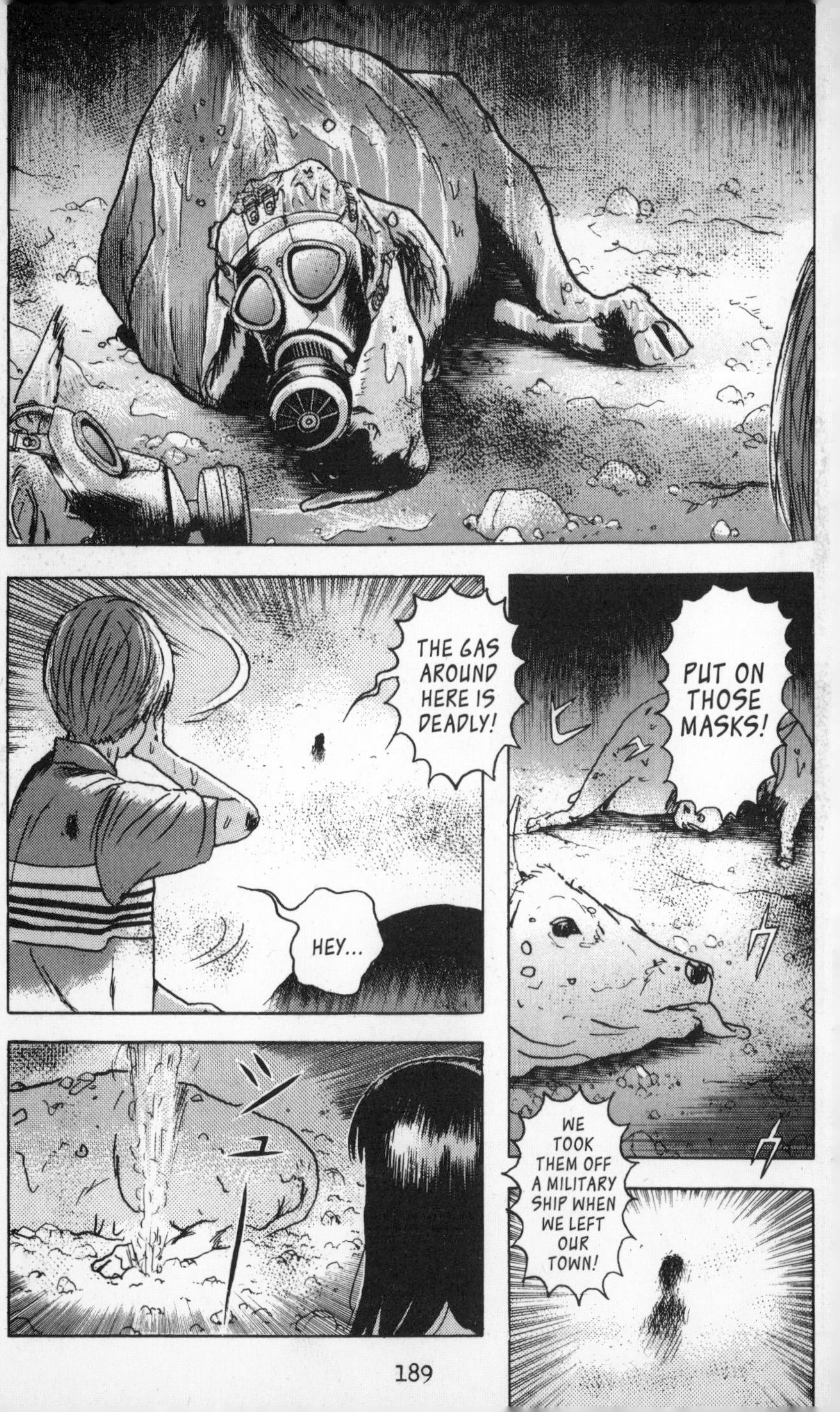
PUT ON THOSE MASKS!
WE TOOK THEM OFF A MILITARY SHIP WHEN WE LEFT OUR TOWN!
THE GAS AROUND HERE IS DEADLY!
HEY...

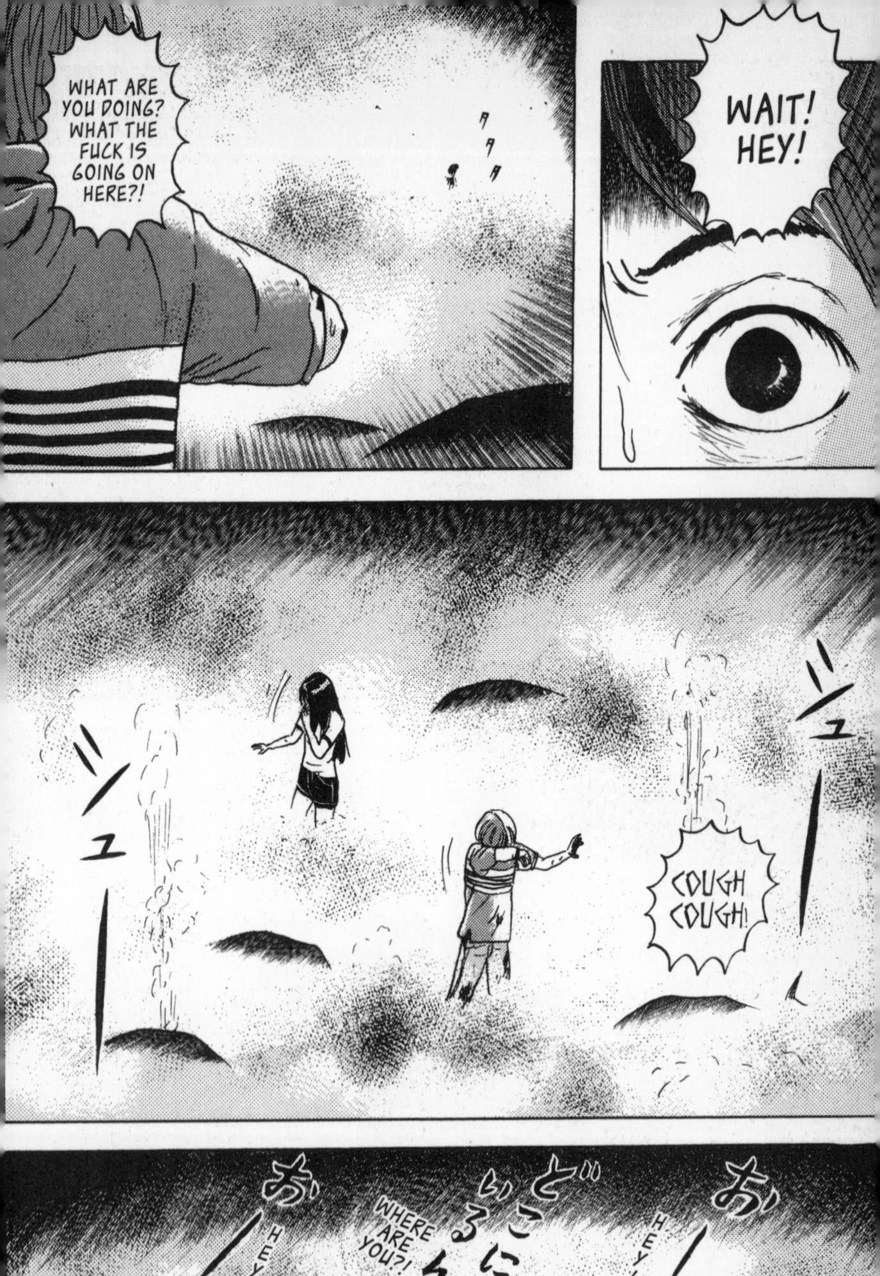
WAIT! HEY!
WHAT ARE YOU DOING? WHAT THE FUCK IS GOING ON HERE?!
ジュー
COUGH COUGH!
ジュー
おーい
HEY!
どこにいるんだ
WHERE ARE YOU?!
おーい
HEYYY!

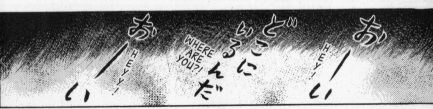

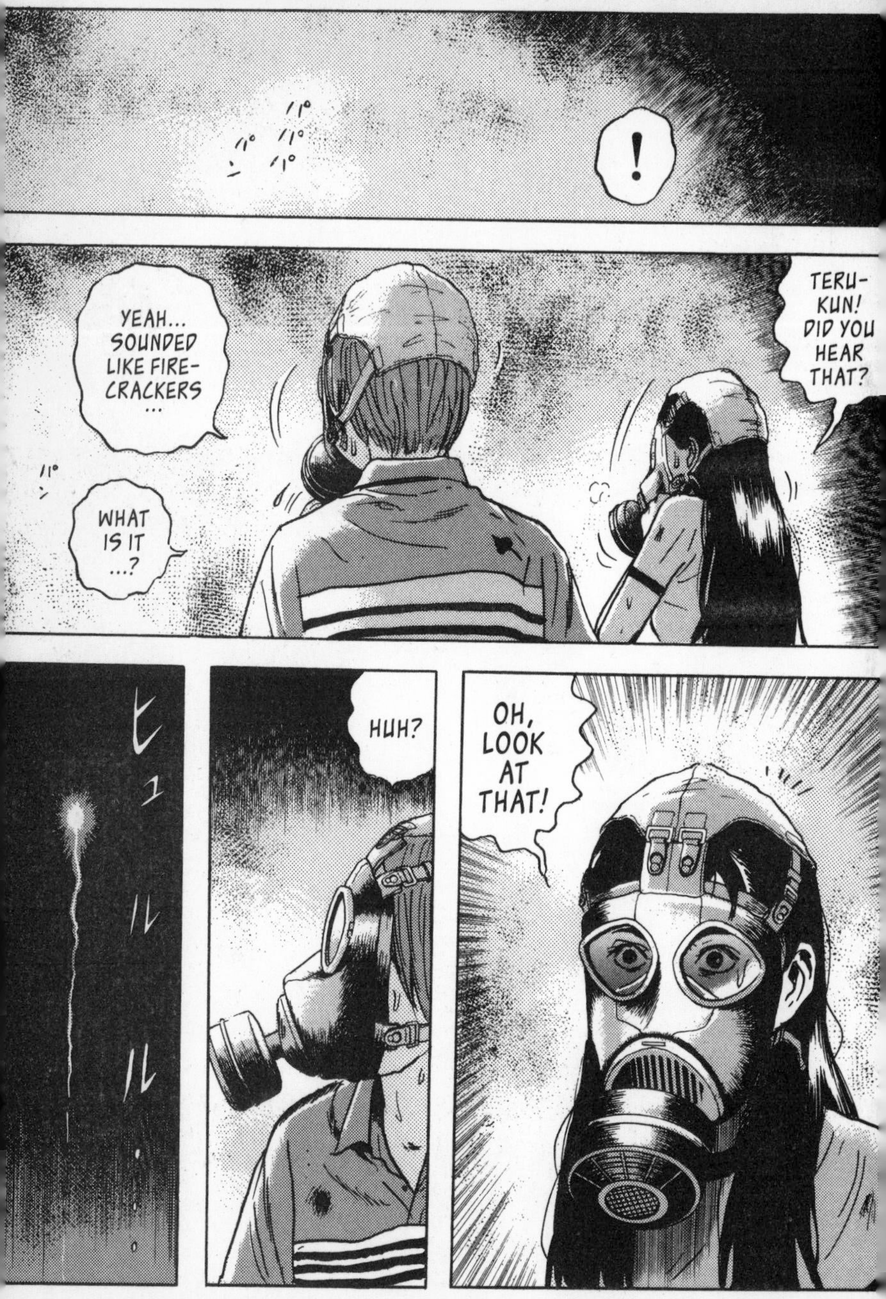
!
TERU-KUN! DID YOU HEAR THAT?
YEAH... SOUNDED LIKE FIRE-CRACKERS ...
WHAT IS IT ...?
OH, LOOK AT THAT!
HUH?
ヒュルル…

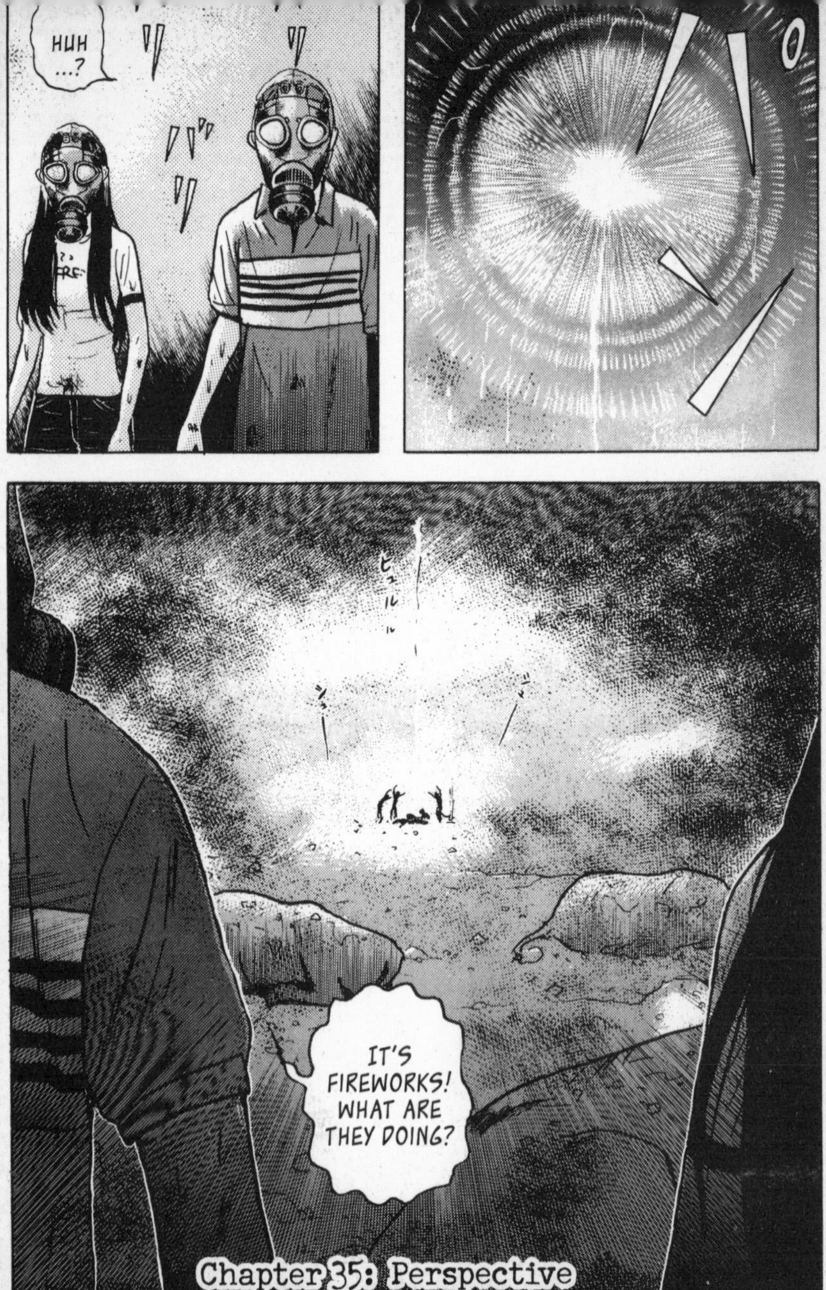
HUH ...?
IT'S FIREWORKS! WHAT ARE THEY DOING?
Chapter 35: Perspective

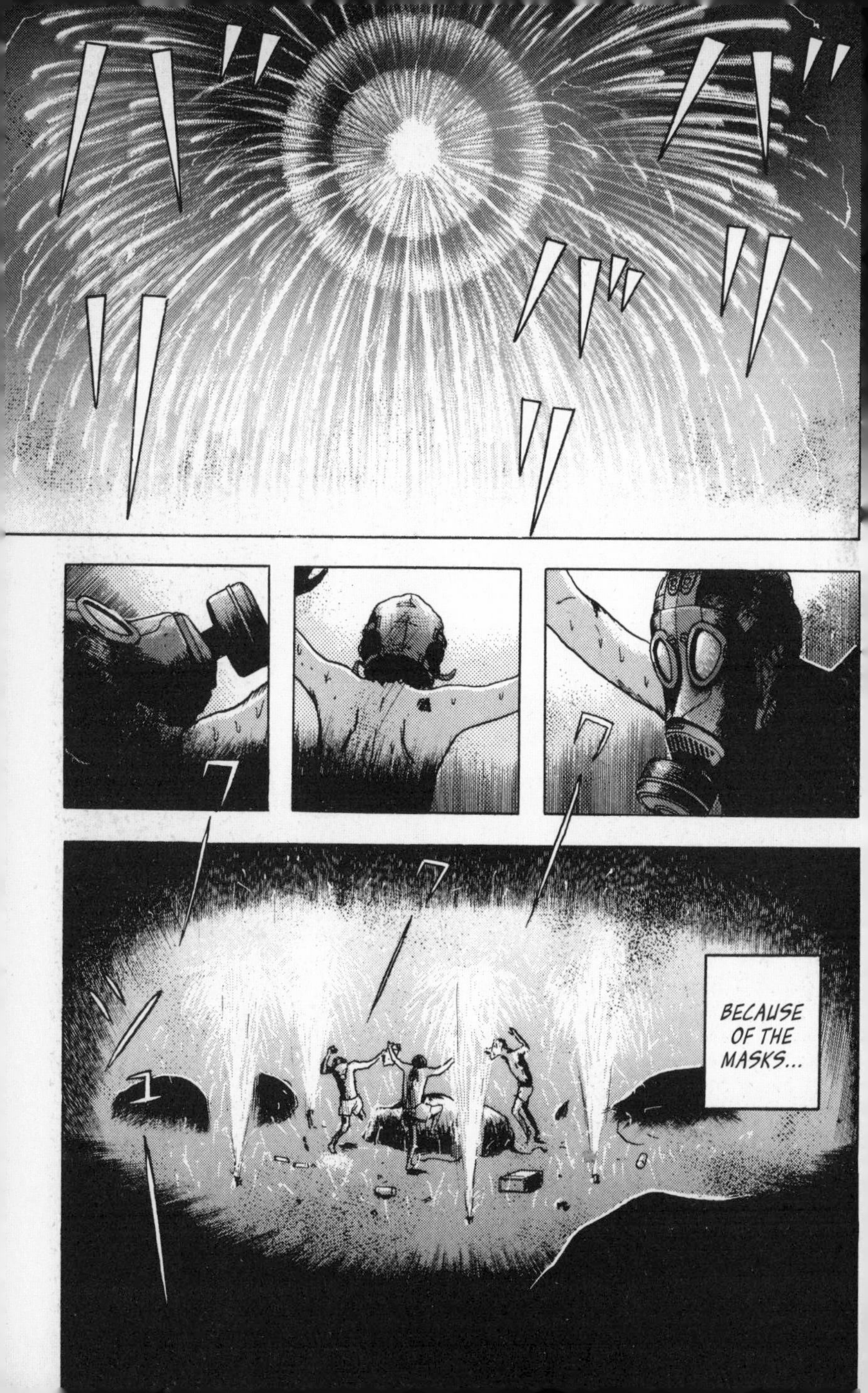
BECAUSE OF THE MASKS...

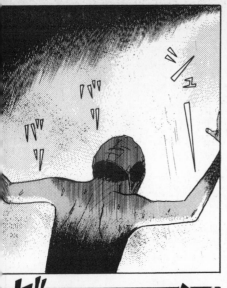

...I COULDN'T EVEN TELL WHO WAS WHO...

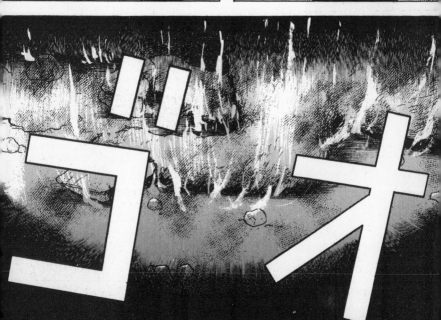

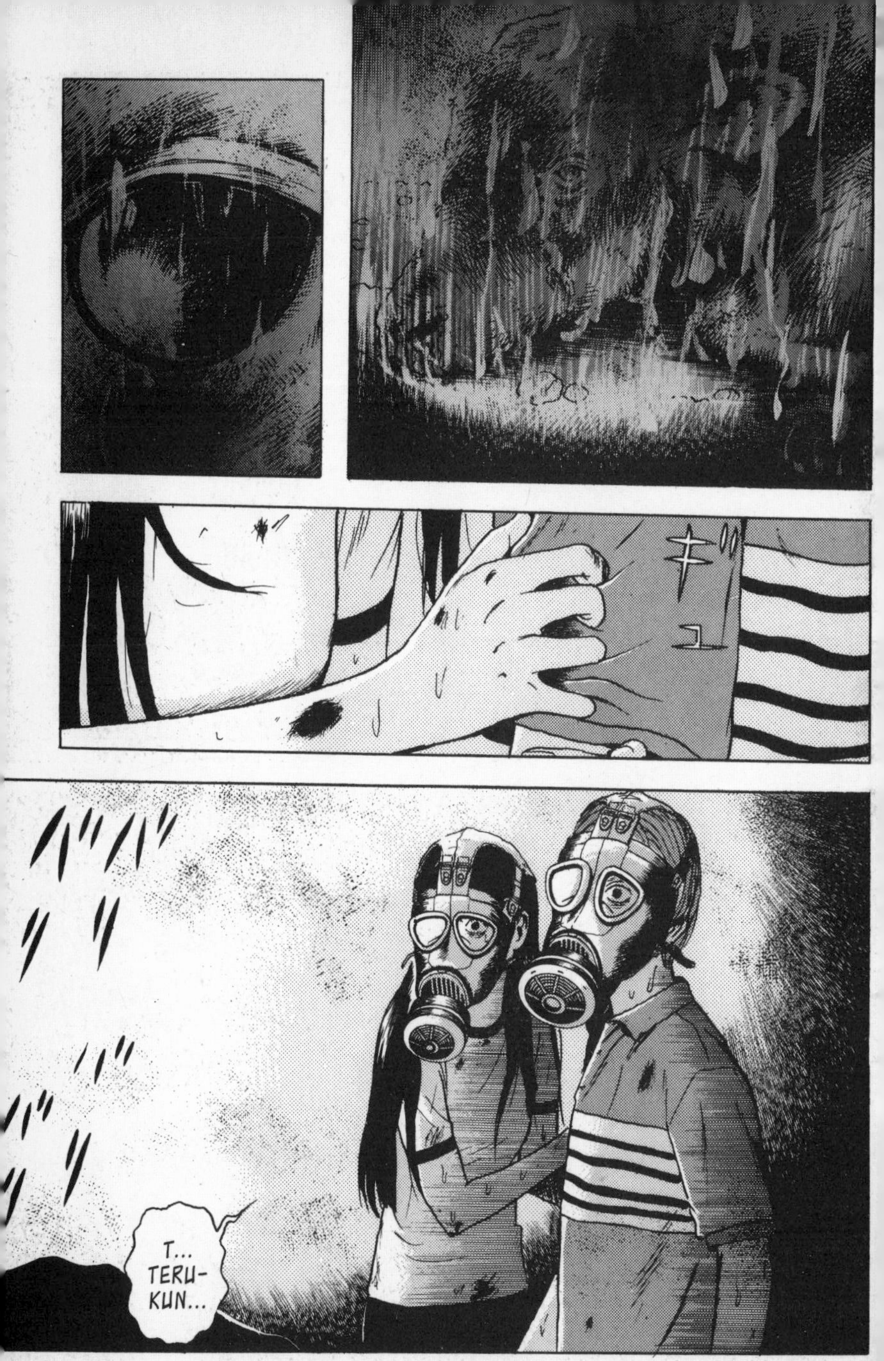
T... TERU-KUN...

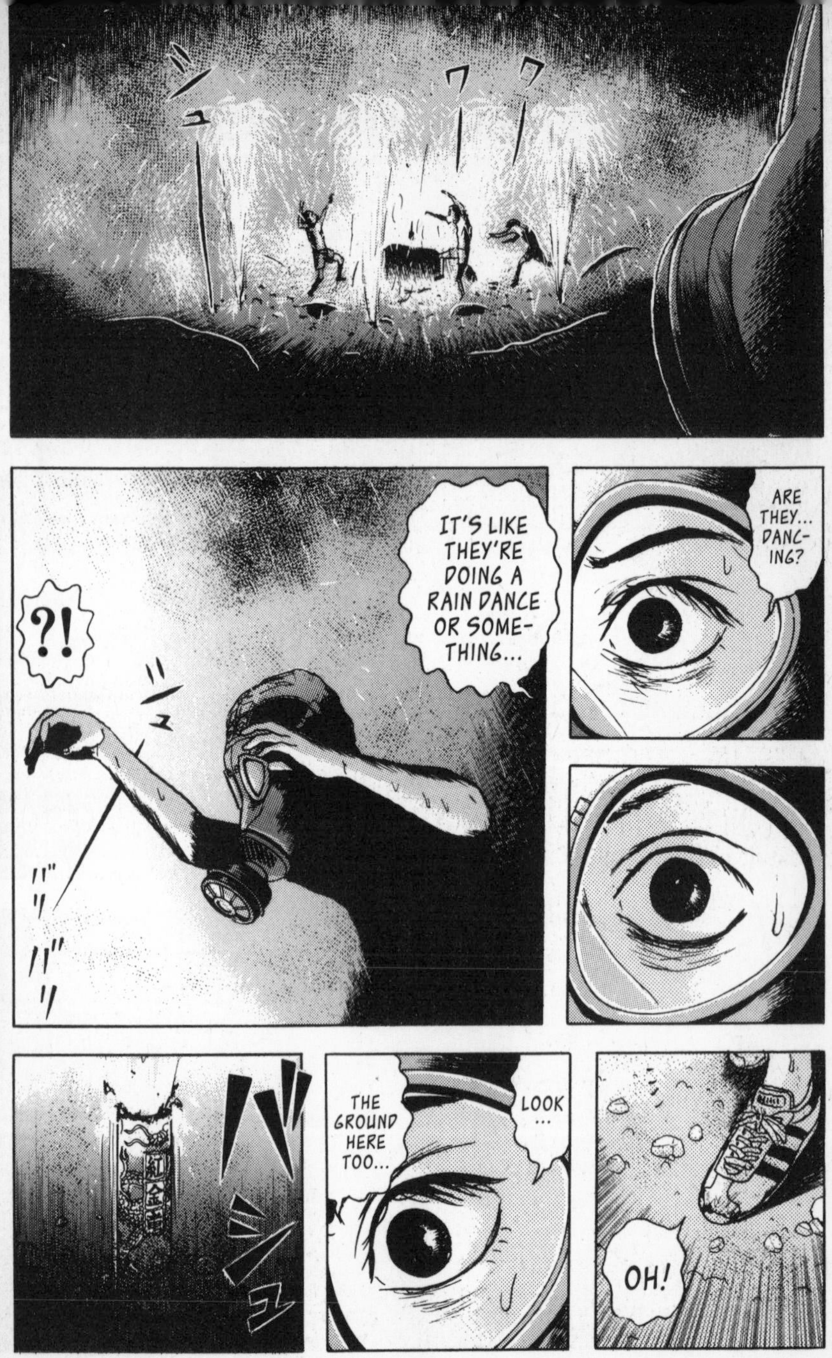
ARE THEY... DANCING?
IT'S LIKE THEY'RE DOING A RAIN DANCE OR SOMETHING...
?!
OH!
LOOK...
THE GROUND HERE TOO...

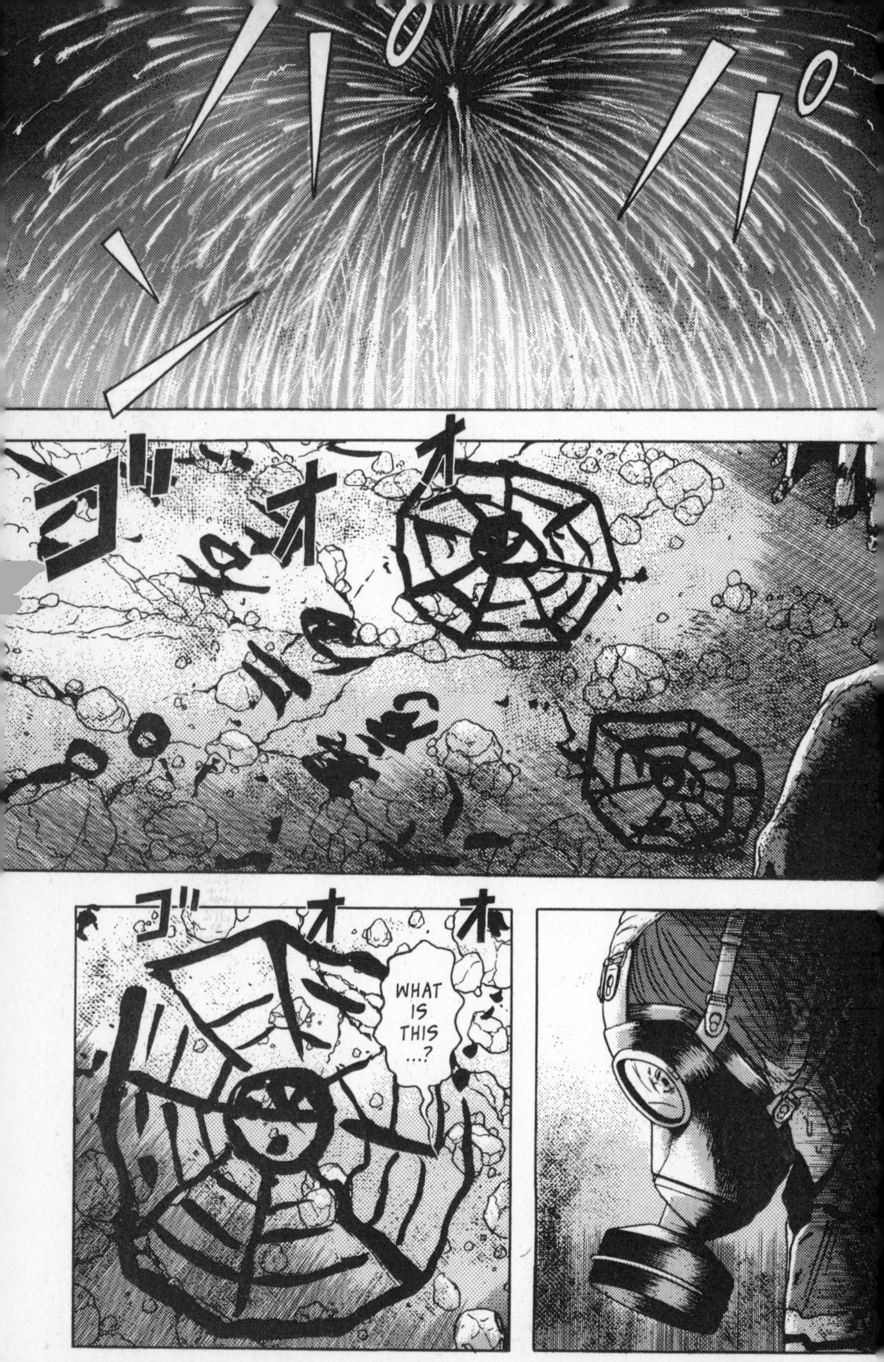
WHAT IS THIS ...?

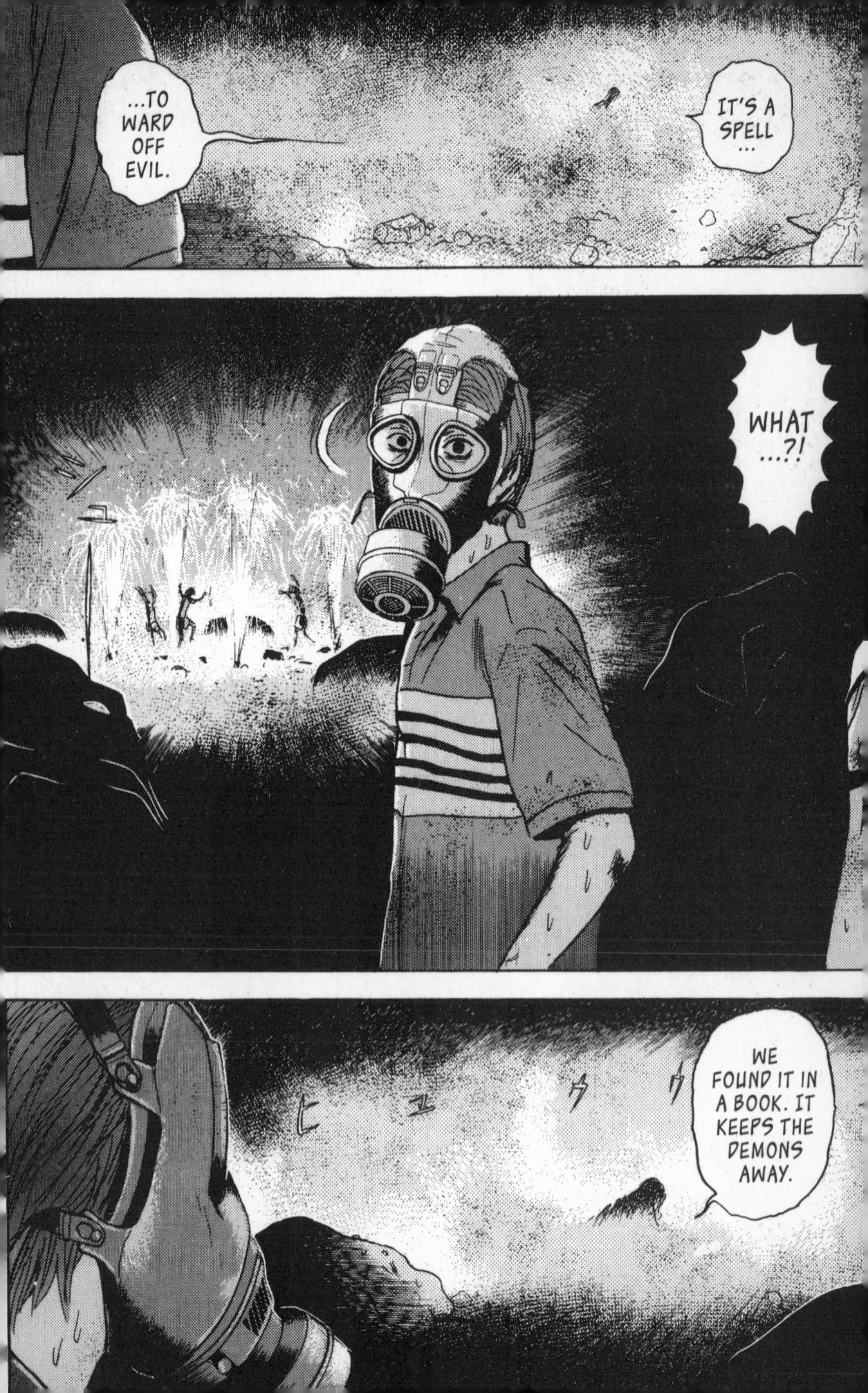
IT'S A SPELL...
...TO WARD OFF EVIL.
WHAT...?!
WE FOUND IT IN A BOOK. IT KEEPS THE DEMONS AWAY.

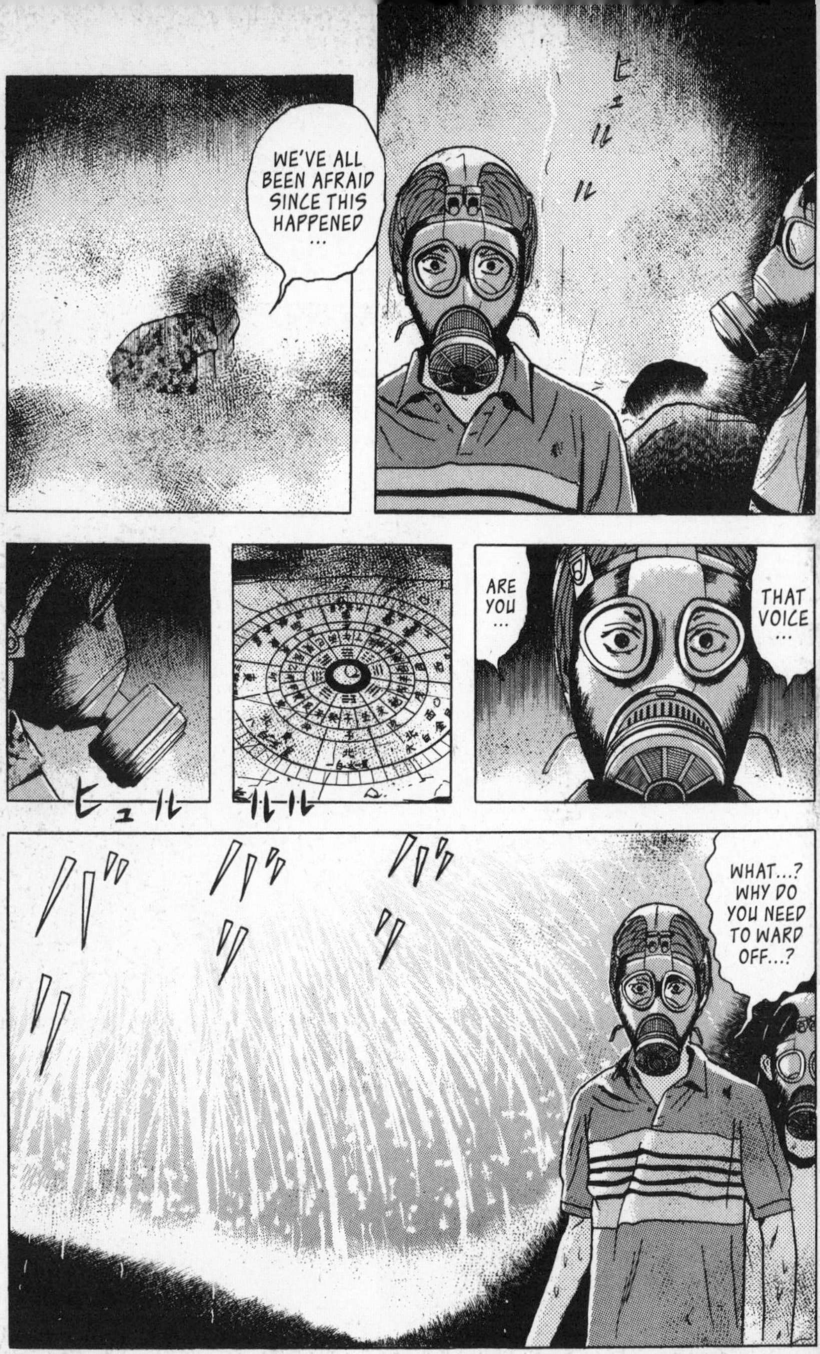
ヒュルル
WE'VE ALL BEEN AFRAID SINCE THIS HAPPENED ...
THAT VOICE ...
ARE YOU ...
ルル
ヒュル
WHAT...? WHY DO YOU NEED TO WARD OFF...?

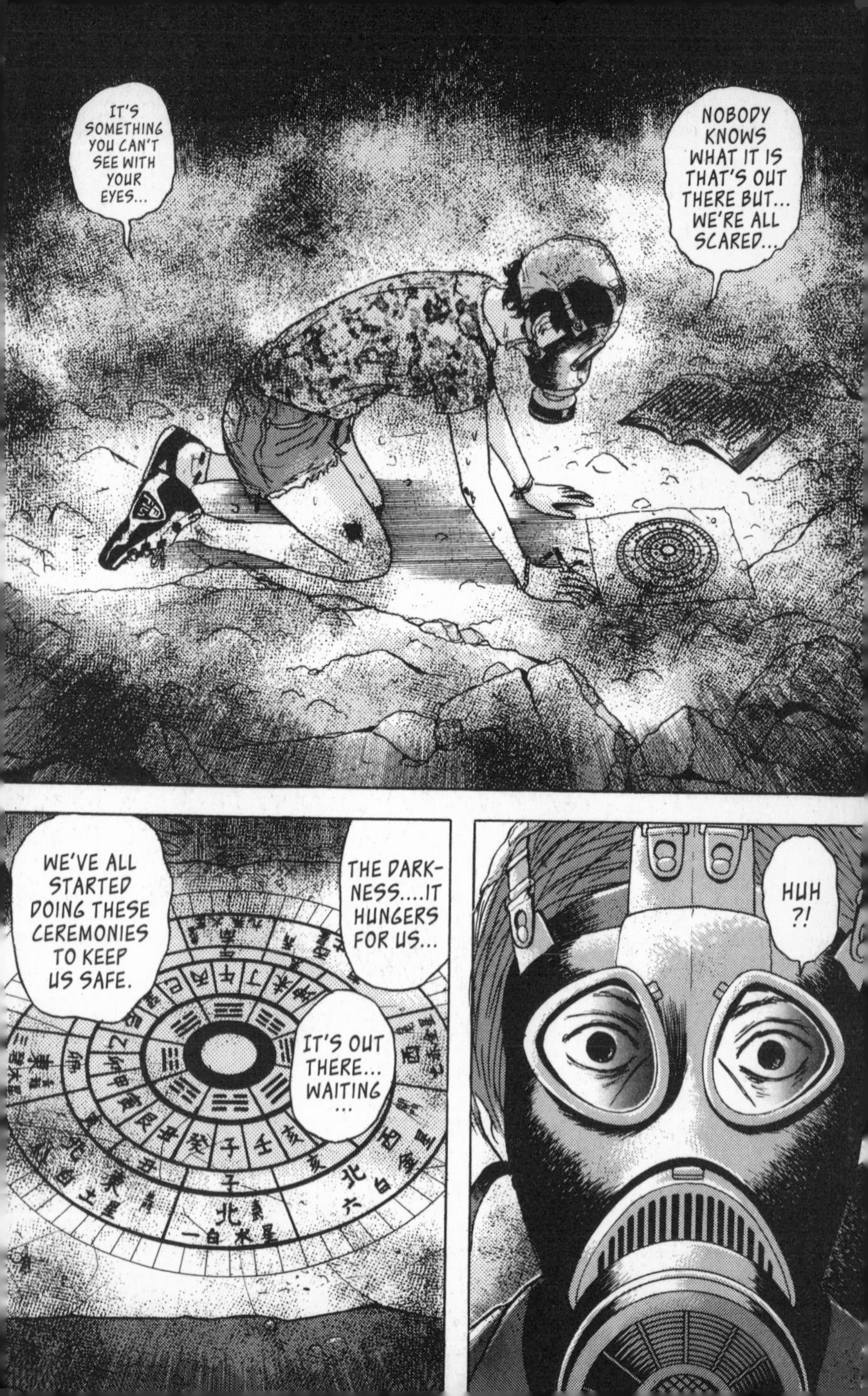
NOBODY KNOWS WHAT IT IS THAT'S OUT THERE BUT... WE'RE ALL SCARED...
IT'S SOMETHING YOU CAN'T SEE WITH YOUR EYES...
HUH ?!
THE DARK-NESS....IT HUNGERS FOR US...
WE'VE ALL STARTED DOING THESE CEREMONIES TO KEEP US SAFE.
IT'S OUT THERE... WAITING ...

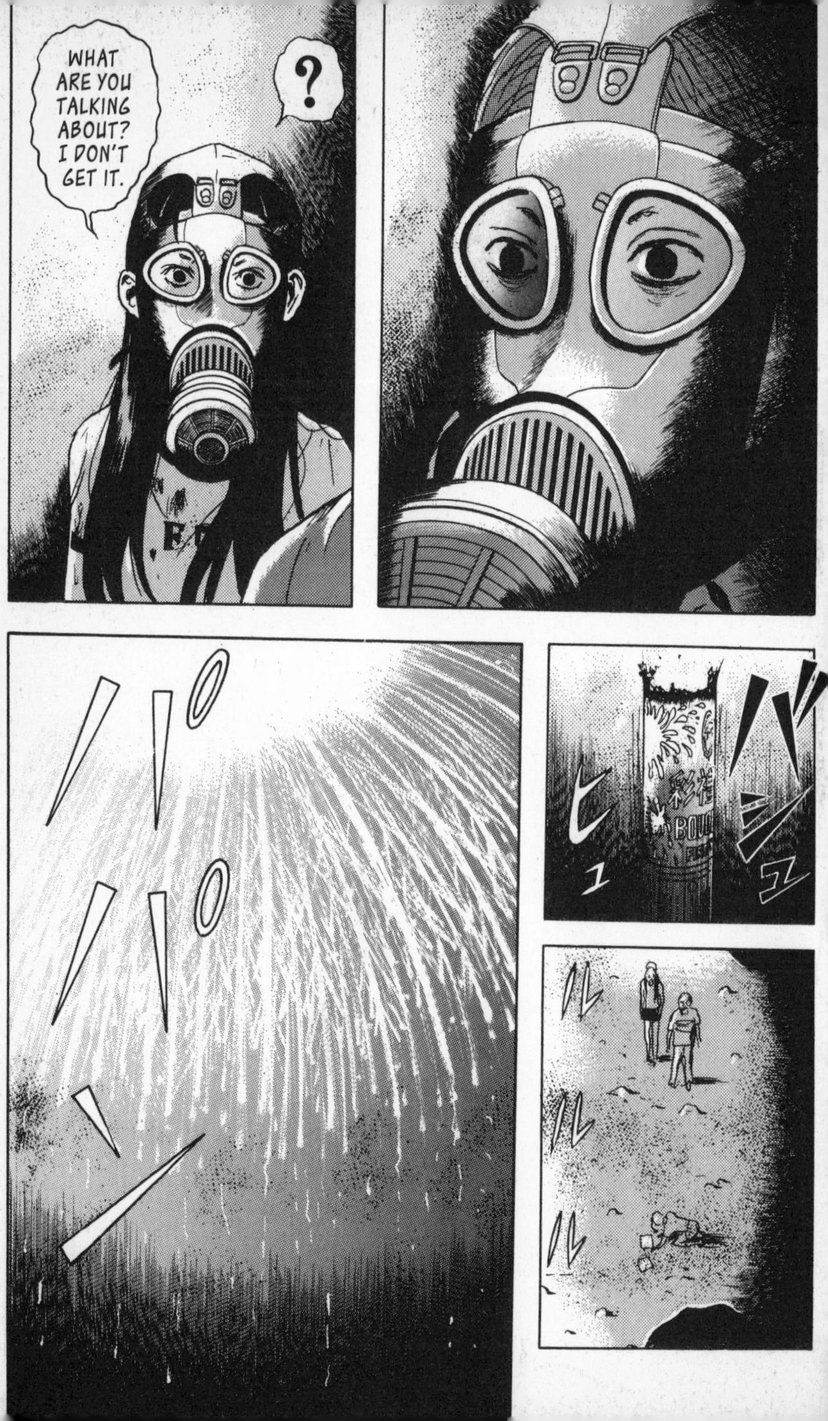
?
WHAT ARE YOU TALKING ABOUT? I DON'T GET IT.

OH
...

ゴォォォォォ

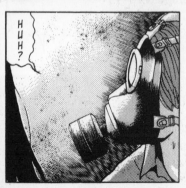

HUH?

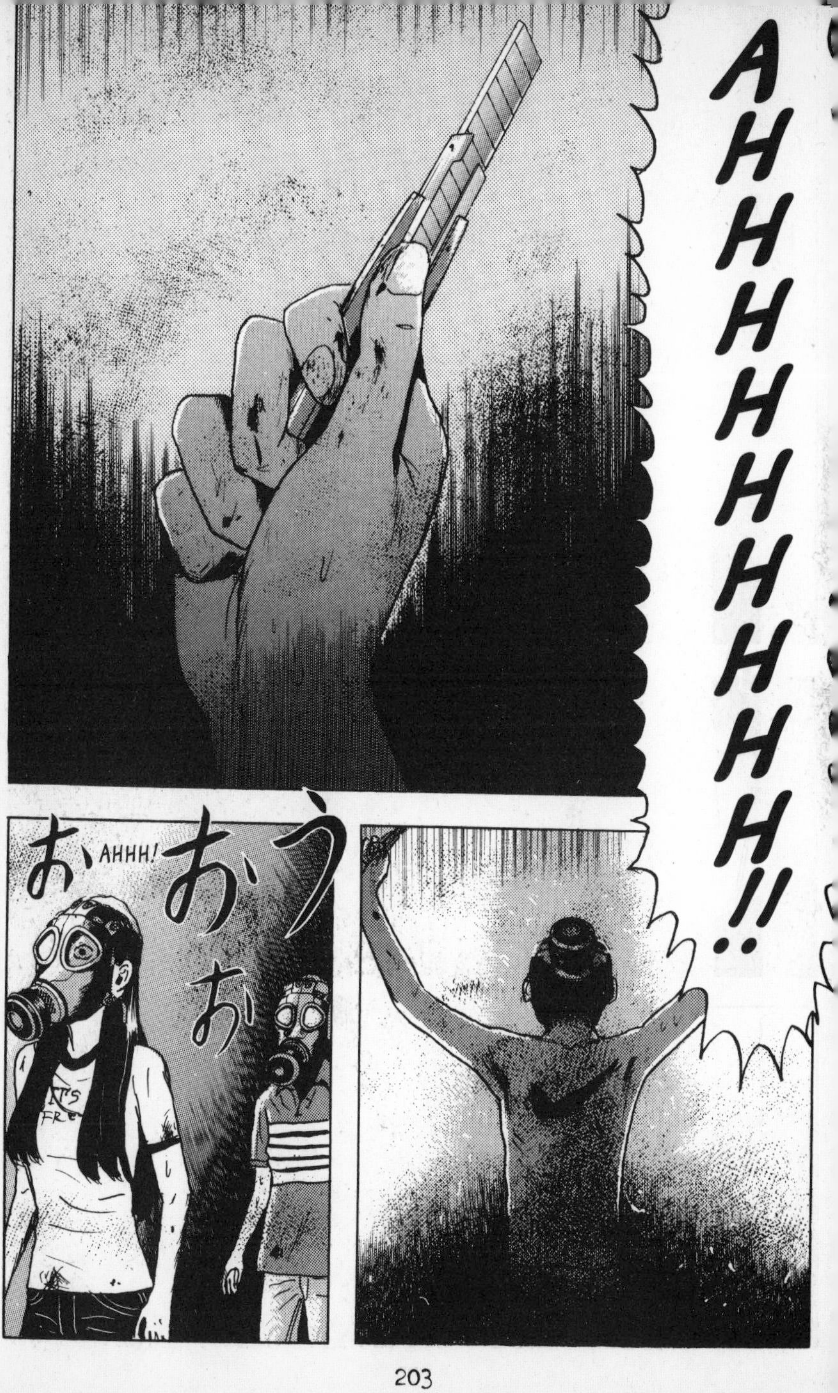
AHHHHHHHHH!!
おおうおお
AHHH!

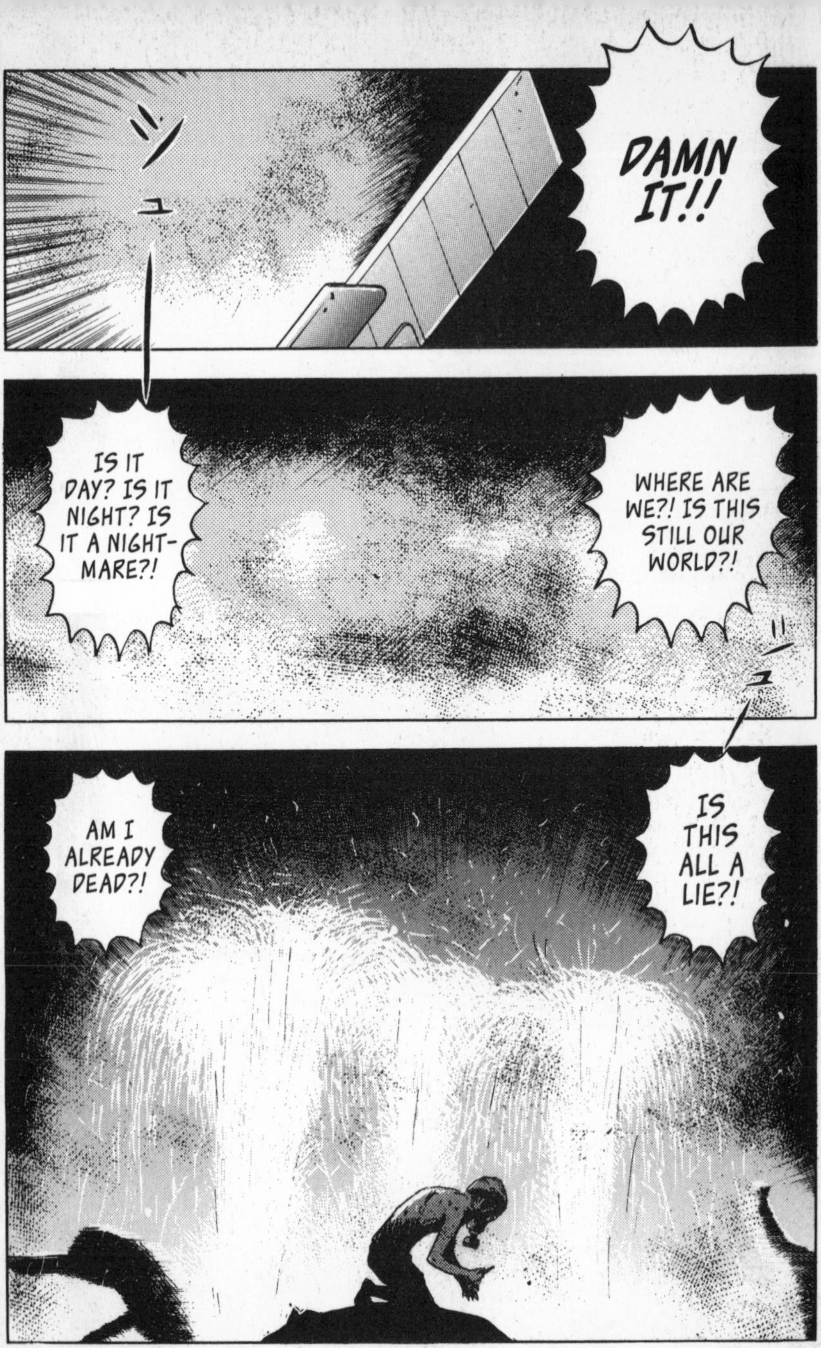
DAMN IT!!
WHERE ARE WE?! IS THIS STILL OUR WORLD?!
IS IT DAY? IS IT NIGHT? IS IT A NIGHTMARE?!
IS THIS ALL A LIE?!
AM I ALREADY DEAD?!

UAAAAAHH!!

AM I REALLY ALIVE?!

NO WAY...

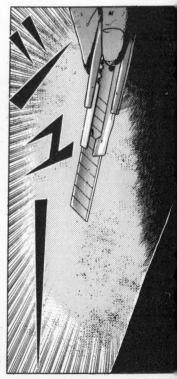

HE ISN'T GOING TO...

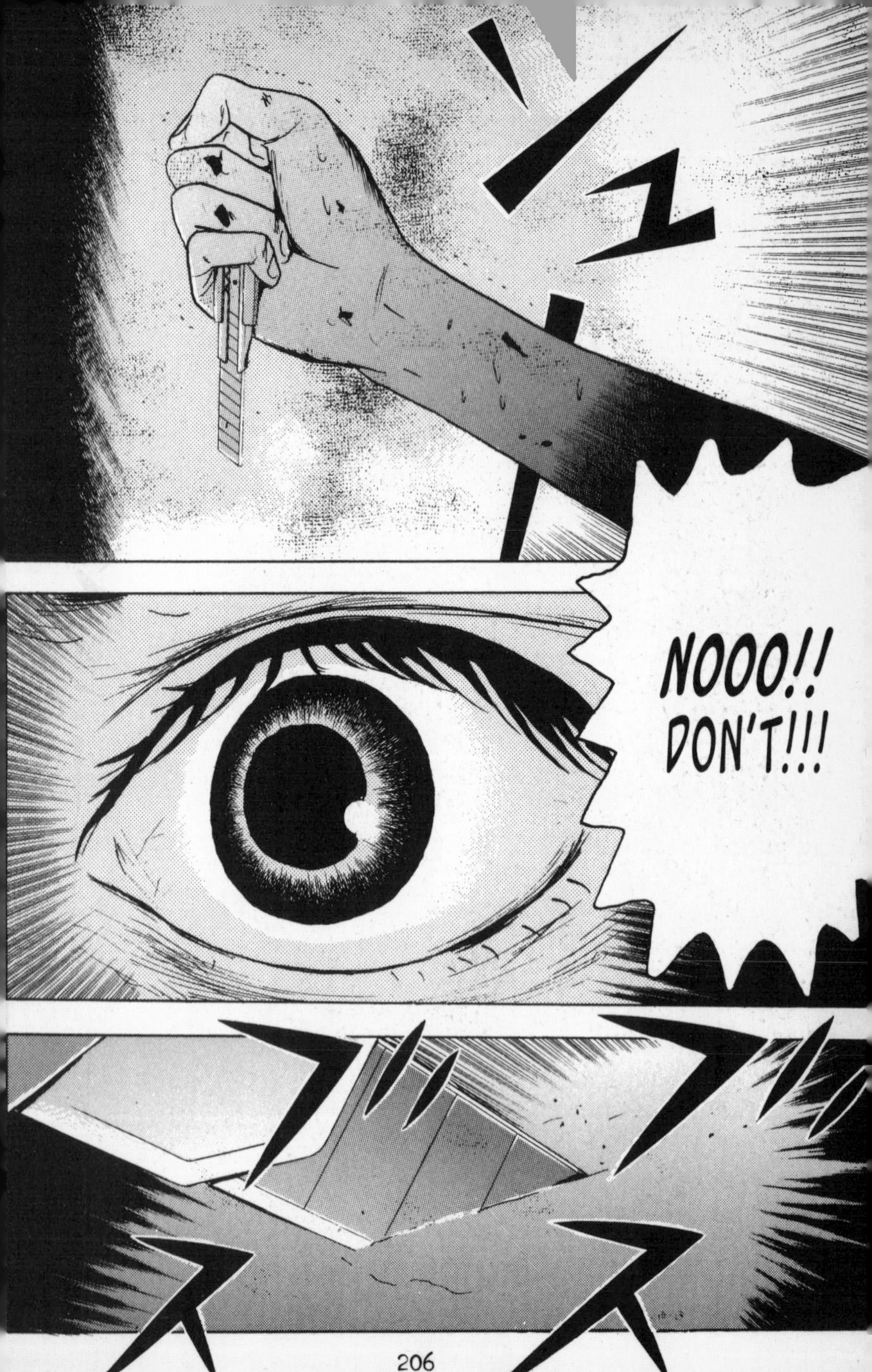
NOOO!! DON'T!!!

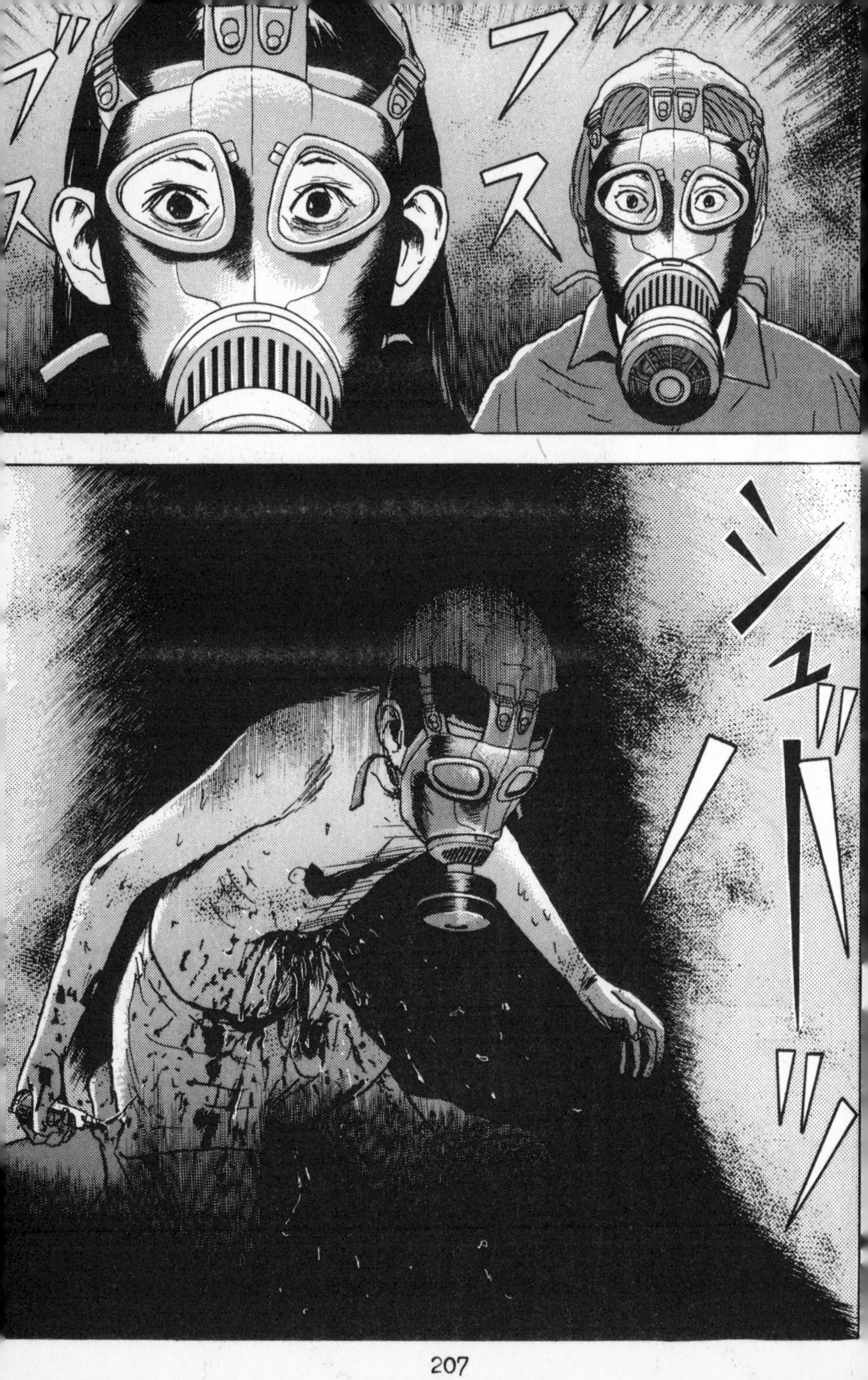
ブス
ブス
シュ゛ーーッ

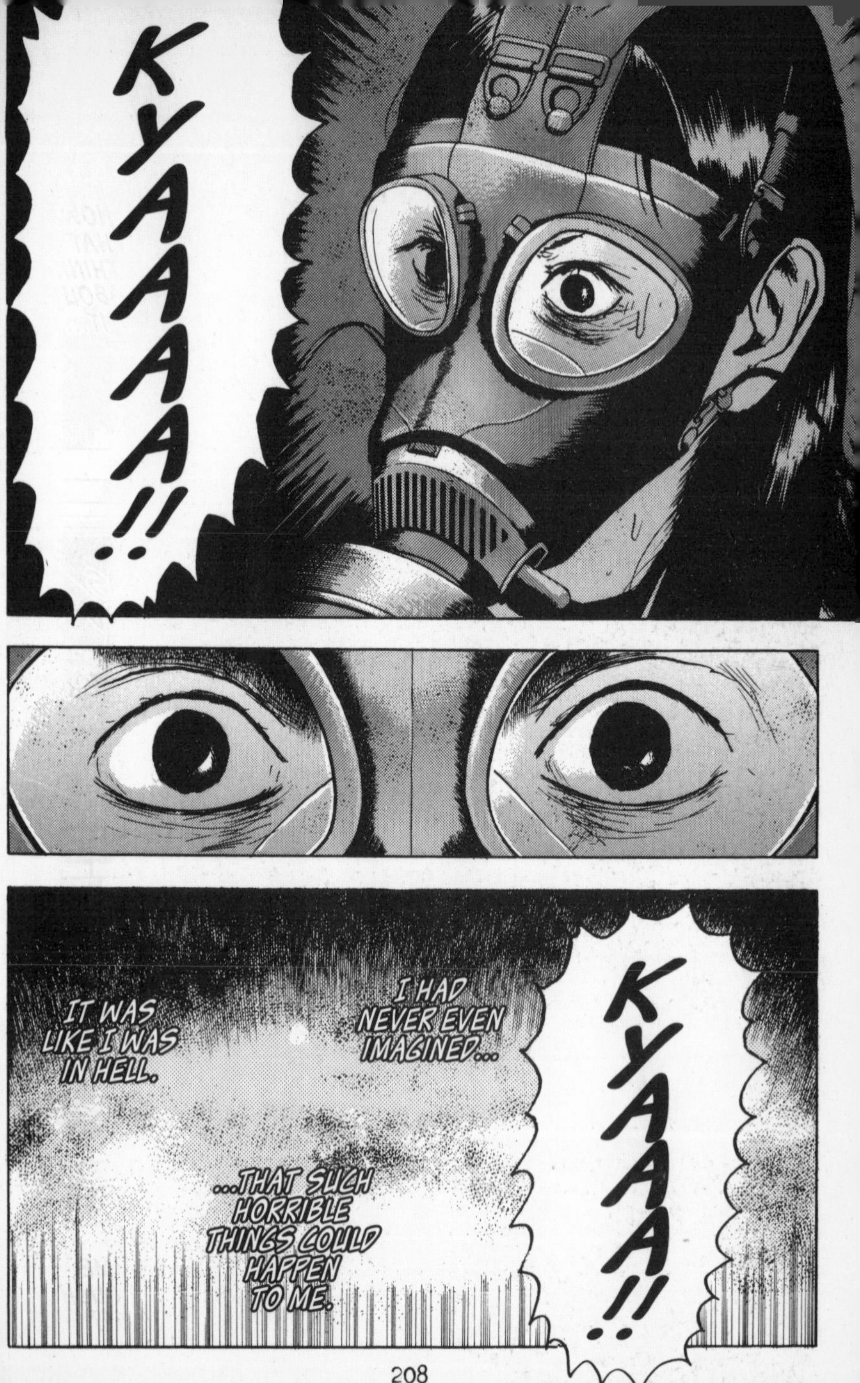
KYAAAA!!
KYAAAA!!
I HAD NEVER EVEN IMAGINED...
IT WAS LIKE I WAS IN HELL.
...THAT SUCH HORRIBLE THINGS COULD HAPPEN TO ME.

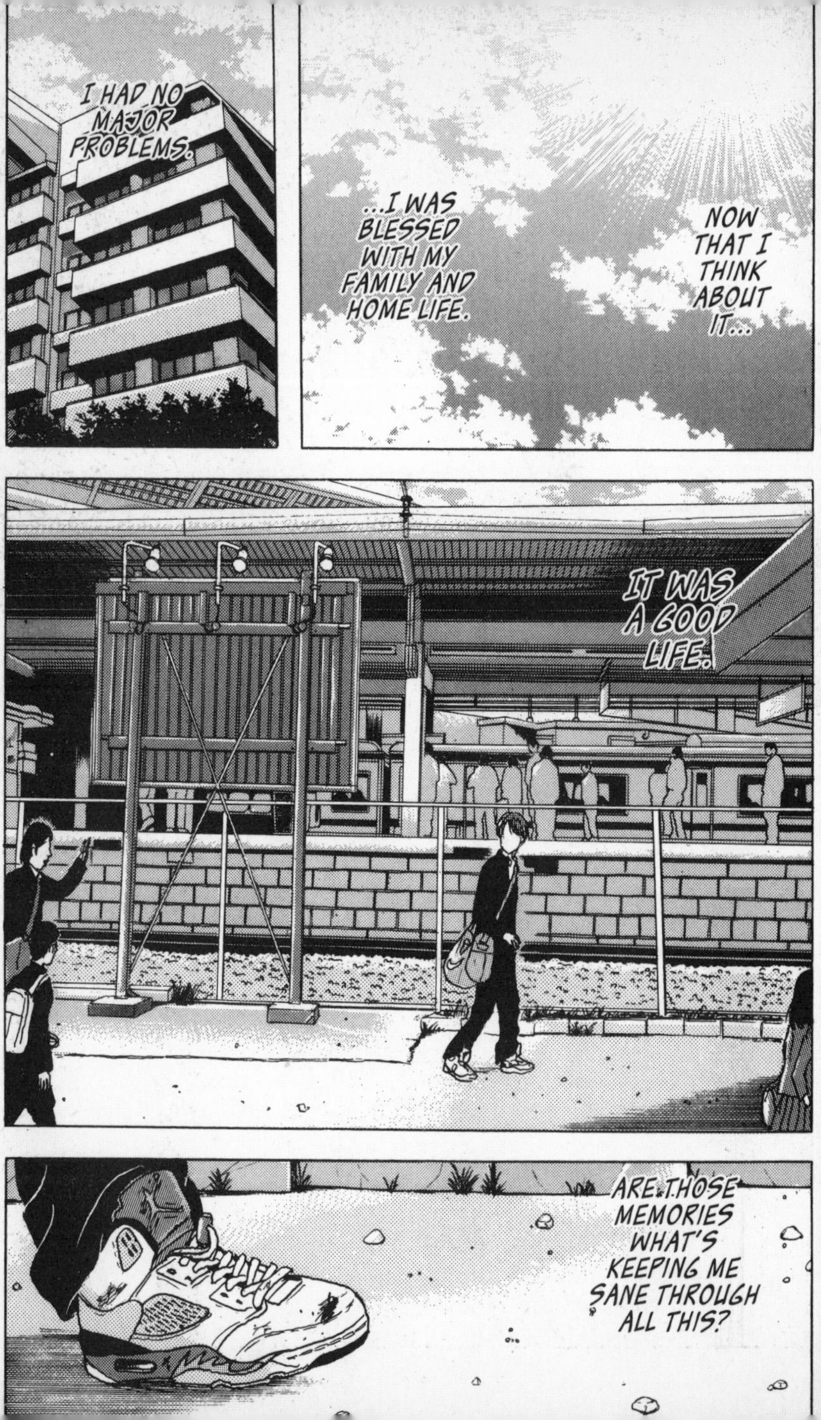
NOW THAT I THINK ABOUT IT...
...I WAS BLESSED WITH MY FAMILY AND HOME LIFE.
I HAD NO MAJOR PROBLEMS.
IT WAS A GOOD LIFE.
ARE THOSE MEMORIES WHAT'S KEEPING ME SANE THROUGH ALL THIS?

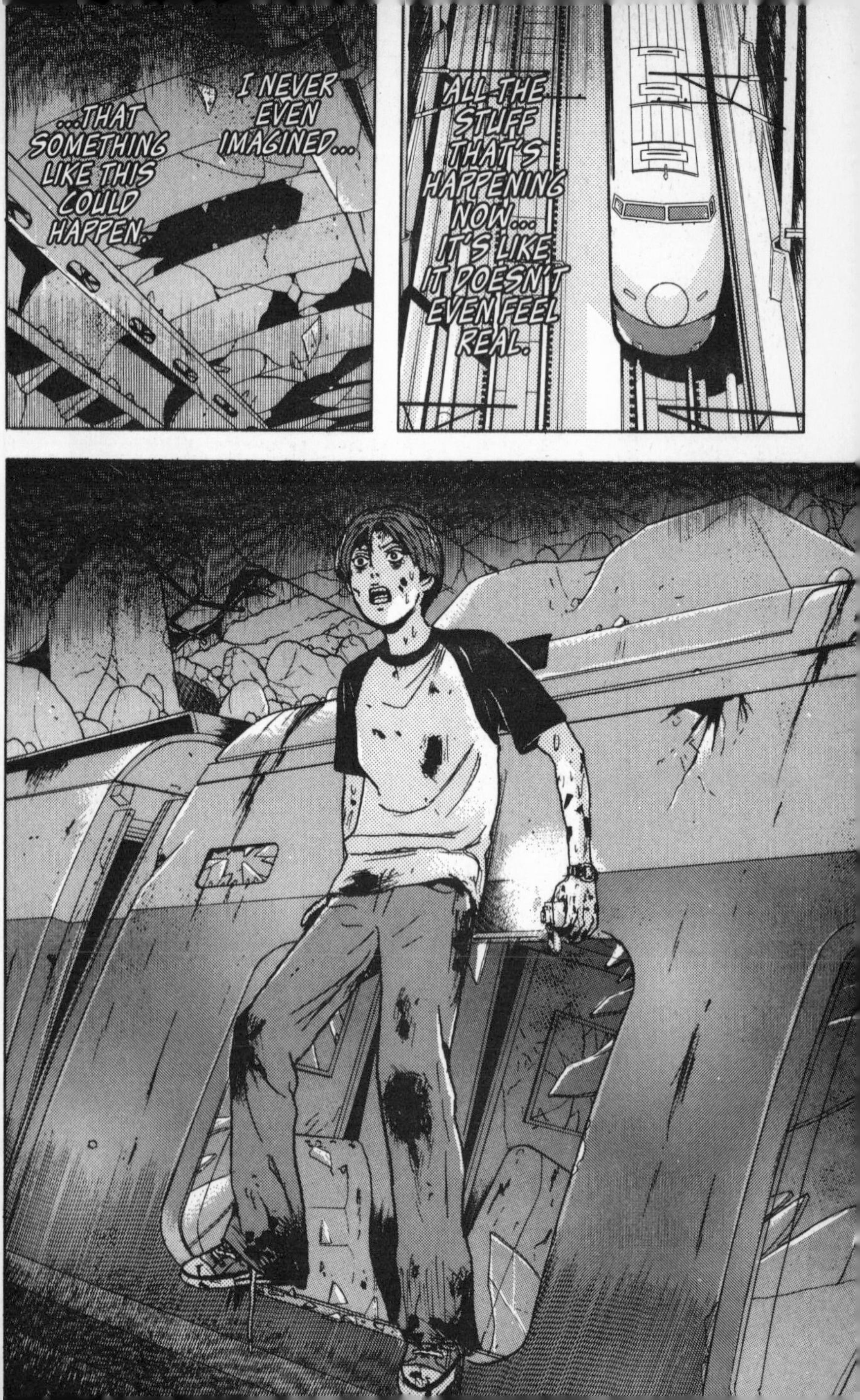
ALL THE STUFF THAT'S HAPPENING NOW... IT'S LIKE IT DOESN'T EVEN FEEL REAL.
I NEVER EVEN IMAGINED...
...THAT SOMETHING LIKE THIS COULD HAPPEN.

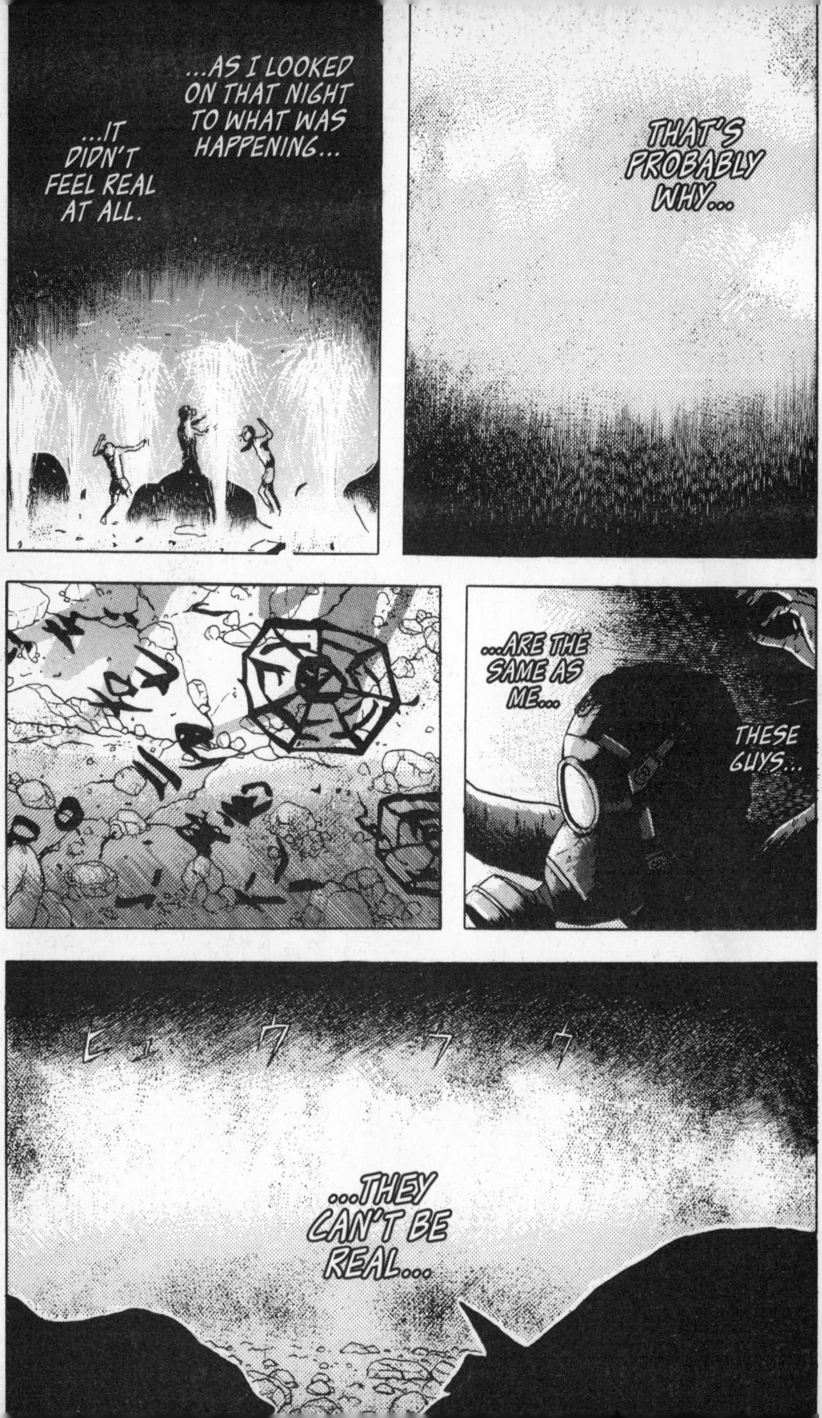
THAT'S PROBABLY WHY...
...AS I LOOKED ON THAT NIGHT TO WHAT WAS HAPPENING...
...IT DIDN'T FEEL REAL AT ALL.
THESE GUYS...
...ARE THE SAME AS ME...
ヒュウウウ
...THEY CAN'T BE REAL...

CUP NOODLE

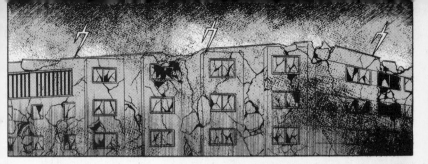

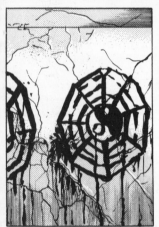

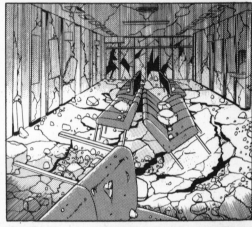

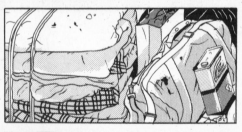

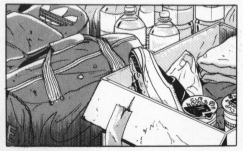

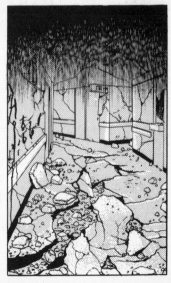

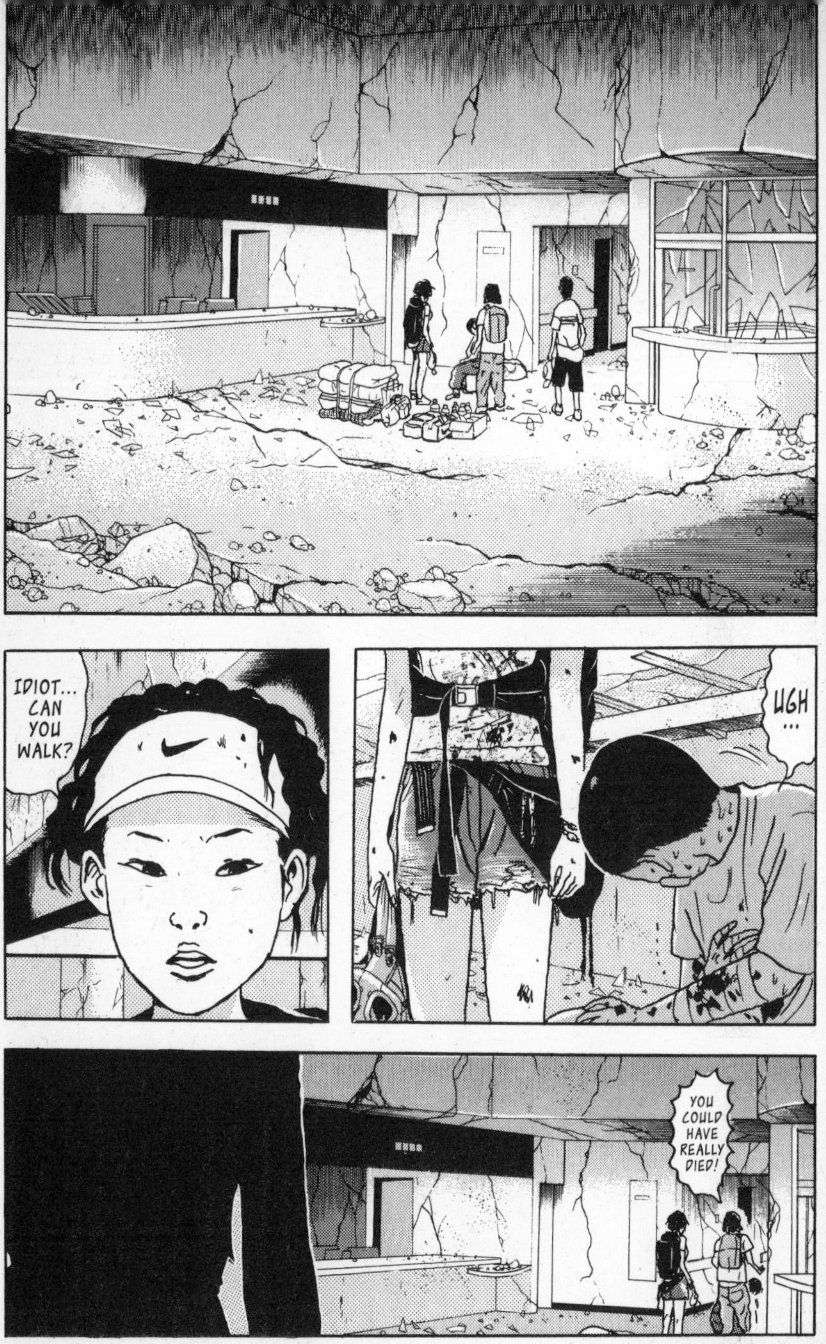
UGH ...
IDIOT... CAN YOU WALK?
YOU COULD HAVE REALLY DIED!

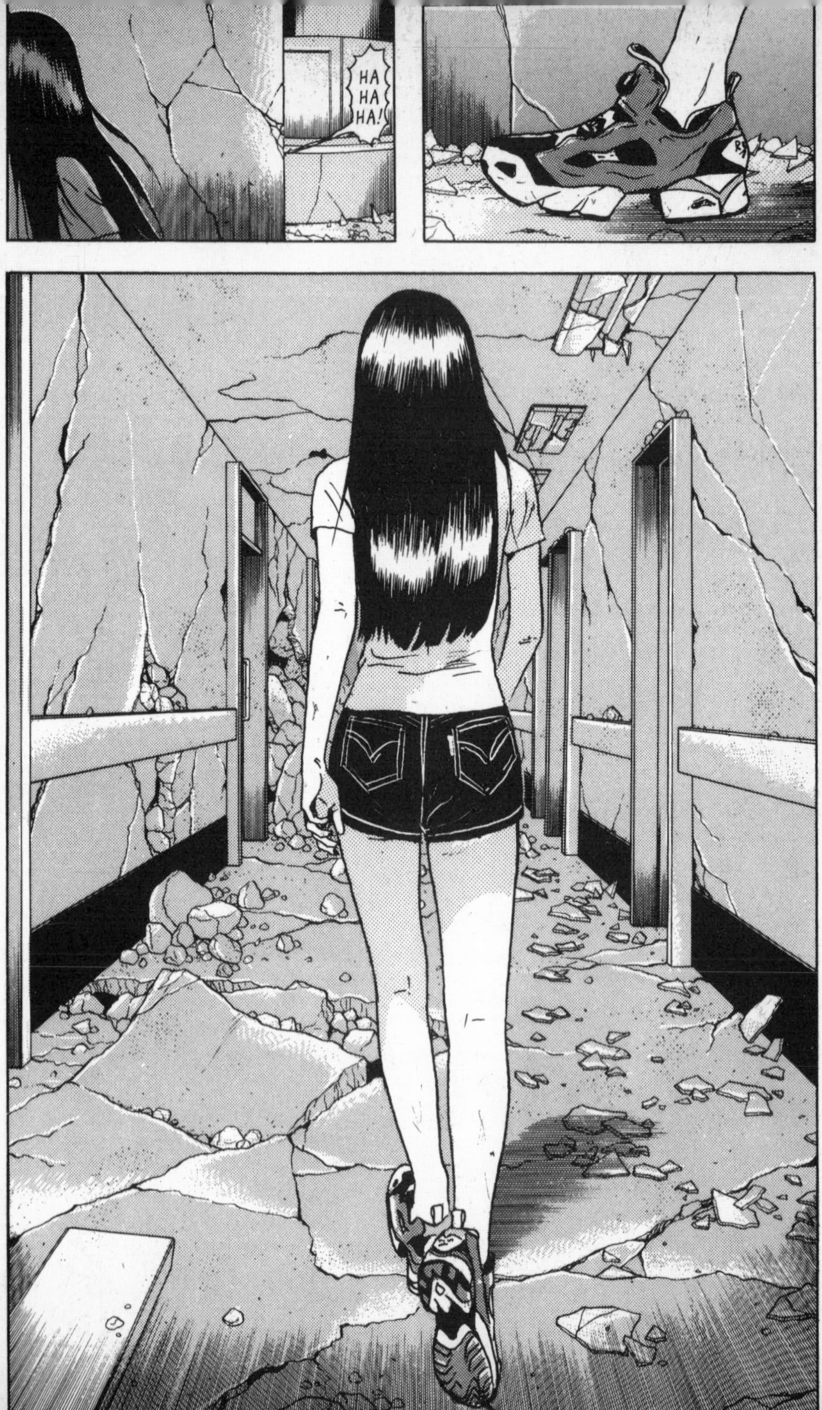
HA HA HA!

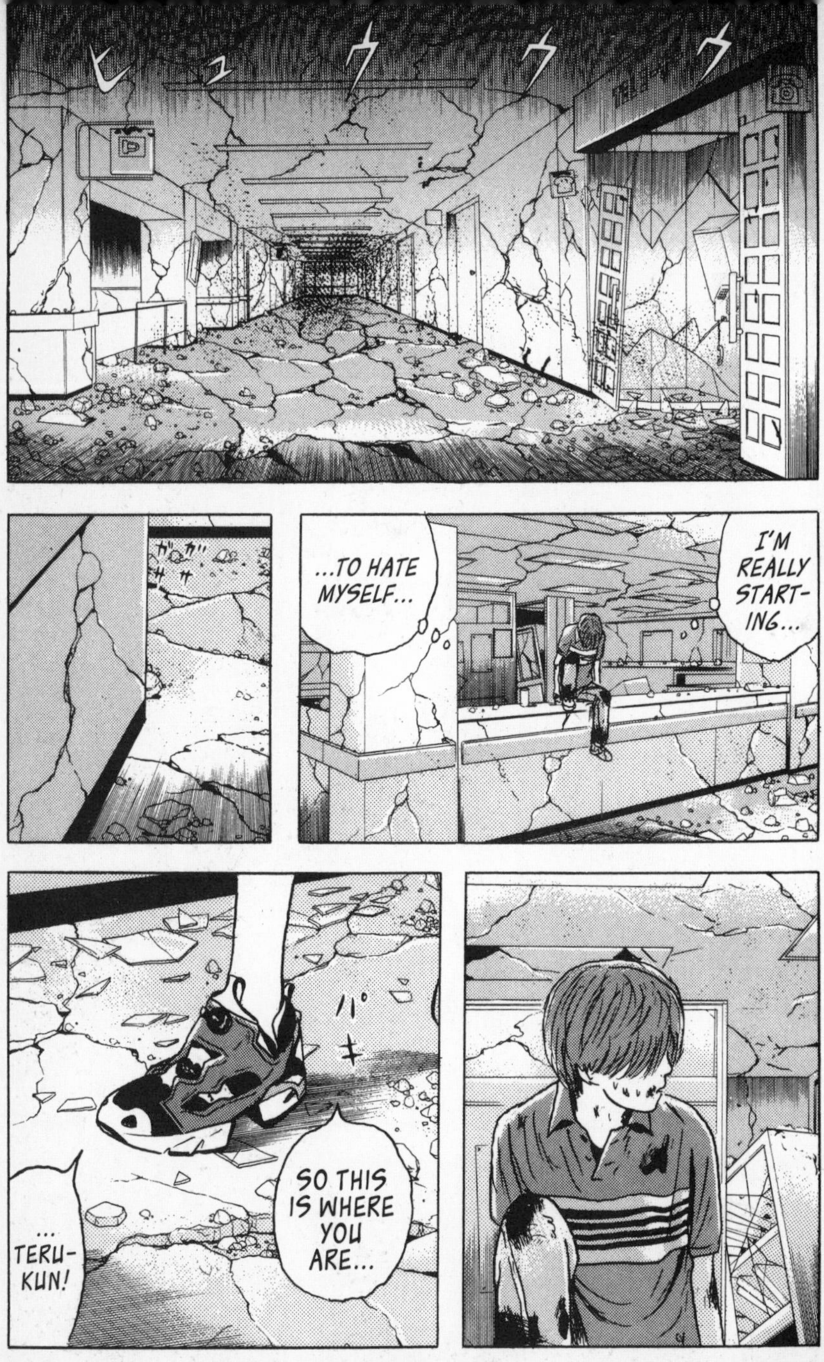
ヒュウウウ
I'M REALLY STARTING...
...TO HATE MYSELF...
SO THIS IS WHERE YOU ARE...
... TERU-KUN!

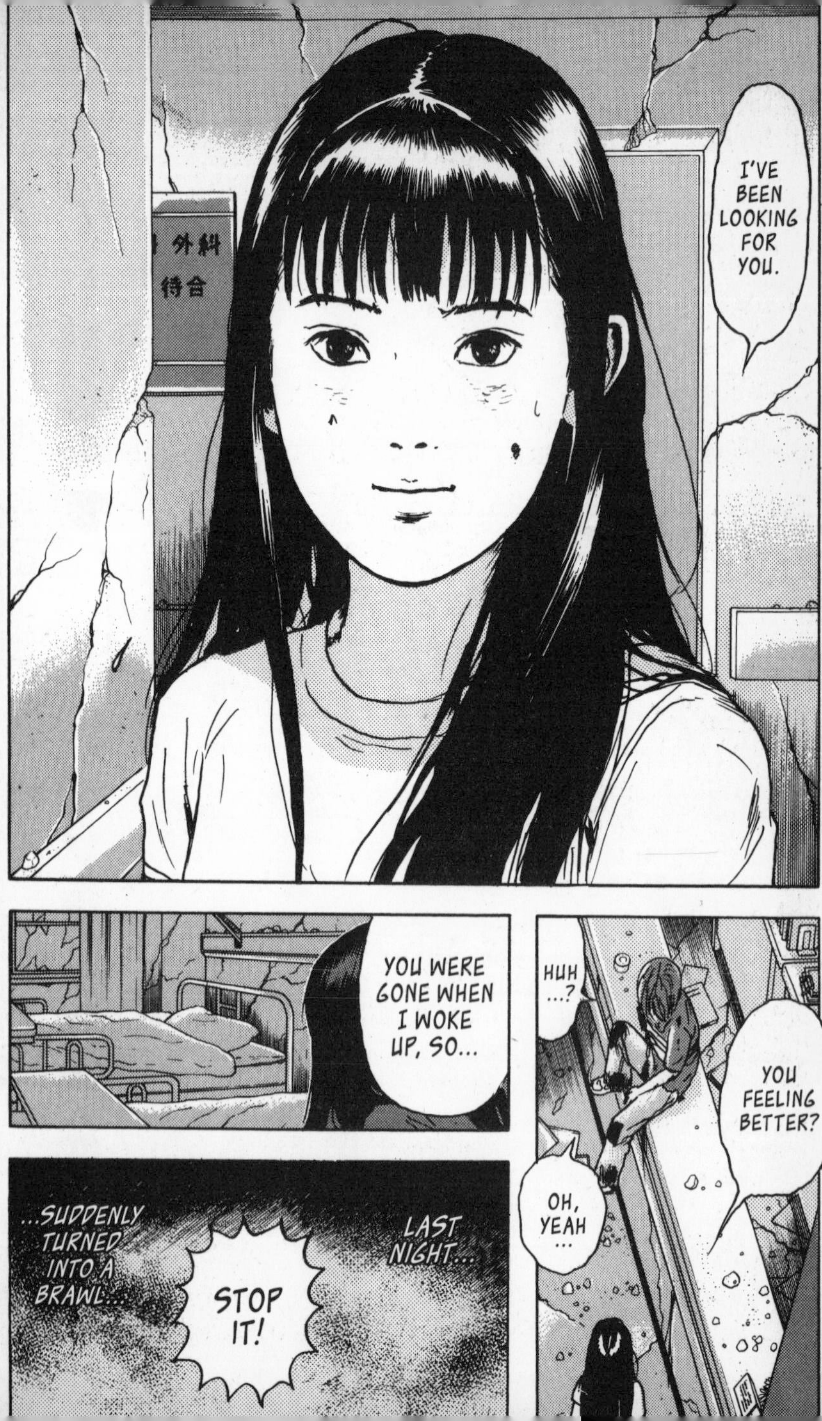
I'VE BEEN LOOKING FOR YOU.
外科
待合
HUH ...?
YOU FEELING BETTER?
OH, YEAH ...
YOU WERE GONE WHEN I WOKE UP, SO...
LAST NIGHT...
...SUDDENLY TURNED INTO A BRAWL...
STOP IT!

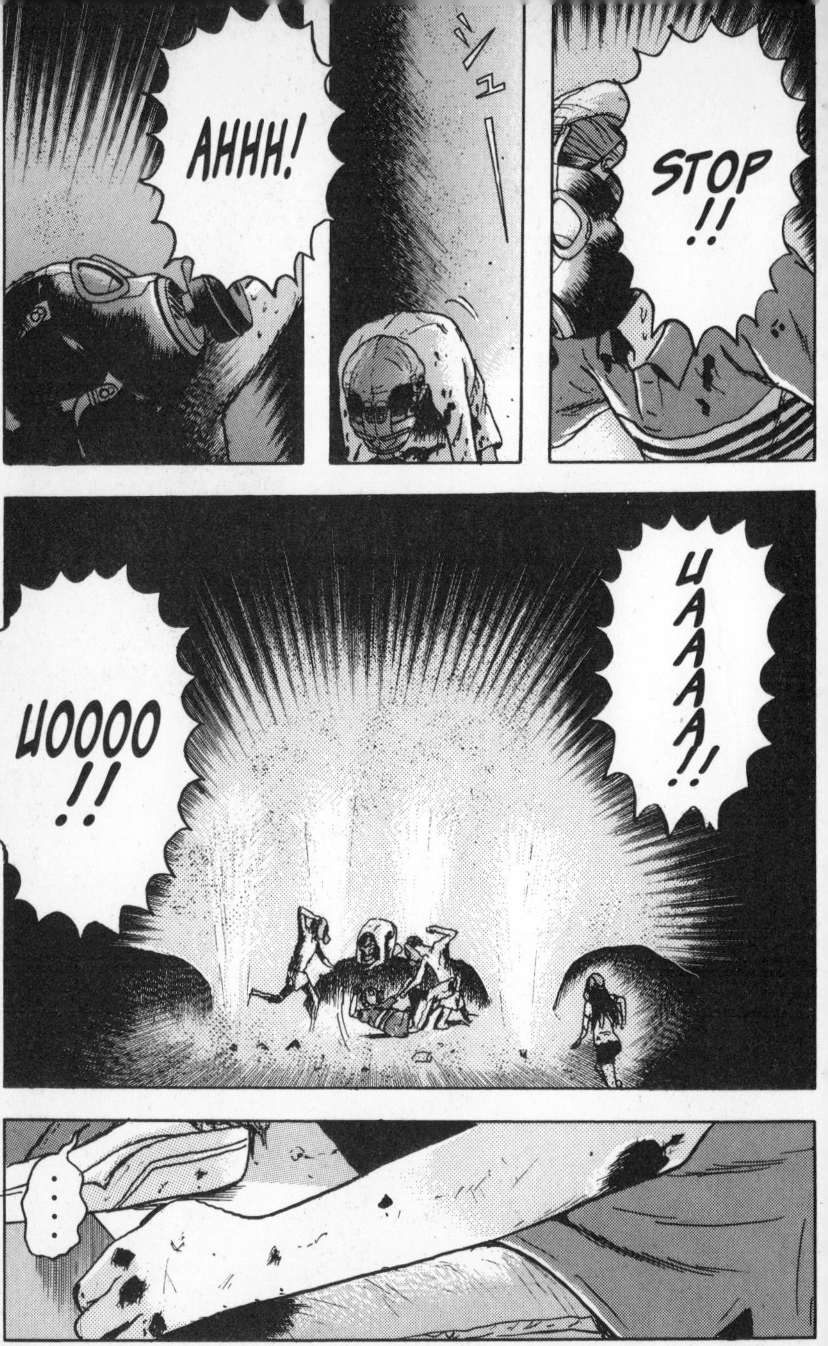
STOP!!
AHHH!
UAAAAA!!
UOOOO!!
.....

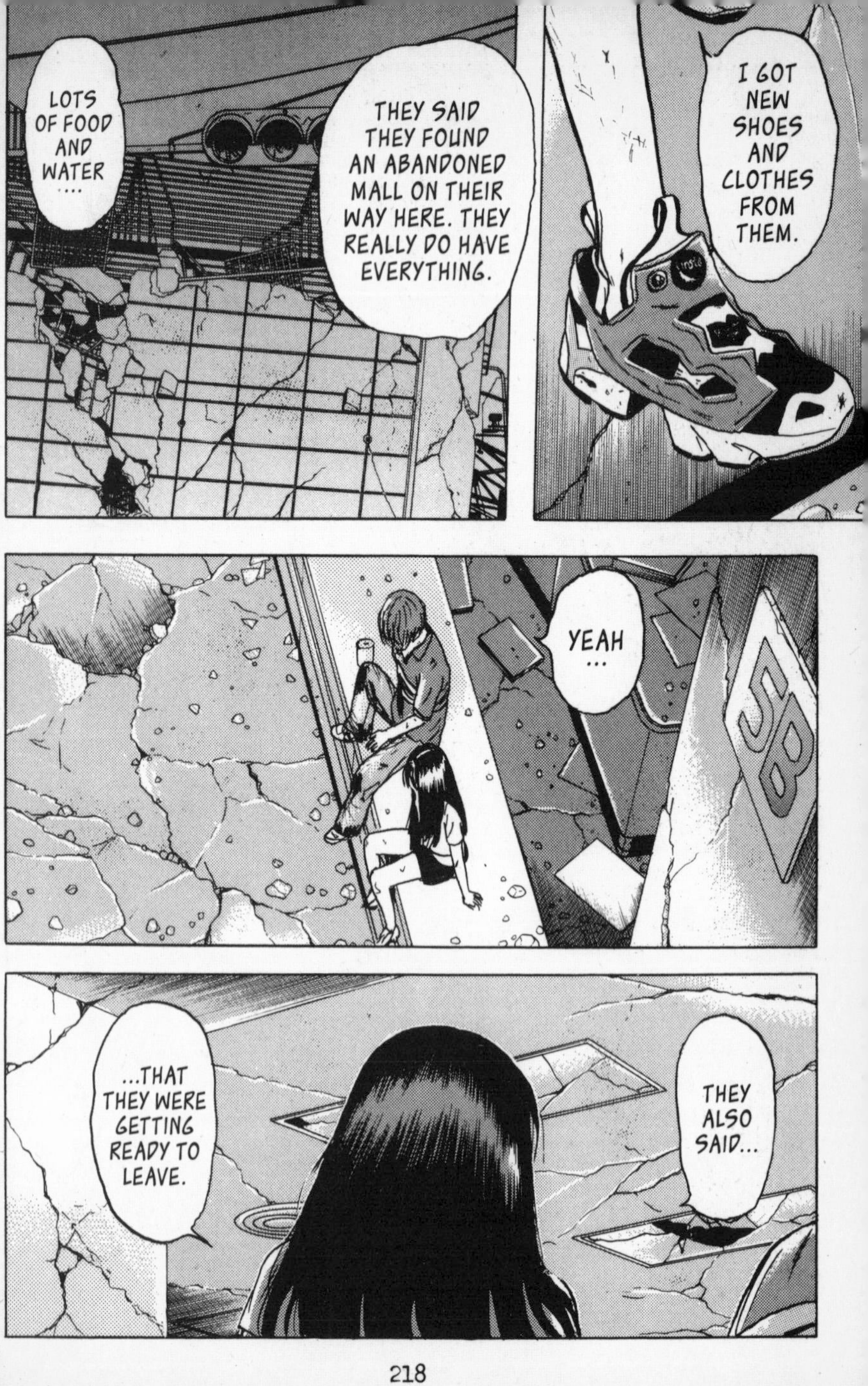
I GOT NEW SHOES AND CLOTHES FROM THEM.
THEY SAID THEY FOUND AN ABANDONED MALL ON THEIR WAY HERE. THEY REALLY DO HAVE EVERYTHING.
LOTS OF FOOD AND WATER ....
YEAH ...
THEY ALSO SAID...
...THAT THEY WERE GETTING READY TO LEAVE.

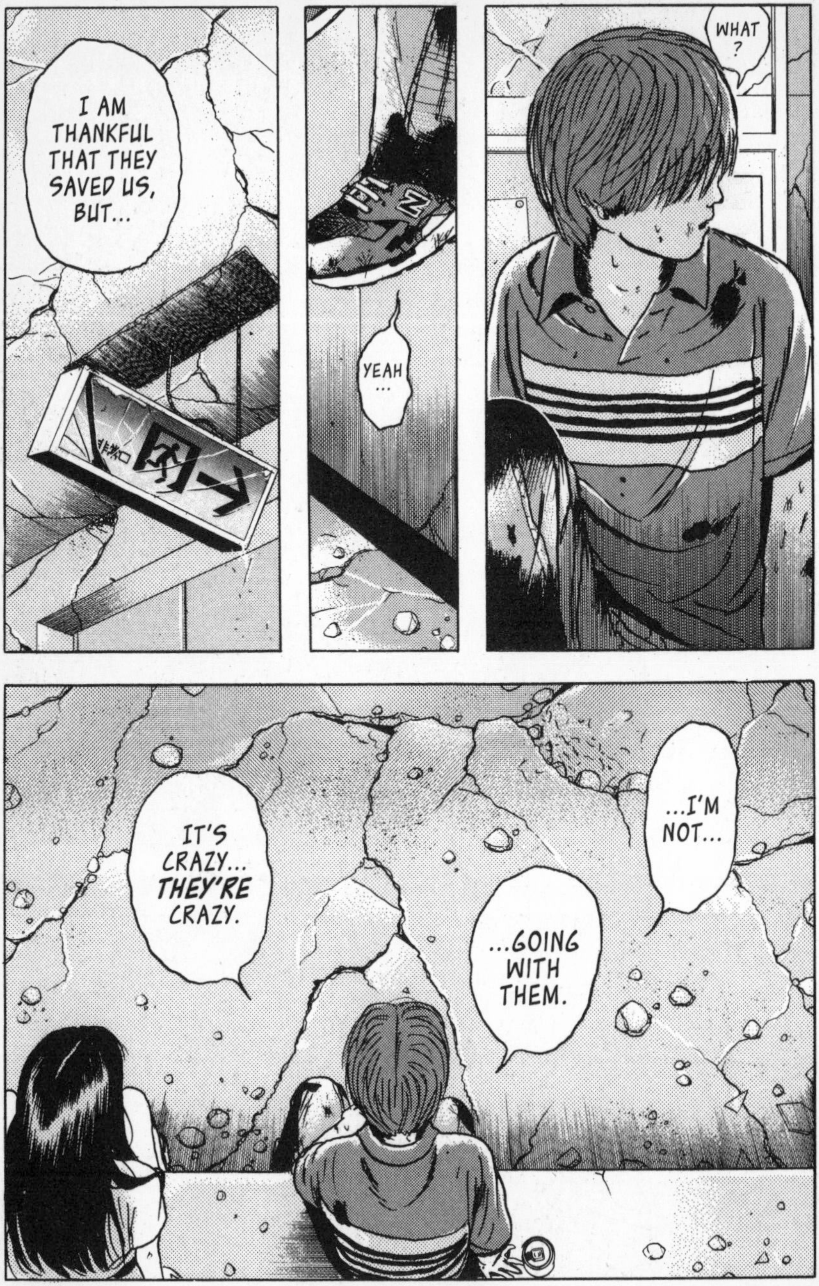
WHAT ?
YEAH ...
I AM THANKFUL THAT THEY SAVED US, BUT...
非常口
...I'M NOT...
...GOING WITH THEM.
IT'S CRAZY... ***THEY'RE*** CRAZY.

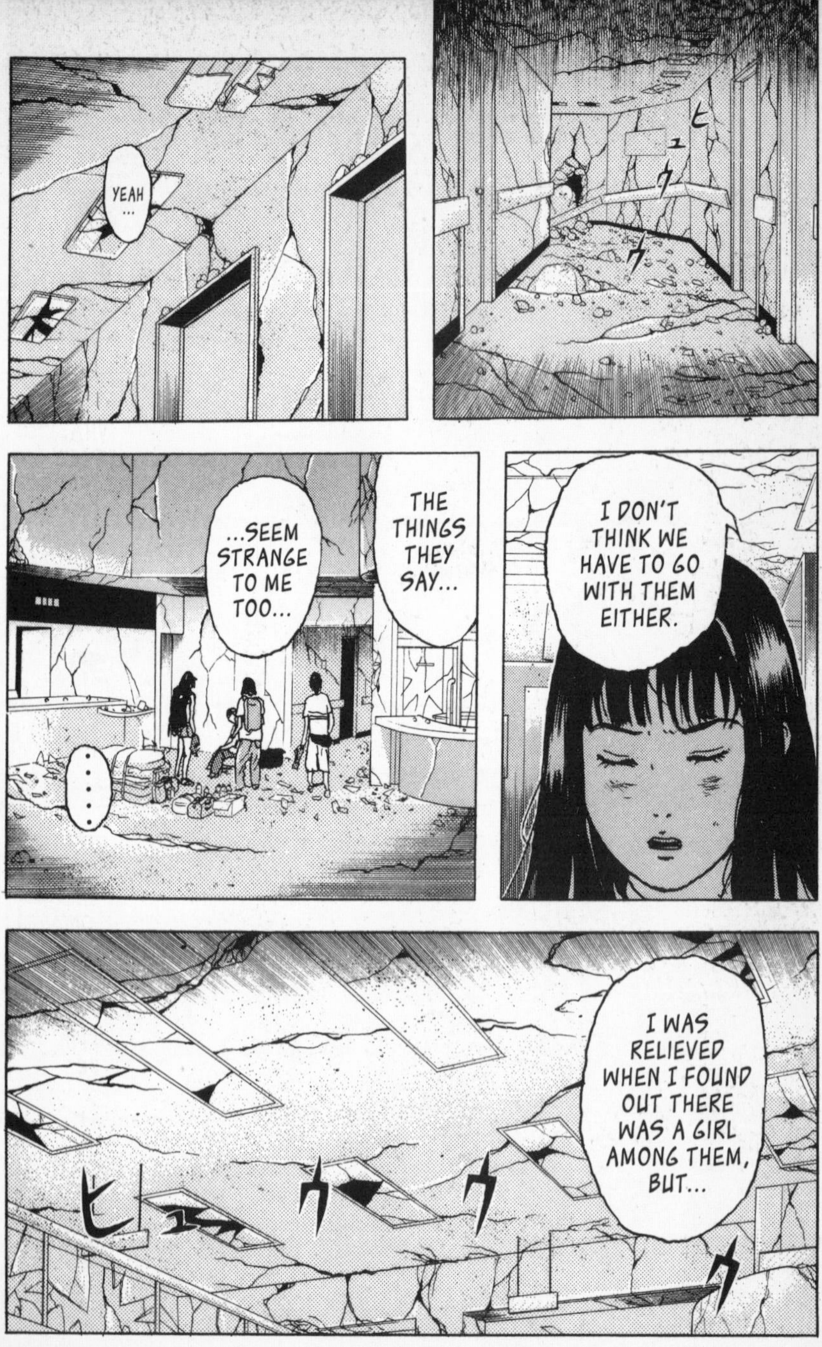
ヒュウウ
YEAH...
I DON'T THINK WE HAVE TO GO WITH THEM EITHER.
THE THINGS THEY SAY...
...SEEM STRANGE TO ME TOO...
.....
I WAS RELIEVED WHEN I FOUND OUT THERE WAS A GIRL AMONG THEM, BUT...
ヒュウウウ

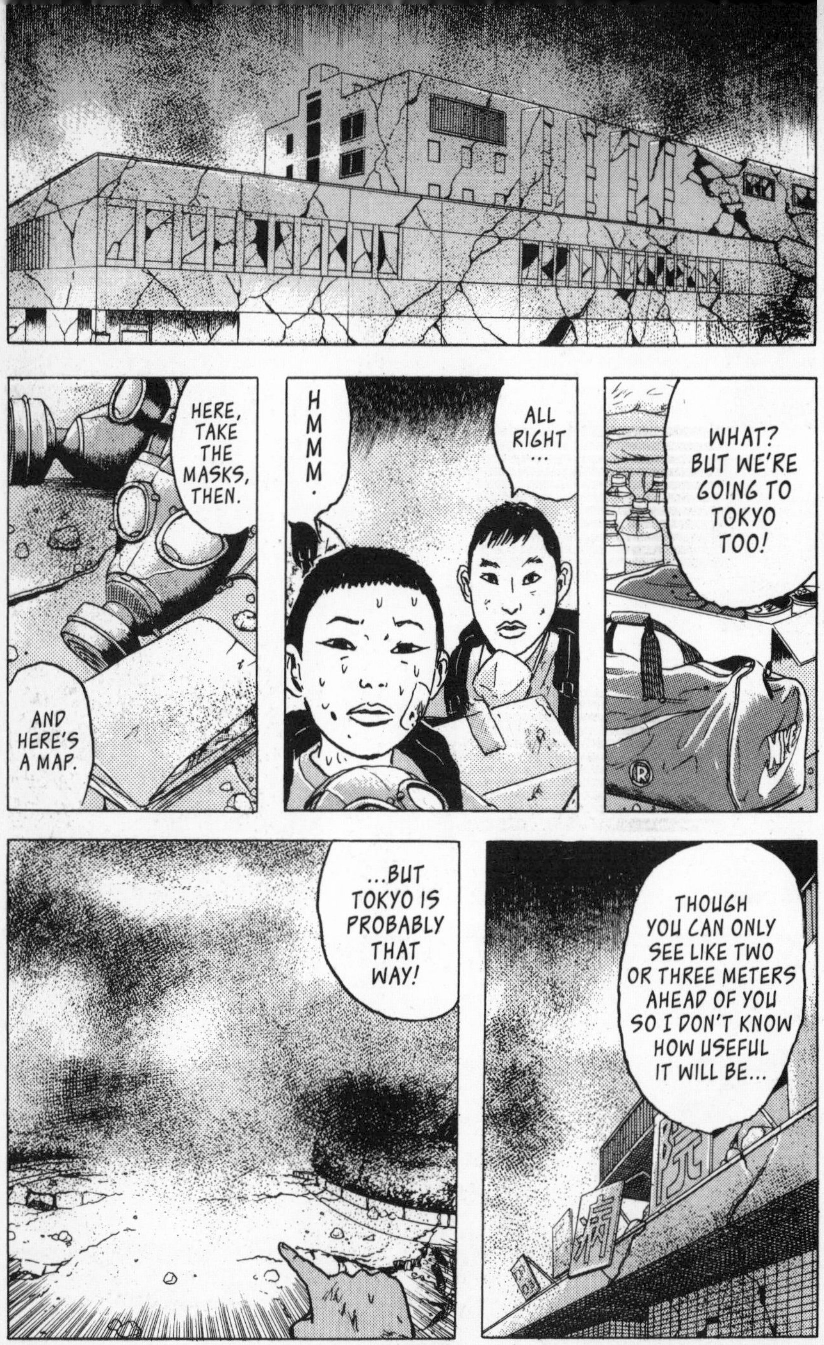
WHAT? BUT WE'RE GOING TO TOKYO TOO!
ALL RIGHT...
HMMM.
HERE, TAKE THE MASKS, THEN.
AND HERE'S A MAP.
THOUGH YOU CAN ONLY SEE LIKE TWO OR THREE METERS AHEAD OF YOU SO I DON'T KNOW HOW USEFUL IT WILL BE...
...BUT TOKYO IS PROBABLY THAT WAY!

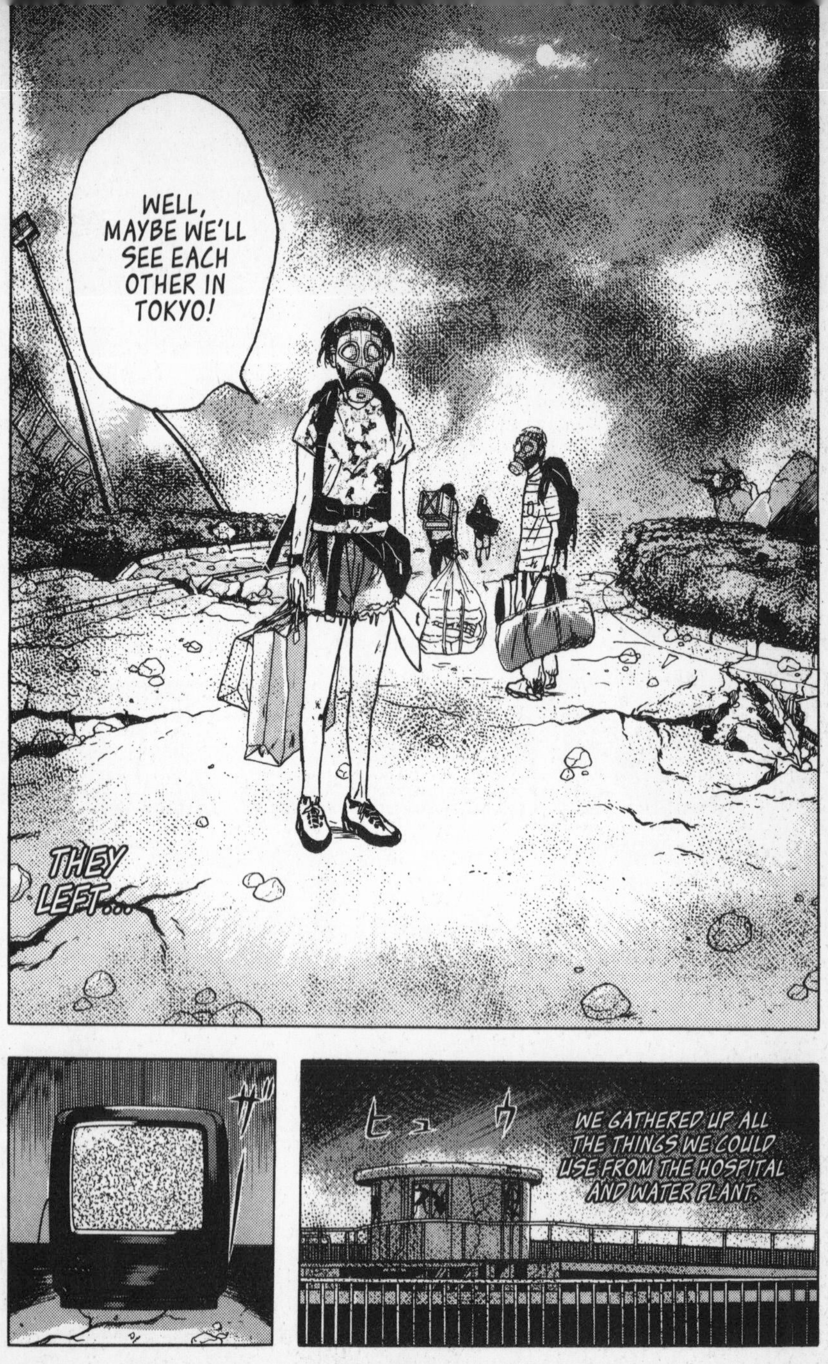
WELL, MAYBE WE'LL SEE EACH OTHER IN TOKYO!
THEY LEFT...
WE GATHERED UP ALL THE THINGS WE COULD USE FROM THE HOSPITAL AND WATER PLANT.
ヒュウ

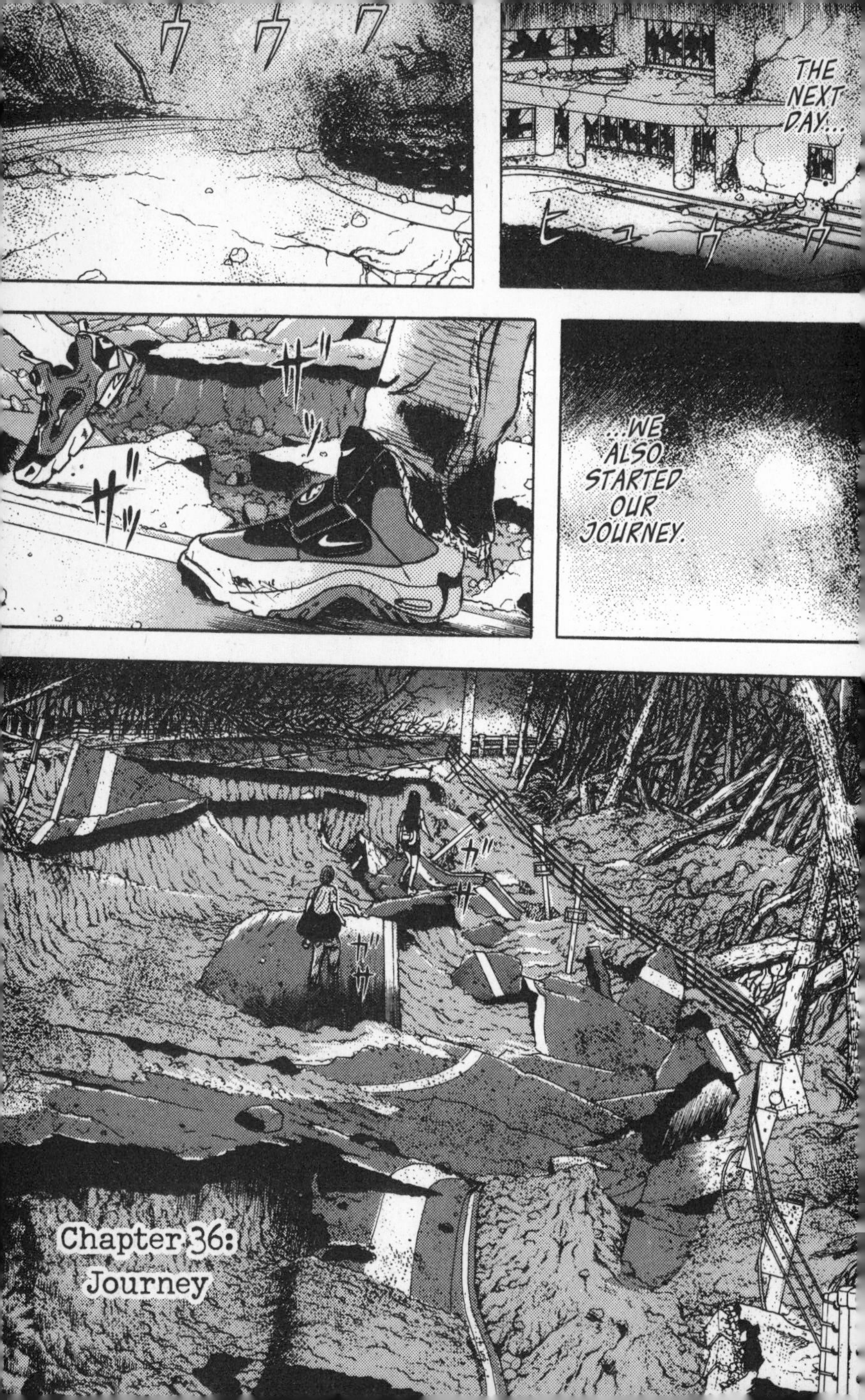
THE NEXT DAY...
...WE ALSO STARTED OUR JOURNEY.
Chapter 36: Journey

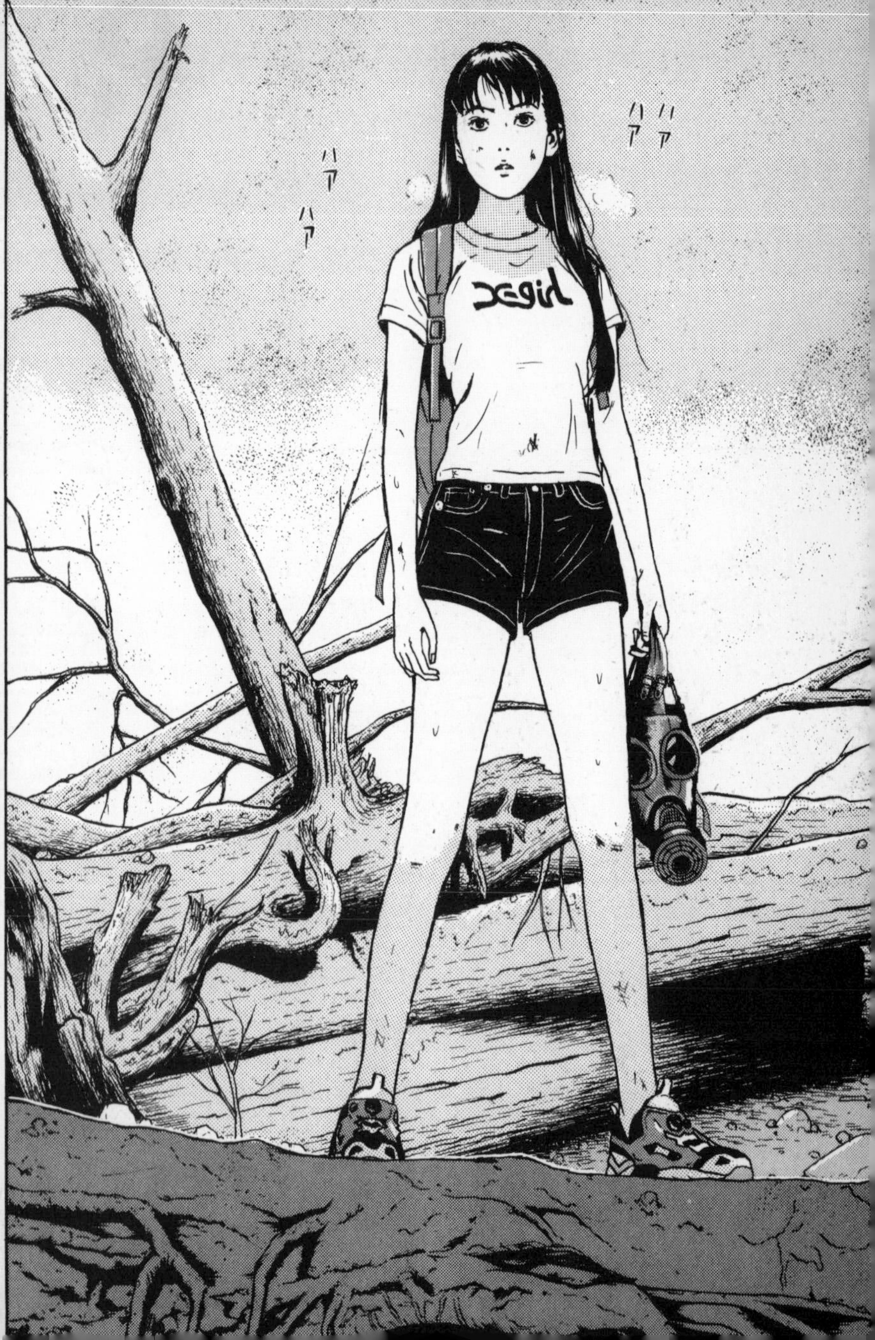
ハァ
ハァ
ハァ
ハァ
X-girl

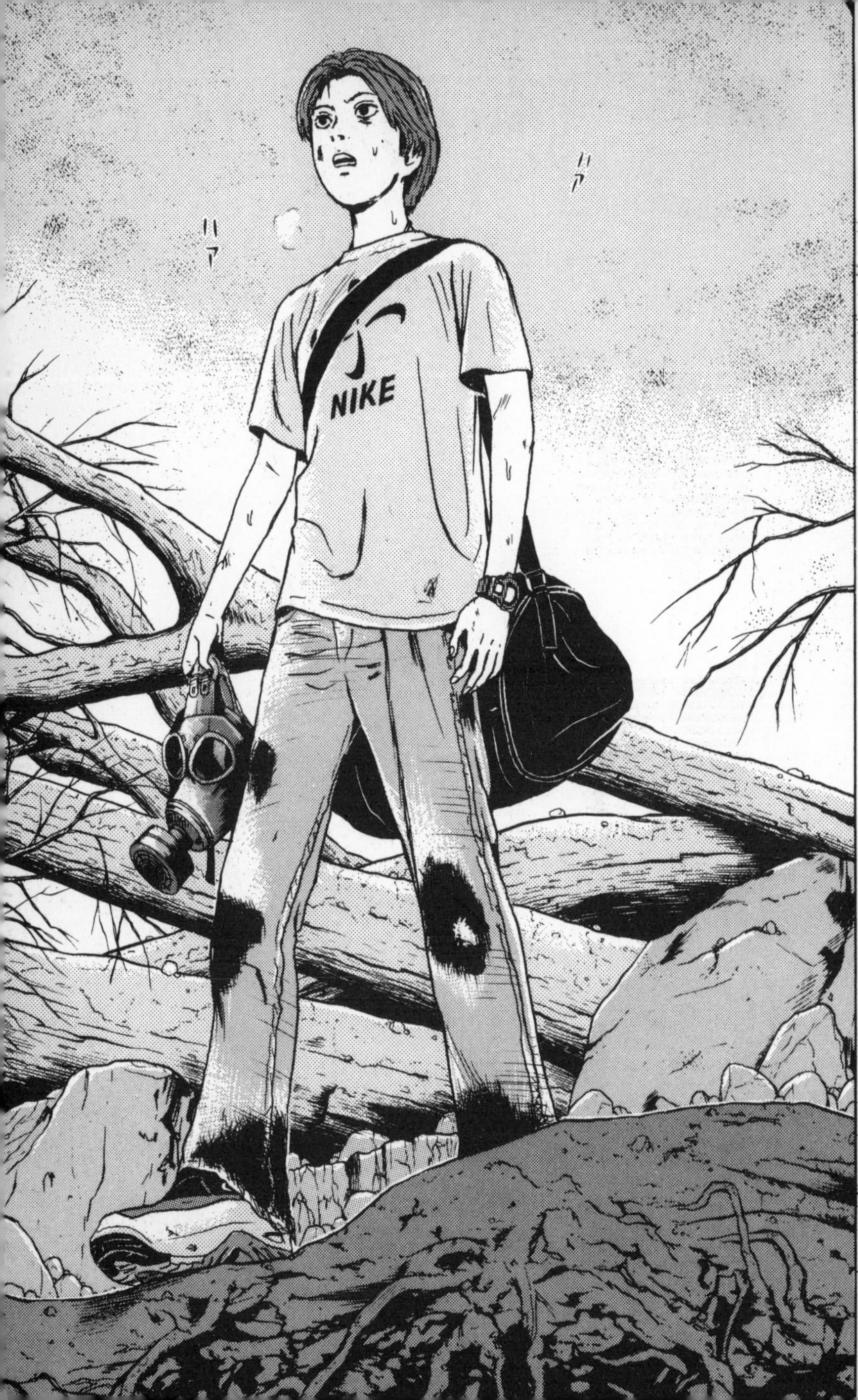
ハァ
ハァ
NIKE

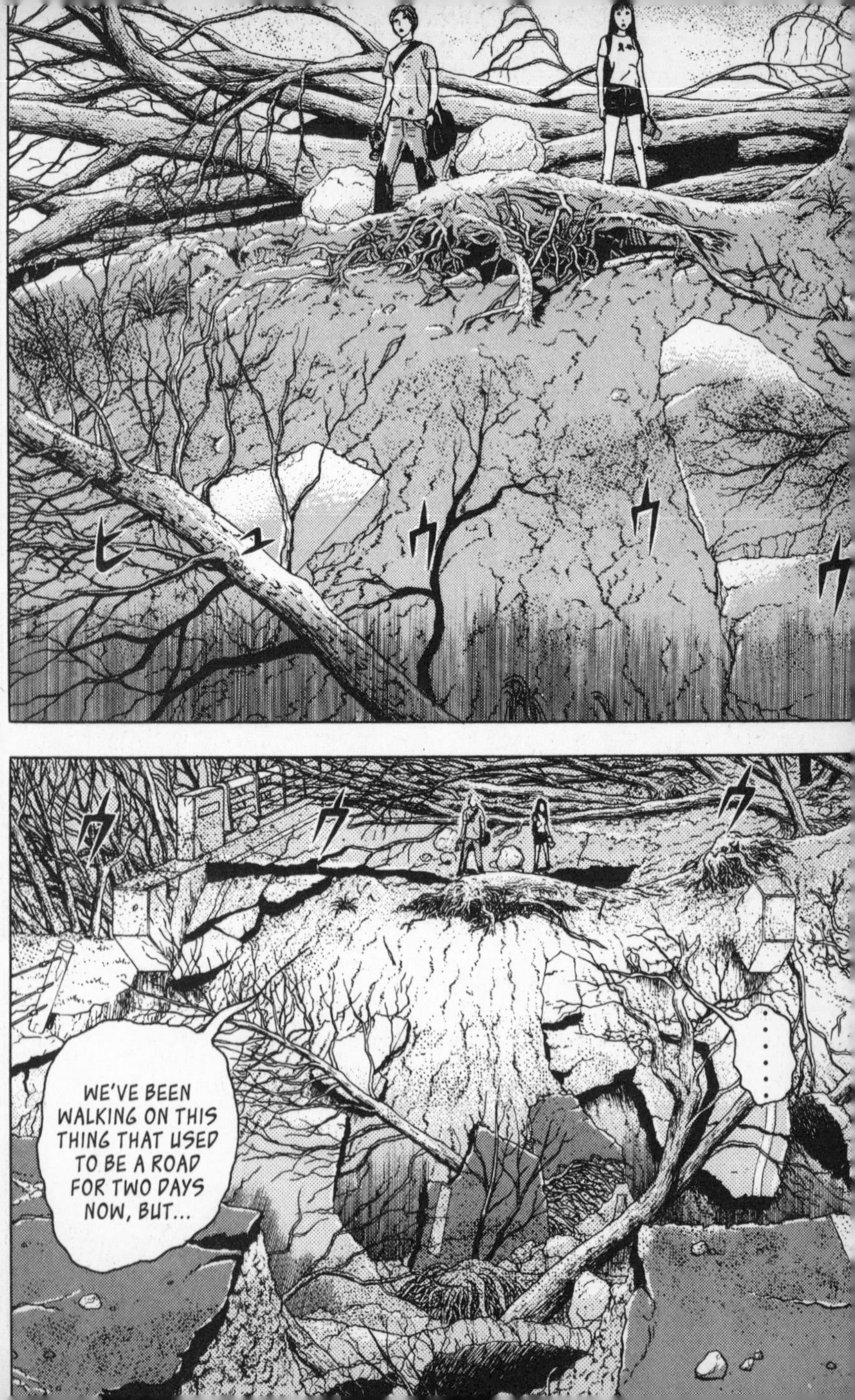
ヒュ
WE'VE BEEN WALKING ON THIS THING THAT USED TO BE A ROAD FOR TWO DAYS NOW, BUT...

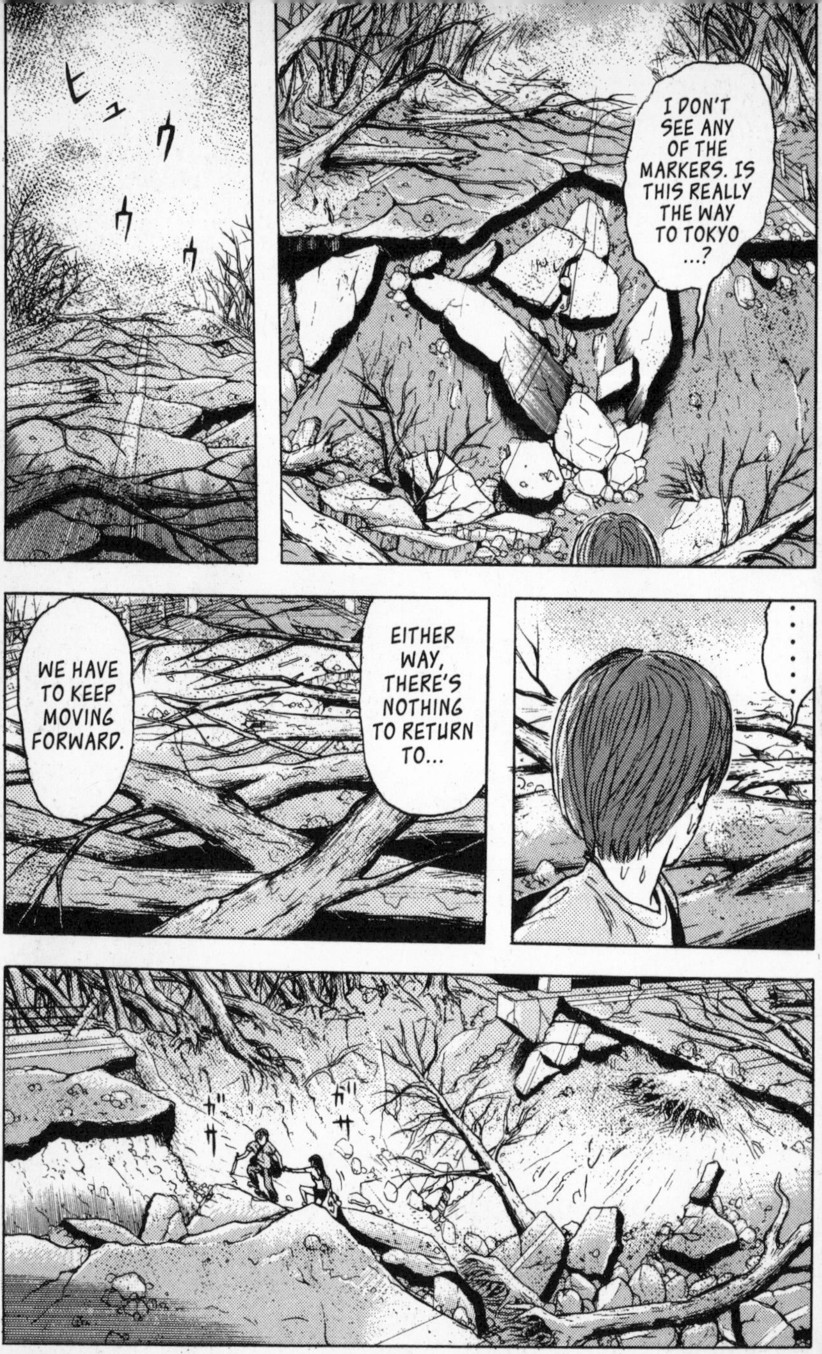
I DON'T SEE ANY OF THE MARKERS. IS THIS REALLY THE WAY TO TOKYO ...?
ヒュウウゥ
......
EITHER WAY, THERE'S NOTHING TO RETURN TO...
WE HAVE TO KEEP MOVING FORWARD.

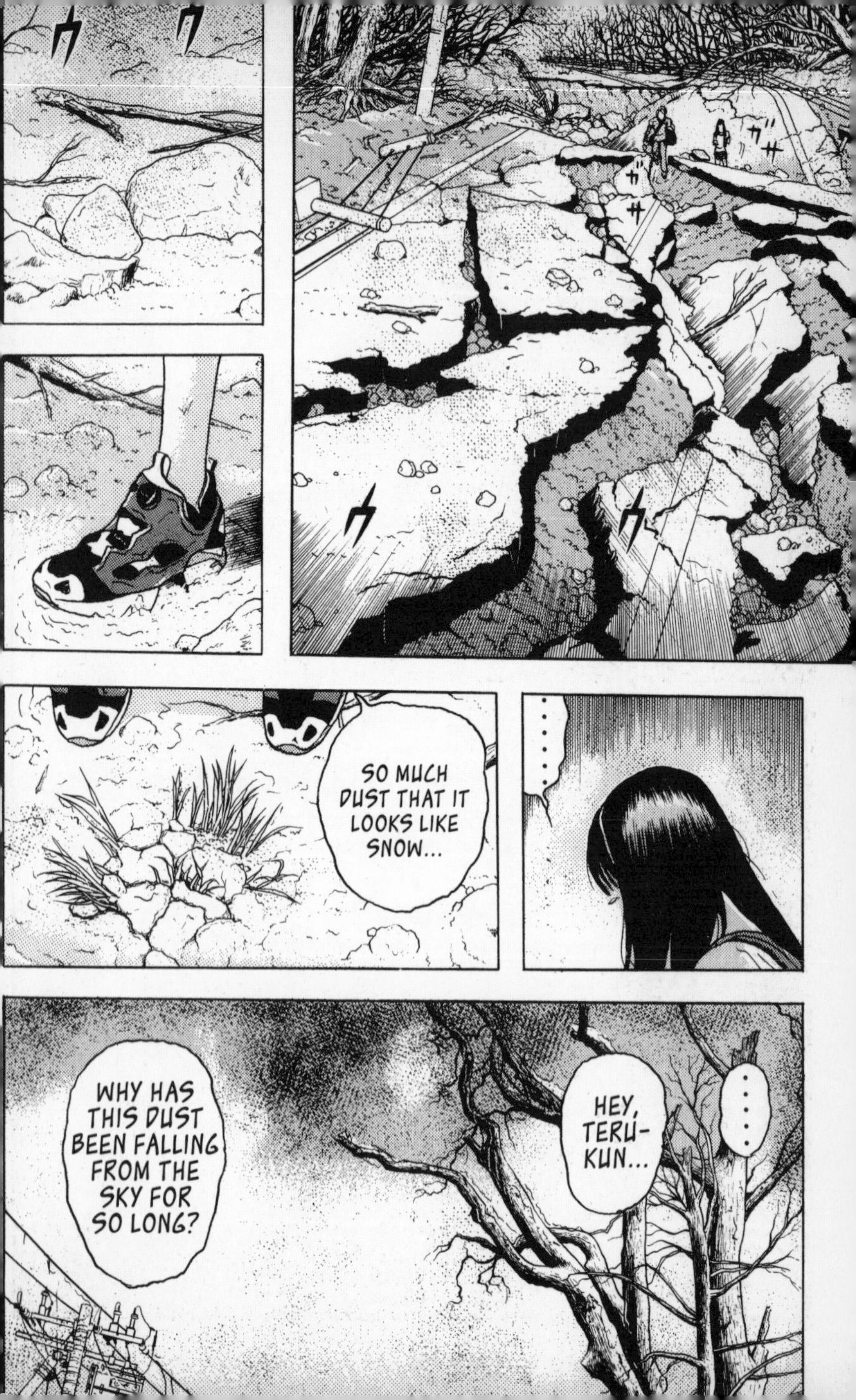
......
SO MUCH DUST THAT IT LOOKS LIKE SNOW...
......
HEY, TERU-KUN...
WHY HAS THIS DUST BEEN FALLING FROM THE SKY FOR SO LONG?

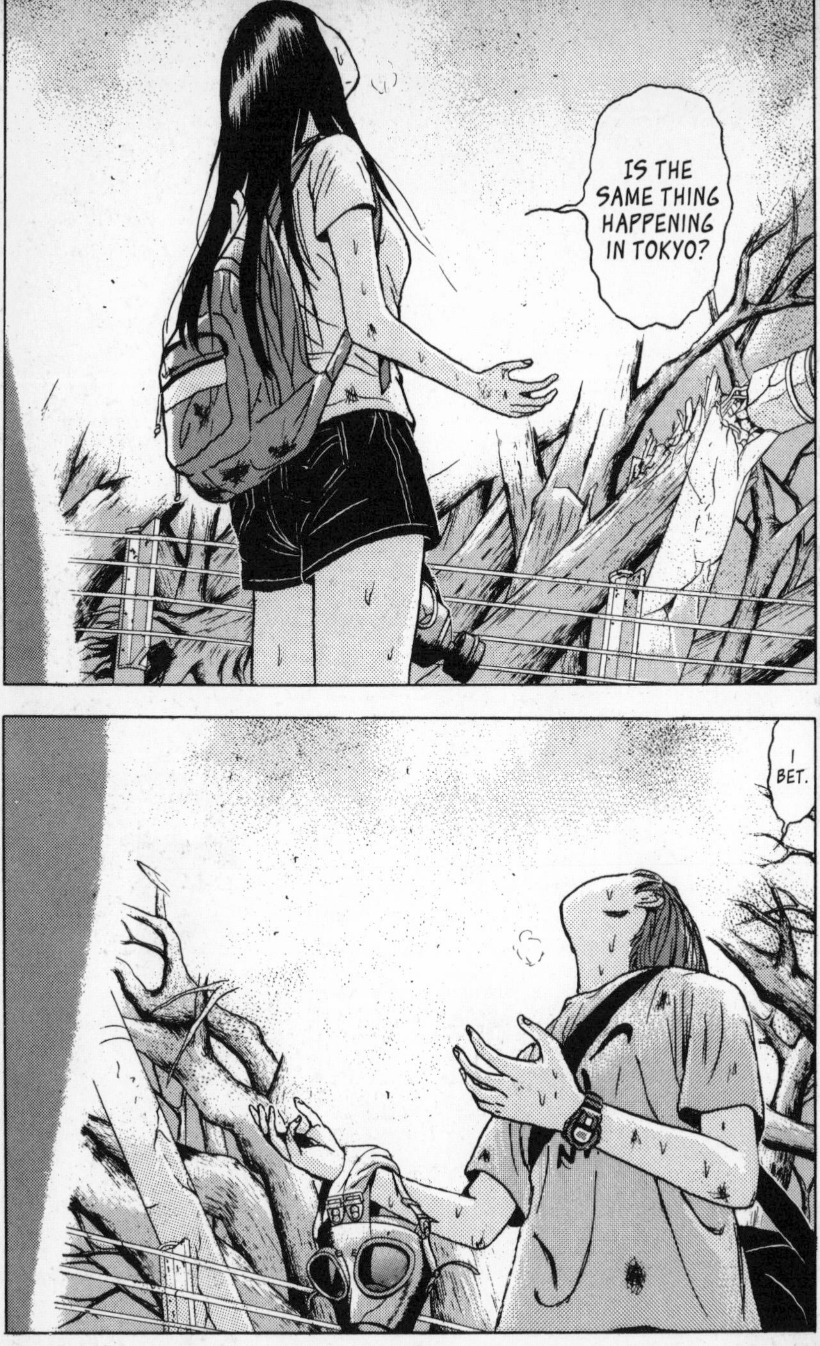
IS THE SAME THING HAPPENING IN TOKYO?
I BET.

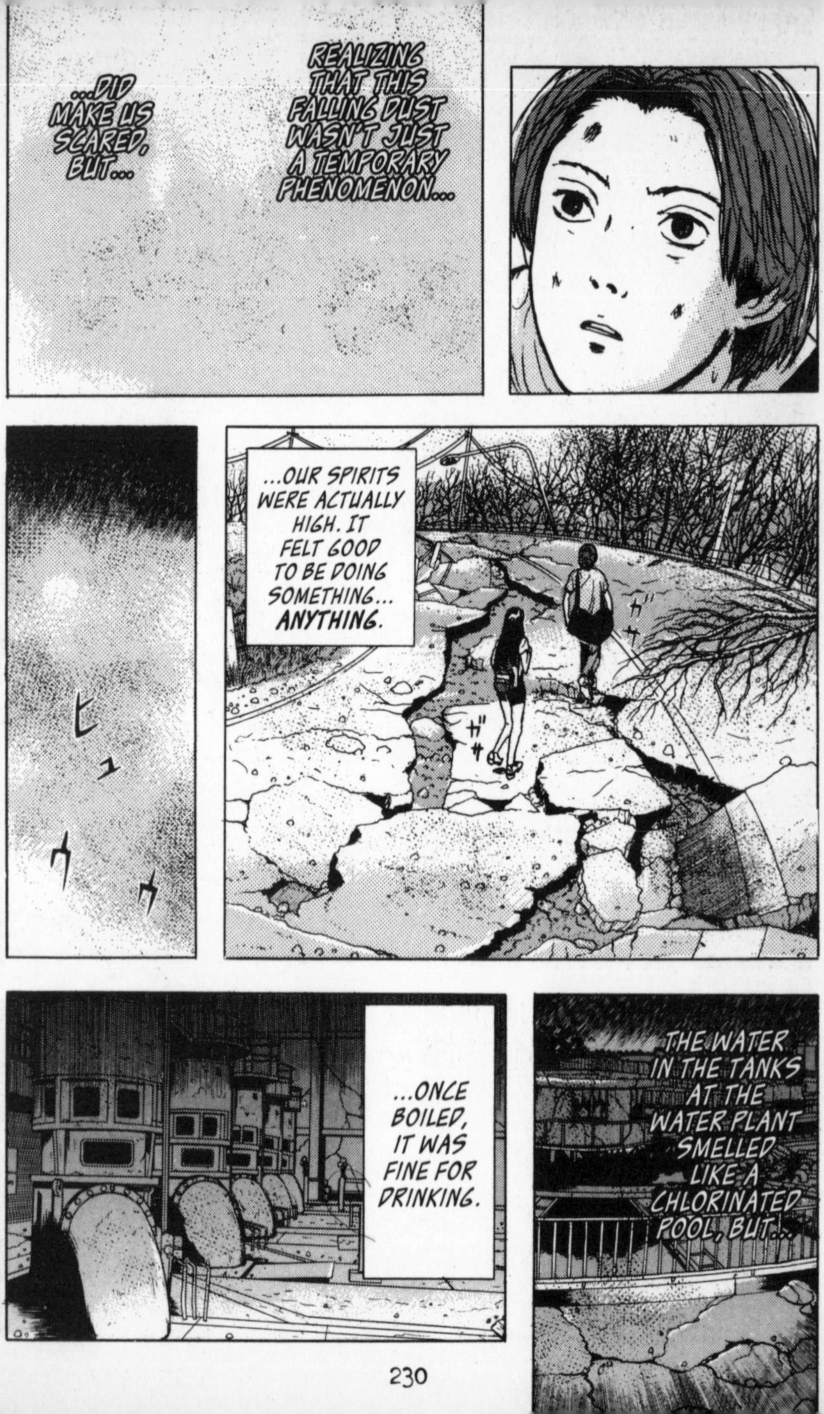
REALIZING THAT THIS FALLING DUST WASN'T JUST A TEMPORARY PHENOMENON...
...DID MAKE US SCARED, BUT...
...OUR SPIRITS WERE ACTUALLY HIGH. IT FELT GOOD TO BE DOING SOMETHING... **ANYTHING.**
ガサ
ガサ
ヒュウウ
THE WATER IN THE TANKS AT THE WATER PLANT SMELLED LIKE A CHLORINATED POOL, BUT...
...ONCE BOILED, IT WAS FINE FOR DRINKING.

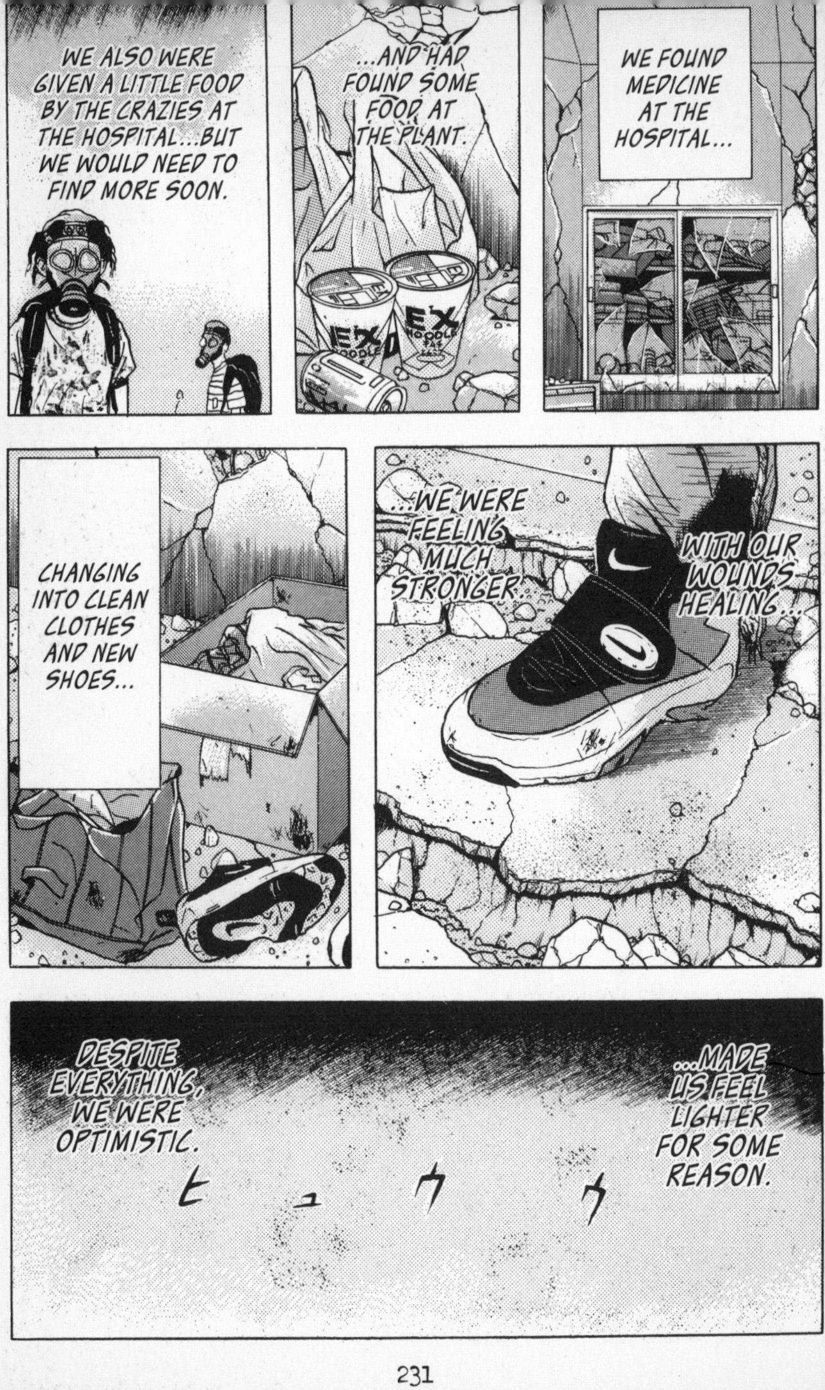
WE FOUND MEDICINE AT THE HOSPITAL...
...AND HAD FOUND SOME FOOD AT THE PLANT.
EX NOODLE
WE ALSO WERE GIVEN A LITTLE FOOD BY THE CRAZIES AT THE HOSPITAL...BUT WE WOULD NEED TO FIND MORE SOON.
WITH OUR WOUNDS HEALING...
...WE WERE FEELING MUCH STRONGER
CHANGING INTO CLEAN CLOTHES AND NEW SHOES...
...MADE US FEEL LIGHTER FOR SOME REASON.
DESPITE EVERYTHING, WE WERE OPTIMISTIC.
ヒュウウ

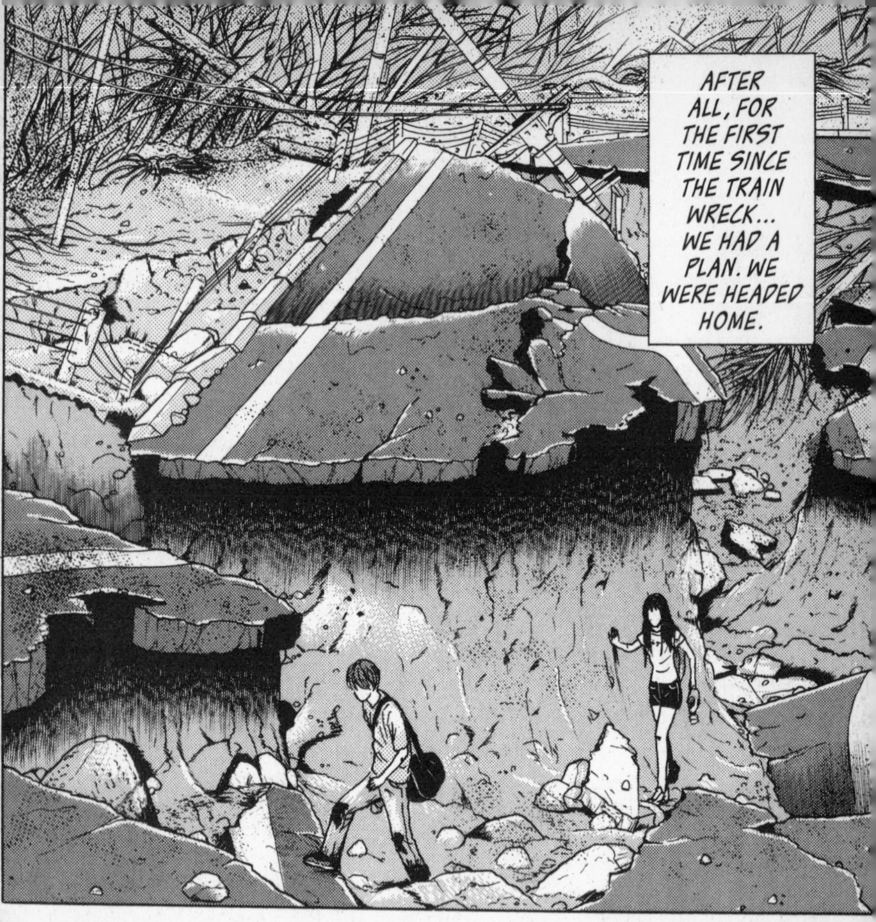
AFTER ALL, FOR THE FIRST TIME SINCE THE TRAIN WRECK... WE HAD A PLAN. WE WERE HEADED HOME.

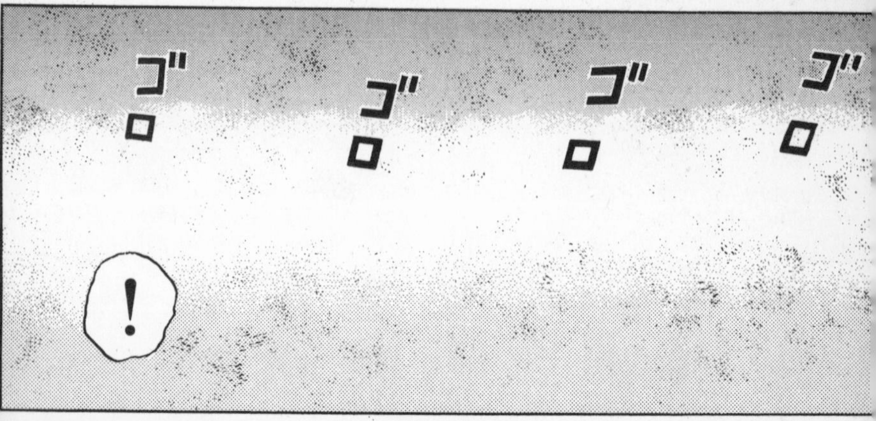
ゴロ
ゴロ
ゴロ
ゴロ
!

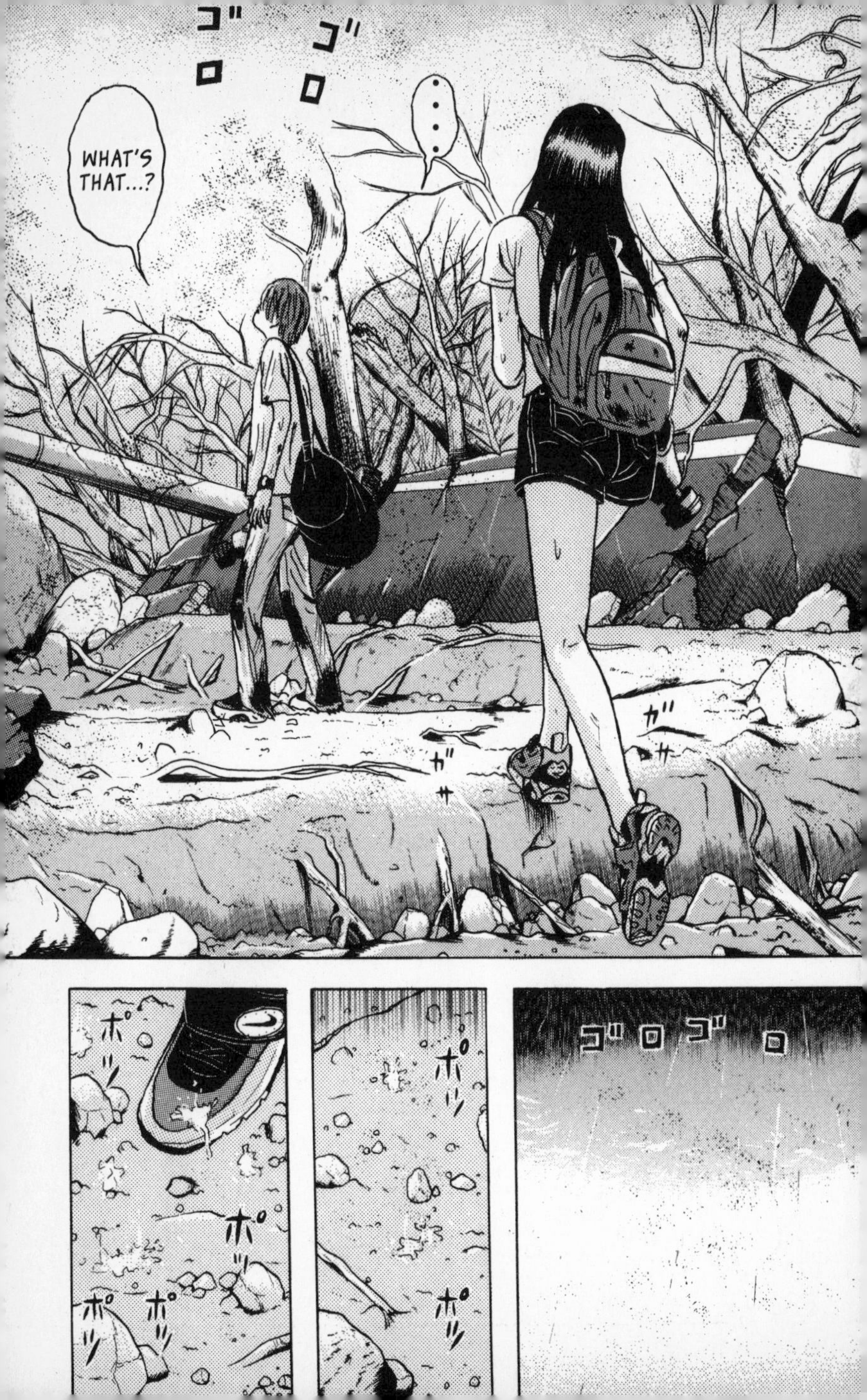
ゴロ
ゴロ
...
WHAT'S THAT...?
ガザ
ガザ
ゴロゴロ
ポツ
ポツ
ポツ
ポツ
ポツ
ポツ

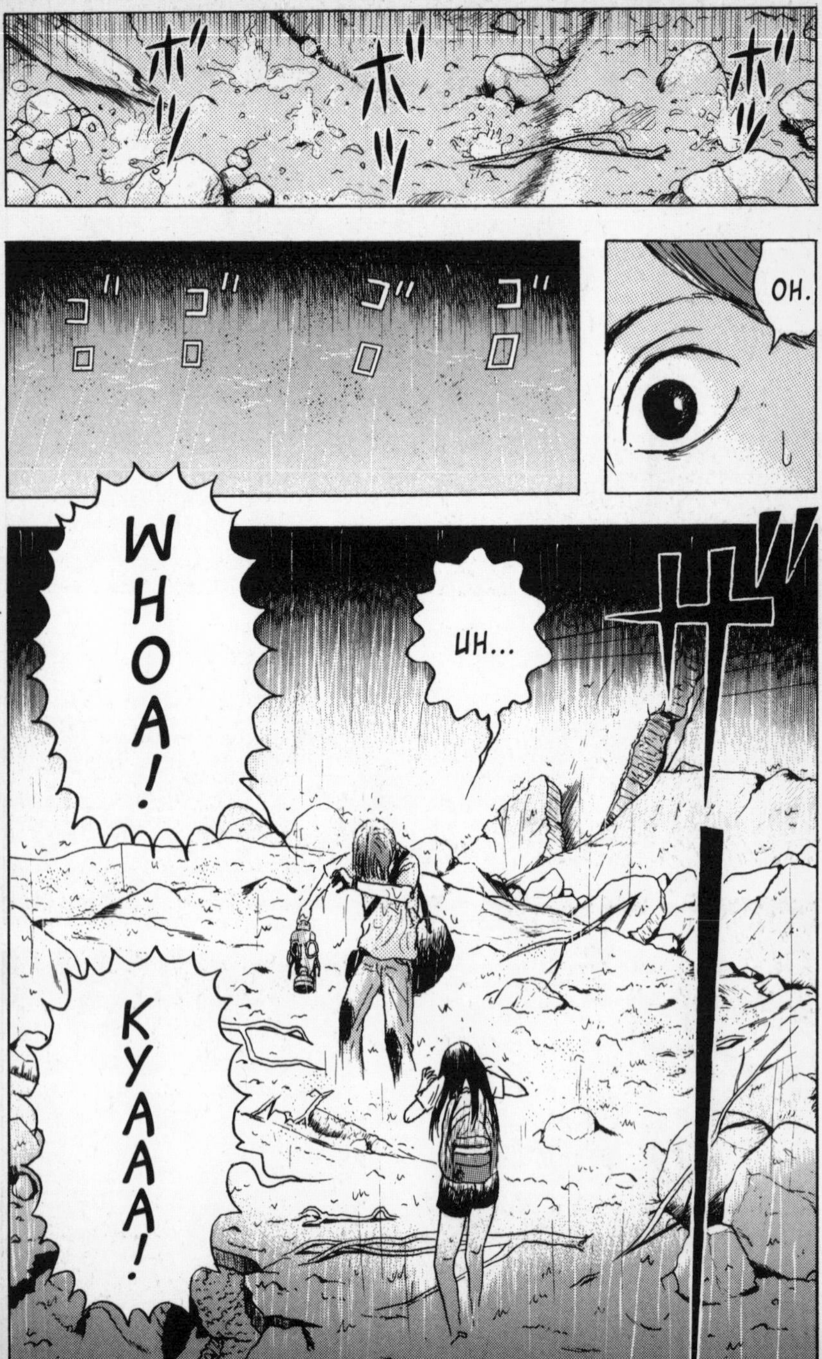
ボッ
ボッ
ボッ
OH.
ゴロ
ゴロ
ゴロ
ゴロ
ザ
UH...
WHOA!
KYAAA!

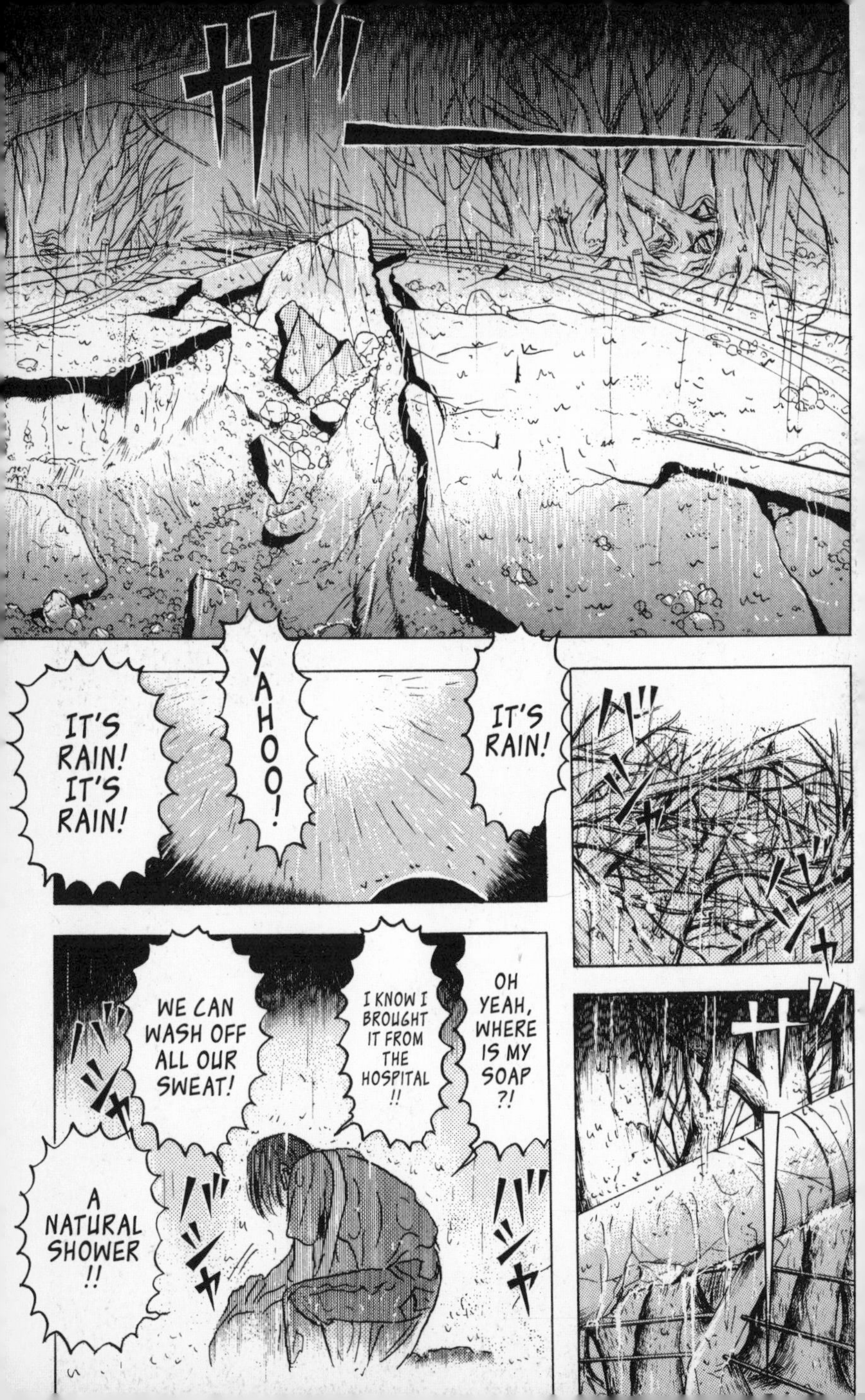
IT'S RAIN!
YAHOO!
IT'S RAIN! IT'S RAIN!
OH YEAH, WHERE IS MY SOAP ?!
I KNOW I BROUGHT IT FROM THE HOSPITAL !!
WE CAN WASH OFF ALL OUR SWEAT!
A NATURAL SHOWER !!

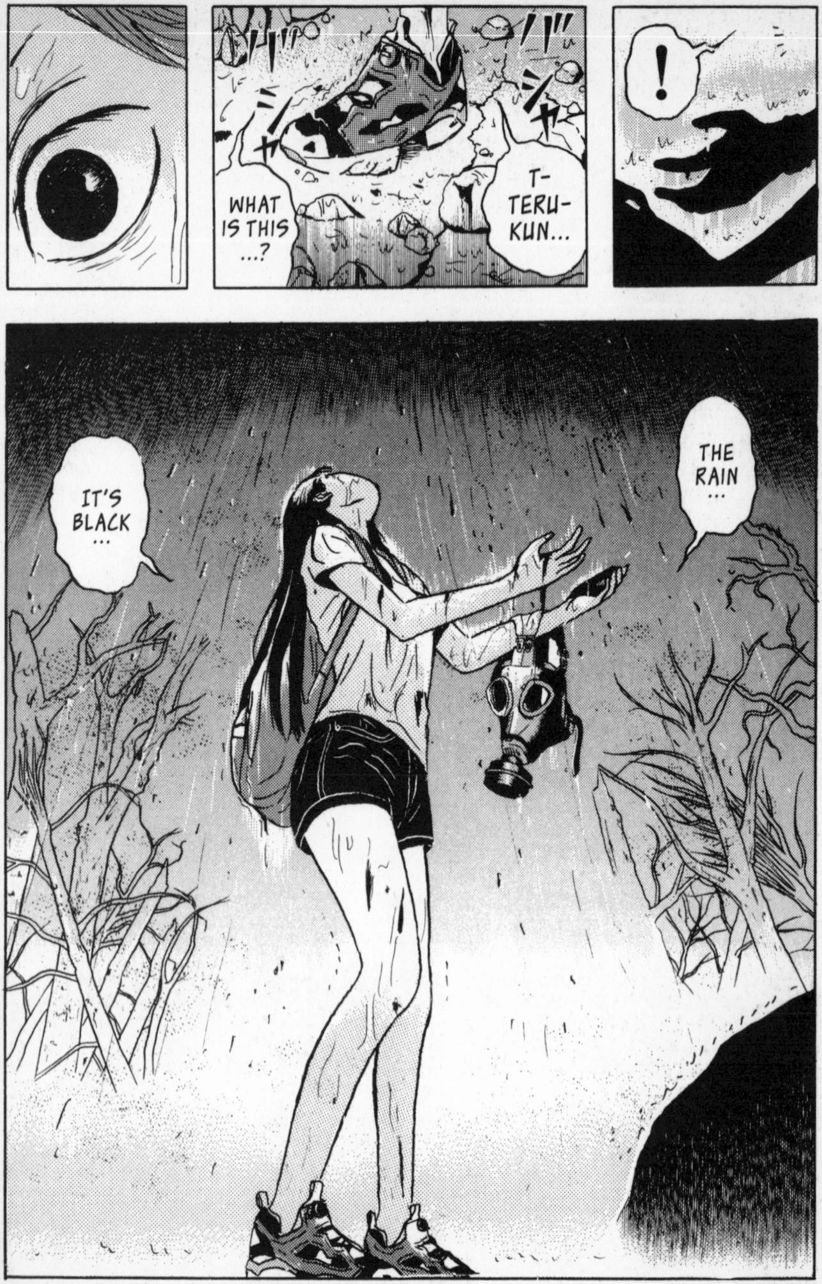
!
T-TERU-KUN...
WHAT IS THIS ...?
THE RAIN ...
IT'S BLACK ...

!
ズブ
....
ALL THAT DUST IS...
...TURNING INTO MUD.
....
ザー

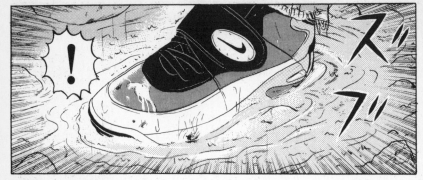

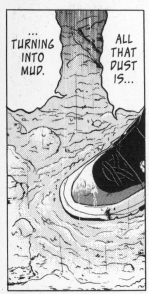

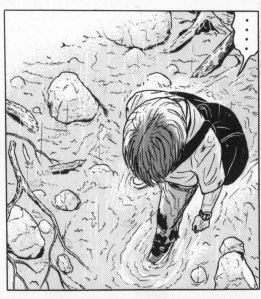

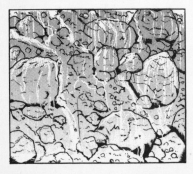

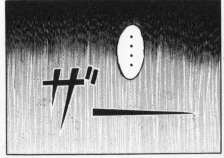

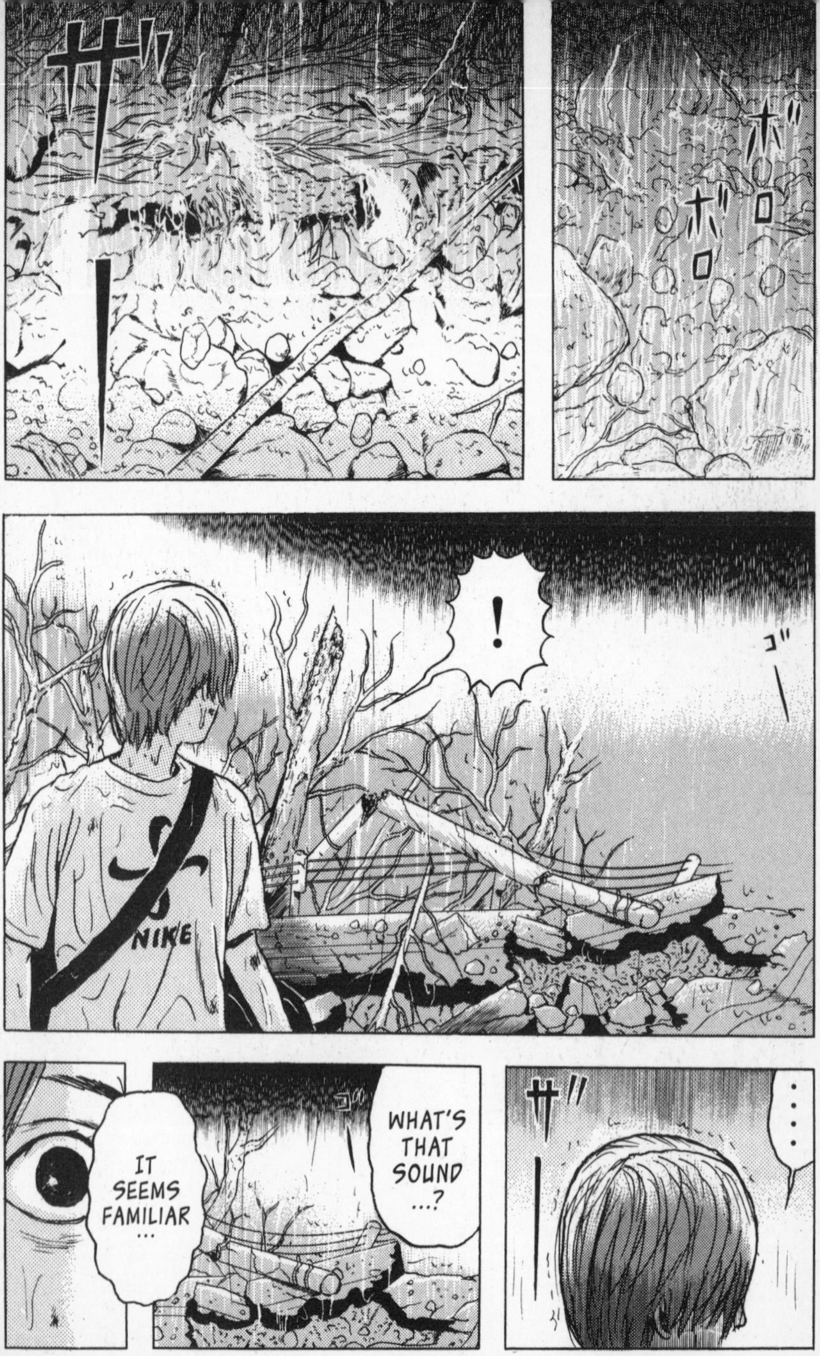
ボロボロ
ザァ
!
ゴー
ザァ
....
WHAT'S THAT SOUND ...?
IT SEEMS FAMILIAR ...

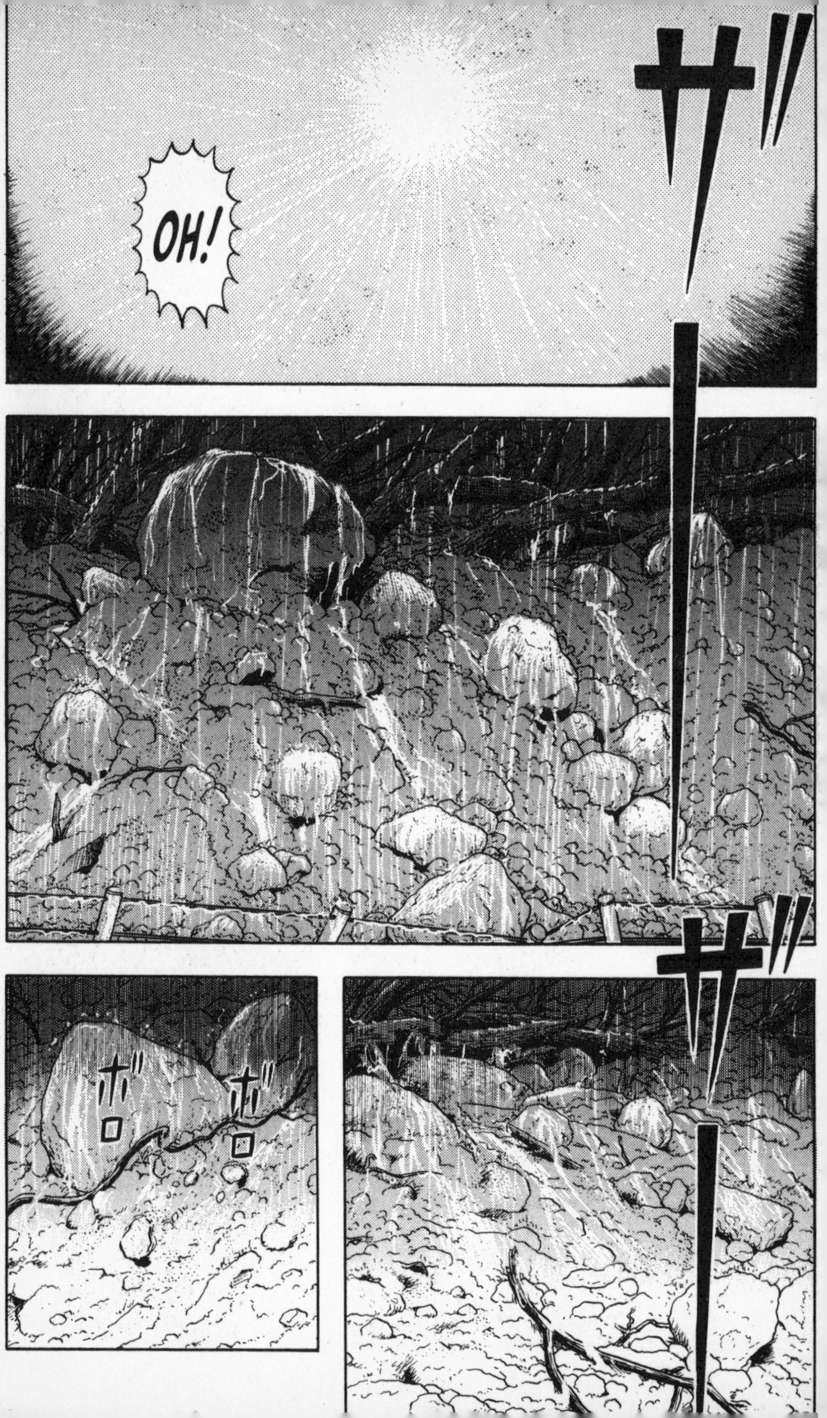

ザー
OH!
ザー
ボロ
ボロ

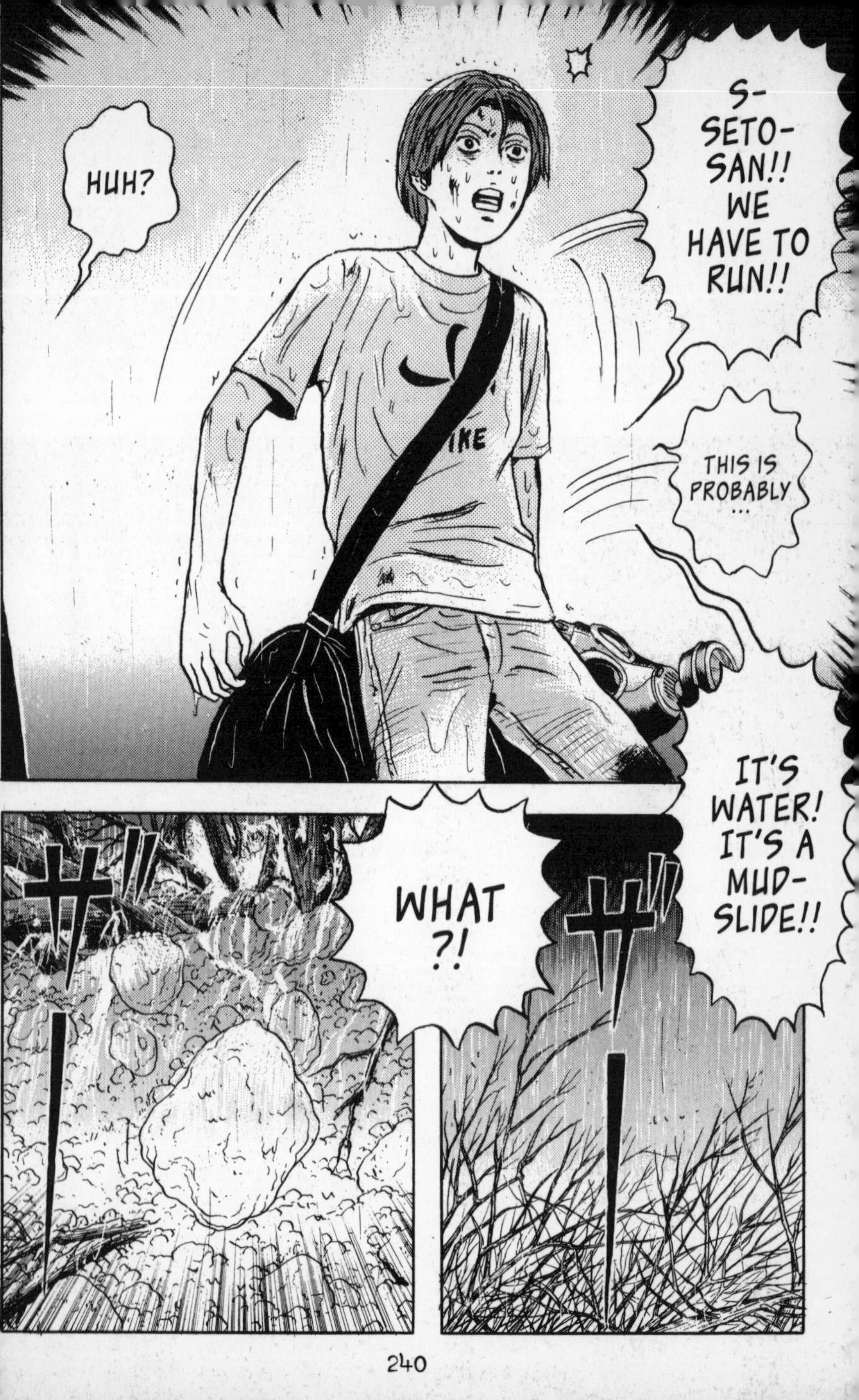
S-SETO-SAN!! WE HAVE TO RUN!!
THIS IS PROBABLY ...
HUH?
IT'S WATER! IT'S A MUD-SLIDE!!
WHAT ?!
ザ
ザ

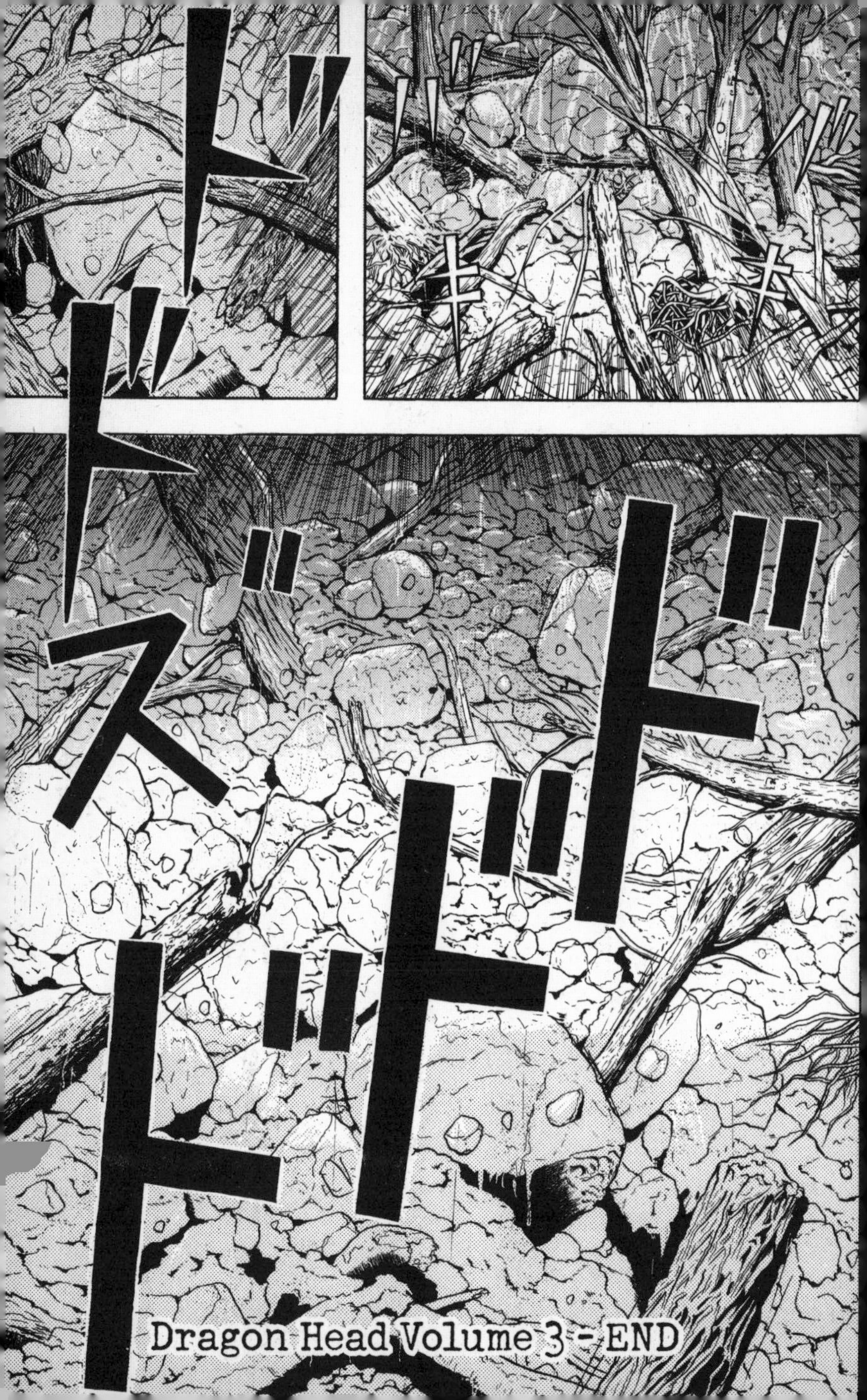
ドドド
ドドドズド
Dragon Head Volume 3 - END

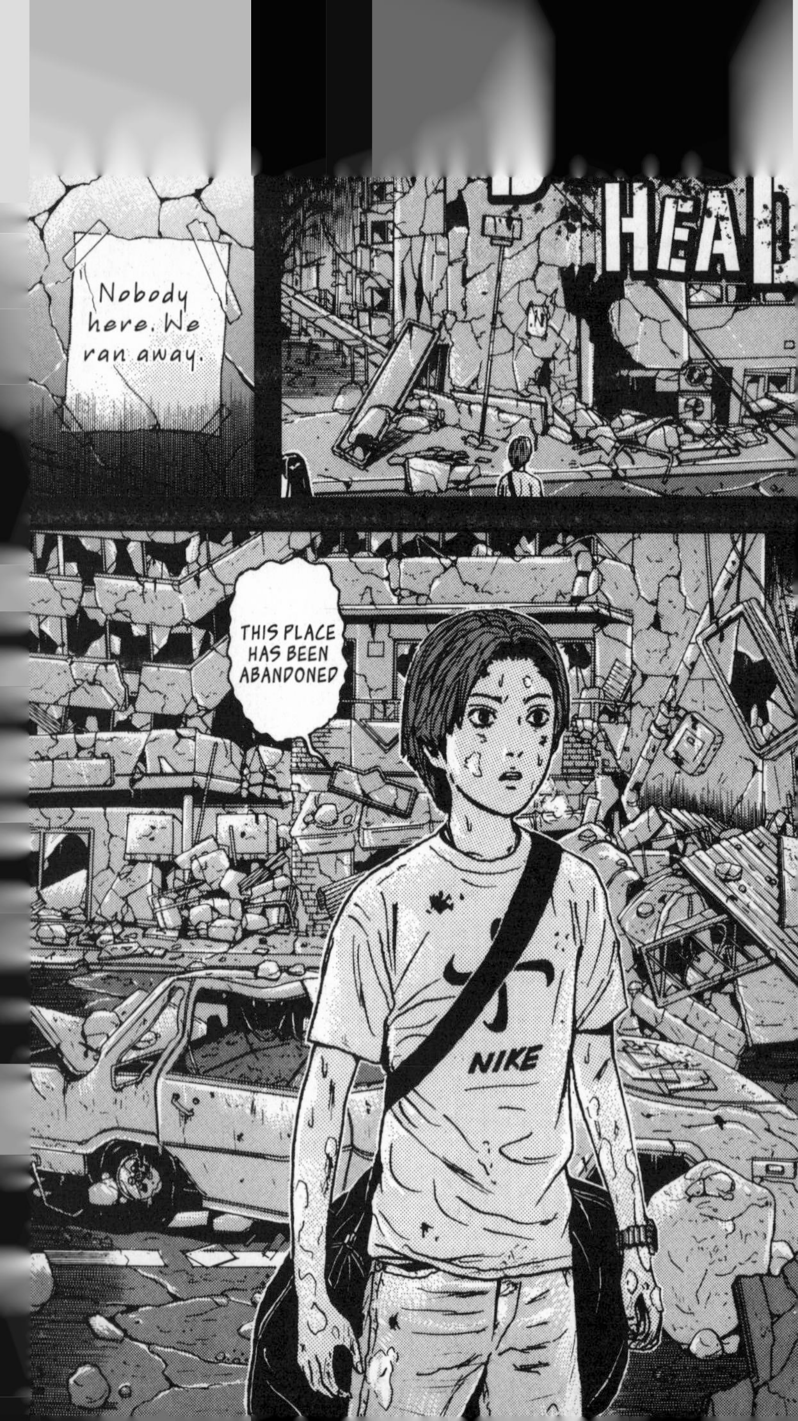
Nobody here. We ran away.
THIS PLACE HAS BEEN ABANDONED
NIKE

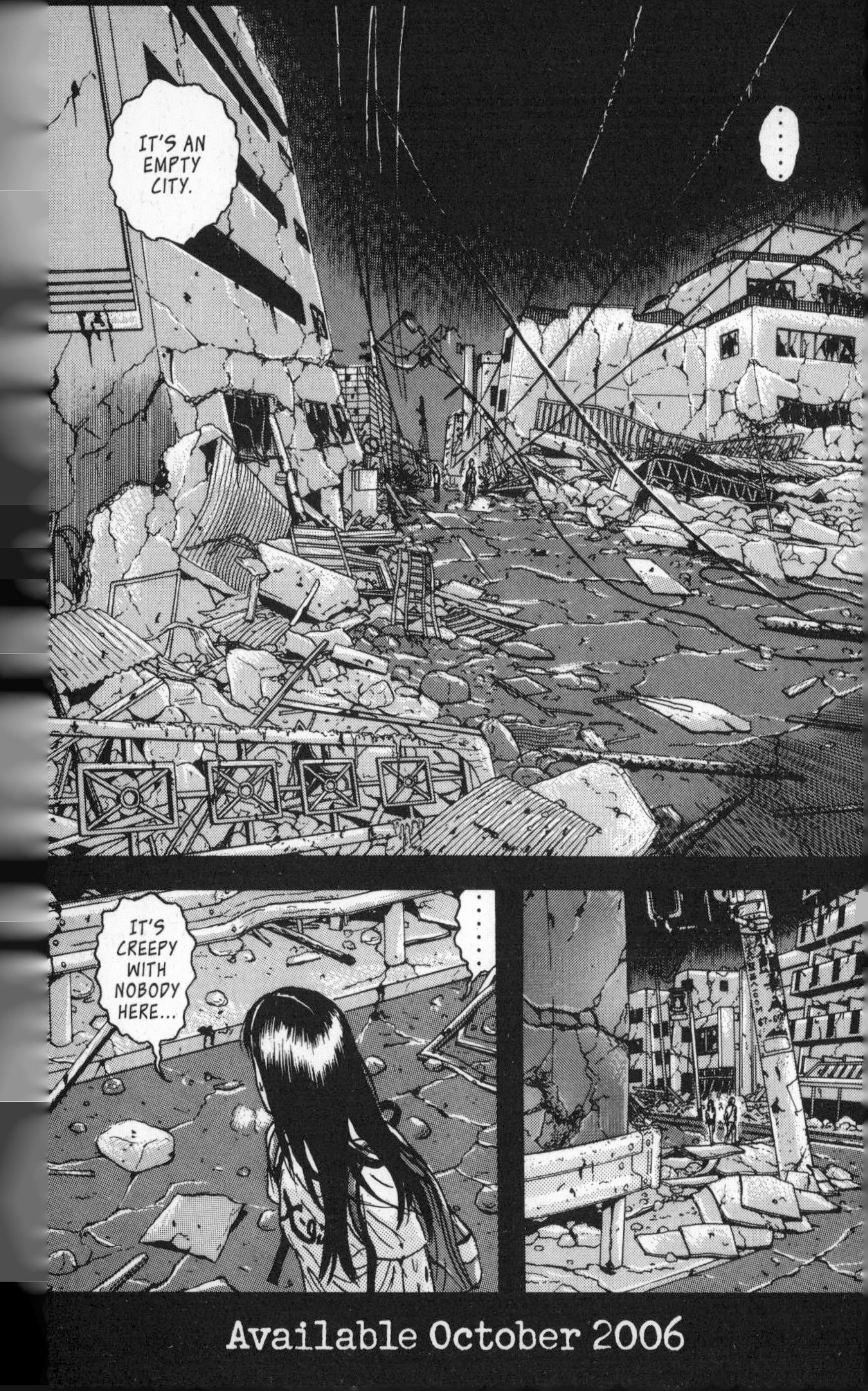
......
IT'S AN EMPTY CITY.
......
IT'S CREEPY WITH NOBODY HERE...

Available October 2006

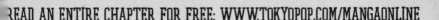

STOP!

This is the back of the book.
You wouldn't want to spoil a great ending!

This book is printed "manga-style," in the authentic Japanese right-to-left format. Since none of the artwork has been flipped or altered, readers get to experience the story just as the creator intended. You've been asking for it, so TOKYOPOP® delivered: authentic, hot-off-the-press, and far more fun!

DIRECTIONS

If this is your first time reading manga-style, here's a quick guide to help you understand how it works.

It's easy... just start in the top right panel and follow the numbers. Have fun, and look for more 100% authentic manga from TOKYOPOP®!